AUG 23 2011

W9-DFZ-080

# CRIME

## & CRIMINOLOGY

HV
6025
.W44
2009

CANADIAN EDITION

# CRIME
# & CRIMINOLOGY
## *An Introduction*

**Rob White**          **Fiona Haines**          **Lauren Eisler**

200101

OXFORD
UNIVERSITY PRESS

NIAGARA COLLEGE LRC

# OXFORD
### UNIVERSITY PRESS

8 Sampson Mews, Suite 204, Don Mills, Ontario M3C 0H5
www.oupcanada.com

Oxford University Press is a department of the University of Oxford.
It furthers the University's objective of excellence in research, scholarship,
and education by publishing worldwide in

Oxford   New York
Auckland   Cape Town   Dar es Salaam   Hong Kong   Karachi
Kuala Lumpur   Madrid   Melbourne   Mexico City   Nairobi
New Delhi   Shanghai   Taipei   Toronto

With offices in

Argentina   Austria   Brazil   Chile   Czech Republic   France   Greece
Guatemala   Hungary   Italy   Japan   Poland   Portugal   Singapore
South Korea   Switzerland   Thailand   Turkey   Ukraine   Vietnam

Oxford is a trade mark of Oxford University Press
in the UK and in certain other countries

Published in Canada
by Oxford University Press

Original edition published by Oxford University Press,
253 Norman Road, South Melbourne, Victoria 3205, Australia.

Copyright © 1996, 2000, 2004.
Rob White and Fiona Haines.

Copyright © Oxford University Press Canada 2009

The moral rights of the author have been asserted

Database right Oxford University Press (maker)

First Published 2009

All rights reserved. No part of this publication may be reproduced,
stored in a retrieval system, or transmitted, in any form or by any means,
without the prior permission in writing of Oxford University Press,
or as expressly permitted by law, or under terms agreed with the appropriate
reprographics rights organization. Enquiries concerning reproduction
outside the scope of the above should be sent to the Rights Department,
Oxford University Press, at the address above.

You must not circulate this book in any other binding or cover
and you must impose this same condition on any acquirer.

## Library and Archives Canada Cataloguing in Publication

White, R. D. (Robert Douglas), 1956–
Crime and criminology : an introduction / Rob White, Fiona Haines, Lauren Eisler.

Includes index.
ISBN 978-0-19-542609-0

1. Criminology—Textbooks. I. Haines, Fiona II. Eisler, Lauren D. III. Title.

HV6025.W44 2008          364          C2008-902986-0

Cover image: iStockPhoto/Mark Wragg

This book is printed on permanent (acid-free) paper ∞

Printed and bound in Canada.

2  3  4 — 12  11  10

**Mixed Sources**
Product group from well-managed
forests, and other controlled sources
www.fsc.org  Cert no. SW-COC-002358
© 1996 Forest Stewardship Council
FSC

# Contents

# List of Tables

# Preface

It is with great pleasure that we present the Canadian edition of *Crime and Criminology*. As each year passes, it is clear that change is fundamental to what is happening in contemporary global society and that this, too, needs to be reflected in a book of this nature. Furthermore, we are aware that the relevance of any particular theory or perspective will vary according to current developments in both the world of academia and in the world outside of the academy. In the light of this, we have modified the text once again, in ways that attempt to make new analytical connections, summarize present trends in criminological theory, and to be of general interest to the reader. Specifically, in this edition we have added important new discussions of peacemaking criminology, restorative justice, cultural criminology, and environmental or green criminology. We believe that we have provided a comprehensive, yet concise, introduction to the major theories and perspectives in criminology. We hope that you find the book of use and interest as you explore the wide variety of explanations for many different types of crime and social harm.

## Acknowledgements

We are grateful to many people for their assistance in the development and further revision of this book. Our special thanks go to fellow lecturers in criminology who helped to mould and shape the ways in which the material was actually developed for teaching purposes. We are also grateful to the many tutors and students over the years who, each in their own way, have assisted us in refining and simplifying the core ideas of the field. Thanks are also due to the academic and general staff in the Criminology Program at Wilfrid Laurier University, Brantford Campus and the Department of Criminology at the University of Melbourne for their ongoing encouragement for projects of this nature, and to support staff at the University of Tasmania for their assistance. Finally, we are grateful once again to all the people at Oxford University Press for their constant enthusiasm and genuine interest in the book.

# CHAPTER 1

# The Study of Crime

## Objectives

This chapter will help you develop an understanding of the:

- social construction of crime;
- impact of media on our understandings of the types and incident rates of crimes committed;
- three major strands within **criminology** that deal with measurement of crime issues; and
- different levels of analysis and the different political orientations that shape criminology.

This book is about the causes of crime. More specifically, it describes the diverse and at times competing perspectives within criminology, and their attempts to explain why certain types of people engage in certain types of behaviour that have been identified as criminal in nature.

The aim of this chapter is to introduce the reader to the study of crime and, in doing so, to explore a series of issues relating to the definition and measurement of crime. A major part of this chapter describes the criteria that serve to differentiate the many perspectives on crime. In particular, we will explore the different levels of analysis used to explain crime and the different political perspectives that impinge on criminological analysis. Thus, one purpose of this chapter is to provide a sense of how we can distinguish between different theoretical perspectives by looking at similarities and differences in broad approaches.

## Criminology as a Field of Study

Before we discuss the nature of crime, it is useful to first say a few words about criminology as a field of study. As we shall see, criminology, like crime, is not a monolith; it contains varied and competing perspectives. This variety of perspectives should be considered in light of the social context of the production of intellectual knowledge.

For instance, the production of knowledge is itself a social and material process. When any kind of knowledge is produced we must ask who has control over this process—not only the production of knowledge itself, but also the ownership and use of the results of research and scholarship. In a similar vein, specific types of 'knowledge' or 'truth' are not always recognized or visible in the public domain. This can happen for a variety of reasons—because there is no market for it, because of publishing rivalries, or because the 'knowledge' is not deemed to conform to particular academic standards or mainstream political agendas.

Knowledge also has distinctive international dimensions. For example, in the field of criminology each country may have its own unique social concerns, intellectual milieux, political traditions, historical development, and, therefore, its own theoretical emphases and biases. In the UK, for example, debates over policing and antisocial behaviour have been prominent in recent years, but in the US concerns have been more focused on ghetto neighbourhoods, unemployment, and the social prospects of the huge numbers of offenders re-entering the community after serving time in prison. Debates in Canada have centred on changes to drug law enforcement, while at the

## Box 1.1   Chief Puts Young Thugs On Notice

Police Chief Mike Boyd has called for action on youth violence, one day after three teens were charged in the beating death of a homeless man.

'Enough is enough,' Boyd said as representatives of the police commission, city hall and both local school boards looked on. 'We have decided to act together because we are not going to tolerate any more of this cowardly, thug-like behavior in our city.'

Boyd said he was concerned by reports from his officers about youths swarming other youth, bus drivers and homeless people in Edmonton. A crucial step, he said, is for victimized youth and others to report such crimes to police, parents, or teachers more often.

'I want to encourage their co-operation to come forward to report this kind of bullying and terrorizing activity,' he said. 'There are witnesses out there, we know that there are.'

On Oct. 21, Russell Ross was found severely beaten in an alley near 109A Avenue and 97th Street. The 52-year-old homeless man survived in the University of Alberta Hospital for three days before dying of his head injuries.

Two 16-year-olds and a 14-year-old have been charged with assault causing bodily harm.

The police and Crown prosecutors, who made a joint decision on the charges, are not saying why the lesser charges were laid.

On Friday, Boyd left the door open to the charges being changed in the future.

From Ryan Cormier and Trish Audette, 'Chief Puts Young Thugs on Notice. . .', *The Edmonton Journal* (Saturday, 28 October 2006). Material reprinted with the express permission of Edmonton Journal Group Inc., a CanWest Partnership.

same time media treatment of criminal justice issues in Canada has featured extensive **moral panics** over young offenders, youth violence, and youth gangs.

Cutting across all of these debates in each of the regions, however, has been a series of general issues relating to the nature and social control of crime. Invariably, analysis of specific issues has employed abstract concepts that are designed to explain why particular phenomena should be dealt with in any particular way. Major themes of this book include exploring the nature of the more generalized statements regarding crime, examining the broad social and historical context within which certain theories and concepts have emerged, and demonstrating the application of these theoretical understandings to selected issues and criminal justice reform.

While '**theory**' informs everything that criminologists do, not every criminologist is a theorist. So what should criminologists actually do, and why is theory relevant to their practice? To answer these questions we need to appreciate the dual nature of much contemporary criminology. On the one hand, many people adopt what could be called a vocational or professional approach to criminology, in which the role of criminology is tied to improving the immediate practices of the criminal justice system. This approach seeks to study, analyze, and research alternative theories in order to institute reform of some kind. Generally, it is directed at making some aspect of the criminal justice system 'better' at some level, be it a programme, an institution, or a strategy. Often this approach is linked to attempts to solve a 'social problem' or an administrative difficulty within the existing system.

On the other hand, there is a strand of criminology in which the emphasis is on a critical or analytical approach. Unlike the vocational approach, this tends not be to a nuts-and-bolts view of the criminal justice system, particularly in respect to making minor changes within the existing institutional frameworks of criminal justice. Instead, this approach suggests that one must stand back from policy decisions and ask bigger questions, such as 'What if. . .?' This approach delves into the deeper philosophical issues of the day; for example, why do we continue to have and use institutions such as prisons when they demonstrably do not work to prevent offending or re-offending? The critical, or analytical, approach does not suggest improvements to the existing penal system, but questions whether it is valid, or even viable, to begin with. Indeed, an informed opinion might simply advocate the abolition of such institutions in their present shape and form.

It is essential to note, however, that often there are strong links between these two approaches. The variability in criminological perspectives in general is due in part to the nature of the relationship between the practical, vocational orientation (with a focus on what can be done here and how to improve the system) and its critical, analytical counterpart (with a focus on why things ought to be done in one way or another). We must also be aware of the uncertainties of knowledge. For instance, whatever area of criminology one may concentrate on, there are almost always unintended consequences that emerge from the knowledge we acquire and the reforms we put forward. Knowledge is a guide to the future—it does not fix the future on a single pathway.

Generally speaking, criminology focuses on three main areas:

- the sociology of law, which examines social aspects and the institutions of law;
- theories of crime causation, which is sometimes referred to as criminogeneisis; and

- the study of social responses to crime, which examine in more depth the formal institutions of criminal justice such as the police, courts, and corrections.

As pointed out earlier, the main theme of this book is the theories that relate to the causes of crime. As will be seen, however, the other domains of criminology often overlap and are inseparable parts of any review of causal theories.

## Defining Crime

What is crime? There is no straightforward answer to this question, as there are constantly changing ideas, perceptions, and conceptions regarding what constitutes criminal behaviour. To a certain extent, both crime and criminology are uncertain in the sense that one's definition of crime is dependent upon one's particular interests and particular worldview. This becomes clearer when we discuss the various definitions put forward for crime.

There are competing views of crime. Crime is always socially defined. This of course, can lead to debate: for example, should crime always be defined by law? Could, or should, it instead be based upon moral and social conceptions such as social harm? To illustrate the difficulties surrounding different definitions of crime, we might consider the film *Schindler's List*. In the movie (and in real life) Schindler broke Nazi law in order to assist Jewish people. What about cases today where people may actively break the law in the name of social justice? There are unjust systems in the world, and it may well be the case that many legal definitions are built on highly contentious, unjust, or unfair propositions.

### Legal and sociological definitions of crime

There are many diverse conceptions of crime, each of which reflects different scientific and ideological viewpoint. Hagan (1987), for example, identifies seven different approaches to the definition of crime, ranging from a 'legal-consensus' definition to a 'human rights' definition. For present purposes, we can summarize broad definitional differences in the following way:

- A *formal legal* definition says that crime is whatever the state identifies as a crime; that is, if something is written into the criminal law, and is subject to state sanction in the form of a specific penalty, then that activity is a crime.
- A *social harm* conception of crime says that crime involves both criminal offences (e.g., assault) and civil offences (e.g., negligence), in that each type of action or inaction brings with it some type of harm. Each should therefore attract some kind of penalty.
- A *cross-cultural universal norm* argument states that crime, in essence, does not vary across cultural norms. Thus, murder is murder regardless of the society, and we can postulate norms of conduct that cut across diverse cultural backgrounds.
- A *labelling approach* to the definition of crime argues that crime only really exists when there has been a social response to a particular activity that labels that activity as criminal. If there is no label, there is in effect no crime.
- A *human rights* approach says that crime occurs whenever a human right has been violated, regardless of the legality of the action. Such a conception also expands

the definition of crime to include oppressive practices such as racism, sexism, and class-based exploitation.

- A *human diversity* approach defines crime in terms of the manner in which deviance represents a normal response to oppressive or unequal circumstances. A major focus here is on power relations, and the attempts by dominant groups to restrict human diversity of experience, language, and culture.

Our intention here is not to explain fully each type of definition of crime, nor to evaluate the explanatory or practical usefulness of each definition (instead, see Nettler, 1984; Hagan, 1987). Rather, we wish to alert the reader to the fact that there are important differences in how people conceive of crime.

Further to these differences, the variation in definition often has real consequences upon how different types of behaviours are dealt with at a practical level. For example, we might consider the issue of violence:

> In the home, parents hit children; on the playing field, sportsmen assault each other; at work, industrial 'accidents' occur; in our community, dangerous chemical are dumped; our governments turn a blind eye to the practices of some police officers; and our governments are responsible for the mass violence of war (Alder, 1991: 61).

How violence is perceived and responded to by criminal justice institutions depends very much upon a range of political and social factors. Crime is not inherent in an activity: it is defined under particular material circumstances and in relation to specific social processes.

## Historical Construction of Crime

While criminologists may argue about the definitions of crime, ultimately it is the legal definition of crime that determines how we, as a society, respond to certain acts deemed to be wrongful. But we might ask: Who actually makes the laws, and why are they made? Whose interests are reflected in those laws and how are they enforced? In line with the broad theme of the variability of definitions of crime, it is also useful to acknowledge that legal definitions of crime themselves change over time. The law itself is thus socially produced and is not static. As it changes, so too does the definition of crime. In this sense we can say that morality itself is a variable, at least insofar as it is reflected in the laws of a country.

What is legally defined as crime varies according to social and historical contexts. This is shown in the following examples.

- As of 1530 in England there existed the crime of being a vagabond, which in effect meant that a person was unemployed and idle. Any person so identified could be branded a criminal—figuratively and literally (through burning of the gristle of the right ear with a hot iron). Vagabonds over the age of eighteen could be hanged if they did not obtain suitable employment for two years. Revived in 1743, the Vagrancy Act expanded the types of persons liable for prosecution to include a wide variety of homeless and poor people (see Chambliss, 1975a). This crime no

longer exists, although one could be tempted to draw similarities with the negative status accorded to the young unemployed today.

- In the seventeenth century, the crime of witchcraft was the most common of all
  crimes in Europe. Crime here was constructed in terms of religion and referred to
  conduct allegedly against (the Christian) God. By and large, such laws pertaining to
  witchcraft targeted women, particularly those displaying eccentric and secretive tendencies, as a means of controlling them and their knowledge (see Inverarity et al.,
  1983). Such laws, of course, are not common in the criminal law today. However, in
  some jurisdictions crimes related to witchcraft are still on the statute books, such as
  reading tarot cards. Similarly, some of the public concern about heavy-metal or Gothic
  'shock rock' music (e.g., Marilyn Manson) appears to have vestiges of the moral and
  religious panics over witchcraft that swept Europe several hundred years ago.
- Prior to 1929, women were not considered legal persons under Canadian law. This
  meant that the rape of a woman was, in effect, a property offence against the
  owner, who was either the father of an unmarried women and the husband of a
  married one. This sense of 'women as property' is evidenced in the rape laws prior
  to 1983; rape was considered to be 'sexual penetration of a woman's vagina with
  a man's penis without the woman's consent, *outside of marriage*' (emphasis added).
  This meant that a man could not be raped, nor could a husband rape his wife. Lob-
  bying efforts by women's groups led to the introduction of Bill C-127 which
  became law on 4 January 1983, making changes to the laws of rape, attempted
  rape, and indecent assault. These laws were replaced with three levels of **sexual
  assault** in an attempt to remove the gender-bias from the law and to improve
  conditions for victims of sexual assault. For example, spousal assault is now
  included in the laws and there is no longer any reference to gender, meaning that
  in the eyes of the law, a man can be the victim of a sexual assault.
- Property and theft are historically and culturally specific concepts. In many traditional Australian Aboriginal and other indigenous communal societies, everything
  is shared. There is no concept of theft—which is premised on the notion of ownership of personal property—because in these cultures property is communal.
  Concepts of land ownership likewise differ from mainstream legal conceptions.
  Some members of indigenous communities hold the belief that they do not really
  own the land, so it cannot be taken away from them. To put it differently, land is
  not a possession; it is something that you have a relationship with. Crime in traditional indigenous communities is associated with the abuse of sacred knowledge, custom, spirituality, witchcraft, and ritual. It is not centred upon property,
  as is most Western law (see Bottomley et al., 1991).

Crime is thus an offence of the time. In European history it was, for a while, intimately linked to moral prescriptions as defined by religious bodies. One reason for this
was that in the 1400s to 1600s, the Church was the body that had access to the tools
of justice administration. This was because literacy tended to be the preserve of the
clergy, who therefore were in a position to construct the laws. Later on, it was the preserve of the state to determine laws. Accordingly, crime became defined as a transgression against the state, not against God. Even today, however, there are vestiges of

conflict between the secular and non-secular laws, as indicated in legal action taken over the ordination of women in some Christian denominations.

## Popular Media Images of Crime

The media have a significant influence on the general portrayal of crime in society. The images that permeate popular consciousness of crime are mainly generated by, and reflected in, electronic and print media. Obviously the media have a tremendous impact in terms of how crime is generally defined in society (see Grabosky and Wilson, 1989; Ericson et al., 1991; Sarre, 1994).

According to the media, in both fictional and factual types of programmes and reportage, crime tends to be defined primarily as 'street crime'. Such crime is thus associated with personal terror and fear, and violence is seen as central. Crime is sensationalized, with important implications for the fear of crime among certain sections of the population. This fear is heightened by the way in which crime is seen to be random in nature, with anyone and everyone a possible target for **victimization**. Consider the number of popular television shows in recent years that deal with crime. Shows such as *CSI* and *Law & Order* (and all of their various permutations and spin-offs), contribute to a distorted view of both the types and frequencies of crimes committed against, and the threat to, the average individual. These shows, for the most part, portray criminal events as violent and random: no one is safe and everyone is a potential victim. George Gerbner's cultivation theory explores this issue and claims that heavy exposure to media—television in particular—may result in a the creation of a vision of society that is more influenced by what is seen on television than by what actually exists. This leads to assumptions being made about types of people, violence, places, and other media-created events that do not accurately reflect real life experiences and events.

As well, there is often the idea that crime is related to morality, and specifically to the decline of that morality. What is 'wrong' is plain for all to see. Furthermore, the 'criminal' is distinctive and identifiably different from everyone else in society. Overall, the idea created is that there is a continuing 'law-and-order' problem in society, and that things are constantly getting worse. Against this tide of disorder and lawlessness, the police and other crime-fighters are generally portrayed as infallible 'superheroes' who use violence legitimately in order to counter the violence of the streets.

The media are important not only in shaping our definitions of crime and crime control, but in producing legal changes and reinforcing particular types of policing strategies. For example, the 'moral panic' generated by the media about problems such as 'youth gangs' may lead to changes in the law (e.g., introduction of youth curfews, school dress codes, and zero tolerance policies) and the adoption of certain police methods (e.g., increasing the use of 'name checks' in particular locales, and the use of dogs in random searches for drugs and weapons in schools). The term 'moral panic'—first used by Stanley Cohen in 1972 to describe a panic or overreaction to forms of deviance or wrongdoing perceived to threaten moral order—describes a situation in which the media creates a perception, and community groups or leaders whose goals are to changes laws or practices then lead the panic and growing concern to achieve their own aims.

## Box 1.2 Saskatchewan Hot Spot for Gang Activity

Saskatchewan is a perfect breeding ground for gangs, particularly its poverty-stricken communities, and denying there is a problem is an open invitation for even more gang activity, Gary Martin told a roomful of teachers on Thursday.

Saskatchewan has the second-largest concentration of youth gangs per capita and many of those gang members are being recruited in our cities, small rural communities, and on reserves, said Martin, who is the director of the youth gang task force in Alberta.

'In 2005, there were an estimated 1,315 Saskatchewan youths involved in gangs. That's 1.3 per 1,000 population,' Martin told delegates attending the Treaty 4 Tribal Council's education conference in Regina.

'You should be concerned because gangs are genocide within your community. A gang killing is the only time someone can kill and get away with it,' he added, referring to the fear and intimidation used by gangs to silence their victims and members within their ranks.

Martin, whose 14-year-old cousin was killed in a gang-related random act of violence in west Chicago in 1971, has spent the last 35 years working with schools and communities to work on gang awareness and strategies to discourage gang involvement. Anti-gang programming goes hand in hand with police enforcement in curtailing illegal gang activity, he said.

'Gangs are a relatively new phenomena is Saskatchewan. People are overwhelmed on one side and on the other side they are deeply entrenched in denial. And so, when you have the denial, no matter where you are, it will result in increased gang activity,' he said.

Gangs are coming into major cities and spreading into rural areas and onto the reserves because people aren't aware gangs exist or what the signs of gang involvement and gang activity are or what they can do to stem future gang violence, Martin said.

Gang activity has been identified in Regina, Moose Jaw, Fort Qu'Appelle, Indian Head, and Yorkton, in the Carlyle and Broadview areas, and as far north as La Ronge, Stanley Mission, and Meadow Lake, he said.

'What affects one will affect all and no matter what color you are we are losing our kids by record numbers to gangs,' he said, referring to a growing problem of gang activity that is closely tied to the illegal drug trade.

'The community has to participate at working to diminish these activities. We are not going to stop (gangs) but if they are not going to get good rewards for their activity, like any other business they will move on. If we do nothing we have lost because they will infiltrate our communities and take over and before we know it going through the school system.'

Youth join gangs to achieve recognition and self-enhancement, and a sense of belonging. Schools can and should work with communities to ensure these youths are provided with self-identity, purpose, and accomplishment, and they are given the chance to be heard and to belong, he said.

From Anne Kyle, 'Saskatchewan Hot Spot for Gang Activity', *Regina Leader Post* (Saturday, 7 April 2007). Material reprinted with the express permission of Regina Leader Post Group Inc., a CanWest Partnership.

It has been demonstrated that the interests of the police and the media are entwined; they have a symbiotic relationship in that the media rely upon the police for much of their information, and the police use the media to portray certain images relating to their work.

The media therefore conveys a sensationalized image of crime, and a protective view of the police and policing practices—and they make unusual events usual events in our lives. As Grabosky and Wilson (1989: 11) comment: 'The most common types of crime according to official statistics, crimes against property, receive relatively little media attention. By contrast, crimes of violence, which are very uncommon in actuarial terms, are accorded much greater coverage.'

Similarly, there is a skewed focus on 'street crime' and bizarre events. Meanwhile, the destruction of the environment, domestic violence, while-collar crimes, and occupational health and safety crimes tend not to receive the same type of coverage or treatment by the mainstream media outlets.

With regard to crime control, the usual implication is that once a crime has been brought to the attention of the authorities, investigation will generally lead to detection and capture of the offender. This is a far cry from the reality of much police work, and in specific cases of serious street crime a significant proportion of cases do not get to the prosecution stage. In fictional accounts of crime fighting, the police are usually endowed with special qualities (e.g., big guns, martial arts abilities, etc.), and violence is both central and always justified because of the nature of the 'criminals' at hand. The nature of actual policing is once again misconstrued and the mundane aspects—interviewing, looking over file material, research, traffic regulation, and so on—are generally absent. Another facet of fictional accounts is that the police are not accountable to anyone; they can even step outside the bounds of the law, because we all know they are on 'our' side. Thus, the police are always honest and incorruptible, even though evidence in real life, such as the Fitzgerald inquiry into police in Queensland, Australia (Fitzgerald, 1989) or the recent inquiries into the interior workings of the Royal Canadian Mounted Police (RCMP) in Canada, reveal widespread and systematic corruption.

As a result, it is important to separate the images and realities of crime in society. The media shape our perceptions of crime and in the process they define crime in particular ways. One aspect of this process is that the media often portray crime in terms of distinct crime waves. 'Crime wave' is a term used to refer to the way in which increased reporting of particular types of crime (usually street crimes such as assault, rape, or homicide) increases the public awareness of this crime. It is greatly significant to point out that there need not have been an actual increase in the crime for a crime wave to occur—the increase, or wave, exists only in public perception.

Nevertheless, 'crime waves' can and do have real consequences, regardless of factual basis. For example, extensive media coverage of child abuse may lead to changes in the law, such as the introduction of mandatory reporting of suspected incidents. Or the fear generated by press coverage of assaults on elderly people may lead to calls for more police, tougher sentences, greater police power, and so on. Given the close relationship between the police and the media, major questions can be asked as to who benefits from the selective reporting of specific crimes, especially around budget time.

## Measuring Crime

Given the limitations and problems of relying upon media definitions and treatment of crime, it is reasonable to accept that any statement made about crime should be tested by referring to the 'facts' about crime. This usually means that we need to confirm particular crime trends and consider official data on criminal activity. However, even here there are difficulties with how crime is defined. For what we 'measure' depends on how we define crime and how we see the criminalization process.

In fact, criminologists are not united in their approach to crime and crime statistics (see Nettler, 1984; Jupp, 1989). For present purposes, we can identify three broad strands within criminology that deal with measurement issues.

- The *realist approach* adopts the view that crime exists 'out there' in society and that the 'dark figure' of crime needs to be uncovered and recorded. There are limitations to the gathering of official statistics (such as reliance solely on police records of reported offences), and the role of criminology is to supplement official statistics (those generated by the police, courts, and prison authorities) through a range of informal or alternative measures). The emphasis is on the *problem of omission*—to uncover the true or real extent of crime by methods such as victim surveys, self-report surveys, test situation, hidden cameras, and so on.
- The *institutionalist approach* adopts the view that crime is a 'social process', and it rejects the notion that we can unproblematically gain a sense of the real extent of crime by improving our measuring devices and techniques. This approach instead concentrates on the manner in which official institutions of crime control actually process suspects and thus define certain individuals and certain types of behaviour as being 'criminal'. The emphasis is on the *problem of bias*—to show how the criminal justice system designates some people and events as being criminal while others are not.
- The *critical realist approach* argues that crime measurement can be characterized as having elements of both 'social process' and a grounded 'reality'. The task of measurement from this perspective is to uncover the processes whereby the crimes against the most vulnerable and least powerful sections of the population have been ignored or underrepresented. The emphasis is on the *problem of victimization*—to demonstrate empirically how certain groups are especially vulnerable to

both crime and the fear of crime, and conceptually to criticize the agencies of crime control for their lack of action in protecting these groups.

As clearly illustrated, there are debates within criminology over how and what to measure, and these ultimately reflect basic divisions within the field regarding the very definition of crime itself. The study of crime is fraught with a wide range of competing viewpoints and perspectives, and it is useful to develop an analytical framework that can make sense of these differences as the basis for different points of view on crime and crime control.

## Criminological Perspectives

The style of questions you ask necessarily determines the answers you receive. As we have indicated, there are competing definitions of crime, and these produce competing answers or explanations of the causes of crime, which, in turn, produce different kinds of responses to crime.

Criminological theory can be presented in abstract fashion as being made up of a series of separate perspectives or approaches. Each approach or **paradigm** attempts to understand a particular phenomenon by asking certain types of questions, using certain concepts, and constructing a particular framework of analysis and explanation. In practice, it is rare to find government departments or academic criminologists who rely solely or exclusively on any one particular criminological framework or approach. Often a wide range of ideas and concepts are combined in different ways in the course of developing policy or in the study of a specific empirical problem.

For the sake of presentation it is nevertheless useful to present **ideal types** of the various theoretical strands within criminology. The use of ideal types provides us with a means by which we can clarify main ideas and identify important differences between the broad approaches adopted in the field. An ideal type does not exist in the real world. The intention behind the construction of an ideal type is to abstract the key elements or components of a particular theory or social institution from concrete situations, and to exaggerate these elements, if need be, in order to highlight the general tendency or themes of the particular perspective (see Freund, 1969). An ideal type is an analytical tool; it is not a moral statement of what ought to be. It refers to a process of identifying different aspects of social phenomena and combining them into a 'typical' model or example. For instance, an ideal type of **bureaucracy** would include such things as impartial and impersonal merit and promotion structures, the following of prescribed rules and regulations, a hierarchical chain of command, and so on. We know, however, that people who work in bureaucracies are not always promoted on the basis of their qualifications, and nor is decision-making always rational. But by constructing an exaggerated 'typical' model of a bureaucracy we are able to compare the actual structure of different organizations and how they actually work in the real world.

If we are to construct ideal types in relation to criminological theory, then it is useful first to identify the central focus of theory, and in particular the level of analysis and explanation at which the theory is pitched. There are three broad levels of criminological explanation: the individual, the situational, and the structural. Different theories within criminology tend to locate their main explanation for criminal behaviour or criminality at one of these levels. Occasionally, a theory may attempt to combine all three levels in order to provide a more sophisticated and comprehensive picture of crime and criminality.

## Levels of analysis

There are three levels of analysis to consider, each of which is discussed below.

- *Individual*. The main focus of an individual level of analysis is on the personal or individual characteristics of the offender or victim, such as the influence of appearance, dress, and public image of the nature of crime causation or victimization (e.g., tattoos or earrings as indicators of a 'criminal' attitude in men). This level of analysis tends to look to psychological or biological factors that are said to have an important role in determining why certain individuals engage in criminal activity. The key concern is to explain crime or deviant behaviour in terms of the choices or characteristics of the individual person.
- *Situational*. The main site of situational analysis is the immediate circumstances, or situation, within which criminal activity or deviant behaviour occurs. Attention is directed to the specific factors that may contribute to an event occurring, such as how the participants define the situation, how different people are labelled by others in the criminal justice system, the opportunities available for the commission of certain types of offences, and so on. Key concerns are the nature of the interaction between different players within the system, the effect of local environmental factors on the nature of this interaction, and the influence of group behaviour and influences on social activity.
- *Social structure*. This approach tends to look at crime in terms of the broad social relationships and the major social institutions of the society as a whole. The analysis makes reference to the relationship between classes, sexes, different ethnic and 'racial' groups, the employed and unemployed, and various other social divisions in society. It also can involve investigation of the operation of specific institutions—such as education, the family, work, and the legal system—in the construction of and social responses to crime and deviant behaviour.

The level of analysis one chooses has major consequences for how crime is viewed, the nature of the offender, and how the criminal justice system should be organized. For example, a biological positivist approach looks at characteristics of the individual offender (e.g., genetic makeup) and sees crime as revolving around, and stemming from, the specific personal attributes of the individual. A situational perspective might consider the interaction between police and young people on the street, and argue that 'crime' is defined in the process of specific types of interaction, behaviours, and attitudes. From a structural perspective, the issues might be seen in terms of the relationship between poverty and crime; that is, the elements of social life that underpin particular courses of action. The individualist, situational, and structural approaches would all advocate quite different policies because of their particular perspective. The vantage point from which one examines crime—whether it is a focus on personal characteristics through to a focus on societal institutions—thus shapes the ways in which one thinks about and acts upon criminal justice matters.

The different levels of analysis apparent in criminology are also partly a reflection of the diverse disciplines that have contributed to the study of crime over a number of years. Researchers, scholars, and writers in areas such as biological science, psychology, law, sociology, forensic medicine, political economy, education, history, and cultural studies have all contributed to the multidisciplinary nature of criminology. Each discipline brings to bear its own concepts, debates, and methods when examining a criminological issue or problem. This means that within criminology there is a natural diversity of viewpoints, as different writers and researchers 'see' the world through very different analytical spectacles. Such differences are also reflected in the adoption of a wide range of different techniques and methodologies in the study of crime. These include historical records, use of surveys, participant observation, interviews, evaluation of official statistics, study of policy documents, and discourse analysis.

Most theories of crime tend to congeal into one of these analytical categories; that is, most lean on one of these particular areas, advancing different theories relating to causes of crime. For example, the classical theory focuses on choice—the offender chooses to offend or not offend; the response is punishment. This approach focuses on the criminal act. The biological positivist looks at the offender's personal characteristics, and focuses on treatment. Some researchers attempt to integrate all three levels of analysis into their approach. The questions one asks will obviously vary according to the approach or combination of approached one adopts, as well as the consequences.

## Political orientations

Differences in broad levels of analysis, and in specific discipline-related perspectives, can also be linked to some extent to differences in the political framework of the writer. The political orientation of a writer can be gleaned, in part, by trying to understand their overall picture of society. For example, consider the following representations of society (see Brown, 1979).

- The *geometric circle* implies society is harmonious, and people share the same values about community and equality. The concept of crime is that perpetrators are deviant, or outside the circle, and thus they need to be either pulled back into the circle or kept outside the circle's confines.
- The *triangle* views society as a hierarchy, in which some people are situated at the top, possessing the wealth and power, and the majority is situated at the bottom. This vision of society implies conflict and inequality. The concept of crime is that it occurs in the context of struggles and hierarchies of control and power. Situated within this perspective are both meritocratic and critical views. A meritocratic view of the triangle argues that within the existing structure anyone who plays by the rules of the game is capable of rising to the top of the hierarchy, and that success is a question of ability and hard work. The laws are seen to exist as a means of sustaining the rules of the triangle. A critical view of the triangle translates inequality into injustice. The laws are seen to be unequally applied; it is argued

that people on the bottom of the triangle are overrepresented in the criminal justice system, and this overrepresentation is questioned.

- The *rectangle* or *square* argues that society consists of a variety of interrelated rectangles representing different interconnecting institutions, such as the family, work, and school. Crime is studied in relation to how these institutions both impact and reflect upon crime. The concern here is not with values, as in the circle, but with the smooth running of the interconnected institutions. The issue is one of administrative efficiency and application of the right kinds of techniques to fix the particular social problem.
- *Non-geometric forms*, such as stick figures, places the focus on individuals, as opposed to society as a whole, and the emphasis is on examining individual creativity and the way individuals construct their realities. The idea is that reality is socially constructed, and that how people act and react in relation to each other has a major impact in terms of defining both behaviour and individuals as being deviant, normal, or whatever. How people think about themselves and each other is a significant factor in how they subsequently behave in their interactions with others.

The manner in which we view society influences the way in which we view crime. The various competing perspectives within criminology reflect different points of view regarding the nature of society. We can identify three major paradigms (conceptual frameworks for understanding social phenomena) in criminology. These paradigms inevitably incorporate specific kinds of value judgment. The motivation, conceptual development, methodological tools, and social values associated with a specific approach are usually intertwined with one of three broad political perspectives: conservative, liberal, or radical.

- *Conservative*. A conservative perspective on society tends to be supportive of the legitimacy of the status quo; that is, it generally accepts the way things are, the traditional ways of doing things, and traditional social relationships. Conservatives believe dissenters should be made to conform to the status quo. They also believe that there is a 'core value system' to which everyone in society should conform. The function of the main institutions is to preserve the dominant system in order to maintain the good of society generally. The values and institutions of society should apply equally to all people regardless of social background or historical developments.
- *Liberal*. A liberal perspective on society accepts the limits of the status quo, but encourages limited changes in social institutions. This approach tends to avoid questions relating to the whole structure of society. Instead it emphasizes the need for action on particular limited 'social problems'. Specific problems such as sexism, racism, poverty, and so on, can be resolved without fundamental changes to the economic or social structure. Rather, policies and programmes can be developed that will serve to inform existing institutions and day-to-day interactions. Problems tend to be studied in terms of their impact on specific individuals (e.g., 'the poor' as the focus of research) and the disadvantages suffered by these individuals or groups.

- *Radical.* The radical perspective on society wishes to undermine the legitimacy of the status quo. Like the conservative perspective, it looks at society as a whole, but its sees 'social conflict' as the central concern. Society is seen to be divided on the basis of class, gender, ethnicity, 'race', and so on. (The use of the term 'race' implies that it is a social rather than a scientific construct, and distinguishes it from any biological connotation the word may otherwise have.) The key issue is who holds the power and resources in any particular community. The focus of the radical perspective is fundamental change to the existing social order. Specific issues, such as poverty, are explained in relational terms (e.g., the relationship between the rich and poor), and the solution is seen to involve dealing with the structural imbalances and inequalities that lead to the problem (of poverty) in the first place.

If we acknowledge the centrality of politics in criminological analysis, then we must accept that there is no such thing as value-free criminology. Values of the right (conservative), left (radical), and centre (liberal) are embedded in the criminological enterprise. The political orientation of the particular approach has major implications for how crime is defined. For example, Table 1.1 presents a radical view of how crime can be defined. As opposed to more conservative approaches, this approach emphasizes both the crimes of the powerful and the crimes of the less powerful. Each particular theory of the causes of crime is generally linked in some way to these broad political perspectives, and thus each sees crime as informed by certain values and philosophical principles.

**Table 1.1   A Radical Definition of Crime**

| Crimes of the Powerful | |
| --- | --- |
| **Typical crimes** | **Examples** |
| Economic | Breaches of corporate law, environmental degradation, inadequate industrial health and safety provisions, pollution, violation of labour laws, fraud. |
| State | Police brutality, government corruption, bribery, civil rights violations, misuse of public funds. |

| Crimes of the Less Powerful | |
| --- | --- |
| **Typical crimes** | **Examples** |
| Economic | Street crime, workplace theft, low-level fraud, breach of welfare regulations, prostitution. |
| State | Vandalism, assault (physical and sexual), murder, resistance via strikes and demonstrations, public order offences, workplace sabotage. |

A further aspect relating to the politics of criminological theory is that the dominant paradigm or approach that is adopted by governments and represented in criminological circles (professional journals, conferences, etc.) varies over time. That is, there are competing general perspectives within criminology, but in different periods particular perspectives will be ascendant over others. For example the conservative perspectives (within which lie a number of related theories, usually associated with classical and positivist views, and which center on punishment and control strategies) held considerable sway at the level of policy formulation and action in the 1950s. By the late 1960s, the liberal perspective (centering on labelling and efforts at rehabilitation) informed much of the reform activity related to the criminal justice system. By the mid 1980s there had been a swing back to the right, which persisted into the 1990s, with strident calls for the adoption of tougher measures to deal with issues of 'law and order'. Simultaneous with the conservative push at the level of policy were both liberal and radical critiques of the effectiveness and fairness of such measures. By the late 1990s and early 2000s, the crime debate incorporated conservative elements stressing offender responsibility and strong state action against anti-social and illegal behaviour, and, as well, liberal perspectives that spoke of the need for restorative justice as a key philosophical principle in responding to crime and criminality.

This melding of conservative and liberal policies may be exemplified in the development of the Canadian Youth Justice System. The Act Respecting Juvenile Delinquents, which later became the Juvenile Delinquents Act (1908), placed the root causes of delinquent and criminal behaviour by juveniles in the child's environment and posited that the solution was to have the state replace the parents who failed to control and properly socialize their children. Judges were guided to treat juvenile delinquents as 'misdirected and misguided' children who needed 'aid, encouragement, help, and assistance' (Juvenile Delinquents Act, S.38.). Over time, dissatisfaction with the Act and its perceived inability to deal with rising juvenile crime rates and to rehabilitate juvenile offenders led to the replacement of the Juvenile Delinquents Act. Other critics of the Juvenile Delinquents Act argued that the civil liberties of juveniles were not protected, and were, indeed, ignored under the Act. The Young Offenders Act was implemented in 1984 in an attempt to deal with the criticisms put forward from both sides. The mandate of the new Act was to ensure national standards in the treatment of youth in the justice system through the establishment of legal principles for the treatment of youth between 12–18 years of age. Each province, however, was given the constitutional right to implement its own administrative organization.

Whereas the Juvenile Delinquents Act (1908) was based on a welfare model that suggested negative environmental influences, such as poverty, difficulties with school and family, and poor moral training, significantly influenced juvenile delinquency, the Young Offenders Act (1984) adopted a more justice-oriented **ideology**. The idea of personal responsibility and accountability for wrongdoing was the core principle of the Young Offenders Act. Bill C-68 was introduced in the House of Commons on 11 March 1999 as the Youth Criminal Justice Act and came into force in April 2003. This new Act attempts to address concerns put forward from both those who argue for more punitive actions and those who argue for the need for special considerations for youth who come into conflict with the law. Public safety and security are at the core of the new

Act, which provides the possibility for strong punitive measures to be employed for youth who are considered dangerous, violent, or habitual offenders. For those youth involved in less serious offences, or who are not considered to be high-risk, the new Act encourages youth courts to utilize community-based sentencing options.

The historical development of a Canadian justice system designed for youth appears to represent a transfer from the notion that children were essentially 'adults-in-training', to a belief that children were in need of protection and welfare, to an attempt to balance the needs of youth with the rights of society in regard to public safety. Criminological theory is thus always related in some way to specific historical contexts, specific material conditions, and specific political struggles.

The objectives and methods of analysis used in criminology reflect certain under-lying ideas and concerns of the writers. In reading criminological material, then, it is important to examine the assumptions of the writers—the key concepts they use, and the methods or arguments used to support their theory—to identify their conceptions of society and of human nature, and the kinds of reforms or institutions that they ulti-mately support. It is also important to identify the silences in a particular theory or tra-dition; that is, what questions are not being asked, and why not? Finally, it is crucial to consider the social relevance of the theory or perspective. What does it tell us about our society, and the direction that our society is, or ought to be, heading? Fundamen-tally, the study of crime involves the values and opinions of the criminologist, and this, too, is part of what the student of crime must be aware of it they are to develop an informed view of the issues.

## Conclusion

The objectives and methods of criminology both reflect and are affected by a wide range of ideas and concerns. This chapter has provided an overview of how the study of crime is built upon a variety of different definitions, how it involves recognition of historical and cross-cultural processes, and that it must acknowledge the impact of popular media images on perceptions of crime. The chapter has also indicated the approaches within criminology to measure crime, and the analytically and politically diverse nature of the criminological enterprise.

The main purpose of this book as a whole is to explore how criminology explains the 'causes' of crime. Our concern is not to discuss general social theory as such, although the influence of specific social theorists, implicitly if not explicitly, permeates many of the discussions. For example, the ideas of Foucault (1980) are particularly evi-dent in certain strands of feminist criminology and critical criminology. In a similar vein, we do not deal with the application of general social theory to specific institu-tional processes as in the case of Foucault (1977) on prisons or Cohen (1985) on com-munity corrections. Indeed, the book is not designed to explain issues relating to the 'responses' of society to criminal behaviour and activity, except in a very general sense and only when directly related to the theories that are discussed. Such questions are considered in greater detail elsewhere, as in the case of Garland (1990) on punishment, Howe (1994) on penality, and White and Perrone (1997) on criminal justice institu-tions generally.

In providing a broad overview of the major frameworks of analysis within criminology we have structured each chapter in the following way: Introduction, Social Context, Basic Concepts, Historical Development, Contemporary Examples, Critique, and Conclusion. By organizing the material in such a fashion we hope to offer the reader a useful guide to the background, development, and core ideas of each theoretical strand in a way that also makes comparisons between the diverse theories relatively easy.

It is our belief that good criminology is that which is self-consciously reflective of the theoretical and political basis of its understandings and analysis. How we view crime, how we define what is harmful or serious, and how we study criminal behaviour all have major ramifications for how we propose to deal with crime at the level of policy, institution, and strategy. It is our hope that this book will assist the reader in situating the social, theoretical, and practical implications of whatever perspective they may draw upon in trying to come to grips with crime and criminology today.

## Key Terms and Concepts

- Analytical criminology
- Conservative political orientation
- Crime waves
- Criminology
- Critical realist approach
- Cross-cultural universal norm approach to crime
- Dark figure of crime
- Formal legal definitions of crime
- Geometric circle view of society
- Human diversity approach to crime
- Human rights approach to crime
- Individual level of analysis
- Institutional approach
- Labelling approach to crime

- Liberal political orientation
- Moral panic
- Problem of victimization
- Problems of bias
- Problems of omission
- Radical political orientation
- Realist approach
- Rectangle or square view of society
- Situational level of analysis
- Social harm concept of crime
- Social structure
- Theory
- Triangle view of society
- Vocational criminology

## Further Reading

W. Einstadter and S. Henry, *Criminological Theory: An Analysis of Its Underlying Assumptions* (New York: Harcourt Brace, 1995).

V. Jupp, *Methods of Criminological Research* (London: Routledge, 1989).

J. Muncie, E. McLaughlin, and M. Langan, eds, *Criminological Perspectives: A Reader* (London: Sage, 1996).

G. Nettler, *Explaining Crime* (New York: McGraw-Hill, 1984).

B. Schissel, *Blaming Children: Youth Crime, Moral Panics, and the Politics of Hate* (Halifax: Fernwood Books, 1997).

B. Schissel and L. Mahood, eds, *Social Control in Canada: Issues in the Social Construction of Deviance* (Don Mills, ON: Oxford University Press, 1996).

I. Taylor, P. Walton, and J. Young, (1973) *The New Criminology* (London: Routledge and Kegan Paul, 1973).

## Websites

*www.canada.justice.gc.ca.* The Canadian Department of Justice website provides current, general information about Canada's criminal justice system.

*www.ciaj-icaj.ca/index.html.* The Canadian Institute for the Administration of Justice is a national non-profit organization that examines the administration of justice in Canada.

*www.scc-csc.gc.ca.* The Supreme Court of Canada website provides a clear overview of the Canadian judicial system.

*www.statscan.ca.* Statistics Canada's website offers access to current statistics to crime in Canada.

## Films/Documentaries

- *Abortion: Stories from the North and South* (National Film Board of Canada, 1984)
- *Acts of Defiance* (National Film Board of Canada, 1992)
- *Crime in the Cities: Public Safety at Risk* (A&E, The History Channel, 2004)
- *Law and Disorder: Animated Justice* (National Film Board of Canada, 2003)
- *Time Machine: Rumrunners, Moonshiners, and Bootleggers* (A&E, The History Channel, 2002)

## Discussion Questions

1. What are the challenges associated with defining crime?
2. Provide an example of a modern-day crime-based moral panic fueled by the Canadian media. Discuss both the real and potential impact this moral panic on public perceptions of the issue.
3. How has capitalism influenced the creation of, and modifications to, our Canadian justice system?
4. What is the 'rule of law'? Is it possible for the rule of law to exist beyond an ideal type in Canadian society? List and provide contradictions to the rule of law in the application of law and the treatment of groups or individuals in society.
5. What are the fundamental and competing differences between an individual and social structural analyses of crime? Are there any ways to find common ground between the two perspectives?

# CHAPTER 2

# Classical Theory

## Objectives

This chapter will help you develop an understanding of the:

- historical context within which classical theory in criminology developed;
- basic principles and concepts found within this perspective;
- influence classical theory has had on current criminal justice issues; and
- strengths and weaknesses of the classic criminological perspective.

## Introduction

The goal of this chapter is to provide students with an outline and review of the classical theory in criminology. Students should understand the historical context from which classicism emerged and the basic principles and concepts of the classical model. Students will also comprehend the contribution of this model to present criminal justice issues and institutions, along with the strengths and limitations of the perspective.

The foundation of the contemporary criminal justice and legal systems were laid down in the eighteenth century. This was the period when the basic principles and practices of classical theory were developed and institutionalized for the first time in Europe. The emergence of classical thought constituted a radical challenge to the institutional and class relations underpinning the system of justice at that time, and resulted in a departure from previous methods of criminal justice adjudication.

## Social Context

The specific contours of legal change associated with the classical perspective in criminology varied greatly depending upon the national context. For example, in England, the seventeenth century was the epoch of greatest importance in the history of political and legal theory. It was a time when the power of the monarch was directly challenged in a number of ways. One outcome of the conflicts over power, authority, and the role of law embodied in this struggle was the development of a body of principles about the supremacy of law, the fundamental rights of human beings, equality before the law, and the democratic basis of political authority (Kelly, 1992). Major political and legal changes were to occur at different times and in different ways in the other

European centres such as France, Germany, Spain, and Italy. The eighteenth-century intellectual movement, the Enlightenment—which looked to rebuild social structures on the basis of purely rational principles—heavily influenced these changes. Assertion of the rule of law, and of the importance of thinking about society and the state in terms of a social contract, were eventually to prevail. As part of the reform processes taking place across Europe, the basis of criminal law and the nature of punishment were called into question.

The development of classical conceptions of law and the criminal justice system was grounded in the transition from **feudalism** to **capitalism**. Major social, economic, and political changes were occurring throughout Europe and were revolutionizing both the institutions of power and social relationships generally. The 'revolutions' were at two levels: economic and political. In production, economies based primarily on agriculture moved to become commercial market economies and then industrial economies; and in the political sphere, the emerging bourgeoisie, or capitalist class, challenged the rule of the landed aristocracy. Thus, over a period of several centuries to the eighteenth century, there occurred a transition from one mode of production, feudalism, to another dominant mode of production, capitalism.

Under feudalism, land, wealth, and power were concentrated in the hands of a small group of people—the landed aristocracy—which maintained its rule through a combination of repression (e.g., putting down peasant rebellions) and appeal to tradition and custom (e.g., the idea of a preordained social order with kings and queens at the top). Ideologically, law was maintained by appeal to such notions as the 'divine right of monarchs', which said that monarchs ruled by God-given right. Since law-making was a matter of birthright and religious conviction, the aristocracy was for a time able to rule with absolute power. Disobedience or challenge to that order was repressed. Basic social patterns, in particular the relationship between serf and lord, were cast as 'natural' and permanent social arrangements.

In the feudal era, there was an absence of formal legal status as such. Rights were not acknowledged as being common to all. Rather, any rights that did not exist were linked to individual station and class. For example, peasants and (most) women were accorded few formal rights while members of the aristocracy and the upper levels of the Christian church had special rights associated with their position in society. One's social rank thus determined the nature and extent of the rights one was able to claim or exercise.

The administration of justice tended to be haphazard, localized, irregular, and unsystematic (see Hall and McLennan, 1986). Just as rights and laws were molded around the specific interests of powerful individuals, so, too, the 'justice' system reflected the personal ties or connections of the powerful (e.g., derived from patronage, familiarity, or business associations) and the personal whim of the local ruling class. Men (women were generally not decision-makers, unless part of royalty) held judicial office as an extension of their wealth and rank in society. Furthermore, there was a proliferation of different types of courts, including local manorial courts, ecclesiastical (religious) courts, and the King's or Queen's courts.

Justice was personalized. That is, decisions regarding whether particular acts were deemed to be criminal or not, and the responses to criminal acts, were essentially a matter of the personal opinion or whim of the presiding judge. Decisions were unpredictable. Persons holding legal office could display mercy if they so desired, but this in itself reflected the absolute power they held in their hands to make decisions. There were few institutionalized checks or balances on this power. The legal system was highly localized, and revolved around the existing power relationships of the landed gentry and church officials.

The penalties for crime were also highly individualized and varied greatly. Torture and death were not uncommon penalties for even minor offences. The brutal nature of the punishment also reflected the fact that the long-term holding of prisoners in particular sites (e.g., prisons) was not used as a general form of sanction. It also reflected the arbitrary use of draconian or extreme measures when the first priority of the day was maintenance of order and orthodoxy, rather than justice and reform.

The exercise of power was, however, circumscribed by certain customs and traditions that, ultimately, served to legitimize the existing social structure (see Fine, 1984). For instance, while the serf or peasant was bound to do extra work or provide an amount of their produce for the lord, the lord was in turn obligated to protect his vassals from outside threat or harm, and to ensure that certain social responsibilities were maintained (e.g., in times of famine to provide a share of social goods to the poor).

The rise of the state, initially linked to the extension of monarchical power, saw the legal and criminal justice systems start to change. Over time, if we take the English case, the monarchs were able to fuse local traditions and customs into a general form of law administration—and hence the development of a '**common law**' system of justice. In other European centres such as France, extensive centralized laws were established (e.g., the Code Napoleon) that were to provide a national structure for the legal system. Each system of law served to entrench and consolidate the power of the monarch over that of the local landowner (e.g., barons), so that the monarch was then able to rule much more absolutely than had previously been the case.

The next stage of legal development was linked to the formation of the capitalist class, beginning with the age of mercantile capitalism (i.e., merchant trading in the context of nation-states). The absolute power of the monarch constituted a fetter on the activities and aspirations of this new class. For example, the ability of monarchs to grant monopoly trading rights to selected companies (e.g., Hudson's Bay Company in North America) was seen to be unfair because it restricted the trading activities of the mercantile capitalists. Furthermore, given that the law was still essentially reflective of personal whim and establishment prerogatives (since decision-making at both national and local levels resided in the hands of the landed aristocracy), a political revolution was necessary to change basic relations of power.

This manifested itself in the form of a series of armed struggles and revolutions, including the French Revolution and the American Revolution. The power of the monarchy was circumscribed, or replaced, by new institutions (e.g., parliaments), and the aristocracy was pushed to the side as the only or major ruling force in society. For economic reasons (i.e., long-term planning purposes) as well as political reasons (i.e., holding of decision-making power), a new form of law and criminal justice system evolved. A central feature of this system was that it was bureaucratic in nature (rather than personalized), and it provided a more systematic and impersonal method of judicial administration.

The concept of individual rights, as opposed to customary and traditional bonds, was central to the political, economic, and social projects of the bourgeoisie. The new class, the capitalists, called for the universalization of rights (at least to those who had wealth and property) against a regime based solely upon hereditary privilege. Accompanying the demand for recognition of the 'rights of man' was an insistence that the state no longer simply rule on behalf of a monarch, or the aristocracy. Rather, the role of the state was to preserve the rule of law. In this system the state apparatus acts as a distinct public authority to guarantee 'equality under the law' in relation to freedom, rights, and obligations. In this conception of law, not only were all equal in the eyes of the law, but the law-makers themselves were likewise bound by the laws they devised.

The claim for universal and equal rights was relevant to the political domain and, as well, to the law and courts. The idea was that all social attributes such as class, rank, and social background should be ignored once a person entered the court. People should not be subject to arbitrary judgment and a justice system based upon different rights for classes of people. Once in court, participants are transformed into 'abstract legal subjects' who, regardless of background, should be treated equally (O'Malley, 1983).

Economically, the demand for individual rights was important in a number of ways (Fine, 1984). First, it helped to bolster the idea that 'private property' was a right that did not have to be seen in relation to customary or traditional obligations. For example, ownership of land had been linked to certain social obligations for those living on the land; it was now absolutely and exclusively a matter for the owner to decide. An owner could decide to plant cash crops for the market, rather than subsistence crops for the peasant residents. Any obligations to help the poor, or find work for the peasants who had been dispossessed of land, were effectively transferred from private hands to the state.

Second, the notion of rights was used to justify a breaking of bonds between peasants and the landed aristocracy. No longer tied by tradition or custom to the land, peasants were allowed the legal right to freely sell their labour. Coupled with the new legal basis of private property, which soon led to the closing of land to the peasant class, the position of individuals as 'free labourers' served to swell the cities as urbanization gathered pace. This provided the capitalist class with a huge reservoir of labour from which to choose, and with which production could be magnified in ways hitherto not seen in the history of humankind. The 'freeing' of people from the land was, in fact, crucial to the later development of full-scale industrialization.

The classical approach in law and criminology was thus born of momentous changes occurring across the political, legal, social, and economic domains. At the core of these changes was the relationship between individual rights, the state, and equality. The rights of human beings, it was felt, should be protected against arbitrary uses of power. Likewise, a rational system of production and exchange (i.e., the capitalist market) demanded a legal system that was predictable, systematic, and regular. Such a system, involving competition between producers, should also ensure that the power of the state be limited, particularly in regard to issues surrounding private property and personal accumulation of wealth.

Canada's governmental structure reflects this historical context. Canada became a country by an act of parliament of Great Britain—The British North America Act (BNA) of 1867—that facilitated the merging of the colonies of Upper and Lower Canada, Nova Scotia, and New Brunswick into a confederation known as the Dominion of Canada. However, this did not mean that the new Dominion of Canada had autonomy. The new country was still part of the British Empire and was governed by monarch-appointed authority. In other words, the BNA Act did not codify a new set of constitutional rules for Canada; any amendments to the BNA had to be enacted by the Parliament in England. This did not change until the Canada Act of 1982 patriated (or brought home) Canada's constitution. The Constitution Act (part of the Canada Act of 1982) declares the Constitution of Canada—with its 30 odd acts and orders—to be the supreme law of Canada and includes the Charter of Rights and Freedoms, which includes provisions for privacy rights, democratic rights, legal rights, and equality rights.

Canada's legal system also reflects the complexity found in state responses to the need for social control of its citizens. Canada's legal system is defined as a bijuralism, which means the coexistence of two fundamental legal traditions; common law and **civil law**. Common law, which developed in Great Britain, was based on the decisions made by judges in the royal court. Over time, this practice evolved into a system of rules based on precedent. In other words, whenever a judge makes a decision that is legally enforced the decision becomes a rule that other judges will follow in making decisions in future similar cases. The tradition of civil law, in contrast, is based on Roman law, which has been found in many places such as books, proclamations, and statutes.

Canada's federal system of government means that the authority to make laws is divided between the Parliament of Canada and the territorial and provincial legislatures. Parliament can make laws for all of Canada in matters assigned to it by the Constitution. Provincial or territorial legislatures can make laws regarding matters over which it has been assigned jurisdiction; these laws only apply within the individual provinces or territories. Aboriginal peoples have also made significant contributions to the development of Canada's legal system. Aboriginal rights, including treaty rights, are recognized and protected under the Constitution. Aboriginal customs have also influenced the ways laws have been applied to people through the development of healing and sentencing circles, restorative justice, and community justice initiatives. In this way, we can see how justice systems develop and are influenced by the historical context in which they exist.

## Basic Concepts

Classical theory is premised upon the notion of individual rights, the human capacity to reason, and the rule of law (see Table 2.1). The theory assumes a particular view of human nature, and the relationship between individuals and that state.

In the classical view, human beings are seen as being essentially self-seeking and self-interested individuals. What we do with our personal talents, skills, and energy is a matter of individual initiative and choice; that is, the classical theory has a voluntaristic view of human nature that emphasized free will and individual choice. We are

## Table 2.1    Classical Theory

| | |
|---|---|
| Definition of crime | *Legal*<br>Violation of law<br>Rights and social contract |
| Focus of analysis | *The criminal act*<br>Specific offence<br>The criminal law |
| Cause of crime | *Rationality*<br>Individual choice<br>Irrational decisions |
| Nature of the offender | *Voluntaristic*<br>Free-will, self-interest, and equal capacity to reason |
| Response to crime | *Punishment*<br>Proportionate to the crime<br>Fixed or determinate |
| Crime prevention | *Deterrence*<br>Pleasure–pain principle<br>Reform of the legal system to make it more accessible. |
| Operation of criminal justice system | *Legal-philosophical approach*<br>Basic principles |

thereby seen as ultimately responsible for choosing what to do with our time and energy, and for the consequences that may arise from our actions.

Rather than analyzing the customary links between people, the theory emphasizes the status of human beings as rights-holders. Individuals are deemed to have an equal capacity to reason and to act in accordance with what is rational from the point of view of their own self-interests. Institutionally, each individual is to be granted equal rights under the law. The fundamental objective of the law is to protect individual rights and to allow the free exercise of choice among individuals as far as this is possible without leading to social harm.

In order to guarantee both individual rights and some semblance of order, classical theory considers the role of the state to be central. Specifically, the theory rests upon the notion of a social contract between individual rights-holders and the state. In this model, there is an implied consensus or agreement that individuals in society give up certain rights to the state in return for the protection of their rights and the security of their person and property from other individuals, and from the state itself. If human beings are seen as essentially self-interested and self-seeking, then there needs to be some kind of mechanism that will, in effect, protect us from the self-interested behaviours and actions of others. Hence, the role of the state is to regulate human interaction, and to be a site where rights in general can be protected by not allowing their infringement in specific instances.

The legal manifestation of the social contract is expressed in the phrase 'rule of law'. The rule of law means that everyone is to be treated equally, without fear or favour, in the eyes of the law. Further, even the law-makers are bound by the law set down for the general populace. Thus, the first principle of the justice system is equal protection of rights. A crucial assumption here is that the social contract will protect each individual against the excesses and corruption of institutions and other individuals by treating all people the same way. For this to occur in practice, it is necessary to have a criminal justice and judicial system that is systematic, predictable, and regular.

The law is seen to be intrinsically good, and to reflect the reasoned beliefs and values of the law-makers. The theory assumes a consensus in society regarding what is considered 'good' and what is 'bad', and this is reflected in the specific criminal laws. Crime is defined in the first instance as simply a violation of the law. Adherence to the law in general, and to specific laws in particular, is seen to be an essential component of the social contract that protects individual rights generally.

In this framework, criminality is seen as primarily a matter of making the wrong choice, by violating the law. Put simply, individuals are to be held responsible for their actions. Since each person is seen to have equal capacity to reason, and given that every effort is made to make citizens familiar with the law, and with its punishments, crime is in essence a matter of free choice. The source of criminality thus lies within the rational, reasoning individual. Crime is the result of individuals either making a calculated decision to do wrong (by weighing up the potential rewards and negative consequences) or engaging in what might be seen as irrational behaviour (by not using their reason adequately or properly).

The social contract is maintained in practice through the use of punishment. The purpose of punishment is to deter individuals from violating laws, which, in effect, means an interference with the person or property rights of another. **Deterrence** should be directed both at the individual (specific deterrence) and at members of society at large (general deterrence) through the use of a wide range of sanctions or penalties appropriate to the offences committed. Punishment was based on the pleasure–pain principle, in which the pain of the sentence would outweigh any pleasure to be gained from committing the crime.

The response of the criminal justice system is focused primarily on the criminal act. The rule of law demands that each violation of the law be treated in the same way—that is, like cases should be treated alike. To put it differently, the emphasis is on equality in legal proceedings (everyone is equal in the eyes of the law) and equality in punishment of offenders (similar crimes are punished in the same way).

The uniformity of the law is guaranteed by set penalties for particular offences. The punishment is thus meant to fit the crime. For the sake of equality, penalties should be fixed prior to sentencing, and be administered in accordance with the actual offence that has been committed. Punishment, therefore, is to consist of determinate sentences, which clearly link specific offences with specific penalties and which are applicable to anyone who has committed the offence in question.

## Historical Development

The two leading figures in the development of classical criminology were Cesare Beccaria and Jeremy Bentham (see Taylor et al., 1973; Bohm, 1999; Schissel and Brooks, 2002; Siegel and McCormick, 2003). The work of Beccaria provided a profound critique of the existing systems of law and criminal justice. He opposed the arbitrary nature of judicial decision-making that was characteristic of the courts of his day, and he was critical of the unduly harsh and barbaric forms of punishment, which included extensive use of the death penalty and the routine use of torture.

According to Beccaria, the basis for all social action should be the utilitarian concept of the greatest happiness for the greatest number in society. Translated into the criminal justice sphere, this meant that crime should be considered an injury to society as a whole (and not explained in terms of 'sin' or dealt with solely on the basis of 'privilege'). The purpose of punishment is not simply social revenge or retribution, but to ensure the greatest overall good for everyone. This means that punishment should be oriented towards deterring individuals or groups from committing crime, rather than wreaking vengeance.

It was felt the prevention of crime was more important than the punishment itself. To this end it was important to make sure that everyone knew the laws. Human beings were seen as essentially rational. For punishment to work in the deterrence sense, it needed to be rationally applied (rather than to be seen as draconian or unfair). It also needed to be applied in a systematic manner that was not subject to the individual whim (including personal granting of mercy) of the judiciary. Further, the deterrent effect of punishment would only be attainable if there was a certainty of punishment, which in turn could be provided only by the establishment of a professionalized police and judicial system.

Ethically, the utilitarian principle demands that the punishment should fit the crime. Hence, the use of torture and the death penalty was condemned insofar as these represented gross violations of individual rights and were disproportionate to the offences actually committed by offenders. Alternatively, incarceration was viewed as a form of punishment that would be particularly effective given the goals of punishment in the classical framework. As Beccaria (1767) put it:

> The end of punishment, therefore, is no other, than to prevent the criminal from doing further injury to society, and to prevent others from committing the like offence. Such punishment, therefore, and such a mode of inflicting them, ought to be chosen, as will make the strongest and most lasting impression on the minds of others, with the least torment to the body of the criminal (43).

Such an approach necessarily was founded upon a heightened importance attached to formal law, which should set out clearly the range of penalties pertaining to particular kinds of infringements. Judicial discretion should be limited to the area of deciding the 'facts' of the case; it should not extend to selection of penalties once guilt had been ascertained.

The classical view was further developed in the writings of Bentham. Likewise seeing human beings and society within a framework of utilitarianism, Bentham argued that all behaviour is reducible to that of seeking pleasure and avoiding pain. Criminal behaviour, in particular, was also seen as reflecting this universal tendency or generalized pleasure–pain principle (see Gottfredson and Hirschi, 1990; Bohm, 1999, Siegel and McCormick, 2003).

Given that human beings were seen as having free will, and having equal capacity to reason, the central question for criminal justice revolved around how to make crime painful and how to reduce the rewards for criminal behaviour. The criminal law reflects a social contract between individuals and the state, a contract that is based upon a rational exchange of rights and obligations. Enforcement of the criminal law should be based on making adherence the most rational thing to do, in the light of the fact that violation would almost certainly mean the experience of negative sanctions. In a nutshell, punishment should offer more pain than the transgression of the law is worth.

To commit or not commit a crime was thus seen as a matter of free choice. Self-interest dictated, however, that if punishment outweighed the potential gain, then crime itself would be the result of either irrational or bad choices. Those who did commit a crime should be punished because the responsibility for doing so in the first place ultimately rests in their own hands.

Although cogent in abstract principle, classical thinking met considerable challenges when put into practice. These came from three directions. The first challenge was to make such general principles serve the interests of justice and equality when faced with a specific defendant in court. Some defendants clearly did not conform to the abstract concept of being rational and equal. Questions could be raised about the rationality of children and people with mental illness, for example. To cope with the reality of life in court, reforms took place (sometimes known as the 'neoclassical' reforms). These developed rules to cope with extenuating circumstances where individuals could be deemed not to be totally responsible for their actions.

The second challenge came from the growing bureaucratization of the state. As capitalism grew, so did the need for a coordinating bureaucracy to ensure the smooth running of commerce. The state fulfilled such a role. The courts, as part of the state, had to fulfill the bureaucratic criterion of efficiency as much as those of justice and fairness. Where the criteria of efficiency and justice were incompatible, conflict resulted. Changes to the state that result from the demands of bureaucracy have been labelled 'corporatization', where procedures are put into place to increase efficiency rather than to emphasize qualities such as justice.

The third challenge to classicism came from vested interests. Those in positions of power viewed classicism as a challenge to their entrenched authority, which they wielded through considerable discretion in application of the law in practice. Codification of legal principles therefore threatened the autonomy of the aristocracy, who naturally resisted such changes. The system that resulted, particularly in the UK and Australia, represents a hybrid of classical and pre-classical models.

## Contemporary Examples

The classical perspective is reflected in many aspects of the contemporary criminal justice system, despite the three challenges outlined above. Classical thinking is evident in legal doctrine that emphasizes conscious intent or choice (e.g., the notion of *mens rea* or the guilty mind) in both sentencing principles (e.g., the idea of culpability or responsibility) and the structure of punishment (e.g., the gradation of penalties according to seriousness of offence).

Philosophically, the classical view sees its modern counterpart in the supporter of a '**just deserts**' approach to sentencing. In this perspective, four basic principles are proposed (see Pitt and Braithwaite, 1993; Siegel and McCormick, 2003; Williams III and McShane, 2004; Bell, 2007):

1. No one other than a person found to be guilty of a crime must be punished for it.
2. Anyone found to be guilty of a crime must be punished for that crime.
3. Punishment must not be more than of a degree commensurate with, or proportional to, the nature or gravity of the offence and culpability of the criminal.
4. Punishment must not be less than of a degree commensurate with, or proportional to, the nature or gravity of the offence and the culpability of the criminal.

Such principles clearly rest on a classical foundation. They encapsulate notions of free will and rationality, as well as proportionality and equality. As we have said, these notions form part of the 'just deserts' understanding of criminal behaviour, and seek to focus on the offence not the offender; to deter the offender from re-offending according to the pleasure–pain principle; and the ensure that justice is served by equal punishment for the same crime. 'Just deserts' philosophy eschews individual discretion and rehabilitation as the aims of the justice system. Justice must both be done (i.e., proportional punishment must be meted out) and be seen to be done (i.e., there should be no exceptions).

The 'just deserts' model has formed the basis for many of the debates surround Canadian reform. The focus of these reforms has been to rationalize the sentencing structure by specifying more clearly the appropriate penalty for the offense. In reality, debate has focused on the perceived need to reduce the discretion of the judiciary by controlling penalties more closely in legislation, dictating length of sentence (or more accurately period of incarceration), and removing or reducing parole and other periods of non-incarceration. The aim is not necessarily to increase penalties (although this may be in fact what happens); rather, the aim is for the penalty to be reflective of the offence and to be administered without favouring one individual over another. This 'just deserts' model is most closely seen in the 2006 election platform of the Conservative Party of Canada, who argued for longer, mandatory sentences for certain offences, a reduction in the use of parole, and the restriction of judicial powers in the use of discretion.

Such sentencing reforms revisit many of the debates that surround the application of classical principles. In particular, debates concern the fairness of a system that has curtailed considerations of extenuating circumstances of the offender and reduced judicial discretion to a large degree. Those who argue for the need to rehabilitate the offender are particularly troubled by the change in legislation, with rehabilitation being irrelevant to both classical and 'just deserts' thinking.

It is perhaps misleading, however, to focus on sentencing as the primary concern of classical theory. Classical theorists were equally concerned with codifying and simplifying law so that the majority of people easily understood it. Both these aims have had limited success. Although there have been some attempts to simplify law, and

## Box 2.1 Conservative Party Election Platform 2006

The following strategies form the basis of the Conservative Party's platform on crime:

- Adopt, in collaboration with the provinces, a national strategy to fight organized crime, including the creation of a joint national task force on security.
- Ensure federal corrections officers have the tools and training they require to do their job as peace officers.
- Repeal the long-gun registry legislation (Bill C-68).
- Reinvest savings from cancellation of the gun registry programme into hiring more front-line enforcement personnel, including filling 1,000 RCMP positions.
- Negotiate with the provinces to create a new cost-shared programme to put at least 2,500 more police on the beat in our cities and communities.
- Invest $100 million per year of new federal money on criminal justice priorities, including working with the provinces and municipalities to hire more police, as well as victim assistance and youth crime prevention programmes.
- Maintain the existing handgun registry and bans on all currently prohibited weapons.
- Introduce mandatory minimum prison sentences with restricted parole eligibility for the criminal use of firearms, trafficking or possession of stolen firearms, or illegal possession contrary to a bail, parole, or firearms prohibition order.
- Strict monitoring, including tracking place of residence, of high-risk individuals prohibited from owning firearms, multiple violent or sexual offences.
- Replace statutory release with earned parole.
- Toughen parole provisions for those convicted of committing a crime while on parole, and eliminate parole for life after the third such conviction.
- Prevent courts from giving extra 'credit' for pre-trial custody for persons denied bail because of their past criminal record or for violating bail.
- Create a reverse onus for bail hearings for anybody charged with an indictable firearms offence.
- Work for a constitutional amendment to forbid prisoners in federal institutions from voting in elections.
- Ensure anyone 14 years or older who is charged with serious violent or repeat offences is automatically subject to adult sentencing provisions.
- Amend the Youth Criminal Justice Act to include deterrence and denunciation as mandatory sentencing principles to be considered.
- Establish national Victims' Ombudsman Office.
- Provide $10 million per year for victim assistance.
- Adopt a zero tolerance policy for child pornography.

- End house arrests and ensure mandatory minimum prison sentences and large monetary fines for serious drug offenders, including marijuana grow operators and producers and dealers of crystal meth and crack.
- Prevent the decriminalization of marijuana.
- Make precursor chemicals of crystal meth, such as pseudoephedrine, harder to get.
- Introduce a national drug strategy to dissuade young people from using drugs.
- Expedite deportation of non-citizens convicted of drug trafficking, drug importation, or running grow operations.
- Restore the Canada Ports Police.
- Support results-oriented, community-based initiatives for addictions treatment, training, and rehabilitation of those in trouble with the law.
- Direct $50 million in funding into community-based, educational, sporting, cultural, and vocational opportunities for youth at risk.
- Work with provinces, municipalities, police, and community leaders in areas threatened by gun and gang violence to support programmes which reach out to young people.
- Require the registration of all convicted sex offenders and dangerous offenders, which will include mandatory DNA sampling of all those convicted or currently in custody on such offences.
- Rename the Age of Consent to the Age of Protection and raise the age from 14 to 16 years of age.
- Prohibit conditional sentences for sex offences committed against children.
- Amend s.810.2 of the Criminal Code to permit the participation of the prosecutors involved in the original trial, as well as the victims of the crime and their families, at the hearing.
- Allow judges to impose residency restrictions on offenders, and extend the term of the order.
- Reduce the backlog of unexecuted deportation orders and swiftly carry out new ones.
- Place top priority on executing existing and new deportation orders against individuals with criminal records, connections to terrorist organizations, or organized crime.
- Amend the Immigration and Refugee Protection Act, the Criminal Code, and the Corrections and Conditional Release Act to permit sentencing courts to order deportation following conviction on select offences and also to prohibit persons already ordered deported from parole eligibility before deportation.

From ctv.ca, 'Election Day, January 2006', 2006a. Based on the official 2006 Conservative party platform and on the Conservative Party's official website.

make it accessible to all, many aspects of law remain obscure and impenetrable to the majority. Furthermore, legal expenses often prove prohibitive to all but the wealthy when it comes to pursuing justice through law. To some extent, though, there have been advances in making law accessible to the general populace. The provision of legal aid and the provisions of small claims courts throughout Canada can be seen to have a least some origin in these concerns of the classical perspective.

## Critique

The limitations of classical theory have been signalled throughout the chapter. Here they will be summarized for clarity. Concerns with classical theory can be broken down into two groups; namely, problems with fairness in the case of individuals, and neglect of inequalities in the broader social structure (see Taylor et al., 1973; Young, 1981).

The problem of fairness in individual cases formed an early critique of classical theory and led to the first wave of neoclassical reforms. Despite such reforms, the problem still remains where a system focuses on the offence and not the offender, coupled with principles of equality and fairness when responding to such criminal behaviour. People are not endowed with equal capacity to reason (e.g., children and people with intellectual disability or mental illness). The decision to offend may or may not be the result of an irrational choice, and the theory gives no insight into how to deal with cases where offending results from an incapacity of reason.

The second critique follows from the first and is concerned with the classical concept of rationality. If offending results from a temporary irrationality, how is it that the distribution of crime (as measured by official statistics) is not spread equally throughout the social structure? Such measures place the bulk of the offending among those with low incomes. The findings suggest that for some people offending may be entirely rational in a manner that is not amendable to the deterrence resulting from punishment. In a world of deep social inequalities, universal equality cannot be realized by treating everyone equally before the law. Rational choice may lead some to offend precisely because of social inequalities. Equality before the law masks this reality.

On a broader level, it has long been recognized that there are clear differences between formal law (that which is written) and substantive law (that which happens in practice). The way law was written tended to assist some individuals who understood the law and know how to exploit it, while disadvantaging others who did not have the same access to lawyers nor understand the way law works in practice. It is a common complaint that a powerful individual or organization appears able to avoid the 'spirit' of the law, while complying with the 'letter' of the law.

The legal process is itself influenced by the broader social inequalities. Some people are more equal than others, and this in turn affects the legal process. The wealthy have access to legal advice that in turn affects how they are dealt with by the justice system. Furthermore, punishments may be proportional to the crime, but will be experienced in markedly different ways—the rich may retain income and wealth, while the poor lose out on income and further work opportunities.

Despite these problems, classical theory had a real and positive effect on the justice system. It did promote a more open, systematic system of justice when compared to the previous system based on the arbitrary whim of the aristocracy. Classical principles argue for the rights of an individual within the system, and place limits of judicial discretion. Finally, the theory espouses a humanitarian approach to punishment when compared to the barbaric practices of the previous era. For example, classical theorists such as Beccaria argued against capital punishment, which was very much a radical proposition for the era.

## Conclusion

Classical theory was developed at a time of great social change, namely the transition from feudalism to capitalism. Just as that transition challenged the pre-eminence of the aristocracy in economic matters, so classicism challenged the aristocracy in matters of crime and justice. Classical theory sought to promote the rights of individuals as equal and rational. According to this perspective, people are inherently self-seeking and endowed with free will. This free will, coupled with a rational system of laws that deters individuals from offending, will ensure few have the motivation to offend. Under this system punishment will be meted out without reference to whom the offender is, in a manner that ensures the pain of punishment outweighs the gain from the offence.

Classical thinking had a profound effect on the justice system, and can be seen particularly clearly in the debates of the 1980s and 1990s concerning 'just deserts' principles in sentencing. However, the focus on the offence rather than on the offender has problems when individuals lack the capacity for reason, or where offending can be seen to reflect the wider inequalities in society. Classical theory can have the effect of masking the reality of these broader inequalities in the social structure, and in this way entrench such inequalities through a pretence of equal access to justice through the legal system.

No system has ever reflected the total demands of the classical system. In Canada, for example, the justice system can be seen as only a partial reflection of the classical model, while retaining large areas of pre-classical processes and procedures, such as case law, in which the law is made not by the parliament but by the judiciary. Even where classical principles hold in practice, there have been continuing neoclassical revisions (i.e., acknowledgment of individual difference).

The classical thinkers initiated a period of lasting debate and controversy over how we should understand crime and criminal behaviour. Although ostensibly focused on the offence and not the offender, the very process of raising issues concerning law and offending inexorably leads to closer scrutiny of the reasons for offending. It is the reasons for offending that form the basis of the theories in the next chapter, namely the positivist perspective.

## Key Terms and Concepts

- Bijuralism
- Capitalism
- Civil law
- Common law
- Feudalism
- Formal law
- Individual rights
- Just deserts
- Rule of law
- Social contract
- Substantive law

## Further Reading

C. Beccaria, *An Essay on Crimes and Punishment* (London: J. Almon, 1767).

B. Fine, *Democracy and the Rule of Law: Liberal Ideas and Marxist Critiques* (London: Pluto, 1984).

M. Gottfredson, and T. Hirschi. *A General Theory of Crime* (Standford: Stanford University Press, 1990).

J. Kelly, *A Short History of Western Legal Theory* (Oxford: Clarendon Press, 1992).

W. O'Grady, *Crime in Canadian Context: Debates and Controversies.* (Don Mills, ON: Oxford University Press, 2007).

I. Taylor, P. Walton, and J. Young, *The New Criminology* (London: Routledge and Kegan Paul, 1973).

J. Young, 'Thinking Seriously About Crime: Some Models of Criminology', in *Crime and Society: Readings in History and Theory*, M. Fitzgerald, G. McLennon, and J. Pawson, eds. (London: Routledge and Kegan Paul, 1981).

## Websites

*www.crimetheory.com.* This website provides an overview of the predominant theory in criminology.

*www.conservative.ca.* The official website for the Canadian Conservative Party.

*www.canada.justice.gc.ca.* The Canadian Department of Justice website provides current, general information about Canada's criminal justice system.

## Films/Documentaries

- *Sentenced to Life* (National Film Board, 2003)
- *Justice Denied* (National Film Board, 1989)
- *Three Strikes: Helpful or Harmful?* (ABC News Production. Princeton, NJ: Films for the Humanities & Sciences, 2004)
- *Punishment DVD* (A&E/The History Channel, 2002)

## Discussion Questions

1. What is meant by the rule of law? Do you believe that the Canadian legal system employs the rule of law? Should it?
2. What, according to a classical perspective, is the cause of crime?
3. How has the classical perspective contributed to the development of the Canadian justice system?
4. What are the criticisms of classical theory?

# CHAPTER 3

# Biological and Psychological Positivism

---

## Objectives

This chapter will help you develop an understanding of:

- how the development of a positivist perspective challenges the classical perspective in criminological study;
- the basic concepts found within this perspective;
- how 'science' was incorporated into the study of crime; and
- the strengths and weaknesses found within a positivist perspective.

---

## Introduction

This chapter discusses **positivism** as a central theoretical and methodological approach in the history and contemporary practice of criminology. As will be seen, the development of positivistic perspectives constituted a major break with the classical tradition that saw crime as primarily a matter of individual choice. For the positivists, crime is explained by reference to forces and factors outside the decision-making ability of the individual. Thus, the classical and the positivist viewpoints are often seen as being directly counterposed.

The rise of positivism represents a shift from what was seen as armchair theorizing or philosophizing to a more rigorous, hands-on, scientific enterprise. The chapter explores the origins of the 'science' of criminology, and discusses two major approaches within positivism: the biological and the psychological. Central to each of these perspectives is the idea that crime can best be explained by examining individual differences between people, and by demonstrating how these differences are, in turn, linked to certain biological and/or psychological factors that predispose certain people towards criminal behaviour.

## Social Context

Positivism as a perspective is associated with a very different view of society and human nature from that expressed in classical criminological theory. It emerged in the nineteenth century, a period of further consolidation of capitalism and the capitalist mode of production in Europe. This was a period that witnessed major technological developments and the entrenchment of mass production (rather than agricultural production or merchant trading) as the dominant form of production and source of profit.

The nineteenth century saw the further concentration of peasants and villagers into large cities, the creation and expansion of the factory system, the introduction of new production technologies and sources of energy (such as the steam engine), and expanded communication and transport networks (e.g., extensive railroad and highway construction). Changes in basic production techniques and relations, and the flow of 'free labour' into employment in the industrial sphere, saw the emergence of a new social class—the working class or **proletariat**.

The rise of the proletariat as a distinct, growing class was accompanied by major industrial, social, and political conflict and upheaval. The previous centuries had been marked by periodic struggles between the aristocracy and the peasantry (in the form of peasant rebellions), and between the established ruling class (the landed gentry) and the **bourgeoisie** (capitalists). Now the dominant class—the capitalist class—was faced with opposition from the working class over the conditions and nature of work, and in some cases over the very ownership and control of production in society.

Life was hard for the members of the working class: child labour was not unusual, and a thin line separated those who worked for a living from those who were condemned to the poorhouse. Living conditions and working conditions were harsh, dirty, and crowded. Meanwhile, the capitalists as a class were amassing huge fortunes and adopting opulent lifestyles. The contrast in circumstances and opportunities was stark.

Not surprisingly, the nineteenth century was also a time when the working class began to organize itself industrially, politically, and, in some cases, militarily. Although banned by law, workers began to combine into industrial organizations, the trade unions. Simultaneously, the material conditions experienced by the working class meant that there was greater analysis of, and sympathetic hearing for, the idea of forging a new type of 'classless' society. This was reflected in the proliferation of alternative working-class publications, pamphlets, and daily press, and in the formation of socialist, anarchist, and labour political organizations and parties. Over the course of the century the ruling capitalist class made a number of compromises. These included, for example, the legal recognition of industrial unions, and the extension of the vote to male members of the working class.

In Canada, one of the most famous examples of labour organization occurred in 1919 and is known as the Winnipeg General Strike. On 15 May 1919 approximately 30,000 workers in Winnipeg walked off the job in the largest strike in Canadian history. The demands of the striking workers included the right to collective bargaining, eight-hour workdays, and a living wage. Civic leaders and employers feared the start of a socialist revolution and moved quickly to break the strike. They formed the Citizens' Committee of One Thousand and hired 2,000 'specials' to replace the striking police.

Parliament also moved quickly to end the strike and amended the Immigration Act so that British-born immigrants could be deported. The federal ministers of labour and justice travelled to Winnipeg and met with the Citizens' Committee but refused to meet with the strikers. After six weeks of sometimes-violent intervention by both the 'specials' and the North-West Mounted Police and the imprisonment of the strike leaders, the Winnipeg General Strike came to an end. However, the stage was set for significant changes to the working conditions for the Canadian working class. While the workers were not successful in their quest for fairer wages and hours, they did accomplish some of their goals. Most importantly, strikers were guaranteed their jobs back, employers agreed to recognize unions, and legislation was enacted to allow collective bargaining (CBC Archives, 2006a).

## Box 3.1   The Winnipeg General Strike

In an era when unions wield as much power as management, it is difficult to imagine a time when they did not even exist. To rely on a employer's goodwill for decent working conditions and a fair rate of pay without any avenue of recourse is a proposition as alien to the modern worker as the idea of commuting to work on a space shuttle. Yet for post-World War I Canadians, a living wage, an eight-hour workday, and the freedom to organize into bargaining groups were rights that had to be fought for.

Individually, none of the contributing factors would have provided sufficient justification for the strike, but, taken together, they created a volatile situation. The relationship between the first-generation, self-made bosses and the immigrant working class was becoming increasingly strained. While manufacturing moguls became wealthy as a result of the war, their employees remained grossly underpaid. The cost of food continued to rise, and it became harder and harder for middle class workers to make ends meet. Soldiers returning home from the war expecting to be received as heroes found nothing waiting for them but unemployment.

On 1 May 1919, the building and metal trades, upon being denied the right to bargain collectively, went out on strike and urged workers throughout the city of Winnipeg to do the same. On 11 May, the Winnipeg Trades Council polled its members for their feelings on the matter. On the 13th, 20,000 organized employees and 10,000 others walked off their jobs.

Initially, the strike proceeded peacefully, its participants doing nothing more but meeting in parks to listen to speakers. But when concerned business owners formed the Citizens' Committee of One Thousand, things began to heat up. Local authorities, fearing a clash of groups, banned public gatherings and hired a scab police force to enforce the ban. But the action backfired when a small riot broke out on 10 June 1919, and the 'special police' received the worst of it.

As the strike went on, distrust grew. Workers and their families found themselves increasingly hard pressed to pay bills and put food on the table, and tempers became short. But it was the government, rather than the workers and their bosses, who brought the situation to a head. Convinced the strike indicated the beginning of a violent revolution, authorities secretly arrested the strike organizers and imprisoned them. Then, on 21 June, what started as a silent parade of protest and solidarity turned into a riot. The event is remembered as 'Bloody Saturday'. Two demonstrators were killed, 34 were wounded, and 80 others were arrested. Dozens of immigrants were deported, and jail sentences were handed out to the strike leaders.

The Winnipeg General Strike proved to be a turning point in labour relations. It sparked a political consciousness of the issues. In 1920, several strike leaders were elected to the Manitoba legislature, and the following year, workers had representation in Ottawa.

From Kristen Butcher, 'Review of On Strike: The Winnipeg General Strike, 1919. (The People's History of the West Series)', *CM Magazine* 7.4 (2000). Available at http://umanitoba.ca/cm/vol7/no4/onstrike.html. Copyright © The Manitoba Library Association.

The nineteenth century in Europe was also a time of new thinking about the nature of human beings, and of society generally. The European powers had been involved in carving up the world's resources for several centuries—from Latin America to Africa, the Indian sub-continent to Asia, the Europeans had been extracting resources and exploiting the labour of indigenous people since the 'voyages of discovery' in the fifteenth century. This was justified initially by the simple expedient that 'might makes right'. However, the justification became more sophisticated with the advent of theories of social and biological evolution.

In particular, the great leaps forward in technology and industrial development, combined with a reliance on and appreciation of the importance of 'science', meant that the European nations asserted their pre-eminence in the global economic and political structure on the basis of a presumed national and biological superiority. Science and technology ensured the expansion of European influence and power into all corners of the globe. Domination was seen as a natural outcome of the fruits of a European 'civilization' founded upon innovation, invention, and technological superiority.

Simultaneously, the work of natural scientists such as Charles Darwin, and especially his general theory of evolution (based upon notions of natural selection and competition), were (mis)appropriated to justify and explain the dominance of the white European over the rest of the world's populace. **Colonialism** and **imperialism** were seen as a consequence of the natural biological superiority of the white European. White supremacy was thus justified and intertwined with notions of a racist biological determinism, one in which white Europeans were at the top of human hierarchy.

The visible presence of class conflict and social misery in Europe, the rise of scientific interest and industrial innovation, and the idea of evolution and stages in human development were all to influence the establishment of positivism as an approach to human affairs. Positivism was founded upon the belief that society ('civilization') is progressing ever forward, and that the social scientist can study society, provide a more accurate understanding of how society works, and ultimately provide a rational means of overcoming existing social problems and ills by using scientific methods.

Social scientists were interested in promoting a positive view of the social order, and in providing positive interventions in social life to make things better. This required systematic study of existing social problems, and the development of a wide range of techniques and strategies to deal with issues relating to schooling, poverty, and family life.

Institutionally, the development of positivism was closely associated with the rise of the professions during the nineteenth century. The passing of legislation in Britain that banned the use of child labour in factories, for example, was accompanied by the introduction of compulsory schooling and expanded welfare concern over the plight of the children of the poor. Under the rubric of positive reform, a wide variety of 'experts'—medical doctors, psychiatrists, health workers, teachers, criminal justice officials, and social workers—began to devise 'scientific' ways to raise children better, to professionalize parenting, to deal with personal troubles and individual deficiencies, to deal with young offenders, and, generally, to engineer wide-scale social reform.

Liberal reform rested upon the idea of progress, humanitarianism, and the active construction of a more caring and supportive society. The main tool of investigation used by professionals and reformers in fostering particular forms of social change was the scientific method. Indeed, the persuasive power of the professionals relied upon the notion that their judgments and strategies were derived from science. That is, people no longer relied upon appeals to God, revelation, faith, or opinion to devise appropriate institutional responses to social problems; rather, social change was to be managed rationally by use of the scientific criteria of logic and empirical study.

The intrinsic appeal of such an approach is understandable, especially since science and technology played a crucial role in industrial capitalism, and a high level of bureaucratization and specialization were a necessary part of an advanced industrial economy. The model of the natural sciences had worked well for capitalist production techniques and manufacturing processes. Now it could be put to use in the social arena as well.

The adoption of concepts and methods from the natural sciences was manifest in several overlapping ideas about the nature of society. For instance, borrowing from the biological sciences, positivist social scientists often viewed society as a type of organism. It was made up of different components, which worked together in order to ensure the proper functioning of the system as a whole. If any one of these components was, or became, 'dysfunctional' then correction was required to restore the social equilibrium. This could apply to specific institutions (e.g., school, family, work) and to particular individuals or groups in society (e.g., the poor, sole parents, the unemployed). Social scientists had the tasks of identifying the nature and source of dysfunctions, and attempting to devise programmes and strategies to alleviate them.

The positivist method in doing so was guided by certain assumptions regarding the applicability of natural science methods to the study of society. Three premises in particular underpinned the scientific approach as conceived by the positivists (see Taylor et al., 1973):

- Social scientists are seen to be neutral observers of the world, and their work is 'value-free'. This is because the world was seen to be 'out there', as an external reality, and the role of the scientist is merely to record the 'facts'.
- The key method of the positivist is to classify and quantify human experience and behaviours through a range of objective tests. This means developing various ways to measure human activity.
- As with the natural world, the social world is seen to obey general laws of operation. The task of the positivist is to uncover the causal determinants of human behaviour (i.e., to identify 'cause' and 'effect' relationships), and thus both to predict and to modify future behaviour outcomes.

The development of positivism was thus related to efforts to adopt natural science methods and concepts in the study of society. This meant accepting certain ideas about the human experience, and attempting to quantify and classify this experience in the expectation that expert intervention could forestall or rectify particular kinds of social problems.

## Basic Concepts

Positivism is based on the idea of a scientific understanding of crime and criminality (see Table 3.1). It assumes that there is a distinction between the 'normal' and the 'deviant', and attempts to study the specific factors that give rise to deviant or criminal behaviour.

One of the hallmarks of the positivist approach is the notion that behaviour is determined; that is, factors and forces outside the immediate control of an individual primarily shape one's activity and behaviour. Behaviour is a reflection of certain influences on the person, whether biological, psychological, or social in nature. It is believed that offenders vary: individual differences exist between offenders, and these in turn can be measured and classified in some way. Rather than seeing people in terms of equal capacities, or equal rights, the positivist view emphasizes difference, which reflects varying conditions affecting each person.

The focus of analysis, therefore, is on the nature and characteristics of the offender rather than on the criminal act. Offenders can be scientifically studied, and the factors leading to their criminality can be diagnosed, classified, and ultimately treated or dealt with in some way. It is the job of the 'expert' to identify the specific conditions leading to criminality in any particular case.

In addition to identifying the specific attributes of offenders, the positivist also sees crime and deviance as something that likewise can be studied in a scientific manner. In other words, the incidence of such behaviour is not assumed to reside only in official violations of the law. This is because the social or moral consensus in society

**Table 3.1   Positivist Approaches**

| | |
|---|---|
| Definition of crime | *Natural*<br>• violation of social consensus<br>• extends beyond a legal definition<br>• deviant behaviour with respect to social norms |
| Focus of analysis | *The offender*<br>• characteristics of offender |
| Cause of crime | *Pathology*<br>• individual deficiency<br>• not a matter of individual choice |
| Nature of offender | *Determined and/or predisposed to certain types of behaviour*<br>• biological and social conditioning and individual differences |
| Response to crime | *Treatment*<br>• diagnosis on individual basis<br>• indeterminate to fit offender |
| Crime prevention | *Diagnosis and classification*<br>• early intervention |
| Operation of criminal justice system | *'Scientific' approach*<br>• measurement and evaluation<br>• essentially neutral |

(which can be described and measured independently of the law) can be violated without necessarily being detected or processed formally in the criminal justice system.

Furthermore, given that deviancy is seen to lie within the (abnormal) individual, and is not always reflected in who actually ends up in court or in the hands of the police, the extent of deviant behaviour is an open-ended empirical question. As such, it requires research into the natural crime that hitherto has been undetected, but that nevertheless is occurring in society. It is necessary, then, to measure the dark figure of unrecorded crime and deviant behaviour through the use of techniques such as large-scale questionnaires, interviews, and various other measures.

A central proposition of positivism is that a moral consensus exists in relation to what constitutes deviant and normal behaviour. Given this, positivists generally see behavioural problems in terms of individual pathology or deficiency. Those who do not conform are seen as having personal difficulties related to biological, psychological, or social factors. The task of the expert is to identify these factors and to correct, or fix, the deficiency.

Rather than being oriented towards punishment, the positivist approach is directed towards the treatment of offenders. Offending behaviour is analyzed in terms of factors or forces beyond the conscious control of the individual. To respond to crime therefore means to deal with the reasons that caused the offending behaviour to occur in the first place.

Since each individual offender is different from all others, treatment must be individualized. This translates at an institutional level into arguments in favour of indeterminate sentences; that is, the length of time in custody should not depend solely on the nature of the criminal act committed, but must take into account the diagnosis and classification of the offender (e.g., severe or not severe problem, dangerous or not dangerous), and the type of treatment appropriate to the specific individual.

## Historical Development

The origins of positivist perspectives in criminology lie in two interrelated developments in the latter part of the nineteenth century. One strand of scientific research attempted to provide biological explanations for criminal behaviour; the other focused on psychological factors associated with criminality.

### Biological positivism

Biological positivism was first popularized through the work of Cesare Lombroso (1911; see also Taylor et al., 1973). Borrowing heavily from evolutionary theories, Lombroso attempted to distinguish different types of human individuals, and to classify them on the basis of racial and biological difference. In a form of 'criminal anthropology', the argument here was that a general theory of crime can be developed on the basis of measurable physical differences between the criminal and the non-criminal. Specifically, Lombroso wanted to establish a link between criminality and the assumption that individuals exhibit particular traits that roughly correspond to the various stages of human evolution.

For Lombroso, the criminal was born, not made; this concept is called '**atavism**'. The idea of a 'born criminal' reflected the notion that crime is the result of something essential to the nature of the individual criminal. In the early formulations of this view, discussion focused on the concept of the 'atavistic criminal'; that is, a person who was biologically inferior in that they represented a reversion to an earlier human evolutionary period. To put it in crude terms, the atavistic criminal was, developmentally, closer to an ape than to contemporary human beings. Such a person could be identified through a series of physical stigmata, including abnormal dentition (protruding teeth), asymmetric face, large ears, supernumerary fingers and toes, eye defects, and even tattoos.

Lombroso later modified his views somewhat, although the element of biological determinism remained. For example, he developed a typology of criminals that divided the population into the 'epileptic criminal', the 'insane criminal', the 'occasional criminal', and so on. In explaining female delinquency and criminality, the argument was put forward that, because of the essential nature of the female sex (which was seen as passive), the female offender was, in fact, biologically more like a man than a woman.

The emphasis on biological factors in explanations of crime was reflected in a number of subsequent studies. Indeed, the search for a single physiological cause of criminality has persisted to this day. Certainly the 'science' of phrenology was popular in criminology for a number of years at the beginning of the twentieth century. This doctrine assumes that the shape and size of the skull correspond to the functions and ability of the brain. A study undertaken in 1912 at the University of Melbourne provides an illustration of this kind of research (Brown and Hogg, 1992). The study was conducted on 355 male inmates of Pentridge prison. The skulls of the prisoners were examined and estimates of the cubic capacity of their brains were made in an attempt to correlate the size of skull to intelligence. It was concluded that cattle stealers had the lowest brain capacity, while forgers and embezzlers had the highest.

The practice of intelligence testing began in France in 1904 when the French government tasked psychologist Alfred Binet to develop a way to differentiate between intellectually normal and intellectually inferior school children. The goal was to identify intellectually inferior children and place them in special schools where they would receive increased individual attention. Binet developed the Binet Scale (also referred to as the Simon-Binet Scale in recognition of the work of Theophile Simon in its creation). The scale measured children on their ability to do specific tasks and it represented a revolutionary new approach to the assessment of individual intellectual ability and level. Binet was concerned with the potential for misuse or misinterpretation of findings and cautioned that the scale was designed to be a guide that should be used only to identify students who would benefit from increased help at school. The scale, he argued, did not permit the measure of intelligence because intelligence could not be considered a single score. Binet also cautioned against the potential to use the scale to assign the child a permanent 'condition' of stupidity, which would negatively impact the entire life-potential of the child (Audioblox, n.d.).

H.H. Goodard (1920) decided that the test would be an effective way to screen students for the Vineland Training School in New Jersey. He translated Binet's work into English and supported a more general application of the scale. Goddard ultimately classified people as 'normal', 'idiot', or 'imbecile'. Each term had differing degrees of developmental potential with 'imbecile' as the lowest; according to Goddard, the imbecile could progress to no more than the level of a three-year old. He also developed a new term—'moron'—to describe individuals who were located somewhere between 'normal' and 'idiot'. In contradiction to the work of Binet, Goddard argued that intelligence was an inborn, fixed, solitary entity that could accurately be measured (Audioblox, n.d.).

In addition to the work of Binet and Goddard, Lewis M. Terman (1916) worked on revising the Simon-Binet Scale. Terman, who also argued that intelligence was fixed and hereditary, published the Stanford Revision of the Binet-Simon Scale of Intelligence in 1916. This test—also referred to as the Stanford Binet Test—become the standard intelligence test for the next several decades. By the 1920s, the mass utilization of the Stanford-Binet Test and other tests had lead to the development of a multimillion-dollar testing industry. The impact of intelligence tests may be understood when one considers that in 1989 the American Academy for the Advancement of Science listed the IQ test among the 20 most significant discoveries of the century. Other scientific discoveries of the century included nuclear fission, flight, the development of the transistor, and the discovery of DNA (Audioblox, n.d.).

Other attempts to measure intelligence, and to argue that criminals were innately less intelligent than the general population, were also popular. In 1913, for example, Charles Goring published the results of his work, which involved examining some 3,000 convicts. He concluded that people with criminal tendencies were endowed with less intelligence and were of a smaller stature than other people. To measure intelligence, he simply talked to people and decided for himself whether or not they were intelligent.

Another type of study looks to physiology, or body structure, as a key determinant of criminal behaviour. In the 1940s William Sheldon (1940) proposed a theory based on body build (somatotype). He wished to establish a link between different body types and criminality. According to Sheldon, human body types can be classified into three broad categories: endomorphic (soft and round), mesomorphic (muscular and strong), and ectomorphic (thin and fragile). Each body type was associated with a particular temperament: endomorphic (relaxed, sociable, and fond of eating), mesomorphic (energetic, courageous, and assertive) and ectomorphic (brainy, artistic, and introverted). It was further argued that mesomorphs were most likely to become criminals. In other words, there was a positive correlation between body type and criminal activity.

As a final example of biological explanation, we turn to research that examined genetic factors (see Taylor et al., 1973). According to the XYY chromosome theory, criminality is related to a deviant genetic make-up. The normal female chromosomal complement is XX; the normal male composition is XY. However, an XYY combination was also discovered. It was held that those who had this kind of chromosomal complement were far more predisposed to criminal activity, due to their 'abnormal' height and mental structures. Fundamentally, a central problem nevertheless remained—that is, how genetic differences actually translate into behavioural traits.

Biological explanations of the kind considered above tend to be fairly pessimistic about positive actions to prevent or deal with crime. This is because crime is seen to be the result of something essential to the nature of the individual. Thus, we are born with certain biological attributes that we cannot change, but that may lock some of us into a life of crime and antisocial behaviour.

**Eugenics** can be viewed as an attempt by society to deal with individuals considered to be mentally or morally defective. The term 'eugenics' was coined by Francis Galton (Charles Darwin's cousin) in 1883 to describe the process of improving—either physically or mentally—the racial qualities of the future generations. Eugenics argued for the use of marriage laws, the segregation of the mentally defective, and sterilization of those with undesirable characteristics. Canadian psychiatrist Charles Kirk Clarke took the lead in linking 'feeble-mindedness' to immigration and posited that the peoples of eastern and central Europe were defectives (in Dowbiggen, 1997). Women's suffrage and temperance groups were especially instrumental in the development of the eugenics movement in Canada, especially in Alberta. Emily Murphy, Canada's first female magistrate lectured widely on the danger of bad genes and argued that insane people were not entitled to have children (in James, 2001). The Alberta Sexual Sterilization Act passed on 7 March 1928 and resulted in the creation of the Eugenics Board, which had the power to authorize the sexual sterilization of individuals. From 1929–1972, when the Act was finally repealed, the Eugenics Board approved 4,725 of the 4,800 cases brought before it; 2,822 individuals were sterilized in Alberta during this period (Canadian Encyclopedia, 2007).

## Box 3.2    Eugenics in Alberta

While large influential groups have brought about change to Alberta's legislation, often a few individuals have achieved justice on their own. Leilani Muir, a victim of Alberta's former sterilization laws, and her lawyers did just that in 1996. They brought before the Alberta Provincial Court a case that set a precedent for many future settlements awarded to other sexual sterilization victims.

Leilani Muir had spent most of her youth living in foster homes. In 1955, at the age of 10, she entered the Michener Centre in Red Deer, which was Alberta's Provincial Training School for Mental Defectives. A year later, the Alberta Eugenics Board gave her an IQ test and a short interview. Based on their findings, she was declared a 'moron' and approved for sterilization. In 1959, she was told that her appendix would have to be removed. While surgeons performed this operation, they also cut her fallopian tubes, making her unable to have children.

Muir was never told about the Eugenics Board's findings or the extent of her operation. After being released from the Michener Centre in 1965, she wanted to start a family. She married at 25, but could not get pregnant. In 1971, her doctor discovered why she could not conceive a child. She and her second husband were heartbroken when they tried unsuccessfully to adopt, and they soon divorced. Her experiences as an orphan had prevented her from ever becoming a parent.

Many thousands of people endured similar experiences under Alberta's Sterilization Act. In 1928, Alberta became one of two provinces and 28 states in North America to pass such legislation. The Act was based on the principles of eugenics, meaning 'good birth'. It was believed that if only those people with desirable genes bore children, the human race as a whole would improve.

The Alberta government and pressure groups including the United Farm Women of Alberta sought to limit the reproduction of many kinds of people, including visible minorities and the 'feeble-minded'. They attributed much of the rise of crime, poverty, alcoholism, and other vices to these people.

Almost 3,000 people were sterilized under Alberta's Sterilization Act. Many more were not released because they would not consent to sterilization. Even in 1972, the year the Act was finally repealed, 55 people were sterilized for their 'danger of transmission to the progeny of mental deficiency' and for being 'incapable of intelligent parenthood'.

Regardless of the reasons in support of sterilization at the time, restricting an individual's ability to reproduce is viewed as a violation of their constitutional rights. Further, studies have shown that mentally handicapped people are no more likely to produce offspring with similar handicaps than the population at large.

Leilani Muir was awarded $740,000 for wrongful sterilization and wrongful confinement. In the following years over 1,200 victims have brought suit against the Alberta government for similar losses. The Alberta government retracted a bill that would have limited compensation to these sterilization victims in 1998. The government has since adopted a more conciliatory stance in attempt to redress the harm caused by the Sterilization Act.

From *Alberta Heritage*. This article can be found on the website Alberta's Political History: The Making of a Province, part of Albert's online Encyclopedia (www.albertasource.ca) created and maintained by the Heritage Community Foundation.

## Psychological positivism

Psychological positivism had different historical origins and a different orientation towards the offender and criminal activity. In this perspective, crime was seen as the result of externally-caused biological problems (e.g., war injury) or internal psychological factors (e.g., mental illness) that were treatable. The criminal was made, not born. And the task of the criminal justice system was to understand the underlying causes of criminality, and to find the appropriate treatment strategy.

This strand of positivism emerged in England from within the criminal justice institutions themselves (see Garland, 1988). Doctors and psychiatrists who worked within the medical-legal framework, and who spent most of their working life with inmates, became increasingly more sophisticated in their classification and diagnosis of offenders. As practitioners within the criminal justice establishment, they had daily contact with a wide variety of 'subjects'. They discovered that there were major differences between individual offenders and, furthermore, that there was a whole range of offenders who did not seem entirely responsible for their actions.

Given their medical background, it is not surprising that these practitioners saw the issue as one of pathology. If offenders were deemed to be 'sick' in some way, then the obvious solution to crime was to find some way to 'cure' them. Thus, an offender might exhibit the conditions of criminality, but these conditions could be dealt with by scientific diagnosis, classification of the condition or illness, and devising the appropriate treatment to fit the condition of each offender.

Such ideas and reasoning were reinforced by the experiences of medical practitioners who treated soldiers returned from the battlefronts of the First World War. Many of these men were shell-shocked and physically disabled, and they presented a number of pathological tendencies, ranging from varying forms of mental illness through to antisocial behaviour. Deviancy in this case was clearly related to trauma of some kind. The problem was not with the innate characteristics of the individual, but with the consequences and impact of the trauma on the individual.

Broadly speaking, psychological theories tended to centre attention on the processes of the mind in explanations of criminal behaviour (see Feldman, 1993). They included several kinds of perspectives:

- Some made reference to psychoanalytic theory, such as analysis of the conscious and unconscious, and how basic emotional and developmental processes affect behaviour.
- Some focused on personality traits, such as studies of aggression and passivity, and the psychological structure of personality as these related to behaviour.
- Some dealt with psychiatric issues from the point of view of childhood experiences, such as analysis that saw deprivation of universal needs during childhood as leading to the formation of certain personality patterns in later life.

## Contemporary Examples

Two major strands can be found in contemporary examples of biological and psychological positivism. First is the field that can be seen as a contemporary variant of early psychiatric interest in criminality, a field that now encompassing both **forensic** psychiatry and forensic psychology. Leading theorists in this field are most often also practising forensic psychologists or psychiatrists. Second are theories that have, to a greater or lesser degree, taken a more academic turn. As suggested in the previous section, there is a wide range of such theories, all of which focus on the characteristics of offenders, but arguably the two most prominent examples are 'control theory' and 'bio-social' explanations, which, as the name suggests, link biological and psychological factors in explaining criminal behaviour.

The predominant concern of forensic psychologists and forensic psychiatrists is in the provision of services to the criminal justice system. Alongside this practical role they have developed a range of theories that both assist rehabilitation and interpret culpability of the offender to the court, as well as predict possible reoffending. This knowledge is required within different aspects of the criminal justice system. In the courts the role of forensic psychologists or psychiatrists is to provide pre-sentence reports and act as expert witnesses. In the corrections area their role is to manage and treat offenders, as well as provide expert advice concerning parole decisions. Perhaps forensic psychology's most contentious application is in police investigations. Here, practitioners undertake **'criminal profiling'**, which, it is claimed, can pinpoint the personality profile of an 'at large' offender as part of the investigation process, or in another variant identify the likely area where the offender lives.

Control theory can be seen as an extension of psychodynamic theories that emanated from Freud. Psychodynamic theories have a common link in that a central concern is how individuals learn self-control. As with Freud, the underlying assumption of these theories is that, left to our own devices and desires, humans are necessarily impulsive and antisocial. We only become social by repressing basic desires. According to Hirschi (1969), and later Gottfredson and Hirschi (1990), the basic question criminologists need to answer is not 'Why do some people offend?' but 'Why do most people not offend?' To put it simply, these theorists argue that individuals learn not to offend through developing self-control. By extension, those who do offend lack self-control. Gottfredson and Hirschi see self-control as a single psychological construct or personal attribute. This single construct is made up of several elements, namely:

- impulsivity, or an inability to defer gratification;
- lack of perseverance;
- preference for risky behaviour;
- preference for physical, as opposed to mental, activity;
- self-centredness; and a
- low threshold for frustration.

Gottfredson and Hirschi argue that child-rearing is critical to the development of self-control, a focus that draws inspiration from the early work of Glueck and Glueck (1960). They propose that poor child-rearing practices, such as lack of supervision (particularly by the mother) and poor attachment to the father, lead to low self-control and higher rates of criminal offending. The theory also asserts that opportunity for offending is important, but only when combined with low social control. Adequately socialized individuals would not succumb to criminal opportunity. It is interesting to note that they see their theory applies as much to white-collar crime as to street offending, since a manager who embezzles company funds has the same problem of low self-control as does a teenager caught shoplifting.

Psychological approaches also include those that focus on 'personality types' (see Farrington, 1996a), and that present typologies of abnormalities in the psychological structure of individuals (for example 'over aggressive' or 'highly strung'). Such approaches often see the formation of particular personality types as linked to certain biological predispositions as well as developmental experiences.

The best known of the bio-social explanations is that provided by Eysenck (1984). He argued that behaviour could be explained by a combination of psychological and environmental influences. Human beings are not totally determined by their biology, but nor are they unaffected by their social circumstances. Behaviour, and in particular criminal behaviour, can be explained in terms of two key variables:

- *The differential ability to be conditioned.* This refers to the way in which genetic inheritance can affect one's ability to be conditioned. That is, the sensitivity of the autonomic nervous system that you have genetically inherited will determine whether you are an extrovert or introvert, and this in turn influences how well you are able to be conditioned in society.
- *The differential quality of conditioning.* This refers to the effectiveness and efficiency of the family in using appropriate conditioning techniques. That is, the content and method of child-rearing will have an impact upon the child's subsequent behaviour.

The argument, then, is that biological potentials (such as the ability to be conditioned or socialized) are set through inheritance. These interact with environmental potentials (shaped by parenting practices), and together these factors determine the overall propensity of individuals to commit crime.

Today, the connection between biological and social environmental influences is seen in very sophisticated terms. It is a case of 'nature' plus 'nurture', rather than one or the other as the sole—or even dominant—factor in producing certain types of behaviour. It is generally argued that human beings have a 'conditional free will', and individuals can choose within a fixed—yet to some degree changeable—range of possibilities (Fishbein, 1990). Human behaviour thus contains a biological and a social element (see, for example, Moffitt, 1996).

Present-day positivists define and identify criminality in a manner geared to establishing those people who are 'at risk' of certain behaviour. There is no longer a one-to-one link between crime and behaviour; rather, certain groups are seen to be more predisposed to crime than others because of biological and social environmental factors. Individuals are not born criminal, but are exposed to baseline biological and psychological processes that shape their personality in childhood. Once the child is introduced to the school, the personality manifests itself in certain types of behaviour. The social influences encountered in the school environment may then further contribute to antisocial behaviour, depending upon initial personality formation.

Contemporary positivists see a dynamic relationship between biological factors (inherited predisposition) and environmental factors (external inputs that modify behaviour). Nevertheless, within this more open and less deterministic framework there has been a resurgence of interest in explanations for crime that are heavily weighted towards the biological. Recent research, for example, has examined the contributions of various factors to criminal behaviour (see Fishbein, 1990):

- *Genetic contributions*. These studies have examined the effect of inheritance on criminal behaviour. Particular traits such as intellectual defects or aggression are seen as genetically given, and as being closely associated with criminal behaviour. Comparisons of identical and non-identical twins, and adoption studies to compare biological and non-biological siblings, are means by which one can test the influence of genetic inheritance.
- *Biochemical contributions*. These studies look at the impact of biochemical differences on human behavioural patterns. Hormonal activity, metabolic processes, and the influence of toxins (such as lead poisoning) are examined in terms of various behaviours such as aggression, and the overall propensity to commit crime. Another strand of research examines psychophysiological variables such as heart rate, blood pressure, brain waves, arousal, and attention levels. It is suggested here that different physiological processes have implications for neurotransmission and psychological impairment.
- *Psychopharmacological inducements*. A third area of research examines inducements such as cocaine, alcohol, amphetamines, and so on, and their effects on human behaviour, especially criminal behaviour.

In a number of these areas it is now possible to conceive of some kind of biological 'corrective' being developed to prevent criminal behaviour from occurring. This could take the form of simply removing the source of the problem (e.g., eliminating lead from one's living environment, or banning alcohol sales), or in the case of more complex responses, regulating the biochemical and physiological operations of the body through appropriate treatment measures (e.g., drugs designed to restore hormonal equilibrium or ensure a regular heart rate).

Whether it is efforts to re-jig the biological balance (e.g., through drug therapy) or to restore a psychological norm or balance (e.g., through parenting classes), a key emphasis in positivist approaches is that of self-control. In other words, efforts will be made to reinforce external and internal regulatory measures so that individuals will conform to the conventional norms of behaviour.

## Critique

Within the positivist aegis then, there exists a plethora of explanations concerning what factors predispose individuals to commit crime. However, virtually all such explanations are concerned with 'street crime', predominantly violent crime or juvenile delinquency of one type or another. The reasons behind white-collar crime and state crime are generally left untouched by positivist criminology (however, see Gottfredson and Hirschi, 1990 for an exception to this).

Furthermore, much positivistic research has taken subjects from incarcerated populations, or those adjudicated as criminal by the law. This poses a problem of the conflict of definitions: the reasoning is that because criminality is the result of psychological or biological abnormality, someone who is adjudicated as criminal by the judicial process must be psychologically or biologically abnormal (Empey, 1982). Thus, all incarcerated populations are, by definition, either psychologically or biologically deficient. This problem results from what is known as circular reasoning where A (criminality) is supposed to be caused by B (impairment), and all those in prison are tested as impaired, and are by definition criminal. Hence impairment is assumed to cause criminality. This conclusion is false for a number of reasons, including:

- It is not clear whether criminality causes impairment, or impairment causes criminality (problem of the direction of causality).
- It is not clear if the imprisonment was the cause of impairment (confounding variable).
- It is not clear whether those in the general population who have the same impairment also offend (i.e. are the two factors simply correlated, or is there a causal connection?).

All explanations of this type thus face considerable challenges in proving the causal connection between biological and psychological factors and criminal behaviour. These challenges concern defining what exactly is being measured (the specifics of a psychological malfunction or chemical imbalance, for example), and designing and undertaking rigorous studies where extraneous variables are excluded. That is, the study must really measure what it says it measures, and there must be no other plausible explanations for what the study found.

While the problem of circular reasoning can be eradicated through the appropriate use of control groups and the application of the scientific method, the possibility of undertaking such experiments has considerable ethical implications and they remain rare. Those that are done face considerable difficulty in matching the variables (such as age, educational attainment, or employment status) of the control group with the experimental group. Unless these factors are carefully matched, the claims of the study can be severely compromised.

Many studies that purported to find biological or psychological reasons for offending have been discredited because of the inability to control all variables (Feldman, 1993). A good example of this problem is the purported connection between violence and the genetically controlled, abnormal metabolism of neurotransmitters that was reported in *New Scientist* (Mestel, 1994). Further research revealed that compounding environmental factors could not be ruled out, and the strength of the relationship between genetics and criminality was greatly downplayed (Aldhous, 1995).

Much of the critique of positivist theory revolves around the blurred distinction between sickness and criminality. Largely undiscussed are the underlying assumptions behind definitions of criminality or, more specifically, deviation from norms. If criminal behaviour is likened to a sickness, it must, like sickness, be undesirable and in need of eradication. There is an assumed consensus within positivism concerning what constitutes criminality and deviation from norms, without adequate discussions concerning whose norms are used as the benchmark for deviation.

The analogy with sickness brings further problems. There is a tendency within positivism to reduce the reasons for criminal behaviour to a single cause, either biological or psychological. It assumes that adult behaviour and personality are totally determined and reducible to single overarching factors (e.g., childhood experiences). This assumption ignores, or fails to acknowledge, that life is a process of continual development, renewal, change, and transformation.

This reductionism to a single cause can lead to both racist and sexist conclusions. Where offending is linked to biology, the logical extension of the line of reasoning can lead to attempts to correlate certain people (e.g., Aboriginal people, poor people, etc.) with certain 'biologically determined' traits (e.g., intelligence as measured by IQ) and so to criminal offending. Without adequate discussion of the assumptions underlying positivism, the search for the causes of criminal behaviour leads inexorably to racist and unwarranted conclusions (see, especially, Gould, 1981).

Once a cause of offending has been isolated, further problems arise. The question of diagnosis, classification, and treatment of offenders becomes important. How is treatment to be administered and on what criteria? Treatment may, for example, require biological 'corrections' (e.g., chemical castration) that raise considerable implications in terms of human rights and human dignity. Even where treatment seems to be relatively benign, such as enhancing parenting skills, there still may be gross assumptions concerning what constitutes adequate parenting. Because of the intrusive nature of treatment suggested by positivist theories, both the theories themselves and the suggested treatments require close scrutiny.

With identification of a biological or psychological cause of crime, positivism suggests that early detection of criminal potential is entirely possible if not desirable. This means intrusive intervention in people's lives may take place long before any crime is committed. Such intervention may be extreme, such as sterilization, or relatively benign, such as pre-school activities in disadvantaged areas. The intrusiveness of the technique must be weighed against the positive outcomes, with each closely analyzed. Do pre-school programmes or pre-natal care really affect behaviour in adolescence and beyond? While there is some evidence that this is the case, should they be conceived of as part of a crime-reduction strategy with the stigma that entails, or are they simply a normal part of society's responsibility to its citizens? Some intrusions, such as sterilization, of course should be disallowed on ethical grounds alone. Alternatively, a focus on the characteristics of an individual also may provide a ready excuse to cut government services; that is, to reduce the level of general state intervention. If violence within schools, for example, can be pinpointed to certain individuals, governments may decide that general programmes to help disadvantaged schools are no longer necessary since the problem has been isolated to individuals and 'dealt with'.

Positivism, with its focus on the scientific method, leads to the production of knowledge that by its nature is inaccessible to the general community. Common-sense understandings of ordinary people are seen as unscientific, and therefore not valid. This reduces the accountability of such professionals, and leaves little avenue for democratic participation in policy that results from positivist research. Specialized knowledge tends to entrench power in the hands of medical or paramedical professionals and other experts.

As we have seen, it is the forensic psychiatrists and psychologists who are most likely to perform this role of the expert. Judges are uniquely sensitive to the concerns of the community regarding the possibility of releasing someone who is a danger to the public at large, and so will draw on this expertise. However, there remain major problems in predicting which person will, and which person will not, pose danger to the community in the future.

The inability to predict dangerousness was dramatically illustrated in New York in the 1970s. A man by the name of Johnnie Baxtrom had been kept in prison after his release date because doctors argued he was dangerous and in need of psychiatric care. All psychiatric hospitals were full, so he remained in prison. Baxtrom challenged the constitutionality of his incarceration beyond the end of his sentence for assault. He won his case, and, as a result, 967 similarly incarcerated patients were released, all of whom were considered criminally insane (that is, they were considered a danger to the community). A team of researchers, led by Henry Steadman, followed up each of these people after four years in order to ascertain how many had re-offended. Only 2.7 per cent of the original 967 had behaved dangerously and were either in a correctional facility or a hospital for the criminally insane (Steadman, 1973). Studies such as these pose tough questions to those who incarcerate individuals deemed to be a danger to the community beyond the term warranted by their criminal offence.

Canada created legislation to deal with dangerous offenders in 1947, with the implementation of the 'habitual offender' designation. The prerequisites for the designation include that the offender had already been convicted of three or more indictable offences and has demonstrated to be 'persistently leading a criminal life'. There have been a number of amendments, but the passage of C-55 in August 1997 was the next (and last) major revision to the legislation. This designation allowed for the discretion of the courts to impose either determinate or indeterminate sentences and is contained in Section 753 of the Criminal Code of Canada. Bill C-55 also created the new designation of 'Long Term Offender' and created the new 'long-term supervision order' that comes into play upon the completion of the custodial order;

a long-term supervision order can be in place for up to 10 years. The goal of this legislation is to provide the state with the ability to deal with individuals who demonstrate a pattern of repetitive criminal behaviour, a pattern of persistent aggressive behaviour, or any behaviour of a brutal nature that indicates that the behaviour of the offender in the future is not likely to be inhibited by normal standards of behavioural restraint, and/or the inability to control his or her behaviour. In other words, dangerous offenders are those who repeatedly engage in criminal activities and seem unable to control their behaviours. The covert assumption made is that perhaps these individuals are lacking in either the moral or intellectual ability to understand good moral conduct and to control their behaviours—a assumption based on biological and psychological positivism.

Certainly there have been improvements in the prediction of dangerousness. Forensic psychologists now estimate that they are right in their predictions of dangerousness in about 50 per cent of cases (Litwack and Schlesinger, 1999). Nonetheless, significant problems remain. The first is that this percentage still remains the same as chance; that is, in one out of two cases the forensic expert will be wrong. The second is that forensic psychologists will readily agree that they are ascertaining the level of risk a particular offender poses to the community, which is separate from a prediction of actual violent behaviour occurring. This is because the context of violence is an important precursor to the occurrence of a violent crime and it is these contextual factors that are impossible to predict. No one can tell if an aggressive person will wake up in a bad mood at exactly the same time that a number of unrelated events occur (such as a chance meeting with an old enemy, losing his or her job, or having a car accident), events that could tip them over into violent behaviour. Finally, such assessments can only be made when the person is found and assessed. In many cases what criminal authorities want is to know the dangerousness of an individual who remains at large—hence the attraction of criminal profiling. This is an entirely separate problem to that of a risk assessment on a person brought to a forensic psychologist or psychiatrist. There remains considerable debate as to the efficacy of criminal profiling. The problem of 'false positives'—bringing under suspicion people who are innocent simply because they match certain personality traits or live in a certain area—remains a major concern.

These criticisms aside, the impact of positivism has been beneficial. It did signal a shift away from hard-line classical thinking concerning individual responsibility. People can act for reasons that are outside their own control, and such factors may mitigate their responsibility for their criminal behaviour. Further, punishment must fail if it does not take account of factors that are beyond the control of an individual's free will.

## Conclusion

Positivism emerged within a specific historical context that promoted the virtues of scientific reasoning over the philosophical approach championed by the classical thinkers. It was assumed that discoveries about the natural world, and natural laws, would find a counterpart within both individual and social human behaviour. The emphasis of positivism is on the scientist as neutral observer with the task of uncovering natural laws that regulate human behaviour, including criminal offending. Specific methods, such as experimentation and survey design, are seen to be able to reveal specific causes of criminal behaviour within the individual, causes that are either biologically or psychologically determined. Once discovered, reduction of offending is seen as possible through treatment programmes aimed at ameliorating or eliminating causal agents. Sentencing should therefore be aimed at rehabilitation rather than deterrence. Further extension of investigation into individuals who are 'at risk' of offending may be seen as preferable, since offences may be prevented before they even occur.

Criticisms of positivism centre on the characterization of criminal offending as akin to a sickness. While criminal behaviour may well be defined as deviation from society's norms, such norms are determined socially, not biologically. Further, society's norms may in fact be the norms of the dominant majority, which marginalize the norms of other social groups within society. In this way positivist research may entrench the current social order by accepting dominant understandings of 'normal' and 'deviant'. Positivism also has a tendency to reduce the complexities of human behaviour to single identifiable causes, and to prescribe treatments that are intrusive, and in some cases unethical.

Recent writing within positivism has tended to move away from overarching generalizations concerning human behaviour (Moffitt, 1996). Fishbein (1990) serves as a good example of a theorist who seeks to establish the place of biological and psychological factors among others as the reasons behind criminal offending. She accepts, for example, the very real place of sociological factors behind offending. It is to these factors that we now turn.

## Key Terms and Concepts

- Biological positivism
- Colonialism
- Criminal profiling

- Eugenics
- Forensics
- Imperialism

- Liberal reform
- Positivism
- Psychological postivism

## Further Reading

A. Binet, *The Development of Intelligence in Children: The Binet-Simon Scale* (Baltimore, MA: Williams & Wilkins Company, 1916).

I.R. Dowbiggen, *Keeping America Sane: Psychiatry and Eugenics in the United States and Canada 1880–1940* (Ithaca, NY: Cornell Studies in the History of Psychiatry, 1997).

H. Eysenck, 'Crime and Personality', in *Psychology and Law*, D. Muller, D. Blackmann, and A. Chapmann, eds. (New York: John Wiley and Sons, 1984).

P. Feldman, *The Psychology of Crime* (Cambridge: Cambridge University Press, 1993).

D. Fishbein, 'Biological Perspectives in Criminology', *Criminology* 28.1 (1990): 27–72.

D. Garland, (1988) 'British Criminology before 1935', *British Journal of Criminology* 28.2 (1988): 1–16.

C. Lombroso, *Crime: Its Causes and Remedies* (Boston: Little, Brown, 1911).

D.C. Masters, *The Winnipeg General Strike* (Toronto: University of Toronto Press, 1950).

T. Moffitt, (1996) 'The Neuropsychology of Conduct Disorder', in *Readings in Contemporary Criminological Theory*, P. Cordella and L. Siegel, eds. (Boston: Northeastern University Press, 1996).

## Websites

*www.crime-times.org.* A non-profit, national publication that explores the links between biology and violent crimes.

*www.crimetheory.com.* This website supplies an overview of the predominant theories in criminology.

*www.civilization.ca/hist/labour.* This federal government website provides information on the Winnipeg general strike of 1919.

*www.eugenicsonline.netfirms.com.* Information is provided about the modern issues surrounding eugenics.

## Films/Documentaries

- *Forensics: The Science of Materials* (Film Media Group, 2000. CD-ROM ISBN 978-0-7365-3847-3)
- *On Strike: The Winnipeg General Strike, 1919* (The People's History of the West Series. National Film Board of Canada, 1991)
- *Origins of Human Aggression: The Other Story* (National Film Board of Canada, 2005)
- *The Man who Studies Murder* (National Film Board of Canada, 2004. 2 DVDs)
- *The Sterilization of Lelani Muir* (National Film Board of Canada, 1996)

## Discussion Questions

1. A central proposition of positivism is that a moral consensus exists in relation to what constitutes deviant behaviour and normal behaviour. Do you agree or disagree with this proposition? Why or why not?
2. What are the fundamental premises upon which biological theories of crime are based? How do these differ from a psychological positivist approach?
3. How do psychological theories of crime support the development and use of criminal profiling?
4. Critics have argued that new technologies like DNA testing allow for the potential development of a new form of eugenics. What might these forms be?
5. What kinds of people or groups of people may be affected by a new form of eugenics? What controls could be put in place to protect individuals who may be deemed 'sub-standard'?
6. In your opinion, what are the central contributions made by positivist theories to the study of criminology? Why are these contributions important?

# CHAPTER 4

# Strain Theory

## Objectives

This chapter will help you develop an understanding of:

- the common concepts found within various types of strain theory;
- the role that subcultures may play in the development of criminal behaviour;
- what is meant by 'social structure' and 'social learning' in the creation of criminal behaviour and attitudes; and
- the strengths and weaknesses found within strain theories.

## Introduction

This chapter provides an overview of various types of strain theory, and includes a discussion of **subcultures** and the ways in which deviant or criminal behaviour is learned in interaction with others. Rather than focusing on factors relating to the individual, these types of theories are sociological in nature. That is, they point to aspects of **social structure** and social learning that contribute to the creation of criminal behaviour and attitudes.

While sharing many of the philosophical and political features of biological and psychological positivism, sociological approaches such as strain theory view crime as manifestations of social pathology, rather than individual pathology. For example, tension or strains are seen to be generated by society itself; they do not reside within the individual (as in the case, for example, of a person feeling strained or pressured by circumstance). The chapter discusses the two main wings of strain theory—those that place emphasis on 'opportunity structures', and those that speak about the learning of particular **norms**, **values**, and subcultural attributes.

## Social Context

The social context in which strain theory emerged and developed can be divided into three key periods. The first period—from the middle of the nineteenth century to the beginning of the twentieth—saw the rise of **sociology** as an academic discipline. As with comparable social sciences (such as psychology), it was felt that one could apply the approaches and concepts of the natural sciences to the study of society. In particular, society itself could be studied as if it were external to the observer. As with positivism in general, most sociology presumed that there existed a **consensus** of values and norms across society. As such, it was supportive of the status quo. The role of the social scientist was to intervene in shaping the direction of social development by providing positive solutions to identified social problems.

The sociological method adopted at this time was one that constructed broad categorizations of different types of societies (e.g., pre-industrial, industrial), and that attempted to show how the structure of a society moulds and shapes individual behaviour. Criminal behaviour, in particular, was seen as a manifestation of a social pathology—the outcome of something wrong in the structures and values of the society generally. Thus, if we are to respond adequately to the incidence of crime, we must go beyond measures that see it as being simply the result of individual malaise. Some type of institutional reform would be necessary if the problem were particularly acute.

The second key period in the development of strain theory was the early 1920s through to the Second World War. The industrial revolution had fostered the development of the professions (including sociology) and was linked to the idea of expert or technical solutions to problems such as poverty and crime. By the early decades of the twentieth century, the conceptual tools of sociology were being turned to examine problems with a specifically modern character.

In 1917 the Russian Revolution occurred, with long and lasting impact on developments in the West. A series of class struggles and armed conflict occurred throughout Europe in the early 1920s, and the example of a successful workers' revolution was creating alarm in the ruling circles of the advanced capitalist countries. Within Russia itself, many people were displaced from their former positions and residences, and later, under the rule of Stalin, a series of purges was carried out that cost millions of lives.

Meanwhile, two further developments were accelerating the tendency towards crisis and war in Europe. On the one hand, one legacy of World War I was a German nation that had suffered impoverishment and deep loss of dignity as a result of the actions of the victors. As in Spain in the 1930s, and later in Italy, there also arose a strong fascist movement in Germany by the early 1930s. Simultaneously, the Great Depression was having a devastating impact on workers and farmers in Europe, North America, and elsewhere.

The developments in Europe and the newly constructed Soviet Union, combined with the dramatic changes in economic fortunes, were to lead to mass movements of people. Events such as the counter-revolutionary war in Russia, the purge of selected classes and social groups across different political systems (e.g., attacks on Jews in Nazi Germany, forced collectivization of farmers in Russia), and the difficulties of economic survival under rampant inflation and high levels of unemployment created large numbers of war, political, and economic refugees in Europe. This led to wide-scale migration to countries such as the USA and Canada, as well as Australia and New Zealand.

A crucial question emerged within the ranks of those who were studying crime as a social phenomenon: How did the successive waves of immigration impact upon crime rates? Furthermore, the issues of unemployment and poverty were put on the agenda in a more systematic and theoretically informed manner by sociologists.

These issues were particularly of interest to researchers in the United States. While such people were unlikely to suggest a Russian-style revolution as an appropriate or desirable response to the depression in the heartland of world capitalism, clear links were now being drawn between unemployment and crime. The economic position of the individual in society was now seen as an important factor in the commission of crime.

The third period of note with respect to the development of strain theory was the post-war period of the late 1940s and into the 1950s. By this time, many of the advanced capitalist countries had entered a long boom period of economic growth. People in these countries were generally optimistic about the future, living standards were rising steadily, and capitalism was indeed appearing, for many, to be the 'best of all possible worlds'. The problem, however, was how to explain persistent crime rates even in the face of apparently good general economic and social conditions. The answer, here, was to examine more closely the distribution of opportunities in society, and also the ways in which people interact with and learn from each other. As with the general orientation of strain theory, the intellectual task was to formulate concepts that would best express the social nature of crime.

## Basic Concepts

The starting point for strain theory is the notion that crime is essentially a social phenomenon (see Table 4.1). It is based upon a sociological understanding of individual and group behaviour—one that sees specific activity, such as crime, as somehow being related to and shaped by wider social processes and structures.

| Table 4.1 Strain Theory | |
| --- | --- |
| Definition of crime | • natural<br>• violation of consensus |
| Focus of analysis | • structure of opportunities<br>• nature of social learning<br>• youth subcultures |
| Cause of crime | • social strain, *viz* opportunity structure<br>• learned behaviour |
| Nature of offender | • determined by social pathology |
| Response to crime | • provide an opportunity to reduce strain, resocialize offender |
| Crime prevention | • expanding opportunity and fostering healthy peer-group activity |
| Operation of criminal | • essentially neutral justice system<br>• individual rehabilitation combined with social programmes |

Rather than looking at aspects of personal psychology or individual biological traits, strain theory argues that crime is socially induced. Thus, a 'criminal' or 'deviant' is a product of a specific kind of social order. In essence, wider societal forces and factors determine the activities and values of the offender, and the offender has few conscious choices regarding his or her available social options.

Crime tends to be defined in conventional terms. However, rather than viewing it as solely the behaviour that formally violates the legal code (as evidenced by court conviction records), this approach sees crime and deviancy in wider terms. In particular, crime is seen as any violation of the general consensus of values and norms in society. Furthermore, given this definition, and given the high levels of activity that go undetected by the formal criminal justice system, it is important to measure natural crime by alternative means, such as victim surveys and self-report studies.

The basic proposition of strain theory is that crime is due to social disjuncture or social processes that represent a social strain within a society. The strains or sources of tensions are social, not individual in nature. That is, the cause of crime is located in social structures and/or value systems that in some way are socially pathological. It is this wider social pathology that best explains crime as a social problem.

The main focus of analysis in strain theory is on strains associated with 'structural opportunities' and 'cultural processes'. The cause of crime is often seen to lie in inadequate or inappropriate means or opportunities to achieve certain goals relative to other people in society. Hence this aspect or type of strain theory is sometimes referred to as 'opportunity theory'. It is argued that restricted or blocked opportunities can lead some people to pursue alternative means, including criminal avenues, to gain desired social goods.

A second broad approach examines how, through various social circumstances, people associate with others who share their cultural understandings regarding acceptable and unacceptable behaviour. The emphasis in this kind of approach is on how criminal behaviour is learned in social situations. Analysis of particular subcultures is undertaken to learn how norms and values are transmitted from one person to another. This type of analysis is sometimes called 'social learning theory' or 'subcultural theory'.

The response to crime according to strain theories is to enhance opportunities in order to reduce social strain. This can take the form of educational programmes, employment projects, and leisure and recreation outlets for particularly 'disadvantaged' individuals and groups. A related crime-reduction strategy is to resocialize the offender into conventional goals and means. This may involve removing him or her from his or her previous associates in order to minimize the learning and/or affirmation of deviant norms and values. Overall, the stress is to combine individual rehabilitation with a series of social programmes.

From the point of view of crime prevention, strain theory leans towards measures that expand educational, employment, and social opportunities, and that foster healthy peer-group activity. The focus is on developing strategies and policies that involve some degree of institutional reform, rather than solely changing or modifying the individual in some way. Since deviance or criminality is related to problems faced by groups of individuals in disadvantaged situations, the solution to crime must be to remedy the disadvantage as far as possible.

## Historical Development

Contemporary strain theories have their origins in the emergence of sociology as an academic discipline and a recognized field of intellectual endeavour. One of the central figures in this process was French sociologist Emile Durkheim, who was writing at the beginning of the twentieth century. His work was of great importance because he consistently presented analysis of society, and of social problems, in a manner that demonstrated the close relationship between social structure (the organization of society) and the norms and values of society (social and cultural life).

Durkheim's analysis was premised upon the notion that there are 'social facts' that can be studied and used to describe social phenomena (see Lukes, 1973). These social facts are seen to be independent of the wishes or actions of individual people. While external to the individual, nevertheless a certain phenomenon has a marked impact upon their behaviour. Thus, for example, one can quantify such social facts as the distribution of population in a certain area or district, or one can ascertain the prevailing norms, rules, regulations, religious beliefs, and legal codes of a society. In either case, these kinds of phenomena represent social facts, which can be measured and which exist as independent entities in their own right.

It order to analyze a particular social phenomenon, it is necessary to acknowledge that different societies give rise to different structures, different beliefs and sentiments, and thus different behavioural patterns. In his famous study of suicide, for instance, Durkheim (1979) demonstrated empirically that suicide rates vary according to whether or not a country is predominantly Catholic or predominantly Protestant in its religious orientation. The point here is that suicide could not be explained simply or solely in terms of individualistic choices or psychological factors. It is a social phenomenon.

More generally, Durkheim employed two basic conceptual tools in analysis of society (Lukes, 1973). On the one hand, it was argued that society is structured around a particular kind of '**division of labour**', with specific types of work tasks and roles. A distinction is made between **mechanical solidarity** and **organic solidarity** as indications of the division of labour. The first describes pre-industrial types of society in which individuals tend to share the same skills, work tasks, customs, beliefs, and religion. The second describes an industrial society, which is far more heterogeneous in terms of wealth, ethnicity, religions, and beliefs, and which has a high level of work specialization.

On the other hand, each society was said to be characterized by a particular form of collective conscience (or consciousness). This referred to a set of beliefs and sentiments common to a whole society, which forms a determinate system. In a nutshell, what we collectively think is greater than any one individual, and the collective conscience has the feature of shaping and regulating our behaviour as an independent, powerful external force. In a society characterized by mechanical solidarity, the emphasis tends to be on rigid conformity and cultural homogeneity. Alternatively, the organic solidarity of industrial society is one in which people are linked though law and interdependence, rather than similarity of life experience.

In applying these concepts to the specific area of criminology, Durkheim was able to argue that the nature of the society in which one lives will determine the manner in which deviants will be dealt with (see Inverarity et al., 1983). A society with mechanical solidarity tends to generate repressive justice, which reaffirms the common beliefs and values by distancing the deviant from the wider collectivity. Conversely, a society with organic solidarity tends to generate restitutive sanctions which aim to restore the social disruption by reintegrating the deviant back into the network of interdependencies.

Fundamentally, the organization of society, as shaped by its division of labour and its collective conscience, determines the nature of crime and the regulation of criminal behaviour. Within differently organized societies, there exists a certain amount of crime since, Durkheim argued, crime is a normal and integral part of any society. Durkheim said that where you have an unhealthy division of labour (e.g., based upon force rather than choice) or an unhealthy regulation of the collective conscience (e.g., norms not well established), there is greater likelihood of widespread crime, and the level of crime will be greater. There is another aspect of Durkheim's view that is not picked up by strain theory, but is related to the idea of the collective conscience: by defining a behaviour or person as criminal, people are reassuring themselves about their own society. In a very real sense, society defines itself by what it is not—and it is this that is defined as criminal.

A normal, healthy division of labour occurs where occupational relationships are in accordance with individuals' aptitudes. In such a situation, two potential types of deviant can be identified: the biological deviant (who is impossible to predict or prevent), and the functional rebel (who acts as a constructive force for limited social change). Where there is an unhealthy or pathological division of labour, there will be conflict between the individual and the social. That is, it will be difficult to regulate the behaviour of individuals in a society under such circumstances.

Societies vary in their ability to impose social regulation, and this is due in part to the nature of the division of labour. The collective conscience may not be developed sufficiently, or may be skewed in some way, and this can affect behaviour as well. The general condition of society (not the individual) may be one where norms and values are in flux or even partially destroyed. We may thus have a situation in which shared beliefs and values have broken down, and where moral guides to and constraints on behaviour have weakened.

Applying these ideas to the specific area of crime and deviancy, it is argued that a healthy society is characterized by a collective conscience that regulates behaviour smoothly. An unhealthy society is one in which values are not well established, or where they work against the aims of integration and regulation (see Taylor et al., 1973).

According to Durkheim, individual desires are unlimited; it is the society that gives direction and a limit to desire. Durkheim drew a distinction between 'egoism' and **'anomie'**, both of which revolve around social norms. Egoism refers to the desires of the 'pre-social self', desires that society must shape and limit. Dysfunctional societies can be characterized by an overemphasis on egoism, where value is placed on the unrestricted pursuit of individual desires. Here, the norms of society itself can produce deviant behaviour. The concept of anomie refers to a lack of social regulation in which the unrestricted appetites of the individual conscience are no longer held in check: we have a state of normlessness in which society fails to impose norms that inhibit such behaviour. This would describe, for example, a society or community at its breaking point, where rapid change has destroyed many of the values and norms. Societies experiencing either kind of normative problem would be expected to have abnormal levels of crime.

The importance of Durkheim as a founding thinker within the strain theory tradition is that he established that crime is essentially a social phenomenon; it is inextricably related to the nature of society itself. And criminality is thus a product of a specific kind of social order.

Moreover, it was Durkheim who emphasized that crime is due to social disjuncture or social strains in a society. These are linked to both the division of labour (later seen in terms of opportunity structures) and the collective conscience (later seen in terms of cultural norms and learned behaviours).

## Crime and opportunity

During the latter part of the nineteenth century and the early part of the twentieth century Chicago underwent a massive social and physical transformation and became the fastest growing city in human history at the time. A fast-growing economy attracted a huge number of new residents from other parts of the country and immigrants from Europe and, as a result, Chicago was transformed from a small city of 299,000 to one of the 10 largest cities in the world with a population of nearly 1.7 million (Grossman, Keating, and Reiff, 2005).

Concentrated in the city core, the newcomers resided in the oldest housing. The resulting concentration of new, predominantly poor, residents led to the development of physically deteriorating areas in the city. This in turn, fueled the fears held by Chicago's wealthy, established residents that the moral fabric of the city was being strained by the influx of new residents. Popular conceptions held during this time was that European immigrants were morally degenerate and crime-prone and that crime was the territory of inferior racial and ethnic groups. Truab and Little argue that 'this belief was rooted in the anxiety of social changes altering the face of 20th-century society: industrialization, urbanization, immigration, and increased geographical and social mobility' (1999: 64).

One of the primary characteristics of the Chicago School—a school of thought favouring free-market economics—was its focus on exploring and recording the diverse aspects of social life located in its immediate geographical environment, the city of Chicago. Basing their theory on concepts found in biology, the Chicago School theorists created an **ecological model** in which to study the impact of urban growth, the lifestyles of residents, and the effects of social change on the city. According to Traub and Little:

> [t]he ecological perspective offered a framework within which these sociologists could study the social order of the city in terms of selection, competition, change, cooperation, and symbiosis. They concluded that these natural processes were affecting and disrupting the mechanisms of social control, with the result that social disorganization and deviance were increasing (1999: 63).

An obvious increase in social disorganization appeared to occur with rapid increases in social complexity, which appeared to lead to higher rates of deviance, particularly in the large urban areas of America. For the Chicago School theorists it was apparent that specific city areas or zones which shared common characteristics including poverty, decaying housing, transient residents, and a myriad of large immigrant groups exhibited greater rates of deviance that more stable areas.

**Social disorganization theory** was popularized by the work of two Chicago sociologists, Clifford R. Shaw and Henry McKay. Building upon the foundation laid by Ernest Burgess and Robert Parks, two earlier sociologists from the Chicago School, Shaw and McKay linked life in transitional slum areas to the inclination to commit crime.

Shaw and McKay (1942; 1972) placed crime and delinquency within the context of the changing urban environment and ecological development of the city. They noted that Chicago had developed into a number of distinct 'natural areas', some wealthy and others characterized by high levels of poverty, and that these various and distinct area represented a series of five **concentric circles**, or zones, in which there were significant and stable differences in crime rates between the zones.

The areas where there appeared to be the highest levels of crime appeared to be in the transitional inner-city zones, which had a large number of recently settled foreign

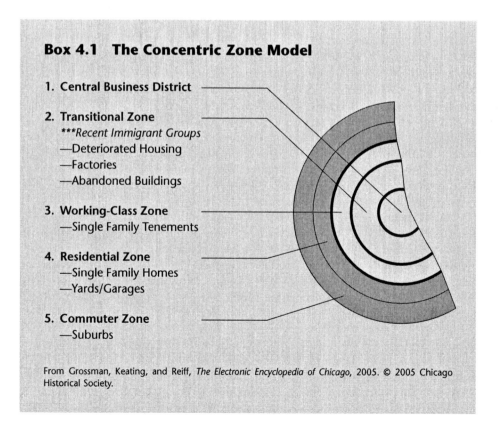

## Box 4.1   The Concentric Zone Model

1. **Central Business District**

2. **Transitional Zone**
   ***Recent Immigrant Groups*
   —Deteriorated Housing
   —Factories
   —Abandoned Buildings

3. **Working-Class Zone**
   —Single Family Tenements

4. **Residential Zone**
   —Single Family Homes
   —Yards/Garages

5. **Commuter Zone**
   —Suburbs

From Grossman, Keating, and Reiff, *The Electronic Encyclopedia of Chicago*, 2005. © 2005 Chicago Historical Society.

immigrants. **Transition zones** were characterized by frequent changes in population composition as new immigrant groups moved into the area, bringing with them divergent cultural and moral standards, and the gradual industrialization of the area. These changes meant that a breakdown in conventional neighbourhood traditions and institutions occurred and that the ability of the neighbourhood to enforce the moral standards of society was diminished.

In contrast, the zones farthest from the city's centre had correspondingly lower crime rates. Analysis of these data indicated a surprisingly stable pattern of crime in the five ecological zones over a 65-year period (Siegel and McCormick, 2003). Based on their data, Shaw and McKay concluded that there exists a blend of cultures and values that, in transitional neighbourhoods, represent conventional and deviant, norms. Young people in these transitional areas often find that adults who have adopted a deviant lifestyle (drug dealer, pimp, gambler) are often the most financially successful individuals in the neighbourhood. Many disadvantaged youths choose to emulate this type of behaviour and adopt similar methods to acquire financial success. These youth join with similarly minded other youth and form deviant or law-breaking gangs. For Shaw and McKay the development of teenage law-violating groups is a fundamental component of youthful misbehaviour in slum areas.

The adoption of deviant values means that slum youths often come into conflict with existing middle-class norms, which are characterized by strict adherence to the legal code. As a result of this conflict the delinquent youth and his or her peers are further distanced from conventional society. The ensuing increase in isolation from conventional goals results in a fuller internalization of deviant goals and behaviour. This isolation translates into the development of neighbourhood street gangs that become fixed institutions and that continually recruit new members and who pass on delinquent traditions from one generation to the next.

Shaw and McKay's comprehensive statistical analysis confirmed their theoretical position. They found that even though crime rates changed, the highest rates were consistently found in zones I and II (central city and transitional areas). This pattern remained; areas with the highest crime rates retained high crime rates even when the ethnic composition of the neighbourhood changed (Shaw and McKay, 1972: 52).

During this time period, Canadian researchers were also involved in the study of social disorganization. Carl Addington Dawson studied sociology at Acadia University and at the University of Chicago; he was later hired as the Director of the School of Social Work at McGill University. Dawson then became the head of the first department of Sociology at McGill University in 1924. Human ecology became the theoretical framework utilized by all McGill sociology courses and it guided the research projects undertaken by Dawson and his colleagues during the 1920s and 1930s (Shore, 1987).

Dawson viewed society as an order that surpassed individual members, and argued that the ultimate goal of social transformation was the creation of harmonious social order. One of Dawson's projects was the investigation of the broader structure of postwar Montreal and the way in which the structure of the city influenced the actions and institutions of its inhabitants. Borrowing strongly from both functionalist theories and social disorganization theory, Dawson viewed the city as an organism, with the business centre as the centre of dominance. Around this centre were a number of zones set up in concentric circles. Each of these zones varied in their use and in the type of occupants according to the value of land and the distance of the zone from the centre.

Dawson and his students examined such factors as industrial development, transportation innovations, immigration, housing, labour organization, crime, juvenile delinquency, family disorganization, welfare work, and child labour. Included in their analysis were detailed mappings of railway property, industrial and commercial frontage, parks, boulevards, and physiographic barriers on maps of the city (Dawson, 1926). Displaying the same growth pattern as Chicago, Montreal experienced a growth explosion that made it the fifth largest city in North American by 1928. Its industries, services, and port attracted both migrants and immigrants by the droves. The introduction of the electric streetcar in 1882 facilitated the movement of thousands of workers from Montreal's inner core out to the newly developing neighbourhoods and suburbs.

While the fundamental concept of concentric circles held true in Montreal, its topographic features distorted the concentric circles into a kidney shape around Mount Royal. As the population grew, businesses that had been originally developed near the river encroached on the residential district adjacent to it. The encroachment of business and industry encouraged the area's more successful residents to move out of the neighbourhood. The area of Montreal that experienced the most disruption as a result was the Dufferin district, a neighbourhood that lay in the city's transitional zone. According to Seigel and McCormick:

> Dufferin district became a slum at the turn of the century, when the commercial sector of Montreal expanded and a flood of Asian and European immigrants poured into the city. Its boundaries were invaded by machine shops, warehouses, and light manufacturing. The more successful among the English, Irish, Scottish, and French families who lived in the district departed, and their vacated homes were remodeled into flats and occupied by the less prosperous (2003: 183).

Dufferin district lacked schools, churches, and other social institutions that were found in more stable Montreal neighbourhoods. Instead, Dufferin district represented the disorganized environment as laid out in the work of Shaw and McKay, with its attendant high levels of poverty, vice, despair, and crime.

The social disorganization concepts first put forward by Shaw and McKay have remained prominent within criminology for more than seven decades. One of the most valuable contributions made by these theorists is the notion that crime is facilitated by the destructive ecological conditions in urban slums. In other words, people do not engage in criminal behaviour because they are biologically, intellectually, or psychologically inferior. Crime instead, is the result of neighbourhood decay and disorganization, and is a natural reaction to adverse social and environmental conditions. This perspective has set the stage for many of the community action and treatment programmes that have emerged in recent times (Siegel and McCormick, 2003).

While Shaw and McKay initially concentrated on the issue of a disorganized and transient population, the impact of the Great Depression prompted them to refine their analysis. They began to look beyond the link between immigration, settlement patterns, and crime. They also acknowledged the social strains caused by poverty and unemployment. Economic deprivation meant that, even where mainstream goals had been internalized, people were denied opportunities to achieve those goals. Thus, a depressed and stratified economic structure could engender conditions that lead to a greater incidence of crime.

While depressed economic conditions, and overall diminished job opportunities seem to provide a reasonable explanation for some types of criminal activity, how are we to explain the incidence of crime in periods of economic growth? This was the dilemma facing sociologists and criminologists in the 1950s.

The first two decades after World War II were characterized by low unemployment levels and high standards of living in the advanced capitalist countries. It was a time of general economic prosperity. Politically, the 1950s was stamped by the contours of the Cold War into which the two superpowers—the United States and the Soviet Union—were locked, along with their allies. This manifested itself in virulent anti-communist campaigns in the West, such as the public attacks on the left in the US by the Senator Joe McCarthy's House Un-American Activities Committee, and in Australia by the attempts of the Menzies government to ban the Communist Party of Australia. It was a time of general political conformity.

It was in this climate that Merton (1957) sought to offer an explanation for the continued existence of crime in the United States. In seeking to explain the prevalence of crime, he embraced the notion that crime rates are related to society's ability to establish norms that regulate the behaviour of the populace. Merton argued that crime could be understood in relation to two main variables: the culturally defined goals of a society; and the institutionalized means whereby one can attain these goals. 'Mal-integration' occurs when there is a disjuncture between the cultural goals and the institutional means.

Merton argued that all individuals basically share in the same cultural goal—the 'American Dream' of wealth, status, and success—but they have different institutional means available to them. In particular, some people experience blocked opportunities and are, therefore, unable to achieve their goals through normal or legitimate means.

In such circumstances, people are perceived as having the capacity to make meaningful choices about how to negotiate their futures. That is, depending upon the opportunities available to them, people decide to accept or reject the cultural goals, and to accept or reject the institutional means to attain commonly accepted goals. The decisions one makes are determined or shaped by one's position or status in society. For example, those people at the lower end of the socio-economic ladder will experience a greater likelihood of blocked opportunities than those from better-off or wealthy families. This has an impact on behaviour.

Merton developed an abstract typology of responses to the means/ends equation. The typology described individual adaptations to goals and means. People can respond in five different ways to the structure of opportunities available:

1. *Conformism*: Those who accept the culturally defined goals (e.g., financial success) and the institutionalized means of attaining them (e.g., education).
2. *Innovation*: Those who accept the culturally defined goals but who lack the institutionalised means to attain them. They therefore resort to innovative means to attain the goals, such as turning to crime (e.g., robbing a bank).

3. *Ritualism*: Those who accept the culturally defined goals but who know they can-not attain them. Nevertheless, they continue pursuing institutional means (e.g., staying at school when no jobs are available), regardless of the outcome.
4. *Retreatism*: Those who reject both the culturally defined goals and the institution-alized means of attaining them. They retreat from society in varying ways (e.g., substance abuse).
5. *Rebellion*: Those who substitute their own cultural goals and institutionalized means in place of the conventional goals and means in society. They create their own goals and means of achieving them (e.g., ecologically sustainable hippie lifestyle).

From the point of view of strain theory, the choices available to people reflect prob-lems stemming from the structure of the society itself. That is, it is the relationship between cultural goals and institutional means that ultimately determines the kinds of opportunities and choices that are available to different groups of people.

## Crime and culture

The structure of opportunities constitutes one part of the criminal behaviour puzzle. The other part, according to some theorists, is the ideas that people hold regarding what is acceptable or unacceptable behaviour. Specifically, attention was directed to issues of culture and the ways in which young people in particular learn certain ways of doing things and certain attitudes towards others.

The work done by Sutherland and Cressy (1974), for example, was directed at explaining the nature and development of youth subcultures. They argued that crime was cultural in nature, in the sense that it is learned behaviour. People in particular neighbourhoods or particular social situations learn about criminal behaviour by inter-acting with other people. The most significant interaction occurs within intimate per-sonal groups, which of course includes peer groups.

Sutherland and Cressy developed the concept of differential association to describe a process in which behaviour is differentially associated insofar as some indi-viduals will associate with carriers of criminal norms, while others will not. They dis-cussed the process that occurs when a criminal association does take place. The learning of criminal behaviour includes:

- the techniques of committing a crime (e.g., how to hot-wire a stolen car);
- the motives, drives, attitudes, and rationalizations associated with crime (e.g., stealing only Porsche cars, because 'the owners can afford it anyway'); and
- definition of the legal code as favourable or unfavourable (e.g., regarding the legal code relating to car theft as unfavourable, since people have car insurance anyway).

Differential associations may vary in frequency, duration, priority, and intensity. Those persons who become delinquent or persistent offenders do so because of a greater num-ber of definitions favourable to violation of the law over definitions unfavourable to violations. This in turn is shaped by group interaction. For example, an individual may associate with a delinquent group, and then later change that orientation by associat-ing with a non-delinquent group.

The essential point of the theory is that criminal behaviour is learned. Because learning takes place in the context of specific types of group formation, and particular types of definitions of behaviour and attitudes, the issues of peer-group pressure and offending cultures are seen as being of central importance.

The idea that people learn to associate certain classes of conduct, either legal or illegal, with the group's approval or disapproval, has obvious links to the analysis of subcultures per se. That is, deviant or criminal behaviour is collective in nature, and is based on shared experiences and perceptions. From within the strain theory tradition, various writers have argued that the strain between cultural goals and institutional means is reflected in specific class cultures.

Albert Cohen (1955) argued that working-class subcultures can be seen as a product of a conflict between working-class and middle-class cultures. Such a subculture is an alternative cultural system that develops because of the blocked opportunities and low self-esteem experienced by working-class young people. Instead of measuring 'success' in conventional terms, the group focuses on alternative goals that are more directly related to their own class experiences. Whereas Merton's typology spoke of the disappointed individual, Cohen saw crime and delinquency in terms of collective behaviour associated with the different aspirations, expectations, and lived experiences of two different class groupings. For Cohen, the school was the point at which lower-class youth understood their choices were constrained by society. His research indicated that youth do not necessarily accept the culturally transmitted social goal of economic success and financial accumulation that appeared to motivate adult offenders.

Cohen posited that instead of financial success, these youth were searching for the status and respect they were unable to command in their schools and communities. These institutions were based on middle-class values and morals and incorporated what Cohen referred to as 'middle-class measuring rods' in order to judge youth. While middle-class youth were able to meet these expectations, status frustration resulted when working-class youth were unable to meet the standards demanded of them by their teachers and communities. The results of this strain could manifest itself in a number of ways. Some youth, according to Cohen, could strive to meet the expectations determined by the 'middle-class measuring rod', while others could reject these standards and develop their own working-class expectations. Still other youth could gravitate towards like-minded youth and form delinquent subcultures that allowed the participant to achieve the status he or she craved. Achieving this status in a subculture could, in fact, involve turning over middle-class values and expectations and doing the opposite of what is expected from successful middle-class youth.

Going one step further, Cloward and Ohlin (1960) put forward the view that, in fact, all classes have the same basic cultural goals (wealth, success, security), but that the working class as a class is disadvantaged in gaining these desired ends. Crime is indeed collective in nature (you learn from your peers), and some groups of working-class children who consider their opportunities to be blocked will adopt criminal or alternative opportunity structures as a result. In other words, illegitimate opportunity structures will develop in those situations where the culturally defined goals are still sought, but legitimate opportunities are blocked or absent. The issue here is not a conflict between middle-class and working-class cultures, but the relationship of certain subcultural practices to specific class backgrounds (i.e., a sense of injustice at the lack of opportunities).

Both Matza (1964) and Downes (1966) provide other explanations of subcultural form. These writers argued that working-class young people neither rejected nor inverted the dominant, culturally prescribed values of society. Instead, they saw working-class youth subcultures as simply accentuating particular 'subterranean values' (risk, adventure, fun) that are part of normal society, but which are sometimes taken too far. In response to restricted access to opportunity, the response of young people is to resort to forms of 'manufactured excitement' of their own.

## Contemporary Examples

The appeal of strain theory is that it attempts to provide a sociological explanation for the causes of crime. As we have seen, crime is usually related to blocked opportunities, combined with the activities of particular subcultural groups.

There are several broad strands to contemporary strain theory. For example, there is a growing body of work in the area of **social ecology**. Part of this research looks at how aspects of the physical and social environment at the local level influence patterns of offending and the fear of crime. The emphasis is on exploring the spatial features of offences and offending by examining the natural and built environments, studying the actions of individuals and groups within certain places at certain times of the day or week, and evaluating the processes of social regulation as these pertain to specific city sites, residential areas, and commercial districts (see Evans et al., 1992; Bottoms and Wiles, 1997). The intention of such research is to explain the uneven distribution and impact of crime, and to develop crime prevention and policing strategies that take into account characteristics of the local environment.

Another related approach is that which provides a theory of crime based upon analysis of community-level social disorganization. Again, the main focus is on particular kinds of neighbourhood areas, such as inner-city ghettos. It is argued that, for example, persistent high crime among African-American youth is due to both structural and cultural factors. Specifically, a 'culture of violence' is sustained among the new urban 'underclasses' through 'structural disorganization and cultural social isolation that stem from the concentration of poverty, family disruption, and residential instability' (Sampson and Wilson, 1993:14). More generally, such perspectives stress the importance of considering the impact of 'neighbourhood effect' when it comes to crime. That is, the social status and crime rate of a neighbourhood have been shown to have an effect on a person's chances of becoming involved in offending behaviour regardless of their specific socio-economic status (Reiss, 1986). For instance, a young person from a low-income background living in a high-crime area is far more likely to engage in offending behaviour than an identical person living in a low-crime neighbourhood. Thus, community context is seen as an integral part of why some unemployed and marginalized young people have a greater propensity to commit crime than other similarly positioned young people.

In Canada, the Jane and Finch neighbourhood, located in the northwest corner of Toronto, is often used as an example of such social disorganization. The neighbourhood saw its start during Canada's post-Second World War immigration wave and was originally settled primarily by Italian immigrants. During the 1960s Toronto needed a space to house its next wave of immigrants from around the world. The original plan was to create a place to house thousands of low-income, high-need families and with this in mind, the Ontario Housing Corporation supervised the construction of a combination of public housing and private high-rise apartment buildings along Jane Street. This geographical 'corridor' attracted an overwhelming number of people and the population in this neighbourhood expanded by more than 2,000 per cent in a decade. Unfortunately, as the population increased the necessary social service infrastructure was not able to keep pace. There was a shortage of settlement, language, and employment services, public transportation was less than adequate, schools were overcrowded, and for many years there were no community centres. Racial tensions also grew as the area morphed from mostly European to a complex mosaic of African, Caribbean, Asian, and Latin American immigrants.

Today the Jane–Finch corridor is a geographically large, socially diverse neighbourhood made up over 75,000 people representing close to 100 different nationalities and spoken languages. According to the San Romanoway Revitalization Association, 75 per cent of residents are new immigrants who are facing an unemployment rate of 40 per cent. Single-parent (primarily women-led) families, poverty, and marginalization are the norm, and crime rates are significantly higher than the national average (Payne, 2005).

Researchers have also explored the impact of social disorganization on levels of fear in a community and the impact this fear has on community behaviours. For example, Pamela Wilcox Rountree and Kenneth Land found that when crime rates were high in areas with social disorganization, levels of fear underwent a significant increase (1996). Others researchers have also come to this conclusion and argue that perceptions of crime and victimization create high levels of neighbourhood fear (LaGrange, Ferraro, and Supancic, 1992). Fear becomes contagious as stories of victimization are shared and people become more fearful about leaving the safety and security of their homes after dark. This leads to a decrease in their participation in outside activities and a withdrawal from community life. When fear starts to impact on community participation, business conditions begin to deteriorate and population mobility increases as people strive to move from the community to areas perceived to be safer. This, in turn, facilitates conditions that encourage 'criminal elements' to move into the neighbourhood, and this increases both the chance of victimization and the level of fear in the neighbourhood. And the cycle continues. Individuals who live in socially disorganized neighbourhoods and experience high levels of fear may also develop a siege mentality where the outside world is viewed as an enemy (Anderson, 1990). This results in both a mistrust of all outsiders, including business and government, and in individuals and communities who become self-conscious and overly sensitive to being disrespected or 'dissed' (Seigel and McCormick, 2003).

Social disorganization researchers have attempted to track the changes that undermine city neighbourhoods. They posit that neighbourhoods may have life-cycles (again, displaying the biologically-based roots of ecology theory) that start with the development of a neighbourhood and moves through to periods of decline. Changes in ethnic makeup and a decrease in population density and socio-economic status mark this period of decline. These areas may then transition to a renewal stage in which housing is replaced or upgraded and the neighbourhood is gentrified. Researchers like Taylor and Covington (1988) argue that neighbourhoods undergoing these transformations see increases in their crime rates.

Other researchers have concentrated on examining the impact of neighbourhood disadvantage on mechanisms of informal social control. Elliot et al. argue that as neighbourhood disadvantage increases, its level of informal social control decreases (1996). This results in the likelihood that children may become involved with deviant peer groups, and then engage in socially repugnant behaviours. This outcome is further supported because of a transient population that makes strong interpersonal relationships difficult, if not impossible, to develop and maintain. As a result, social institutions such as schools and churches are not able to effectively work in an atmosphere of mistrust and alienations. According to Bursick and Grasmick: 'In these areas, the absence of local political power limits access to external funding and police protection. Without money from the outside, the neighborhood lacks the ability to 'get back on its feet' (1993: 270). Social control is further weakened by the presence of unsupervised peer groups and gangs that disrupt or block the influence of neighbourhood control agents (Skogan, in Reiss and Tonry, 1986). As a result, young people who live in socially disorganized neighbourhoods find that their ability to participate in conventional social institutions, such as school, is blocked and they are instead exposed to recruitment into gangs (Gottfredson, McNeil, and Gottfredson, 1991).

Most recently, social disorganization theories have been applied in an attempt to create buildings and neighbourhoods that discourage criminal behaviours through design and may be referred to as **environmental criminological theory**. This undertaking can be seen in the work of architect Oscar Newman. His book *Defensible Space: Crime Prevention through Urban Design* (1972) considers the impact that the actual physical environment of different neighbourhoods can have on crime rates. He posits that better designed projects found within low and middle-income housing projects have significantly lower crime rates than poorly designed projects that have comparable types of residences and population densities. Defensible space then becomes the model for projects designed to inhibit crime by increasing levels of surveillance and the creation of environmental spaces that discourage criminal activity. This can be accomplished through a variety of measures that include 'real and symbolic barriers, strongly defined areas of influence, and improved opportunities for surveillance' (Bohm, 2001: 71) and it can include elements such as the use of strategically placed lighting to discourage deviant activities or loitering, the use of play areas and benches to encourage people to go out in their neighbourhoods, and by encouraging residents to take charge of their own neighbourhoods. The goal of the creation and implementation of defensible spaces is to decrease criminal activities by bringing the environment under the control of its residents. This idea of increased surveillance and resident control has been the foundation for the development and implementation of the popular neighbourhood watch programmes throughout North America (Stark, 1987).

A second spin-off from ecological theory is the **routine activities theory** put forward by Lawrence E. Cohen and Marcus Felson. Routine activities theory seeks to expand the ecological explanation of criminality to an exploration of crime and victim rates over time. For them, structural changes in the routine activities undertaken in everyday life influences crimes against both property and individuals. According to Cohen and Felson three factors play a primary role in how structural changes to routine activities can, and do, affect types and rates of crime. The first factor is the presence of 'motivated offenders', such as teenage males, drug addicts, or unemployed individuals. A second factor is the presence of 'suitable targets', such as unlocked cars or homes. The last factor is the absence of 'capable guardians', such as police officers, homeowners, or security systems (in Chamlin and Cochran, 1997). Cohen and Felson argue that all three factors must be present for the successful completion of crime; by removing one or more factors, communities and individuals can significantly reduce the potential for successful criminal activities.

The focus of routine activity theory is not on criminal motivation but is instead on methods to prevent criminal activities. Inherent in this theory is the assumption that all people will engage in criminal behaviours unless prevented from doing so. For Cohen and Felson, criminal activities are so fundamentally located in the legitimated opportunity structure of modern society and in the freedom and prosperity that some people enjoy that the only way to reduce crime is to significantly modify our everyday way of life (Hilbert, 1989).

Crime prevention strategies based on routine activity theory concentrate on potential crime victims who must instigated lifestyle changes in order to ensure that they are no longer easy targets for criminal offenders. Much of the focus is therefore placed on protecting the immediate environment through the creation of defensible space, target hardening, and increasing the presence of capable guardians (Siegel and McCormack, 2003).

Social ecology and social disorganization perspectives combined can provide important insights into how and why certain communities are stigmatized and disadvantaged as communities. For example, research undertaken in the United States (Wilson, 1996), Germany (Heitmeyer, 2002) and Australia (Collins et al., 2000) has pointed to the fusion of class and ethnic dynamics that has direct and indirect negative consequences for ethnic minorities. A crucial factor appears to be the location of specific minority groups in segregated ghettos, a process exacerbated by selected government policies and programmes. The result of a concentration of ethnic minority groups in heavily disadvantaged areas is the systematic exclusion of these groups from mainstream social, economic, and political life. It can also be associated with alternative forms of gaining social status, including the use of violence and reliance upon criminal or illegal activity.

An area of particular and growing interest to criminologists today is that of the study of youth gangs and youth in groups. This research has concentrated on providing detailed descriptions of specific types of youth group formations in places such as the United States (Klein et al., 1995; Huff, 1996), Europe (Klein et al., 2001), Australia (White, 2002), and Canada (Gordon, 1995; Gordon and Foley, 1998). This kind of work has generally attempted to provide more precise definitions of different types of youth groups, to examine the kinds of activities and associations associated with diverse group formations, and to explain the origins, dynamics, and changes in group formation as these relate to social, economic, and policing factors. Significant issues include not only those of poverty and unemployment, but racism and the impact of ethnic divisions and inequality on group behaviour. Attention is also directed at patterns of policing, and how these impinge upon different populations of young people in different ways.

A large body of literature has also emerged that is informed by what can be called social development theories. This literature deals with the personal, family, and social factors that influence the life chances and life decisions of young people. This research and theorizing draws upon elements of strain theory, as well as ideas and findings more closely associated with biological and psychological research. For example, in a review of empirical research on the predictors and correlates of offending, Farrington (1996b) provides a systematic outline of the key 'risk factors' associated with youthful offending. Among the many factors cited are:

- prenatal and perinatal factors (e.g., early child-bearing, substance use during pregnancy, low birth weight);
- hyperactivity and impulsivity (e.g., hyperactivity, impulsivity, attention deficit, inhibition);
- intelligence and attainment (e.g., low non-verbal intelligence, abstract reasoning, cognitive and neuropsychological deficit);
- parental supervision, discipline, and attitude (e.g., erratic or harsh parental discipline, rejecting parental attitudes, violent behaviour);
- broken homes (e.g., maternal and paternal deprivation, parental conflict);
- parental criminality (e.g., convicted parents, poor supervision);
- large family size (e.g., insufficient parental attention, overcrowding);
- socio-economic deprivation (e.g., low family income, poor housing);
- peer influences (e.g., male group behaviour, delinquent friends);
- school influences (e.g., use of praise and punishment, classroom management);
- community influences (e.g., high residential mobility, neighbourhood disorganisation, physical deterioration, overcrowding, type of housing); and
- situational influences (e.g., specific opportunities, benefits outweigh expected costs, seeking excitement).

The combination of these factors, and their association with certain categories of young people, are seen to explain variations in the propensity for criminal behaviour and criminalization among young people. However, these risk factors are seen to coincide and to be interrelated in complex ways, and as such they do not yield easy or simple answers to the question of crime causation. The emergence of life-course criminology can also be traced to recent developments within the field of developmental criminology, which focuses on subdividing the offender population into specific stages of a criminal career and assumes that different causal factors are present within each specific stage. According to Sampson and Laub (2005):

> . . . it is now commonplace to assert that certain childhood factors uniquely explain persistent adult offenders, whereas another set of causal factors explain desistance in adolescence. A variation on this theme is that a small group of offenders continue to

commit crimes at a persistently higher rate as they grow older. In direct contrast, another view posits an 'invariant' effect of age—that regardless of stable between-individual differences, all offenders will commit fewer crimes as they age (13).

Life-course criminology presents a revised theory of social control which posits that development must be viewed as a constant series of interactions between individuals and environments and includes an examination of the role human agency plays in the development of criminal behaviours. In general terms, the emergence of life-course criminology has resulted in time, context, and process, being understood as more significant dimensions of theory and analysis (Elder, 1985). In other words, life-course criminologists posit that crime is an evolving process that cannot be fully explained by neither individual nor environmental factors. According to Elder:

> Unlike the focus of single careers, so widely studied in the past, the life course perspective offers a framework for exploring the dynamics of multiple, interdependent pathways. . . . With an eye to the full life course, analysis is sensitive to the consequences of early transitions for later experiences and events. . . . The implication of early choices and pursuits brings up a core premise of life course study: developmental processes and outcomes are shaped by the social trajectories that people follow, as through advancement and demotion. Causal influences flow in the other direction as well (in Piquero and Mazerolle, 2001: 3).

Life-course criminology relies on two fundamental concepts in the study of criminal behaviours. The first concept is that of trajectories. A trajectory is a pathway or line of development over the life span of the individual and can include such elements as work, career, and family pathways. Trajectories represent long-term patterns of behaviours but they are subject to changes in condition and future options (Elder, 1985). The second concept is that of transitions which represent specific life events, such as leaving school, the birth of a child, a first job, or retirement. Transitions evolve over a shorter time-span and are entrenched in trajectories. In other words, as Elder states, transitions are 'changes in state that are more or less abrupt' (1985: 31–2). Transitions are not necessarily age-graded (although some are) and what is often the focus of life-course analysis is the timing, ordering, and duration of major life events and the impact these factors have on later social development (Jessor et al., 1991). Behavioural stability also plays a fundamental role in life-course analysis. Research has indicated a fairly consistent relationship between early transitions and later experiences and events. It has been shown that the implications of early adult choices can extend as far as the later years of retirement and old age (Clausen, 1993)—'the implication of early choices and pursuits brings up a core premise of life-course study: developmental processes and outcomes are shaped by the social trajectories that people follow' (Elder, 1985: 32).

According to Elder (1985), the inter-relationship between trajectories and transitions may spawn turning points in the life-course, which may alter its directions. He argues that the ability to adapt to life events is crucial because the same event or transition followed by different adaptations can lead to different trajectories (Elder, 1985:

35). Sampson and Laub (1992) point out the importance of trajectories to the life-course when they state that:

> The long-term view embodied by the life-course focus on trajectories implies a strong connection between childhood events and experiences in adulthood. However, the simultaneous shorter-term view also implies that transitions or turning points can modify life trajectories—they can 'redirect paths'. Social institutions, and triggering life events that may modify trajectories include, school, work, the military, marriage, and parenthood (71).

While much of the focus in life-course criminological research is on trajectories and the relationship between childhood behaviour and later adult outcomes, three other important themes are incorporated into this perspective. The first theme concerns itself with the social meanings of age throughout the life-course. The second explores the intergenerational transmission of social patterns, while the third additional theme focuses on the effects of major events, such as the Great Depression or the Second World War, and structural location (i.e. class and/or gender) on the life histories of individuals. As Elder notes, a primary goal of the study of the life-course is to connect social structure and social history to the unfolding of human lives. Therefore in order to explore these themes, individual lives are studied through time, with particular attention paid to aging, cohort effects, historical context, and the social influence of age-graded transitions (Elder, in Piquero and Mazerolle, 2001: 24; Sampson and Laub, 2005). This focus means that the primary methodology employed by life-course researchers is longitudinal studies of individuals over the course of many years. This form of data collection is necessary in order to collect the information that allows researchers to examine the pathway, trajectories, and transitions of their subjects.

Researchers within this broad framework attempt to identify not only the range of 'risk factors' (such as drug abuse), but also those 'protective factors' (such as family cohesion) that influence whether or not an individual engages in criminal or antisocial behaviour (Catalano and Hawkins, 1996). Resilience factors focus on positive adaptation to adverse conditions and are 'concerned with the successes, social competence, good academic adjustment' in youth who are considered at-risk (Palmary, 2003: 4). This focus on protective or 'resilience' factors has increased in recent years with many researchers now looking at the combination of risk and resilience and how this combination impacts a young person's decision to engage in deviant or criminal behaviour. The exploration of the relationship between risk and resilience has had a profound impact on the development of interventions aimed at youth in high-risk situations. This can be seen in the creation and implementation of programmes such as the four million dollar Safe Haven plan announced in the *Toronto Star* on 6 June 2007. The plan called for schools in troubled and poverty-stricken neighbourhoods in Toronto to be open during the summer of 2007 in an attempt to keep at-risk youth busy and off the streets by offering a variety of programmes and by providing summer jobs to students.

More generally, there is seen to be an overlap between offending behaviour and other types of problem behaviour, and a close connection between immediate social context and the developmental pathways of, in particular, serious and violent young

## Box 4.2 $4 million safe haven plan opens schools for summer

More than 150 schools in troubled and poverty-stricken neighborhoods across Toronto will open their doors this summer to keep kids busy—and safe.

Today, the provincial government is expected to announce $4 million for schools in neighborhoods like Lawrence Heights, Malvern, as well as Jane-Finch, where Jordan Manners was shot and killed in his school, the *Toronto Star* has learned.

Manner's school, C.W. Jeffreys Collegiate, is one of the locations that will offer youth programmes all summer long.

'Kids that aren't going to go off to summer camp or kids who don't have cottages to go to need to have a community place they can feel they're a part of,' said Education Minister Kathleen Wynne, when asked about the plans.

'One of the determinants of safety in communities is having public space that's accessible with programmes,' she said.

The proposal put forward by the Toronto Public and Catholic school boards, which was still being finalized last night, involves stretching the provincial dollars as far as possible by adding programmes, like basketball camps and mentoring classes, to many schools already scheduled to be open for part of the day.

'This is big,' said Toronto board trustee Bruce Davis, who chaired the planning group. 'There will be a range of recreation, school readiness, tutoring, mentoring, swimming—every single one of them will be customized,' he said.

The proposal also involves providing summer jobs for 380 students, with 80 being hired by the school board to do full-time maintenance, care-taking, and painting.

'The kids would be earning money and picking up a skill,' said one trustee involved in the planning. 'They might work for eight hours and then slip into the school pool that's open all summer, for longer hours, under the initiative.'

The remaining 300 students will be hired for community programming— as camp counselors or coaches—at the same hourly rate.

Three years ago, after a spate of youth violence, the Toronto board opened school doors in a handful of neighborhoods.

This time the money will be spread more broadly and rather than opening a few schools 24–7, about 150 schools will have some increased weekly access.

A community group offering a basketball camp one day a week, for example, will be asked to expand it to two or three days. A morning swimming programme could be extended to the afternoon.

'Each school will be different,' Davis said.

> The schools are in the 13 priority neighborhoods identified by the city and United Way as desperately in need of social and recreational programmes and economic opportunities, and some other areas of Toronto with pervasive poverty and social dysfunction.
>
> Last month, 15 year-old Manners was shot dead in his school hallway, prompting questions about school safety and the need for programmes to reach out to troubled youth.
>
> 'I know everyone is thinking this is all about C.W. Jeffreys but I can tell you we've been aching to do this. . .we just didn't have the money,' Davis said, adding that the school board passed a motion a week before Manners was killed asking staff to develop a community access plan for the summer.
>
> 'Everyone is keenly aware of the need to keep kids active and busy with healthy choices. Has there been an increased awareness and urgency by everybody? Yeah, probably,' he said.
>
> From Kerry Gillespie and Kristin Rushowy, '$4 million safe haven plan opens schools for summer', *The Toronto Star*, 6 June 2007. Reprinted with permission—Torstar Syndication Services.

offenders (Loeber and Farrington, 1998; see also Rutter et al., 1998). This type of multifactoral perspective leans towards a quantitative and empirically based analysis of offending. As such, it pitches causal explanations not at the more general level of wider social structures, but at the immediate and observable features of society and behaviour. For instance, poverty is treated as a risk factor, rather than a phenomenon stemming from, and requiring investigation in terms of, systemic social inequality.

The sophistication and complexity of the explanations broadly influenced by strain theory are mirrored in the incorporation of elements of the theory into other distinctive explanatory models. For example, the notion that there are distinct criminal subcultures is an important component of republican theory (discussed in Chapter 10).

## Critique

Strain theory represents a broad array of differing perspectives. In the light of this, the critique offered here highlights some of the problems with the main thrust of strain theory. In general, for example, a critique is possible of strain theory's almost exclusive focus on working-class crime. Despite understanding the need to gauge levels of crime not reported to police within communities, strain theorists largely accepted the 'shape' of the official crime statistics, namely that the majority of offences are perpetrated by the working class. An exception to this was Sutherland (1983), who undertook ground-breaking work in the area of white-collar crime. The majority, however, accepted that the crime in working-class neighbourhoods was that which needed explaining and eradicating.

This reflected an acceptance of a consensus of values in society. Ultimately, all people in society want to achieve the same goals and share the same lifestyle (again there are exceptions to the general view; see, for example, Miller, 1958). In this way, strain theory accepts the status quo. Rather than seeing the goals and aspirations of society as moulded by those in positions of power, strain theory sees such aspirations as a genuine consensus of values. Others argue that this is not necessarily the case at all. The acceptance of the genuine nature of the consensus is subject to challenges today, for example, by many churches, which argue against the materialistic nature of the 'American Dream'. Still others argue against the notion of any consensus by looking at entrenched conflicts of values and interests, as indicated for example in the work of Marxist, feminist, and radical environmentalist writers.

The concept of a general social consensus has several consequences. First, it denies pluralism of values in society. By definition, since there is consensus, a conflict of values must mean that one group's values are wrong. Second, strain theorists tended to accept that the gender roles in society were part of this consensus. Working in the 1950s, Cohen, for example, felt that the major strain in the lives of young women was the tension associated with wanting an ideal husband (Naffine, 1987). It did not occur to him that the roles of young women in the 1950s were imposed, or that, given the choice, they might have a genuine desire to pursue a career outside the home. Furthermore, Cohen's view was distinctly middle-class, since many working-class women needed to work to bring money into the family home. In working-class areas the strain of unemployment could be as great on working-class women as on their male counterparts.

It can also be argued that by accepting the status quo, in terms of 'core values', strain theory fails to take account of structural inequalities—the way the capitalist system by its very nature renders some people 'marginal' and so criminalizes their activities. As theories in later chapters suggest, the system itself can be responsible for labelling some people and their activities criminal, while leaving alone other individuals whose activities are equally, or even more, harmful to society as a whole. The process of criminalization is such that only those who challenge the status quo are labelled as criminal.

Without tackling issues relating to the inequalities of the system itself, some argue that strain theory simply attempts to adapt the individual to a system where structurally he or she has no place. Furthermore, there is often inbuilt resistance to this kind of change. Periodically, for example, the system will actively react against any (limited) attempts to 'adapt' marginalized groups and to provide them with equal opportunity. A good example of this 'reaction by the system' or 'backlash' is shown by the eventual collapse of the 'War on Poverty', a major initiative by the Kennedy, and later the Johnston, administrations in the United States. The aim of the initiative was to empower the poor in order to enable them to assimilate into the opportunity structure of American society. Part of the reason for the lack of effectiveness of this programme was the resistance by those in power to the new realities created by the movement towards empowerment. While various factors led to the demise of the 'War on Poverty', including some ill-conceived programmes it spawned, the resistance by the status quo—and particularly politicians who were now faced with an organized, aggressive inner-city urban population—was certainly a major factor in sealing its fate.

Finally, it can be argued that some variants of strain theory oversimplified the link between lack of opportunity and crime. Subsequent studies have shown the link between unemployment and offending to be a very complex one (see especially Weatherburn and Lind, 2001). There are also numerous additional factors, such as attachment to school, family, and peers who also offend, which are not accounted for in many of the theories discussed above. While there may indeed be some generalized strain that underlies offending, how this affects individuals, and why some individuals respond with offending behaviour and others do not, is not explained adequately by strain and subculture theories.

Criticisms of life-course criminology are similar to the criticisms levelled at strain theories in general. Critics argue that life-course criminology ignores the potential influences of biological and/or psychological factors on criminal behaviours. In addition, life-course criminology is unable to offer a comprehensive explanation for why some individuals who are faced with negative surroundings and poor role models avoid becoming involved in criminal behaviours and activities. What factors come into play to make it possible for some individuals to resist the impact of negative experiences, poor family interactions, or peer group pressure while other are unable to escape the impact? Or, to put it another way, how are these individuals able to desist from 'learning' from what they are surrounded by (Schmallager and Volk, 2005: 271).

Having said this, these theories did highlight aspects of offending that were clearly absent from psychological and classical perspectives. They raised the level of debate away from a focus on the individual to the influence society has on the behaviour of the members of the working class who offend. In doing so it established a strong link between societal context and the nature of criminal or deviant activity. Furthermore, it recognized that criminal activity for those who lack opportunities is meaningful for those involved, given their reduced opportunities and/or peer-group supports. Finally, it opened the way for more progressive reforms politically, and against knee-jerk punitive approaches or intrusive psychological rehabilitation.

## Conclusion

From a strain theory perspective, crime is seen to be more a matter of 'normal' people in 'abnormal' situations, rather than disturbed individuals acting out their pathology (Gibbons, 1979). This is clearly a sharp break from individualistic perspectives that locate deviant behaviour squarely in the choices or defects of each offender. These theories took as a base the sociological concepts of Durkheim, which steered them away from looking at individual characteristics, and towards concepts such as anomie and social solidarity that could not be reduced to an individualistic frame of reference.

Within the aegis of strain theory there is a wide range of perspectives that share some similarities, yet also clearly differ in their detail and emphasis. Early theorists such as Shaw and McKay emphasized the disorganization of the poor and lack of cohesive identity that lead to offending. Later theorists, such as Merton, emphasized the strain between goals and means, and the way criminal means would be used to attain goals in the absence of legitimate avenues, such as access to employment and career.

Sutherland and Cressy shifted attention to the interaction between individuals that leads to offending behaviour, and looked at the way criminal associations supply the techniques, motivations, and rationalizations necessary to act criminally. Subcultural approaches, such as the work of Cohen, and Cloward and Ohlin, took association between individuals a step further and emphasized the formation of subcultures as a response to the lack of opportunity supplied by society to working-class youth.

The relationship between lack of opportunity, alienation, and criminal behaviour is, if anything, more important in the current economic climate. Levels of youth unemployment are high, and the inequalities between rich and poor continue to grow at an alarming rate. If strain theorists are right, then the levels of youth crime and the levels of gang formation should also increase. These concerns are, in fact, being reflected in the formation of new international networks of researchers. The Eurogang Research Network, for example, comprises researchers from over 24 different countries spanning Europe, Russia, North America, and Australasia. A key task of this network is to provide grounded, specific research into the nature of youth group formations within the context of global processes relating to consumption, immigration, youth identity, employment trends, and educational opportunities (see also White and Wyn, 2004).

Strain and subculture theories saw movement of analysis of criminal behaviour away from concentration on the conditions of the offender, to the circumstances of criminalization itself—that is, crime as a social process in response to the inequalities in society. What was left unchallenged was the legitimacy of basic structures of society, and the way society itself influenced the way some activities were criminalized, and others not. This 'labelling process', the process of being seen as criminal, is the subject of the next chapter.

## Key Terms and Concepts

- Chicago School
- Cultural processes
- Defensible space
- Ecological theory
- Norms
- Positivism
- Resilience factors
- Risk factors
- Routine activities theory
- Subcultures
- Social disorganization
- Social learning
- Social structure
- Strain theory
- Structural opportunities
- Transition zones

## Further Reading

J. Bryne and R. Sampson, eds, *The Social Ecology of Crime* (New York: Springer Verlag, 1985).

M. Bulmer, *The Chicago School of Sociology* (Chicago: University of Chicago Press, 1984).

R.J. Bursik, Jr, 'Social Disorganization and Theories of Crime and Delinquency: Problems and Prospects', *Criminology* 26.4 (1988): 519–52.

R. Cloward and L. Ohlin, *Delinquency and Opportunity: A Theory of Delinquent Gangs* (Chicago: Free Press, 1960).

D. Farrington, 'The Explanation and Prevention of Juvenile Offending', *Delinquency and Crime: Current Theories*, J. Hawkins, ed. (Cambridge: Cambridge University Press, 1996).

R. Merton, *Social Theory and Social Structure* (New York: Free Press, 1957).

O. Newman, *Defensible Space: Crime Prevention through Urban Design* (New York: Collier, 1976).

R. Park, E. Burgess, and R. McKenzie, *The City* (Chicago: University of Chicago Press, 1925).

A. Reiss, 'Why Are Communities Important in Understanding Crime?', in *Communities and Crime*, A. Reiss and M. Tonry, eds (Chicago: University of Chicago Press, 1986).

C. Shaw and H. McKay, *Juvenile Delinquency and Urban Areas* (Chicago: Chicago University Press, 1942).

C.R. Shaw and H.E. McKay, *Juvenile Delinquency and Urban Areas*, rev. ed. (Chicago: University of Chicago Press, 1972).

W. Spelman, 'Abandoned Buildings: Magnets for Crime?', *Journal of Criminal Justice* 21 (1993): 481–93.

E. Sutherland and D. Cressy, *Criminology* (New York: Lippincott Company, 1974).

F. Thrasher, *The Gang: A Study of 1,313 Gangs in Chicago* (Chicago: University of Chicago Press, 1927).

W.J. Wilson, *When Work Disappears* (New York: Knopf, 1996).

## Websites

*www.cdc-efc.ca*. The Child and Family Canada website is a public education site that is sponsored by 50 non-profit organizations committed to providing resources for children and families; there is also access to an extensive library of research materials.

*www.crime-prevention.org*. The National Crime Prevention Council of Canada website that provides information on federal government crime-prevention initiatives.

*www.cssn.org*. The Canadian Safe School Network (CSSN) is a national, charitable organization dedicated to reducing youth violence and making our schools and communities safer.

*www.deltapolice.ca/community/cpted.php*. This website provides an overview of policies based on crime prevention through urban design.

*www.designcentreforcpted.org*. A website for a non-profit organization based in Vancouver, British Columbia, whose mission is to provide resources for CPTED design and concepts, increased awareness, and education of this approach, which is based on environmental criminology.

*www.crimetheory.com*. This website provides an overview of the predominant theories in criminology.

*www.hewett.norfolk.sch.uk/curric/soc/durkheim/durk.htm*. A detailed resource for information on Emile Durkheim's work.

## Films/Documentaries

- *A Call to Action* (National Film Board of Canada, 2004)
- *Boys will be Men* (National Film Board of Canada, 1980)
- *Clockers* (Universal Studios, 1995)
- *Girls and Aggression* (National Film Board of Canada, 2002)
- *Learning Peace: A Big School with a Big Heart* (National Film Board of Canada, 2002)
- *The Street: A Film of the Homeless* (National Film Board of Canada, 1996)
- *Wednesday's Children: Vicky* (National Film Board of Canada, 1987)
- *Romper Stomper* (Australian Film Commission, 1993)
- *Zero Tolerance* (National Film Board of Canada, 2006)

**Discussion Questions**

1. According to Durkheim, what is the cause of crime?
2. Do you believe that theories based on the idea of social disorganization are relevant to contemporary criminological study? Why or why not?
3. What kind of person might be more likely to respond to strain by engaging in deviant or criminal behaviour? Why?
4. What doesn't everyone exposed to significant risk factors engage in deviant or criminal behaviours? What may mediate the risk for some individuals?
5. What do you believe would be included today in a definition of Cohen's 'middle-class measuring rod'? In other words, how would we define success for youth today? Has our definition changed over time?

CHAPTER 5

# Labelling Perspectives

---

### Objectives

This chapter will help you develop an understanding of the:

- fundamental concepts found with the labelling perspective;
- objective and subjective dimensions to the criminal justice experience;
- influence that labelling perspectives have had on the criminal justice system; and
- strengths and weaknesses found with labelling perspectives to criminology.

---

## Introduction

The aim of this chapter is to discuss how labelling perspectives view issues relating to crime and criminality. Borrowing conceptually from sociological approaches such as 'interactionism', the labelling perspective introduces us to the idea that to understand crime.we have to explore both objective and subjective dimensions of the criminal justice experience.

In the previous chapter we examined how strain theory explains crime in terms of blocked opportunities and cultural or learned behaviour. One of the hallmarks of positivist criminology—whether it be biological, psychological, or sociological—is that crime is basically seen as a given. That is, it is assumed that crime exists 'out there' in the real world, and that all we have to do is record it, through classifying behaviour and searching for determining causes. Such criminology assumes that much criminal behaviour is due to forces beyond our control (genetic, psychological, institutional). Generally speaking, it is further assumed that there is a consensus in society regarding core values and norms, and that the role of the social scientist is to provide an objective investigation into the factors that underpin why certain people commit crime.

The labelling perspectives challenge this view of crime and criminal justice. Instead, it is argued that crime is a social process. As such, it involves different perceptions of what constitutes 'good' or 'bad' behaviour (or persons), and particular power relationships that ultimately determine what (or who) is deemed to be 'deviant' or an offender. Crime is not an 'objective' phenomenon; it is an outcome of specific types of human interaction.

## Social Context

The development of labelling perspectives within criminology was due to a combination of the influence of certain intellectual currents, and wider changes occurring in society generally. We shall explore the intellectual foundations of labelling theory in greater depth later in the chapter. For now, it is enough to say that a central concern of the 'new deviancy' theory was the issue of subjective meaning, and how this impinged upon objective social relationships. Or, to put it differently, the concern was with how human beings actively create their social world.

Part of the impetus to the rise of labelling perspectives lies in the changes that were taking place in the advanced capitalist countries, particularly the United States, in the 1960s and 1970s. The dominant image of the 1950s was one of shared collective interests, consensus on core values, economic prosperity for everyone, and standards of **'deviance'** and **'conformity'** that were clear for all to see. The **social order** was thus viewed as monolithic—everyone was dedicated to common goals, and everyone had a stake in the status quo. Any problems that did arise were dealt with through adequate research and application of appropriate technical responses and programmes.

By the 1960s, however, the presumed consensus was disintegrating. The phenomenal popularity of Elvis Presley in the 1950s signalled a new cultural form that was premised upon energy, separateness, novelty, and rebellion. The birth of rock-and-roll music in the post-war period led to the creation of a leisure-based **'youth culture'**; one that generally represented a sharp break with the existing 'culture' of the parents. Music, fashion, language, appearance, and activities—all were forged in a manner that departed from existing conventions (and, yet, in the end were linked to the creation of new youth-related and commercialized conventions). 'Deviancy' in the youth cultural revolution was consciously perpetrated and, simultaneously, hotly contested by the young themselves.

If conventional family relations involving the generations were undergoing massive change, so too they were put under pressure by the public campaigns of women, and gay men and lesbian women, to have their collective needs and human rights acknowledged in society. The Second Wave of feminism, in the form of a militant Women's Liberation Movement, actively challenged traditional, conservative notions of the female role and place in society. Similarly, conventional ideas regarding sexuality and sexual preference were subject to increasing analysis and condemnation by feminists and by gay and lesbian activists. Conflict went to the heart of mainstream society and, in particular, the basic assumptions concerning the 'American way of life'.

The idea of a uniform social consensus was further sundered by the coming to prominence of the civil rights movement. The radicalism of Malcolm X and Martin Luther King Jr and the dream of creating a more just, equal, and free society for African Americans were both crucial components in a mass social movement for fundamental social transformation. The movements for equal rights, and indigenous rights, were echoed in Australia with the establishment of the Aboriginal Tent Embassy on the lawns of Parliament House in 1970. People of colour, native people, and migrant groups could no longer be easily silenced, nor could their demands be ignored. Social division was now on the political agenda.

The breakdown of convention, and the elevation of social difference to cultural and political prominence, was further entrenched through the fierce public resistance to the Vietnam War, particularly among the young, in a number of countries and especially in the US and Australia, where conscription into the conflict was an ever-present reality for young people. The events of May 1968, in which students and then workers took to the streets of Paris and paralyzed France for a period of weeks, underscored the fact that social change was not only unavoidable, but was happening here and now.

One consequence of these great movements for change and reform was that social scientists started to rethink their conceptions of society, social order, and deviancy. Society was now seen as pluralistic in nature; made up of a number of diverse interest groups and classes. It was not immutable, but subject to constant pressures to change. Furthermore, what was deviant one day might not be the next. Likewise, what one group thought of as deviant might well be acceptable to another. Social reality thus is contingent—how we view the world very much depends upon where we are situated within that world.

One of the characteristics of the social movements of the time was the emphasis and stress placed upon human creativity, liberation, and free will. The libertarian ethos emphasized choice and rebellion over passive acceptance and conformity. Translated into social theory terms, this broad orientation was reflected in the idea that meaning is part of an ongoing social process. Social life is not fixed and immutable. It is made up of constant interactions between groups. The meaning we give to events and situations depends upon how we negotiate definitions of each event or situation.

## Basic Concepts

Labelling perspectives generally start from the premise that crime and criminal behaviour are a social process (see Table 5.1). The focus of concern is with the nature of the interaction between 'offender', 'victim', and criminal justice 'officials'. What counts as a 'crime' is, in essence, determined by the activities of the criminal justice system and its officials; that is, the definition of particular behaviour or an individual as criminal depends upon who does the labelling. Those who have the power to label, therefore, confer the official designations of 'crime'.

The measurement of crime is a process in which the particular actions of certain people are defined by those in power within the criminal justice system as being 'deviant' or 'criminal'. This institutionalist perspective on crime measurement stresses that crime is not in fact 'objective': it is shaped by the nature of interactions and selective labelling by members of the criminal justice system in their dealings with the general public.

A key area of analysis is the relationship between the offender and those who have the power to label. The consequence of this relationship, and especially of the labelling process itself, is that stigmatization can occur. Negative effects can arise from labelling, such that the person labelled takes on the role prescribed in the label. In other words, if a person is branded officially as a 'deviant', 'offender', or 'criminal', then this may result in the person acting in a manner that fits the label.

## Table 5.1   Labelling Perspectives

| | |
|---|---|
| Definition of crime | • defined by social action and reaction<br>• conferred by those who have power to label |
| Focus of analysis | • relationship between offender and those with power to label |
| Cause of crime | • stigmatization and negative effects of labelling |
| Nature of offender | • determined (by) labelling process |
| Response to crime | • diversion from formal system |
| Crime prevention | • decriminalization<br>• radical non-intervention |
| Operation of criminal | • system should not have stigmatizing effect<br>• justice system<br>• greater tolerance and minimal intervention |

In effect, the labelling perspective points to the impact of labelling on the psychological and social development of offenders. The **self-concept** and social opportunities of the offender are determined or influenced by the labelling process. The **stigma** sticks to the offender, and it affects how others see them, as well as how they perceive themselves.

One result of stigmatization is that some persons who have been negatively labelled not only engage in further criminal, offending, or deviant activity, but they also seek out or find comfort in the company of others who have likewise been cast as outsiders. Another consequence of the labelling process, therefore, is that it creates an impetus for similarly labelled people to associate with each other—generally in the form of delinquent or criminal subcultures.

From a labelling perspective, the potentially negative outcomes of the labelling process are seen to outweigh the necessity to intervene in the first place. That is, for young people in particular, the stigmatization of official criminal justice intervention may well propel them into a criminal career for activity that, for most people, is generally transitory in nature.

The response of the criminal justice system to offending behaviour, therefore, should be based upon a policy of diversion from the more stigmatizing aspects of the criminal justice system. The idea is that every attempt must be made to divert certain offenders from contact with the more formal elements of the system, and thus to reduce the chances of stigmatizing them.

Less serious offences, for example, should not warrant arrest, court appearance, and incarceration. Rather, the response should be based upon the principle of (radical) non-intervention, or at the least minimal intervention. In a similar vein, in order to reduce the possibility of unwarranted or unnecessary stigmatization there may be calls to decriminalize certain 'victimless' or 'non-predatory' activities.

Overall, there is a general demand that criminal justice officials should tolerate many different types of behaviour and activity. The power to label is substantial, and has lasting impacts; it should be used judiciously and only where absolutely necessary.

## Historical Development

Labelling perspectives have a wide range of intellectual influences. These include social psychology, **phenomenology**, and **ethnomethodology** (see Taylor et al., 1973; Muncie and Fitzgerald, 1981).

Broadly speaking, labelling perspectives have strong links to the '**symbolic interactionist**' perspective in sociology. This perspective employs concepts such as 'self' and '**symbol**' in order to explain social behaviour and social action. The logic of such a perspective revolves around the diversity of individual responses to social situations (see, for example, Berger and Luckmann, 1971).

A symbol can be said to be anything that stands for something else (e.g., a badge, a gesture, a word). All human beings have to learn how to respond to different situations by accurately 'reading' the symbols around them.

The self is not a psychological concept (like personality), but refers to how people see themselves. This in turn is built through social interaction. In this sense we can talk about the 'looking-glass self'; that is, that your image of yourself is simply what you see of yourself reflected in those around you (see discussion of the work of Cooley and Mead, in Coser, 1977).

Part of human interaction involves role-playing. For role-playing to occur, each individual has to be able to 'take the role of the Other'—to see things as others see them. In other words, interaction can occur only because each person is able to attribute appropriate meaning to the symbols—words, gestures, and so on—of the other.

But the 'self' does not simply passively respond to events and people around it. It also plays an active part in selecting how it responds. How we respond to other people in our social interactions depends upon how we define the situation. The symbolic nature of behaviour means that the first stage of any interaction is one of definition. When people share the same definitions, communication is likely to be straightforward and clear, allowing us to interpret the significance of the interaction itself.

The taken-for-granted world may appear to us as the 'real world' that exists outside us as hard, concrete objective fact. However, in actual fact we are collectively involved in constructing reality through the use of signs and symbols that each of us generally interpret the same way. The basis of our interaction with other people is the use of **typifications**, which are drawn upon as part of our recipe knowledge that we use in order to make sense of the world (Berger and Luckmann, 1971).

The first step in communication therefore is one of defining situations in a process of interaction. Sometimes situations are misinterpreted if we define them incorrectly. For example, if we see two men embracing and kissing each other, a variety of explanations may suggest themselves: it could be a greeting (at an airport), a congratulatory gesture (on a sports field), or a love affair (in a club). What is important in terms of our behaviour is not the circumstances, but whether we have defined the situation in the same way—that is, whether we share the same definition of a situation.

From these types of propositions it is concluded that, at one level, it does not matter what the actual situation is: what matters is how we define it. For instance, a blazing light in the sky could be seen as a comet, or as a sign from a supernatural being. In either case, how we collectively define the situation will still have real consequences for our behaviour and actions.

While human beings are not passive, how other people perceive us does have real and immediate effects on how we see ourselves and how we behave. This social process can be negative or positive. This has been demonstrated in work that has been done in the study of hospitals, asylums, schools, and prisons.

An important concept here is that of the self-fulfilling prophecy. The idea behind this is that who I am is determined by who defines my reality and how this is done. People who are labelled 'stupid', 'bright', 'dumb', 'genius', and so on will respond accordingly.

For example, in the so-called Pygmalion experiment, a group of school students was split into two. One half of the group was publicly labelled 'slow and stupid', while the other half was told they were 'brilliant'. After a while, the school grades of the two groups began to deteriorate and to improve respectively. The argument was put forward that each group had internalized the self-concepts framed for them, and had responded to the public labels by playing the role of 'stupid' or 'brilliant' (Rosenthal and Jacobson, 1968).

It is further suggested that once a person has been labelled a particular kind of person, they are liable to be treated in a different kind of way from others who may engage in the same kind of behaviour, but who have not been so labelled. This general process can be represented as follows:

1. negative labelling;
2. stigmatization;
3. new identity formed in response to negative labelling; and
4. commitment to new identity based on available roles and relationships.

Labelling perspectives in general are based upon this kind of processual model (see Rubington and Weinberg, 1978). In essence, this says that in association with labelling, stigmatization occurs. A person who is stigmatized is seen by others predominantly in terms of one particular character trait or behavioural pattern, based upon the content of the initial negative labelling.

For example, the negative label may be 'juvenile delinquent' because the person was alleged to have stolen an item from a shop. The person becomes subject to stigmatization when the negative 'juvenile delinquent' label becomes a master public definition of 'what they are like'. Everyone then responds to the person according to the terms of the label, regardless of what the person may now actually be doing with his or her life, and with little regard for the other positive qualities they possess. Over time, if the stigma attaches, then the person may commit himself or herself to the new label and hence change his or her identity to fit the label. Within labelling perspectives, labelling is usually seen to produce negative consequences.

The broad interactionist perspective thus focuses on how people typify one another (e.g., as 'mentally ill' or 'young offender'), how people relate to one another on the basis of these typifications, and what the consequences are of these social processes (Rubington and Weinberg, 1978).

From the point of view of criminology, the influence of perspectives that wish to examine the 'social construction of reality' is manifest in two major questions:

1. How do individuals come to be labelled deviant or criminal?
2. How do individuals come to be committed to a deviant or criminal label, and ultimately, career?

Deviance or criminality is not something that is simply objectively given (as in the positivist framework); it is subjectively problematic (Plummer, 1979). For example, it can be argued that deviancy itself can be the result of the interactive process involving individuals and the criminal justice system.

In early versions of the labelling perspective, it was asserted that deviancy is not an inherent property of behaviour. Rather, deviancy is something that is conferred upon an individual by society. According to Becker (1963: 9), the impact of social reaction to certain types of behaviour or particular categories of people is crucial to explaining the criminalization process. Social groups create deviance by making the rules whose infraction constitutes deviance, and by applying those rules to particular people and labelling them as outsiders. From this point of view, deviance is not a quality of the act the person commits, but rather a consequence of the application by others of rules and sanctions to an 'offender'. The deviant is one to whom the label has successfully been applied; deviant behaviour is behaviour that people so label.

Becker's research focused on people considered to be on the margins of society, and on the margins of conformity (e.g., the homeless, alcoholics, prostitutes). According to Becker, the key reason why these people are placed on the 'outside' is because their particular behaviour has been labelled deviant by more powerful interest groups in society. There is nothing in the behaviour itself that is necessarily 'deviant' or 'conformative': it only becomes so in the actual process of labelling.

The importance of this view was twofold: first, it called into question the social nature of the definitions of crime by alerting us to the variability in human behaviour, and second, it showed us that 'crime' is as much as anything a matter of who has the power to officially label behaviour or persons as criminal (see Cicourel, 1976). According to labelling theorists, the use of **self-report** and victim surveys indicates that crime and victimization are ubiquitous—that is, they are found in all social classes and across gender and ethnic boundaries. Hence, the crucial issues are (1) who gets labelled by whom, and (2) what are the consequences of this labelling.

Lemert (1969) provided one explanation of the importance of labelling on people's future behaviour. In this case, the main concern is with the social-psychological level of analysis. That is, we want to know the reasons why a person engages in a deviant act to begin with, and furthermore, what maintains their commitment to deviant activity. According to Lemert, in order to describe the process of labelling we can distinguish between primary deviation and secondary deviation.

Primary deviation refers to initial deviant behaviour. The proposition here is that most of us, at some stage in our development, engage in activities regarded as deviant (e.g., underage drinking, smoking cannabis, petty shoplifting), but we do so because of a wide variety of social, cultural, and psychological reasons. Little is said about the primary causes of deviant behaviour, except that these are wide-ranging and involve a multitude of individual factors. However, the important point is that at this initial stage of deviation, when people engage in deviant activity they do not fundamentally change their self-concept; that is, the individual's psyche does not undergo a symbolic reorientation or transformation (e.g., we do not see ourselves as a drunk, a pothead, or a thief). There is no change in identity, and deviance is seen as nothing more than a passing event.

The main focus of labelling perspectives is with secondary deviation. This occurs when the individual engages in some kind of primary deviation (e.g., shoplifting) and there is an official reaction to that behaviour (e.g., the police are called in). If the police apprehend a person, that person may be officially labelled as 'deviant' (e.g., 'young offender'). The individual may begin to employ a deviant behaviour or role based upon this new status, which has been conferred upon them by state officials, as a means of defence or adjustment to the overt and covert problems created by the public social reaction to their original behaviour. For example, the person may start to 'act tough' to counter ridicule from peers, taunts from neighbours, and persistent surveillance by police when they go out. Secondary deviation is said to occur when, because of the social reaction to primary deviation, the person experiences a fundamental reorientation of their self-concept, and thus their behaviour.

Labelling perspectives were to have most application in the area of juvenile justice. It was argued that young people are particularly vulnerable to the labelling process, and thus more likely to respond, for better or worse, to official social reaction. In their work on juvenile delinquency, for instance, Sykes and Matza (1957) and Matza (1964) described the motivational accounts provided by young people themselves as to why they engage in certain types of activity. They argued that young people use certain techniques of neutralization as a way of denying the moral bind of law (e.g., 'they started it', 'no one got hurt'). Furthermore, Matza argued that the actions of the juvenile justice system, and especially youth perceptions of the competence of officials and the application of sanctions, also affect the 'will to crime' of young people and form part of the ways in which they neutralize their moral restraint.

In studying the values, perceptions, and emotions of young people, Matza (1964) explored the reasons that propelled some youth into further criminal activity. Although most people at some stage engage in some form of criminal, antisocial, or deviant behaviour, not all young people experience offending and criminal justice in the same way. Matza found that juveniles generally 'drift' between the two poles of conventional and unconventional behaviour (including crime), without being fully committed to either. In the end, most young people drift towards conventional lifestyles and behaviours as their permanent pattern. However, if during the teenage years of drift there is official intervention and social reaction to specific kinds of unconventional behaviour, this may well precipitate the movement of the juvenile into a more permanent state of delinquency.

The idea that young people who are subjected to public labelling may be propelled into criminal activity or careers also features in the work of Schur (1973). The solution, according to Schur, is to adopt a policy of radical non-intervention. This means that we should take a hands-off attitude to juvenile offending as far as possible. Young people should be free from official intervention, and they should be diverted from the formal systems of juvenile justice in order to avoid stigmatization.

## Contemporary Examples

Labelling perspectives have become an ingrained part of how we think about juvenile justice institutions and processes (see Cunneen and White, 2002). As will be explored in more detail later on, many of the core ideas of labelling perspectives have spurred further conceptual development in the areas of 'restorative justice' and 'reintegrative shaming' that are at the heart of the republican theory of criminal justice (Chapter 10).

### Cultural criminology

The idea of reaction being important to crime is also found in the work of Katz (1988). In an unusual twist to the labelling perspective, Katz has argued that knowledge of labelling processes (and in particular, the notion of shaming) may itself constitute part of the impetus to engage in deviant or offending behaviour. Katz was interested in the relationship between crime and the emotional states of offenders. He turned his attention to the seductions of crime and the compulsions that are felt by people as they engage in various types of criminal projects. Crime, in emotional terms, is exciting and exhilarating. It represents a transcendence of the mundane, an opportunity to creatively explore emotional worlds beyond that of 'normal' rational behaviour. Part of the thrill of crime is seen to lie precisely in the risk that one will be shamed if caught. Thus, being successful in an activity such as shoplifting or joyriding is not only about 'getting away with it'; it is also about avoiding the shame they would feel if they did get caught. These risks thus constitute an important part of the excitement of the deviant experience. If an arrest does occur, Katz sees this as a kind of 'metaphysical shock' in that it implies that persistence in the activity would now signal a commitment to a deviant identity. This, in turn, would undermine the emotional impact of knowingly being deviant, particularly since such thrill-seeking deviance is seldom tied to the notion of criminal identity or criminal career.

As with the themes and issues raised by Matza (1964), for Katz (1988) it is important to examine the lived experiences of criminality, to consider the emotional and interpretive qualities of crime. Emotions such as humiliation, arrogance, ridicule, pleasure, and excitement are often central to why we act as we do. Indeed, the study of the emotions of crime is capturing greater interest within criminology, particularly since criminal behaviour is deeply and ambiguously emotional. It is argued that different states of emotional arousal, from fear and anger through to pleasure and excitement, have major bearings on individual and group behaviour, and for the policies and practices of criminal justice institutions (see De Haan and Loader, 2002). Locating activity within an emotional universe is one of the characteristic features of what is broadly known as cultural criminology.

Cultural criminology refers to a body of scholarship that tends to focus on the pleasures, excitement, and opportunities for 'psychic resolution' involved in certain modes of criminality (Ferrell and Sanders, 1995; Hayward, 2002: 80). The focus, therefore, tends to be on the varied emotional dynamics and experiential attractions that constitute an essential element of much crime and antisocial behaviour. For example, Presdee (2000) writes about the spectacle of violence in popular movies, sexual activities such as sadomasochism, the attractions of rap and rave, and so on. Ferrell (1997) describes the liberating feelings and sense of power and resistance associated with graffiti. A common theme in much of this work is that deviance offers the perpetrator a means of 'self-transcendence'—a way of overcoming the conventionality and mundaneness of everyday life (Hayward, 2002).

More sophisticated accounts also make the link between the loss of **ontological** security (a sense of place and belonging) at an individual level that makes people feel at risk in an unstable world, and achieving a sense of 'controlled sense of loss of control' by engaging in risky practices (see Hayward, 2002). Consider car surfing, for example. This involves a person standing on top of a speeding car and putting oneself at considerable personal risk in so doing. So why do it? The emotional answer is that it is fun and exciting; the analytical answer is that it represents a choice to engage in a controlled sense of loss of control. According to cultural criminologists, as everyday life becomes more routinized, sanitized, and criminalized, so too will there be greater propensity among people to transgress the boundaries of what is deemed to be acceptable behaviour.

In addition to having a major influence on perspectives such as Marxist, feminist, republican, and cultural criminology, the labelling approach has had a marked impact at the level of policy development. This is particularly the case with respect to young people and children. For example, diversion programmes operate in many jurisdictions. These take the form of pre-court programmes (such as police cautioning schemes) and alternatives to court (such as juvenile conferencing projects). The emphasis here is to divert the young person away from the more formal aspects of the criminal justice system, and therefore to reduce the likelihood of stigma and negative labelling.

Another example of the systemic response to labelling perspectives is the way in which a number of jurisdictions attempt to protect the young person from being stigmatized and penalized for the rest of their life for offences committed when they are young. Canada's youth justice system has implemented steps to address this very issue with the Young Offenders Act of 1984 and, later, with the Youth Criminal Justice Act of 2003. While media are allowed to report on the court appearance of a youth, they are not allowed to reveal the name of the young offender nor the names of any juvenile witnesses. The only exception is if the young offender is transferred to an adult court or is at large and considered to pose a considerable threat to the community. The anonymity of young offenders is further protected under Sections 40 through 46 of the Young Offenders Act, which places restrictions on access to the criminal records of youth. Records are kept by the RCMP in a central repository and are only accessible to the young offender, his or her lawyer or parent, and a select group of others. Records are to be destroyed three years after the completion date for a summary offence or five years later for an indictable offense.

The Youth Criminal Justice Act of 2003 further continues this protection of youth by also prohibiting the publication of names or any information that could lead to the identification of a young person charged with an offence. The exception to this rule is similar to the provision in the Young Offenders Act in that the name may be published if the youth has received an adult sentence or if he or she is unlawfully at large and considered dangerous. These provisions have been put into place because the protection of anonymity of young offenders is considered to be paramount to their successful rehabilitation and reintegration into the community upon the completion of his or her disposition.

## Box 5.1  **Double Murder**

The victims of a double murder at a Scarborough home this week had gone there hoping to score some crack. But instead of getting high with stolen crack, the two men each ended up with a bullet in the chest. And now there's a 16-year-old boy on the run who Toronto police believe to be armed and dangerous.

'He's so young and he's out there with a gun,' homicide Det.-Sgt Pauline Gray alleged of Livingston Lewis. 'It's just so scary.'

Lewis is wanted on a Canada-wide warrant for the city's 37th and 38th murders of the year.

'We just want to get him off the street before he makes things worse for himself,' Gray said.

In an effort to bring the teen suspect in, police obtained a court order allowing them to release his name and photo for five days.

Police have spoken to Lewis's family but he remained on the loose last night, Gray said.

The victims have now been identified as Shawn Day, 33, and Clifford Charles, 43.

It's believed the pair drove to 108 Rylander Blvd., near Port Union and Kingston Rds., just before 4am Wednesday hoping to steal some crack cocaine. But Gray said something went 'terribly wrong'.

She said Day and Charles entered the two-storey, brick home in the normally quiet neighborhood, knowing there were drugs inside. Lewis was allegedly inside the home along with five others, including the man who rents the house and his family.

There was 'an altercation' and Day was shot. Charles ran out of the house and was gunned down as he tried to flee in the SUV.

'I don't care what they did, nobody deserved to die like this,' Charles' estranged wife, Linda Derocchis, 43, said tearfully after leaving a heartfelt note on the tree he crashed into after being shot. She and Charles were together 10 years before they split up five months ago. Derocchis said her ex, who had four kids and two grandkids from a previous relationship, was normally 'a great guy'.

'But he had an addiction problem,' the grief-stricken woman admitted.

A close relative, who did not want his name used, say Day had similar troubles.

'Shawn was a big guy and he had an even bigger heart,' the family member said. 'He just made some really bad choices.'

Relatives of both men said they hope the accused gunman, wanted for first- and second-degree murder, is eventually tried as an adult.

From Chris Douchette, 'Double Murder', *Sun Media*, 6 July 2007. Reprinted by permission of the publisher.

One of the more unusual and controversial applications of labelling theory was the Tattoo Removal Scheme. This was part of an Australian young offender programme in the State of Victoria which attempted to reshape the public image of certain young people. The presence of tattoos was seen as part of the problem for these young people. They were too easily branded as 'crims' or 'toughs', and this fed into a long-term scenario of heightened police intervention, offending activity, and criminal careers. In order to reduce the stigma attached to these young people, the detention centres introduced a scheme whereby they could have their tattoos removed (Ross, 1985).

Tattoo removal schemes are not unique to Australia or to young offenders. New Zealand implemented programmes in the 1990s to assist in the rehabilitation of convicted offenders in prison. The Department of Corrections introduced an inmate employment programme to provide inmates with the opportunity to develop skills and work experience by working in approved establishments outside of prison. Along with this initiative, the Department of Corrections established a programme that would allow offenders to have visible tattoos removed. This programme applied most directly to Maori inmates whose tattoos signified tribal or gang affiliations and were seen to adversely affect their employability. Again, the idea was that how 'others' respond to a person is an integral part of how people see themselves and how they behave. These types of programmes are not without critics, who argue that they are a waste of tax-payers monies and that they do little to change the behaviour of individuals or the rates of recidivism.

## Box 5.2   Call to Scrap Free Removal of Criminals' Tattoos

Tax-payer funded removal of criminals' tattoos helps them re-offend and evade capture after they are released, opponents of the scheme say.

Calls are being made for the Corrections Department to scrap the tattoo programme, which runs in Auckland and Waikato and aims to help rehabilitate prisoners.

Gangster John Gillies has had his 'Mongrel Mob Forever' tattoo removed from his face during 15 $300 laser sessions paid for by tax-payers, the Dominion Post reported today.

The 34-year-old, one of New Zealand's most dangerous criminals, was convicted of assaulting two policemen and supplying Class A drugs in May last year. He had barely been out of jail a year, after serving 10 years of his 12-year sentence for stabbing former Gisborne police sergeant Nigel Hendrikse with a screwdriver in 1993.

Last Monday, at a Wellington High Court, Gilies was acquitted of raping a woman in Hawke's Bay last year.

During the rape trial Gillies told the court the laser treatments on his facial tattoos were done over 2-1/2 years. Remnants of the tattoo remain visible.

Gillies claims to no longer be a patched Mongrel Mob member. However, during the trial he showed the jury a gang-related bulldog tattoo on his torso.

Auckland lawyer David Garrett supports ditching the free tattoo removal, saying the fact that Gillies was chosen showed 'how stupid and gullible the people that make decisions are.'

'The tax-payer paid between $5,000 and $10,000 to help him elude capture—what a disgrace—no one forced him to get the tattoo,' Mr Garrett said.

'You would have to be an idiot not to think he did it to evade capture. . . He is an outlaw, he believes the law doesn't apply to him.'

National MP Tony Ryall said the scheme was a waste of money.

'There are a lot of good law-abiding people who would love to remove their teenage tattoos but can't afford it,' he said.

'Criminals are getting a red carpet to the car as well.'

Sensible Sentencing Trust chairman Garth McVicar said criminals like Gillies already cost the taxpayer enough. He did not believe rehabilitation efforts such as tattoo removal worked.

Canterbury University associate professor of criminology Greg Newbold, a former prison inmate, said it appeared a 'bad prediction' was made in the Gillies case.

Dr Newbold said though he supported the tattoo scheme, he believed it should be used only for prisoners at low risk of offending.

'I think it is probably a good policy to invest in inmates who show determination to reform to help them on their way—I wouldn't do it for everyone, not by any means.'

But Dr Newbold said the cost of tattoo removal was insignificant compared with the cost to society of jailing someone repeatedly. It costs $55,000 a year per prisoner.

Most criminals were capable of stopping offending, with 35 the age many turned their lives around, he said.

'People get older and more mature and their values change, they get sick of being in jail—crime is not so much fun anymore.'

Corrections Department public prisons service general manager Phil McCarthy said some inmates had disfiguring tattoos in highly visible parts of their body and removal increased employment prospects and decreased reoffending.

Mr McCarthy said those who had had tattoos removed showed a decrease in reoffending compared with prisoners with visible tattoos.

Prisoners must be on good behavior in the 12 months before they are accepted on the scheme, and be drug and alcohol-free.

From 'Sensible Sentencing Trust Story: Call to Scrap Free Removal of Criminals' Tattoos', *New Zealand Herald*, 10 October 2005. Copyright © 2007, APN Holdings NZ Limited.

## Critique

One of the first criticisms that often comes to the mind of students is the fact that the labelling perspective does not provide any explanation as to why people offend in the first place—so-called 'primary deviation'. The theory concentrates on social reaction to deviant behaviour. While this is true, those using the labelling perspective argue that they did not set out to explain why primary deviation occurred. They do not see labelling theory as a discrete theory but rather as a perspective, a part of the overall picture that is able to explain the negative consequences of criminal justice intervention.

Some would argue, however, that there is a problem with focusing exclusively on crime as defined by social reaction. There are a number of crimes that are characterized by high social agreement concerning both their harmfulness and their criminality. Crimes such as rape and murder are seen to possess intrinsic qualities that make them a part of criminal law across cultures (Hagan, 1987). Focusing exclusively on social reaction with respect to such crimes would seem to distort the reality of such criminal behaviour.

So, while labelling theory seems plausible in explaining minor delinquency, there are some crimes, such as rape and murder, where the labelling perspective is less useful. It is hard to conceive of these crimes as purely defined on a subjective basis, or as simply a by-product of the confirmation of a 'criminal identity' by the state. While some serious offences, such as murder, are committed by those with an extensive history within the criminal justice system, and could be seen as a result of secondary deviation, for others murder is a first offence, or a **primary deviance**. It is hard in these cases to conceive of these as resulting entirely from **secondary deviance**.

Nonetheless, even under the terms of the labelling perspective itself, it is not always clear what gives people the capacity to reject particular labels. While some seem to succumb to labels and easily slip into deviant identities, others reject the labelling process even after repeated contexts where 'labelling' has taken place. There is extreme variability in how people respond to labels in practice. This has many implications for labelling theory, and republican theory, which we shall consider in chapter 10. Fundamentally, labelling is unable to explain what gives one person the capacity, or the will, to reject the label, while another lacks such a capacity.

There is, then, considerable variability in how people respond to a labelling process. For example, an individual may persist in shoplifting in the absence of overt or immediate social reaction. This same individual, when caught, may cease shoplifting precisely because of the stigma of being caught (and possibly not even because they think that what they were doing was 'wrong'). Others, such as political activists, may be arrested several times for their activities, yet continue to protest. This is because they see official policy—such as the destruction of the rainforest or bias against homosexual lifestyle—as the deviance, not their behaviour. They actively reject the labelling of the criminal justice system. Finally, for some people the act of going through the criminal justice system and its labelling processes may be seen as an important rite of passage, as has been suggested is the case with some indigenous young people in northern Australia (see Johnston, 1991). The labelling perspective cannot explain this phenomenon on its own, since it is bound up with broader issues such as colonial relationships, and in particular the relationship between Aboriginal people and the police.

However, it is important not to oversimplify the labelling process, for example, by suggesting that it only takes one event and a person is labelled for life. The process of acquiring labels is far more subtle, and, as Plummer (1979) points out, labels are used by a wide range of institutions, such as family and school, which extend far beyond the reaches of the criminal justice system. By the time someone reaches the criminal justice system they may well have an entrenched set of negative labels. It may be this labelling process, not that which occurs in the criminal justice system, that determines the fate of a young person. Labelling by the criminal justice system remains important, however, since as Polk (1993, 1994a) points out, it can wield only negative labels—'graduating' from a criminal justice institution has very different connotations in mainstream society to graduating from high school.

For this reason there has been much discussion of the concept of 'net-widening' in the literature. Those with concerns about the policies that emanate from labelling theory argue that diversion, rather than turning people away from formal involvement in the criminal justice system, actually draws more people into its purview. Thus, the negative labels wielded by the system reach further into the juvenile population. This is particularly the case where diversion results in greater intrusion into individuals' lives, for example, through the use of juvenile conferencing in cases of minor offending (see Alder and Wundersitz, 1994; Cunneen and White, 2002). 'Failure' in the context of such diversionary programmes can mean re-entry into the justice system, possibly with harsher penalties involved. Alternatively, this possibility is minimized where diversion involves no further action, such as in the police cautioning programme in New Zealand.

The concept of diversion then needs critical evaluation. Cohen (1985) argues that analysis of diversionary programmes reveals several recurrent problems. First, diversionary programmes can be more intrusive of individual lives (denser nets). Second, people may be brought into the criminal justice system where previously they would have had no contact (broader nets). Finally, while the institution of social control may change, the nature of social control may remain—that is, control that marginalizes and alienates the person (different nets). For example, some form of medical or psychiatric control may replace the criminal justice agencies.

Ultimately, however, to explain criminality it is necessary to go beyond interaction at the level of individuals and social groups. Explanation of how power is wielded within the labelling perspective is limited to the immediate institutional level (e.g., the individual police officer), which begs analysis of the wider distributions of power in society. The analytical gaze of the labelling perspective is on the 'underdogs' and their reaction to their position, not on how they are positioned, and regarded by the more powerful in society.

## Conclusion

The labelling perspective can be seen as a radical break from earlier positivist and classical explanations of criminality and criminal behaviour. It was the first time that the notion of a consensus in society was challenged by criminologists and sociologists. With this challenge came the understanding that 'crime' and 'criminal' were themselves subjective, and depended as much on context and social reaction to give them meaning, as on the nature of the actual behaviour.

Labelling theorists were ultimately concerned with the nature of action and reaction that resulted in an individual taking on a deviant identity, and pursuing a deviant lifestyle. The central problems that inform the labelling perspectives have been usefully summarized by Plummer (1979: 88) and include:

- What are the characteristics of labels, and their variations and forms?
- What are the sources of labels, both societally and personally?
- How, and under what conditions, do labels get applied?
- What are the consequences of labelling?

Through these questions, crime is seen as a process. Becoming successfully labelled as 'criminal' involves taking on a negative label that is primarily applied by the criminal (or juvenile) justice system. This system is full of symbols, or cues, that denote who is criminal (the one in the dock) and who sits in judgment on them (those on a raised platform, the judge or magistrate). The consequences of this process include an individual taking on a criminal identity and then acting according to the expectations of that label; that is, committing more offences. Labelling theory has important issues to raise about the social reaction process, and how best to intervene or not to intervene.

Finally, the labelling perspective raises the importance of power and competing interests in society. This combination of the power differential and conflict of interest between some groups in society often results in the powerless being labelled as deviant. Those without power are thus more vulnerable to the labelling process. It is this issue of the power differential in society that is taken up in radical and feminist theories.

### Key Terms and Concepts

- Conformity
- Deviance
- Primary deviance
- Secondary deviance
- Social order
- Stigmatization
- Symbolic interactionism
- Typification
- Youth culture

## Further Reading

H. Becker, *Outsiders: Studies in the Sociology of Deviance* (New York: Free Press, 1963).

A. Cicourel, *The Social Organisation of Juvenile Justice* (London: Heinemann, 1976).

K. Hayward, 'The Vilification and Pleasures of Youthful Transgression', in *Youth Justice: Critical Readings*, J. Muncie, G. Hughes, E. McLaughlin, eds (London: Sage, 2002).

J. Katz, *Seductions of Crime: Moral and Sensual Attractions in Doing Evil* (New York: Basic Books, 1988).

K. Plummer, 'Misunderstanding Labelling Perspectives', in *Deviant Interpretations*, D. Downes & P. Rock, eds (Oxford: Martin Robertson, 1979).

M. Presdee, *Cultural Criminology and the Carnival of Crime* (London: Routledge, 2000).

G. Sykes, and D. Matza, 'Techniques of Neutralization: A Theory of Delinquency', *American Sociological Review* 22 (1957): 664–70.

P.G. Zimbardo, *The Lucifer Effect: How Good People Turn Evil* (New York: Random House, 2007).

## Websites

www.canada.justice.gc.ca. The Policy Centre for Victims' Issues is a Department of Justice site that provides information on federal government initiatives regarding victims of crimes.

www.crcvc.ca. The Canadian Resource Centre for Victims of Crime is a national, non-profit victims' rights advocacy group.

www.justice.gc.ca. This website provides information about the youth justice system in Canada and about the roles and responsibilities of the federal, provincial and territorial governments.

www.prisonexp.org. This website features an extensive slide show and information about the Stanford Prison Experiment.

## Films/Documentaries

- *Brother 2 Brother* (National Film Board of Canada, 2004)
- *Colour Blind* (National Film Board of Canada, 1999)
- *Quiet Rage: Stanford Prison Experiment* (Phillip G. Zimbardo Inc., 1971)
- *The Street: A Film with the Homeless* (National Film Board of Canada, 1996)
- *It's a Girl's World* (National Film Board of Canada, 2004)

## Discussion Questions

1. Why do you think it is so challenging to overcome successfully imposed negative labels? Provide examples to support your answer.
2. How can a label such as 'gang member' affect others associated with the stigmatized individual? What impact might this have on the ability of the labeled individual to create a new self-concept?
3. How is crime defined through a labelling perspective?
4. Do you think the names of young people charged with serious offences should be made public? Why or why not?
5. What do you believe is the most significant contribution or contributions labelling theory has made to the study of deviant or criminal behaviour? Support you opinion with examples.

CHAPTER 6

# Marxist Criminology

## Objectives

This chapter will help you develop an understanding of:

- the basic similarities and differences found within Marxist criminology;
- how **power** and **inequality** contributes to the development of criminal behaviours and attitudes;
- the relationship between economic and political power and different types of criminal behaviours;
- the contributions Marxist criminology has made to the study of how and why crime occurs; and
- the strengths and weaknesses found within Marxist theories in criminology.

## Introduction

The labelling perspective represented a major challenge to existing orthodoxies of crime, particularly positivist assumptions regarding the straightforward existence of crime as fact. Labelling perspectives instead saw the creation of crime as an active social process. When such notions were first mooted in the 1950s and 1960s, a number of significant questions were raised that created further critical waves within criminology. For instance, why are some groups in society labelled more than others, and why are some groups more vulnerable than others to the labelling process? One answer to such questions was provided by perspectives that analyzed the structure of society itself as a major source of inequality and differential treatment. These were the Marxist and broad conflict perspectives in criminology.

This chapter will focus predominantly on the Marxist perspective in criminology. The key aspect of this approach is that it views crime as an outcome and reflection of basic class divisions in society. The focus of analysis, therefore, is on power and inequality, especially insofar as these embody class-related processes associated with the overall distribution of social wealth.

The chapter begins with a brief discussion of the differences and similarities between a Marxist and a broad conflict perspective within criminology. This is followed by a review of the core concerns of Marxist writers, and the particular attention they pay to crimes of the powerful, as well as crimes of the less powerful. The relationship between economic, political, and criminal processes is a central theme of the chapter.

# Social Context

Terms such as 'critical', 'conflict', and 'radical' have all been applied interchangeably to theories that acknowledge the importance of power and social inequality in the construction of criminality. However, the terminology can be misleading. Regardless of the label, there exist important conceptual boundaries between **liberal-conflict theories** and Marxist analyses of crime.

The work of social scientists in the 1950s was largely conservative in nature. Writers of the period had either overtly bought into the Cold War ideology, which defended the 'American way of life' (based upon defence of capitalism), or were afraid to voice a critical response to such ideology. Their fear was created by state-sponsored attempts to stifle social criticism that bore any resemblance at all to communist ideas, such as the House Un-American Activities Committee (HUAC) in the United States. HUAC was formed in 1938 to investigate claims of disloyalty and propaganda made against individuals. Such well-known people as Ronald Reagan and Walt Disney, who blamed Hollywood labour conflicts on communist infiltration, were 'friendly' witnesses who provided information to the Committee. In 1947 the Committee began a series of formal inquiries into charges that the Communist Party of the United States had penetrated the American film industry. During these inquiries dozens of 'friendly' Hollywood witnesses denounced over 300 individuals as secret members of the Communist Party. Many of these individuals were subsequently blacklisted and did not work again in Hollywood for over a decade. The most famous of the black-listed individuals were the original group of 'unfriendly' witnesses—primarily screenwriters who refused to provide political information about themselves to the Committee, and who became known as the 'Unfriendly Ten' or the 'Hollywood Ten'. This situation was similarly reflected in the criminological writings of the time, many of which were premised upon the idea that there was a consensual social order and a core set of societal values. Deviance meant deviation from consensus and from the presumed accepted core values and norms.

This consensus perspective adopted a **functionalist approach** in which everything was conceived as operating to sustain society as a whole. We all have shared values and interests in society. If an individual deviates from the social norm, then we bring them back into line, and thus restore the equilibrium. In this fashion, individuals are socialized into the core set of values and common interests. This view of society characterized most of the criminological perspectives until the 1960s.

The 1960s was a period that saw sustained critique of many of the dominant social institutions. There was a general rebellion against the norms, values, and activities of mainstream society. This took the form of resistance to the Vietnam War in the United States and elsewhere, student militancy, the rise of the Women's Liberation Movement, demands for civil rights by Black and indigenous minorities, and so on. By this stage, as well, the anti-communist fervour had died down, permitting a more open and critical analysis of society. The readiness to adopt a conflict perspective of society is reflected in the literature of the time. It is essential to note here that a conflict perspective is not necessarily radical; it does not necessarily have to question the status quo, including the processes and institutions of society.

In the 1960s, labelling theory emerged as the precursor to more profound critiques of the existing orthodoxies; it questioned the prevailing worldviews, and emphasized that not all was as it appeared to be. Indeed, some of the writers who had subscribed to the consensus view of society, such as Lemert (1969), changed their views and began conceiving of society in terms of **pluralism** (see Pearce, 1976). Society was no longer seen as a homogenous, unitary whole, but one made up of various competing interest groups. One could identify diverse ethnic, class, and religious groupings; divergent economic and political interest groups; conflicting lifestyle approaches; and subcultural values.

The recognition of social difference was translated at the level of theory into several conceptions of the relationship between social interests and power. Some theories suggested that competing groups are more or less equal in power, and that power is more or less evenly distributed throughout the social structure. Other theories suggested that conflict exists between different elite groups in society. These theories were based on the assumption that there will always be powerful minority groups, and the less powerful majority. The question then was: What is the nature and composition of those elites in society who are able to move up or down the power hierarchy?

While these conflict perspectives acknowledged the competitive nature of society, they were not necessarily radical. In many cases, for example, they still assumed a basic consensus in society in relation to the appropriate means of dispute resolution. That is, a 'consensus' still existed, but this related to the methods of resolving disagreements, rather than to a commonality of values and interests. The basic institutions of society therefore were not challenged. The state is seen as essentially neutral and detached from the competing interest groups. An appropriate forum for change, for example, would be the existing parliamentary procedures. At any time, there is conceived to be a plurality of opportunities to move in and out of parliament. The balance of power is therefore in a constant state of flux.

Radical pluralists held a different view of competing interest groups in society. Becker (1963), for instance, observed that there is not a constant movement up and down the power ladder. Instead, it is always the same composition of people on the bottom; it is always the poor, the Black, and the disadvantaged. A key concept here is that of the 'underdog' (see Pearce 1976). According to this view, the solution to the problem was to assist the disadvantaged—who were locked out of the process of acquiring wealth in society—via the assistance of piecemeal management programmes. This strategy does not challenge society's basic institutions, however: it merely tries to ameliorate the more blatant negative aspects and inequalities of the system.

Marxist conceptions of society are rooted in the analysis of social power. A crucial aspect of the theory is the notion that power is concentrated increasingly into fewer and fewer hands; there is a ruling or capitalist class. There is therefore not a plurality of power. Those who ultimately wield power are said to be those who own the means of production—the factory owners, landowners, and media owners; it is these individuals who will dictate the nature and shape of society.

A liberal-conflict conception of the state sees it as a coordinating body within society. It recognizes that conflict exists within society between competing groups, but sees the state as acting in the capacity of a neutral arbiter or umpire, independent of and not aligned to any particular class interest. Marxist theory disagrees with this view. From the more radical perspective, power is concentrated in a capitalist society, and the state and its personnel are not neutral. The argument here is that if one conducts a class analysis of the state's personnel and analyses critically the state's policies, including economic and military ones, it becomes apparent that the state is far from neutral and impartial.

Ultimately, the state apparatuses (the courts, judiciary, police, prisons, and community programmes) operate in the interests of capitalism. Questions were therefore raised in relation to the criminalization process. Structurally, if the state reflects the interests of capitalism and the capitalist class, then who is subject to what kind of state sanctions, and why?

## Basic Concepts

Marxist conceptions of society are based upon an analysis of structural power in society (see Table 6.1). As mentioned, those who wield decisive power in a society are those who own and control the means of production—the factory owners, the landowners, the media owners, and the owners of information technology. An individual in a class society is defined not so much by personal attributes or by reference to universalizing statements regarding 'choice' and 'determinism', but by their position and opportunities in society as dictated by class forces.

| Table 6.1  Marxist Criminology | |
|---|---|
| Definition of crime | • human rights conception<br>• class interests |
| Focus of analysis | • economic and state crimes of the powerful<br>• economic and socio-cultural crimes of the less powerful |
| Cause of crime | • institutionalized inequality, exploitation, and alienation<br>• **marginalization** and **criminalization** of working class |
| Nature of offender | • choices of offender dictated by structural imperative to maximize profit, or by subsistence pressures<br>• alienation |
| Response to crime | • challenge state repression of working class<br>• expose extent and nature of social harm by the powerful |
| Crime prevention | • radical democracy<br>• collective ownership and control over means of production<br>• redistribution of societal resources according to need |
| Operation of criminal | • democratization of institutions<br>• justice system<br>• public accountability<br>• upholding of human rights<br>• law reform to reflect working-class interests |

To understand crime, we need to examine the actions of the powerful in defining and enforcing a particular kind of social order, and the activities of the less powerful in the context of a social structure within which they have fewer resources and less decision-making power than the owners of the means of production. Power is concentrated in a capitalist society, and the activities of the state reflect the interests of capital-in-general in fostering the accumulation of capital, in maintaining the **legitimacy** of unequal social relations, and in controlling the actions of those who threaten private property relations and the public order. The general tendency of state institutions (such as the police, the judiciary, the prisons, and community programmes) is to concentrate on specific kinds of behaviour (usually associated with working-class crime) as being more 'deviant' and 'harmful' than other kinds of destructive or exploitive behaviour (usually associated with crimes of the powerful), which is deemed to be less worthy of state intervention.

In determining what is 'crime', the initial difficulty is that if the laws reflect the interests of the ruling class, then many types of social harm may not be incorporated into the criminal law if they go against capitalist interests. In such circumstances there is a need to establish wider criteria relating to the nature of offences. Thus, for example, crime has been redefined in a broader sense to encompass any activity that interferes with basic human rights and causes social injury.

Marxist criminology directs attention away from an exclusive focus on 'street crimes' or working-class crime towards the social harms perpetrated by the powerful within society. It attempts to demonstrate how class situation is linked to specific types of criminality.

According to the Marxist view, a broad distinction can be made between the crimes of the powerful and the crimes of the less powerful:

- Crimes of the powerful are linked to both a personal desire to augment one's wealth and a structural imperative to get an edge in the overall capitalist economic competition. They include economic crimes (e.g., fraud, violation of labour laws, environmental destruction) and state crimes (e.g., misuse of public funds, violation of civil rights, corruption).
- Crimes of the less powerful stem from a combination of economic and social motivations. In the first instance, they are related to efforts to bolster or supplement one's income relative to subsistence levels; in the second, they may represent antisocial behaviour linked to varying types of socio-cultural alienation. They include subsistence-related crimes (e.g., shoplifting, workplace theft, welfare fraud) and socio-cultural crimes (e.g., vandalism, assault, public order disturbances).

Thus, the cause of crime is found in the structure of unequal class relations in a society. It is institutionalized inequality, the intrinsic economic exploitation of workers by the capitalist class, and the alienations associated with consumer capitalism that form the context for criminality under capitalism. In essence, where you are located in the class structure will influence the kinds of criminal activity you engage in, the propensity for you to engage in such activity, and the intensity of that involvement.

The pressures and limits of circumstance—and thus offender choice—vary according to class position. For example, economic forms of criminality involve different motivations, propensities, and characteristics, depending upon class background and circumstance. Crimes perpetuated by the working class are largely the result of a need to ensure economic subsistence; that is, a need to live. This situation can be contrasted with motivations based on accumulation rather than subsistence. Hence, the choices open to an offender are dictated by wider structural imperatives to maximize profit, or by immediate subsistence pressures. In addition, both individuals who are powerful and those who are less powerful in society can be deeply alienated from other members of the human community.

For a Marxist, to respond to crime is to expose the extent and nature of the social harm perpetrated by the powerful in society. It is argued that crimes of the powerful have a much greater economic and social impact than 'street crime' and working-class crimes generally, and that if coercion is to be used it should be directed at those doing the most harm.

Simultaneously, effort is put into challenging the manner in which the state apparatus is used to repress the working class. This extends to such issues as public-order policing—especially of the unemployed, poor, and minority groups—and the policing of class conflict in the form of union strikes and industrial disputes. As discussed in Chapter 3, the Winnipeg General Strike of 1919 provides a clear example of how Marxist criminology incorporates an analysis of social conditions into the study of deviance, criminality, and social control.

In ideal terms, the operation of the criminal justice system should be based upon full public accountability of each apparatus of the state (e.g., the police, courts, prisons), a genuine upholding of human rights, law reform that is designed to protect the interests of the working class (e.g., enshrining the right to strike), and a democratization of institutions (e.g., by a combination of participatory involvement of citizens and election to decision-making positions within the criminal justice system).

The best form of crime prevention is one that addresses the basic problem of a concentration of wealth and power into a small number of hands in society. Crime is seen to flourish in a context of inequality and structural pressures towards capitalist accumulation and profit. Alternatively, it is felt that much crime can be eliminated or reduced through the extension of radical democracy throughout society and its institutions, the collective ownership and control over the means of production (e.g., various forms of nationalized industry), and a redistribution of societal resources according to human need.

## Historical Development

Within the Marxist framework it is argued that history can be seen in terms of a succession of different 'modes of production' (see, for example, Cornforth, 1987). Each mode of production encompasses particular forces of production (e.g., tools, techniques), relations of production (e.g., lord–serf, capitalist–proletariat), and social institutions (e.g., monarchy, parliamentary democracy). So, as societies move from, for example, feudalism to capitalism, we see a shift in the mode of production across these areas: from agriculture to industry; from power concentrated among the aristocracy to power concentrated among the bourgeoisie or capitalist class; from institutions built upon the notion of the divine right of monarchs to those based upon rule of law that binds the ruler as well as the ruled.

The emergence of different modes of production has been associated with the rise of different kinds of class societies, where the central dynamic of each society is that of the expropriation of surplus from the direct producers and into the hands of those who own and control the overall means of production. For instance, in a slave-based economy (as in ancient Greece or Rome) the slave owner appropriates the surplus product of slave labour; in a feudal society the lord appropriates the surplus product of the serf; and in capitalist society the factory owner appropriates the surplus labour of the worker. Hence, the concept of economic exploitation and class struggle are central to the Marxist view.

In order to place the rise of conflict approaches and Marxist criminology into perspective, we need to acknowledge the impact of recent historical developments. In the last century and a half, for example, we have witnessed the birth and growth of a new class—the working class or proletariat—and with this the rise of distinctively working-class political organizations (e.g., trade unions) and theories (e.g., social democracy, socialism). In particular, the philosophies and analyses provided by Marxism and anarchism voiced the concerns of working people to forge a new kind of social order in which the working class, rather than the capitalist class, was in power. Revolutionary ideas were in a number of instances accompanied by actual revolutions. Some of these were successful (as in the overthrow of the Tsar in Russia in 1917) and some were not (as in France in 1871 and Germany in 1918–19).

As the twentieth century unfolded, rebellion and revolution were to be features of many peasant and working-class revolts around the world. Class conflict was an ingrained part of life for many people. Class conflict was manifest in the form of periodic economic recessions that disproportionately affected the working class (e.g., in Canada in the 1930s, and the mid 1970s), and in the form of struggles over industrial issues (e.g., strikes and lock-outs) and political activism (e.g., with the formation of the Cooperative Commonwealth Federation and later the reformation to the New Democratic Party of Canada). It was a time of conflict, revolution, and change.

Early Marxist writings on crime in the first few decades of the twentieth century discussed the ways in which crime is an outcome of the precipitating economic and social conditions of capitalism. Bonger (see Taylor et al., 1973), for example, argued that 'criminal thought' is generated by the conditions of want and misery foisted upon sections of the working class, and is also the result of the greed that underpins the capitalist competitive process. In Australia, the work of Wood on convict history provided an important stepping stone for later radical historians who likewise saw crime as stemming from the twin evils of poverty and a savage and unjust criminal code (see Garton, 1991). However, generally speaking, these writings went against the mainstream of criminology of the time. It was not until the 1970s that Marxist criminology was incorporated into the field as a significant and popular perspective in its own right.

During the 1960s and 1970s, American criminologists such as Quinney and Chambliss directly challenged the prevailing approaches in criminology. Clear distinctions were drawn between a conservative ('functionalist') and a radical ('conflict') perspective on the nature of crime and law enforcement. It was argued that where there are class divisions in a society, there are also different capacities to determine the content of the laws of that society. The powerful ruling class will be able to shape the criminalization process in such as way as to protect its own collective interests, which reflect the interconnection between this class and a particular state form (see Chambliss, 1975b; Chambliss and Mankoff, 1976; Quinney, 1970, 1974).

How issues are constructed, how crime is defined, and how crime is responded to all relate directly to one's position in the class structure. If social power is concentrated in the hands of those who own the means of production, then they will influence and generally dictate what behaviour will be defined as criminal and what will not. For example, shoplifting may be considered theft, but false advertising may be viewed as only a trade practices violation. Similarly, those with power are capable of influencing the nature of societal reaction to behaviours deemed to be socially harmful; for example, whether to prosecute industrial homicide as murder or simply to see it as accidental or a product of negligence.

One of the classic cases in this area is the Ford Pinto case. During the 1960s demand increased for subcompact cars and Ford Motor Company President, Lee Iacocca, was determined to meet this demand. Iacocca pushed for the design and production of a new subcompact car that was not to exceed 2,000 lbs and that would cost no more than $2,000.00. This car was the Ford Pinto. In order to have the Pinto in the showrooms in 1971, engineering vice-president Bob Alexander was instructed to oversee an extremely short production period. The normal time span from conception to production for a new car is approximately 43 months. The schedule for the design and production of the Pinto was just under 25 months. During the design and production stage crash tests discovered a serious defect in the automobile. In crashes at speeds over 25 miles per hour, the gas tank always ruptured, which led to the possibility of explosions and fires. To correct the defect would have cost the company $11 per vehicle, would have meant changes to the design and production of the Pinto, and would have made it virtually impossible to meet the goal of having the cars in the showroom in 1971. Production went ahead without correcting the defect and the Ford Pinto debuted on time.

Conservative estimates state that crashes involving the Ford Pinto led to over 500 burn deaths (some argue the number is closer to 900) to individuals who would not have otherwise sustained serious injuries if the gas tank had not burst into flames. Hundreds more sustained serious burns. Law suits against the Ford Motor Company began and one of the most damming pieces of evidence against the company was the discovery of a memo containing a cost/benefit analysis that compared the cost of fixing the defective gas tank to the potential cost of paying out victims of accidents (Birsch and Fielder, 1994). The Ford Motor Company had determined that it would be less damaging to their bottom line to pay victims than to correct the faulty gas tank on the Pinto.

In February 1978, a California jury awarded a record-shattering $128 million payment in a lawsuit stemming from an accident. In May 1978 the Department of Transportation announced that the Pinto fuel system had a 'safety related defect' and demanded the product be recalled. Ford agreed and on 9 June 1978 the company recalled 1.5 million Pintos. In a landmark case—State of Indiana v. Ford Motor Company—Ford became the first American corporation to be prosecuted or indicted on criminal homicide charges. While the company was acquitted of this charge in March 1980, the Pinto's reputation had been irrevocably damaged and Ford stopped production of the model five months after the trial.

---

**Box 6.1  Summary table of the Cost/Benefit Analysis of the Ford Pinto, by the Ford Motor Company**

*Benefits*
Savings: 180 burn deaths, 180 serious burn injuries, 2,100 burned vehicles
Unit Cost: $200,000 per death, $67,000 per injury, $700 per vehicle
Total Benefit: (180 x $200,000) + (180 x $67,000) + (2,100 x $700) = $49.5 million

*Costs*
Sales: 11 million cars, 1.5 million light trucks
Unit Cost: $11 per car, $11 per truck
Total Cost: (11,000,000 x $11) + (1,500,000 x $11) = $137 million

From Birch and Fielder (1994).

---

In developing a new typology of crime—one that dealt with both crimes of the powerful and crimes of the less powerful—Quinney (1977) argued that analysis of the relationship between class, state, and crime is essential. It was put forward that, on the one hand, there are crimes of domination. These are crimes committed by the capitalist class, the state, and the agents of the capitalist class and the state. They include crimes of control (e.g., police brutality, violation of civil liberties), crimes of government (e.g., warfare, political assassination), and crimes of economic domination (e.g., pollution, price-fixing). On the other hand, there are crimes of accommodation and resistance, which are associated with the working class. These include predatory crimes (e.g., burglary, robbery), personal crimes (e.g., murder, assault, rape), and crimes of resistance (e.g., workplace sabotage, protests).

Criminality is intimately tied to class position, and the logic of a system that is geared towards capital accumulation rather than the meeting of social need (see Greenberg, 1993). According to Quinney (1977) crime must be understood from the point of view of the political economy of capitalism:

Those who own and control the means of production, the capitalist class, attempt to secure the existing order through various forms of domination, especially crime control by the capitalist state. Those who do not own and control the means of production, especially the working class, accommodate and resist in various ways to capitalist domination (60).

A crucial concept within the Marxist framework is that of surplus population, in that much of the existing forms of criminalization and public concern with 'street crime' are seen to be targeted at those layers or sections of the population that are surplus to the labour market and the requirements of capitalism generally (Spitzer, 1975). A broad political economic analysis of capitalism set the scene for research and writing on more specific aspects of class conflict and class processes relating to crime.

For example, arising from concerns with class and class analysis of society, attention was drawn to the specific ways in which the activities of working-class juveniles have been subject to particular processes of criminalization. The research of the Birmingham Centre for Contemporary Cultural Studies in England, for instance, re-examined the issue of youth subcultures from the point of view of the unequal material circumstances of working-class boys and girls (Hall and Jefferson, 1976). It was argued that class was central to any explanation of the experience of 'growing up', and that the relationship between young people and social institutions such as school, work, and the legal system is characterized by different forms of class-based resistance to the relations of power and domination. Certain youth subcultures were seen to 'solve', in an imaginary way, problems experienced by working-class young people (e.g., unemployment, educational disadvantage) that at the material level remained unresolved (Clarke et al., 1976; Brake, 1985).

From the point of view of social control and policing, various studies pointed to the ways in which the media portrayed certain types of youth subcultures, which in turn led to a form of 'deviancy amplification' (Cohen, 1973; Young, 1971). That is, the sort of public labelling that pertained to some groups of young people actually generated further 'deviant' behaviour in the group so labelled. More generally, the link was made between the actual experiences of working-class young people—culturally, socially, and economically—and the manner in which the state, particularly the police, intervened in their lives both coercively (e.g., arrest rates) and ideologically (e.g., through the promulgation of 'moral panics' over their behaviour and attitudes).

By providing a structural perspective on social institutions, social processes, and social outcomes, Marxist approaches argued that revolutionary or profound social transformation is needed if 'crime' is to be addressed in a socially just manner.

## Contemporary Examples

In Marxist criminology the concern is to highlight the inequalities of a class society (e.g., wealth and poverty; business profits and low wages), and to show how these impact upon the criminalization process. The powerful are seen as designing the laws in their own collective interests, while having greater capacity to defend themselves individually if they do break and bend the existing rules and regulations. The less powerful in society are propelled to commit crime by economic need and social alienation. They are also the main targets of law enforcement and wider criminal justice agencies. This is reflected in statistics that show an overrepresentation of the unemployed and poor in prisons, police lock-ups, and the courts. In Canada, statistics show that Aboriginal people are over-represented in the prison population, where, in 2006, they accounted for 18.5 per cent of the federal inmates while representing only 2.7 per cent of the Canadian population.

## Box 6.2  Overrepresentation of Aboriginal People in the Canadian Federal Prison System

Canada's correctional investigator is sounding an alarm about discriminatory treatment of aboriginal offenders in federal penitentiaries.

Howard Sapers said Monday that while the Correctional Service of Canada isn't responsible for the disproportionate numbers of aboriginals in the prison system—the incarceration rate for natives is nine-times higher than for non-natives—it is responsible for discrimination within its walls.

He pointed to statistics that aboriginal offenders are routinely over-classified—for example, being routed to maximum security instead of lesser classifications—compared to non-aboriginals.

'This over-classification is a problem because it means inmates often serves their sentences far away from their family, their community, their friends, their supports, their elders,' he said.

Natives get released much later in their sentences and have a harder time getting rehabilitation programming, he said.

'In short. . .the general picture is one of institutionalized discrimination,' Sapers said.

Some of his other points:

- On a proportional basis, far fewer aboriginals get community supervision than non-aboriginal offenders.
- Aboriginals are more likely to get their parole yanked for technical breached than non-aboriginals.
- The correctional system must do a better job of preparing aboriginals for release and better support while they are in the community.

The service's own statistics show that despite all the studies and task forces, outcomes for aboriginal offenders haven't improved in 20 years.

'To the contrary, the gap in outcomes. . .continues to grow.'

Sapers calls for more commitment and resources to address these problems. He wanted more aboriginal workers hired, especially in institutions where there were high numbers of incarcerated natives. In the West, 60 per cent of federal prisoners are native.

He also noted that given the predominantly young aboriginal population, if current trends continue, the native proportion of the prison population will rise from 18.5 per cent to 25 per cent in the next 10 years.

Aboriginals make up 2.7 per cent of Canada's population.

'Clearly the need to do better is obvious and urgent,' said Sapers, a one-time Liberal MLA in Alberta.

Public Safety Minister Stockwell Day said he will take the report under consideration.

However, he said there is no evidence of systemic discrimination against aboriginals in the prison population.

Phil Fontaine, grand chief of the Assembly of First Nations, said in a news release that his organization called on the service to implement all of Saper's recommendations.

Beverley Jacobs, president of the Native Womens' Association of Canada, said in a release that there is a clear correlation between poverty and over-representation of aboriginals in the justice system.

From Graham Richardson, 'Report: Prison System Discriminatory to Aboriginals', *CTV.ca News*, 16 October 2006. © 2007 All Rights Reserved. Reprinted by permission of ctv.ca.

Due to a range of academic institutional factors (e.g., the rise of postmodernism as a perspective) and external political changes (e.g., the collapse of Stalinism, the demise of large Marxist-oriented political parties in the West), the Marxist perspective waned within criminological circles in the 1980s. In its stead there developed a broader and more inclusive radical approach that we describe in Chapter 11 as critical criminology, and various liberal strands of criminology such as Left Realism and republican theory. Nevertheless, there are ongoing attempts to restate and make applicable the basic propositions of Marxist criminology today, especially in the light of the increasing polarization of wealth and poverty on a world scale, and the further concentration and monopolization of production.

The ongoing contribution of a Marxist framework to understanding contemporary developments in society, and to criminal justice specifically, has long been highlighted in the work and writings of Jeffrey Reiman (1998). Reiman first published his book *The Rich Get Richer and the Poor Get Prison* in 1979. As the title suggests, the book is an analysis of the economic biases, ideological processes, and social inequalities associated with the criminal justice system. In later editions, the book includes an appendix that provides a detailed outline of the Marxist critique of criminal justice. Marxism as an analytical framework may have declined in popularity among academic intellectuals, but Reiman (1999) argues that the issues with which it is concerned have not lost any of their potency or relevance. For example, a report issued by Statistics Canada in 2006 indicates that the gap between the rich and poor widened between 1999 and 2005. According to news article by CBC:

> Rising home values are behind much of the widening gap between Canada's wealthier citizens and its poorest, Statistics Canada said Wednesday. Those with a net worth that places them in the top 20 per cent saw their wealth grow by 19 percent between 1999 and 2005, while those in the bottom 20 per cent gained no ground at all. The median net worth of the country's top fifth came to $551,000 last year. It was $465,000 in 1999 and $336,000 in 1984. The surging price of housing explains much of the increase. Most of those (95 per cent) in the top 20 per cent bracket owned a home, and the median value of that home grew by $75,000 between 1999 and 2005. Only six per cent of those in the lowest wealth group owned a home. Statistics Canada said the median net worth of the poorest group has stagnated over the past two decades. 'The value of their assets never exceeded the value of their debts during the 1984 to 2005 period,' the agency said. Of the total household wealth in Canada in 2005, the top 20 per cent possessed 75 per cent of it (CBC, 2006b).

As Reiman (1999: 1) states: 'Economic bias is still with us. What has changed is that the attention and concern that was once focused on economic bias as a serious problem that threatened to undermine the legitimacy of the criminal justice system has steadily diminished.' For Reiman, economic bias has continued and, in some respects, deepened. The lack of attention to the contours and dimensions of this bias among social scientists and political leaders is explained in terms of the power of ideology, and specifically what he refers to the 'angle of moral vision'. Reiman says that the 'awareness' of economic bias may well still be there, but its 'acceptance' indicates that differences in wealth are perceived simply as morally irrelevant differences (1999: 4). Thus, analytically Marxism is seen to continue to provide important insights into class inequality, and the ideologies and institutions that sustain this. The political attractiveness and criminological implications of the perspective, however, tend to be bound up with the degree of social upheaval and social movement within society at large. In other words, the social context within which Marxist analysis takes place forms an important part of how it is received in the wider intellectual and political communities.

An article by White and van der Velden (1995) provides another example of contemporary Marxist writing on issues of class and criminology. It argues that there are typical patterns of crime associated with specific classes. This is because class position embodies diverse material circumstances and capacities of people to marshal economic and political resources, and this in turn depends upon one's relationship to the means of production. To put it differently, the wealth and power one had determines the kind of crime in which one might engage. Thus, the crimes of the capitalist class are linked both to augmentation of personal wealth and to attempts to secure an advantage in the process of 'doing business'. This translates into various types of criminal fraud and illegal business transactions. By way of contrast, working-class criminality is seen as based on subsistence, designed to supplement income or in some cases to be of a survival nature (e.g., theft, shoplifting). Further, working-class crime also includes a range of activities that reflect the various alienations experienced by workers, such as vandalism, rape, racist attacks, and so on.

The impact of the crimes of the powerful is often diffuse, yet they affect a large number of people directly or indirectly simply because of the capacity of the capitalist to do harm on a large scale. For example, tax avoidance or environmental destruction may have a considerable social cost, but not be 'visible' in the public domain in the same way as 'street crime'. In defending themselves against prosecution, the powerful have greater social resources at their disposal with which to protect their interests. Furthermore, the sheer costs associated with investigation and prosecution of white-collar and corporate crime often make it prohibitive for the state to proceed, or to cast a wide net to catch other violations similar to the exceptional few that are prosecuted. Crimes of the powerful may have significant structural effects in terms of lives lost and financial impacts. Because such crimes are usually directed, in the first instance, against other capitalists or against the rules governing the marketplace, the general public rarely perceives them as being of special interest to them personally (except in the case of events such as industrial homicide).

By way of contrast, the crimes of the less powerful tend to be highly visible and to be subjected to wide-scale state intervention involving police, welfare workers, social security officials, tax department officials, the courts, prisons, and so on. A feature of relative powerlessness is that the crimes committed tend to be individualized and thus to have a discrete impact. There is usually one victim (or a few), whether personal or business or household, and the impact of the offence is limited to the actual household or person violated. The response of the major institutions in society is largely oriented towards stopping these kinds of crimes, regardless of the comparatively greater amount of damage caused by crimes of the powerful. The lack of access to resources, such as control of the media and legal experts, means that working-class people are more vulnerable to apprehension, prosecution, and punishment at the hands of the capitalist state. They are exposed to societal control mechanisms in such a way that they feel the full force of the state for any transgression they might commit.

In this analysis, issues of the regulation of an 'underclass' and the policing of working-class communities is bound up with the cyclical and long-term deterioration of the social and economic conditions of life for the majority in capitalist society (see White and van der Velden, 1995). The structural conditions producing working-class crime (e.g., unemployment, cutbacks in welfare spending) are seen to have implications, as well, for the capacity of the state to respond other than coercively to 'street crime'. Because the state is undergoing a fiscal crisis (a crisis around a real or perceived lack of government funds), it cannot use welfare-type measures as a means to deal with the social fall-out arising from capitalist restructuring. Harsher 'law-and-order' strategies will thus only make worse the political isolation, socio-cultural alienation, and economic immiseration of the marginalized layers of the working class, thus causally feeding the very criminality that the campaign for enhanced social control is designed to overcome.

Most criminological theories focus their attention on crimes perpetrated by the working class. Marxist theory, however, redirects our attention away from 'street crimes' and compels us to examine crimes of the powerful. The question then arises of how we are to do this, given the concentration of power and the ability of the powerful to define crime in their interests. For example, within capitalist society there are contested definitions concerning criminal behaviour (what ought to be criminalized), and instances where criminal offences exist but are not enforced (what is actually criminalized). In other words, the criminality of this behaviour is perceived as ambivalent within the capitalist system—there is uncertainty whether or not an activity is really criminal—and whether or not the powerful in some instances should be labelled as criminal (e.g., industrial homicide).

Alternatively, Marxists argue that there is a need to broaden the definition of crime. This entails establishing wider criteria relating to the nature of offences (see Schwendinger and Schwendinger, 1975). The definition of crime would accordingly extend to encompass any activity that interferes with one's human rights, including things such as racism, sexism, and so on. Ultimately, Marxists argue that wherever economic exploitation exists, a crime has occurred.

## Critique

Despite the overview given above, it is clear that Marxist criminology—like many other strands of criminology—has variations on a particular theme. The theme here is that capitalist exploitation leads to criminal behaviour and criminalization of one group (the workers) to a greater extent than the powerful in society. While there are considerable areas of agreement between Marxist criminologists, there are also considerable areas of disagreement.

One concern of some Marxist criminologists relates to the use of the term 'criminal'. For example, Steinart (1985) argues that the term 'crime' has lost any useful meaning it might once have held. It is too imbued with the capitalist ethos, so that the symbolic emotive aspect of the label cannot be separated from its capitalist connotation. For this reason the term is of no use to Marxists. Rather, he argues that the term should not be used; instead, the aim of Marxist criminology should be to highlight those who are harmed the most (the proletariat) and devise policies that have the sole aim of reducing harm, without recourse to criminal law or criminal process. Those advocating Left Realism label this position as 'left idealist', a theory discussed in Chapter 9.

While some would see this position as extreme (including many Marxists), it does overcome a central problem in Marxist criminology; namely, how to define crime. Is there a qualitative difference between the harm that is labelled 'criminal' and other sorts of harm? Traditional perspectives in criminology insist that crime consists of both 'the harm' and 'the guilty mind'. One of the problems with this definition is that 'the guilty mind' takes actions out of context, in particular a context where the powerful dictate the conditions under which the powerless act. Furthermore, harm in the white-collar area results, in many cases, from many negligent minds rather than one guilty mind. For these reasons Marxist criminologists have moved away from the notion of *mens rea*, and focused on the degree of harm.

The problem then becomes what harm to define as criminal. This has led, as we have seen, to very broad definitions of what constitutes criminal activity: for example, 'any activity that interferes with one's basic human rights', or 'wherever economic exploitation exists', a crime has occurred. Some would argue such definitions are so broad that they lose any useful meaning (Cohen, 1993), and alienate wide sectors of society that may be sympathetic to the general thrust of Marxist criminology. This raises big issues for criminology generally; that is, the terms 'crime' and 'non-crime' are dichotomous, whereas in reality degrees of harm can be considered along a scale. Definitions of crime that are broad (or narrow) do not solve this problem of trying to squeeze a variable that exists on a continuum (such as harm) into dichotomous categories, such as criminal/not criminal.

Furthermore, Cohen (1988) argues that there is a tendency for those who argue for greater use of the criminal law against white-collar crime, such as the Marxists, to forget the problems associated with using the criminal law to curb harmful behaviour. Earlier research has mapped out a multitude of problems associated with processing people through the criminal justice system, such as the problems associated with stigmatization and the costs involved in criminal prosecutions. There is also the issue of the politics of criminalization. Any push to criminalize behaviour is subject to political contingencies that result in unintended consequences of reform: instead of ameliorating the harm, it may indeed exacerbate it.

Marxists have been subjected to further criticism as well. It has been argued that aspects of Marxist writing in criminology have a romantic image of the criminal as 'primitive class rebel'. These conceptualizations understate the real harm caused by such 'rebels'. Those who are the victims of antisocial behaviour, often poor themselves, suffer considerable hardship at the hands of those who commit 'street crime'.

Some Marxists have been criticized for conspiratorial overtones in their analyses regarding, for example, the direct involvement of members of the ruling class in dictating the operational activities of the police (Hall and Scraton, 1981). Critics argue that there are many examples where laws are enacted to fetter the activities of specific capitalists (e.g., insider trading). There are many laws in existence that restrain the activities of individual capitalists, which would seem to refute the Marxist argument of the criminal law always defining the activities of the powerless as criminal and never those of the powerful.

This criticism, however, highlights a debate within Marxism itself concerning the precise nature of the state. Some, such as Miliband (1969), have argued that the state can be viewed as an instrument of class rule by virtue of the close social relationship between the top members of the state apparatus (such as high-level bureaucrats and members of the military establishment) and members of the capitalist class (such as bankers, media owners, industrialists, and other corporate leaders). Others such as Poulantzas (1972) have argued that the state exists to promote the interests of capital-in-general, not individual capitalists. In the end, both Miliband and Poulantzas would be unfazed by the criticism above that laws impact negatively on individual capitalists. They would see that the state exists to maintain conditions for capital accumulation, and defend those conditions, whether threatened by individuals of the ruling class or the proletariat. However, the state, by defending the conditions of capital accumulation, ultimately enhances the prospects of the ruling class as a whole.

In terms of crime, it is clear that one cannot reduce crime to a simple equation with poverty or alienation. If this were so, then we would need to explain why it is that not every person living in poverty commits crime, and why some people who appear to be well-off do engage in crimes such as vandalism, homicide, etc. This does occur. However, Marxists are more interested in general trends and broad predictions, based upon the notion that social context shapes the choices or options actually available to a person. The choices for the poor concerning whether to steal or not are categorically different to the choices for the rich; furthermore, these conditions are structurally determined.

Not all criminal laws can be defined as 'class' laws, however, in that some deal with class-neutral questions such as rape. This suggests that power may not be totally encapsulated or explainable in class terms. Power and powerlessness can exist in a sense outside the class structure, such as the power of men over women. Similar concerns have been expressed in relation to issues of racism and the relative position of different ethnic groups in society. In either case, however, there are usually strong class factors that shape the contours of the power relationship between men and women, and different ethnic and 'race' groups.

There are many diverse interpretations and explanations for crime from within the broadly Marxist framework. Some of them offer rather simplistic formulations (e.g., the ruling class directly defines what is criminal or not) and some of them provide detailed, sophisticated accounts as to how class power is exercised via the state to enforce basic class rule (e.g., through analysis of personnel, decision-making processes, limits to reform). Overall, however, it can be said that the strength of such approaches is that they attempt to locate social action within the wider structural context of a class-divided society. In doing so they elevate the issue of power and control to the foreground of criminological analysis, and they stress the ways in which social background and social processes give rise to certain propensities (on the part of the powerful and on the part of the less powerful) to engage in criminal activity.

## Conclusion

Marxists argue that within contemporary capitalist societies, the capitalist mode of production operates at many levels, both national and global, and this has economic, social, and political impacts. There is a concentration of wealth and power into the hands of transnational corporations, which control both material and cultural production. The penetration of capitalist relations and enterprises (e.g., in Russia), and the concentration of economic power into fewer hands (e.g., Murdoch), is apparent on a world scale. Internationally and at the national level, the number of poor is growing and the rich are getting richer.

Marxist criminology argues that the concentration of wealth and power into the hands of a small capitalist class has ramifications for the definition of, and responses to, crime. If power is concentrated in the hands of those who own the means of production, they will influence, and to a certain extent dictate, what behaviour will be defined as crime and what will not. Those with power are likewise capable of influencing the nature of societal reaction to behaviours deemed to be criminal. There is thus an ability here to influence how the state will intervene, for example, on issues relating to environmental destruction.

According to a Marxist perspective, if we wish to examine crime and class in the global context, we must determine who it is that controls the finances (e.g., the banks, the International Monetary Fund); we must evaluate trade agreements that define how the benefits of trade are to be distributed, and the conditions of trade that will be adhered to; and we must consider the impact of mass production and technology (including new information technology) on the lives of workers. Class divisions exist both within and between countries. The existence of the rich and the poor, the divide between the North and the South, are symptomatic of processes of polarization that fundamentally determine the distribution and definition of crime. For a Marxist, the fundamental questions revolve around the implications of such divisions for the nature and causes of crime, and for the manner of state intervention into people's lives.

## Key Terms and Concepts

- Alienation
- Criminalization process
- Functional approach
- Liberal-conflict theory
- Marginalization
- Moral panics
- Political economy of capitalism
- Radical pluralism

## Further Reading

J. Bakan, *The Corporation: The Pathological Pursuit of Profit and Power* (New York: Simon & Schuster, 2003).

P. Edwards, *One Dead Indian: The Premier, the Police, and the Ipperwash Crisis* (McClelland & Stewart, 2003).

W.M. Evans and M. Manion, *Minding the Machines: Preventing Technological Disasters* (New York: Prentice Hall PTR, 2002).

D. Greenberg, ed., *Crime and Capitalism: Readings in Marxist Criminology* (Philadelphia: Temple University Press, 1993).

R. Quinney, R. (1977) *Class, State and Crime: On the Theory and Practice of Criminal Justice* (New York: David McKay Company, 1977).

J. Reiman, *The Rich Get Richer and the Poor Get Prison* (Boston: Allyn and Bacon, 1988).

H. Schwendinger and J. Schwendinger, 'Defenders of Order or Guardians of Human Rights', in *Critical Criminology*, I. Taylor, P. Walton, and J. Young, eds (London: Routledge and Kegan Paul, 1975).

S.S. Simpson, *Corporate Crime, Law, and Social Control* (Cambridge: Cambridge University Press, 2002).

S. Spitzer, 'Toward a Marxian Theory of Deviance', *Social Problems* 22 (1975): 638–51.

R. Vaughn, *Only Victims: A Study of Show Business Blacklistings* (New York: G.P. Putnam & Sons, 1973).

R. White, and J. van der Velden, 'Class and Criminality', *Social Justice* 22.1 (1995): 51–74.

## Websites

*www.civilization.ca/hist/labour.* Information about the Winnipeg general strike of 1919 is provided.

*www.crimetheory.com.* An overview of the predominant theories in criminology is presented.

*www.parl.gc.ca/information/library/PRB.* A website presenting the Final Report of the Royal Commission on Aboriginal Peoples.

*www.saskndp.com/history.* An archive providing documents, articles, and resources from the history of the CCF and the New Democratic Party.

*www.statcan.ca.* The Statistics Canada website provides free and for fee economic, social, and census data, and daily overviews of statistical releases.

*www.TheCorporation.com.* The official website for the film by the same name.

## Films/Documentaries

- *A Call to Action* (National Film Board of Canada, 2004)
- *No Place Called Home* (National Film Board of Canada, 2003)
- *No Turning Back* (National Film Board of Canada, 1996)
- *One of the Hollywood Ten* (Bloom Street Productions, 2000)
- *Roger and Me* (Warner Brothers Inc., 1989)
- *The Corporation* (Big Picture Media Corporation, 2003)
- *The Street: A Film with the Homeless* (National Film Board of Canada, 1996)

## Discussion Questions

1. How would a Marxian perspective explain why crime occurs?
2. How is this different from a radical pluralist explanation of crime causation?
3. How do the main assumptions found within a Marxian perspective differ from a functionalist approach to the study of crime?
4. How would a Marxist theorist explain the events of the Ford Pinto disaster?
5. What do you believe to be the strongest contributions Marxist criminology has made to the study of crime and crime causation? The weakest? Provide examples to support your answers?

# CHAPTER 7

# Feminist Perspectives

## Objectives

This chapter will help you develop an understanding of the:

- social context that gave rise to the development of feminist theories;
- various strands of feminist perspectives within criminology;
- position of women and girls within the criminal justice system;
- impact feminist theory has had on the criminal justice enterprise; and
- strengths and weaknesses found within feminist approaches to criminology.

## Introduction

The intention of this chapter is to discuss and review issues pertaining to feminist perspectives in criminology. To do this adequately, we need to know something about the position of women and girls generally within the broad criminological discipline, and how gender differences or similarities have been theorized within the field.

The previous chapter outlined the impact of class structure on the construction of criminality, and fundamental motivational distinctions were drawn between crimes of the powerful and those of the powerless. Generally, crimes of the powerful are said to be committed in order to enhance competitive advantage or to augment personal wealth. Additionally, these individuals are said to possess, or have access to, social resources that enable them to resist detection or prosecution attempts. By contrast, working-class crimes are tied to issues of economic subsistence and alienation—be it economic, social, political, or cultural. Furthermore, it is the activities of this class that are excessively regulated; given the lack of access to social resources, they are in the most vulnerable position.

This chapter shares some themes in common with Marxist criminology. Namely, feminist criminology has been centrally concerned with issues of power, the distribution of economic and social resources, and the differential position of selected groups in society, which has implications for their activities as either 'offenders' or 'victims'. According to feminist criminology, the sexist nature of the criminal justice system is an ingrained part of that system, and is long overdue for reform.

## Social Context

Marxist criminology put questions of power on the agenda in a forceful way during the 1970s. Feminist criminology also looks at who holds and wields power in society, and questions how this impacts on women. Feminist criminology developed in the late 1960s and into the 1970s, and was closely associated with the emergence of the Second Wave of feminism at this time. History reveals that women have long been oppressed as a group, denied rights, and subjected to violence. The new movement was called the Second Wave of feminism in recognition that the First Wave of feminism had surfaced in the form of the suffragette movement towards the end of the nineteenth century. This movement had been expressly concerned with attaining political power through gaining the vote for women.

The advent of the Second Wave of feminism in the 1970s saw the formation of a dynamic social movement that projected many issues into the public domain, highlighting both the structural oppression of women and the general abuses and crimes directed at them. In its radical phase, the Second Wave of feminism was called the women's liberation movement. The social agenda was radical social transformation. The key demands were:

- equal pay;
- equal education and job opportunities;
- free contraception and abortion on demand;
- free 24-hour nurseries, under community control;
- legal and financial independence;
- an end to discrimination against lesbians;
- freedom from intimidation by the threat or use of violence or sexual coercion, regardless of marital status; and
- an end to the laws, assumptions, and institutions that perpetuate male dominance and men's aggression towards women (Feminist Anthology Collective, 1981).

In any discussion of feminism, there is a fundamental distinction to be made between sex and gender. This distinction is likewise at the nub of explanations of male and female offending and victimization. Sex (male/female) is a biological classification indicated primarily by genital characteristics. Gender (masculine/feminine) is a **social construct**, not a biological given. Concepts of masculinity and femininity are part of the learned culture of the actor indicated by dress, gestures, language, occupation, and so on.

In a review of feminist thought and criminology, Daly and Chesney-Lind (1996: 343) describe what they see as the key defining elements of feminism as a mode of analysis:

- Gender is not a natural fact but a complex social, historical, and cultural product; it is related to, but not simply derived from, biological sex difference and reproductive capacities.
- Gender and gender relations order social life and social institutions in fundamental ways.

- Gender relations and constructs of masculinity and femininity are not symmetrical but are based on an organizing principle of men's superiority and social and political-economic dominance over women.
- Systems of knowledge reflect men's views of the natural and social world; the production of knowledge is gendered.
- Women should be at the centre of intellectual enquiry, not peripheral, invisible, or appendages to men.

Feminism has much to contribute to our understanding of both biological and social constructions of the female (see, for example, Eisenstein, 1984). Early feminist works, for instance, looked at sex roles and distinguished between the differences between males and females in a biological and social sense; they essentially sought to explore whether sex roles are biological or social.

This questioning was followed by a period in which feminists looked not at the polarizations between men and women, but rather at the similarities. The focus of analysis here was on **androgyny**. Males and females were said to exhibit characteristics that were similar as a whole. For example, rock stars such David Bowie, Grace Jones, and Michael Jackson have all, at times, presented an androgynous image that combined elements of 'femininity' and 'masculinity'.

Another approach adopted a women-centred analysis, which explored the specifically different characteristics of women stemming from their biology or physiology. The emphasis here was on the fundamental, special divisions that separate men and women. For instance, the ability of women to give birth—to perpetuate the human race—was viewed as rendering women essentially superior to men in regard to aspects of caring, sharing, and loving another person.

Regardless of specific orientation, feminism deals with the structural position of women in society. For example, there is a call for greater **autonomy** and the advocacy of rights for women in social, political, and economic spheres. Feminist movements were initially motivated for change because of a perceived inequality of autonomy and rights. This can be generalized to all women in society or can be applied to specific categories of women. Aboriginal women, for instance, tend to be over-represented in the criminal justice system. Some groups of women therefore experience specific concerns related to or stemming from their ethnicity, class position, and national background.

Feminism itself has many different strands, and this has implications for how we view the world and respond to it. There are a number of competing explanatory frameworks focusing specifically on the place of women in society that need to be acknowledged (see Eisenstein, 1984; Segal, 1987; Tong, 1989). These various feminist strands are primarily concerned with autonomy, rights, and power. The different perspectives within feminism broadly include the liberal, Marxist, radical, socialist, and cultural approaches, which are each discussed below.

## Liberal feminism
**Liberal feminism** views the individual as the most important part of society. There is talk here about rights, dignities, and freedoms of the individual. The hallmark of this perspective is the need to value reason, not to discriminate against anyone. In the view

of liberal feminists, the question of rights is paramount in the context of competitive views of the individual. Hence, the laws should be changed to ensure that women have equal rights. For example, it is seen as necessary to change legislation in order to provide equal opportunities in the sphere of paid work. There was a recent example of the assertion of such rights in a Western Australian case of female construction workers. The argument was that sexist violence (e.g., pornography and abusive language) existed in many forms on the worksite, and that female workers should not be exposed to this. The Equal Opportunities Board decided in this instance that the women were being denied the right to participate in the workforce.

In Canada, both the Employment Equity Act of 1986 and the revised Act of 1995 were implemented to legislate the rights of minority groups for equal opportunity of employment. The creation and implementation of this legislation can be credited in large part to the efforts of feminist individuals and groups who successfully lobbied the Canadian government in an effort to increase and strengthen to rights and opportunities for women and other minorities in Canada. An excerpt from the Employment Equity Act's overview (1986, 1995) states:

> Any examination of salaries, occupations, career patterns, unemployment and labour force participation rates indicates serious disparities between the labour force experiences of women, Aboriginal peoples, persons with disabilities, and members of visible minorities and those of other working age individuals. To address these disparities, the government passed into law the *Employment Equity Act* to ensure that no one is denied employment opportunities and benefits for reasons unrelated to ability. The Act states that this is achieved by correcting disadvantages in the workplace experienced by the four designated groups mentioned previously. It is also achieved by implementing the principle that employment equity means more than treating people in the same way but also requires special measures and the accommodation of differences (Government of Canada, 2007a).

### Marxist feminism

The **Marxist feminism** perspective is not so much concerned with traditional rights, but instead analyzes the structural position of women in society in terms of paid and unpaid labour. The key category of employment for women is seen to be that of domestic labour, which is unpaid. This situation is viewed as exploitative. Even in those instances where women participate in the paid workforce, they tend to be lowly paid relative to their position and their male counterparts, and to be concentrated in insecure positions such as part-time and casual work. The argument advanced here is that if we want to deal with gender inequality then we need to do something to fundamentally transform class societies such as capitalism that are organized around the exploitation of female (and male working-class) labour. Marxist feminists would point to a recent Statistics Canada report as evidence of the gender inequality currently found within the paid workforce. The report, released in June 2007, stated that while the number of university-educated women has increased significantly between 1991 and 2001, the gender-earning gap between men and women has narrowed only marginally:

From 1991 to 2001, the proportion of 25-to-29-year-old women holding university degrees went to 34 per cent from 21, while the proportion of men with degrees in their 20s rose only moderately, to 21 per cent from 16 per cent. Yet the gender earnings gap narrowed only slightly—with women in their 20s earning 20 per cent less than men in 1991 while that number dropped to 18 per cent in 2001 (Frenette and Coulombe, 2007).

## Radical feminism

**Radical feminism** stresses the common experiences of women; it is basically involved in collective consciousness-raising about the oppressions shared by all women. The assertion here is that all aspects of women's lives (both personal and political) are touched and shaped by patriarchal relations. The personal is viewed as inherently political. Women are viewed as an oppressed class, and all women are said to be subject to the oppressive structures of male domination. At the same time, all men share in some way in the benefits of that oppression. This approach examines the historical exclusion of women from political, social, and economic spheres. The social institutions of home, the law, the workforce, the courts, etc. are examined in order to expose the victimization of women across all spheres and institutions of life. The issue of male violence—physical, verbal, and psychological—is of major significance.

## Socialist feminism

**Socialist feminism** agrees that women have been, and continue to be, exploited and oppressed in both the public and private spheres, but this perspective views the exploitation and oppression within the framework of capitalist society. There is an emphasis here on the necessity of examining the commodification of women's bodies as a capitalist enterprise (e.g., the pornography and advertising industries). It is contended that the nature of a class-divided society and the issue of male domination need to be considered in tandem. Women as a broad social category are subject to oppressive images and practices, but the specific nature of concrete instances of exploitation and inequality needs to be examined from the point of view of capitalist accumulation. In essence, the social and economic needs of women have been subordinated to the requirements of profit-making institutions, a process that directly affects many men as well. It is possible, therefore, to think of alliances with certain sections of the male population on some issues as a means to institute social change to the benefit of women.

## Cultural feminism

**Cultural feminism** adopts a women-centred analysis that is often not tied to any specific economic or political programme. It concentrates instead on the development of a separate women's culture and the special nature of women's relationships to each other and to society. This perspective manifests itself philosophically in the appeal of New Age religion, magic, and mysticism. Women are seen as intrinsically and fundamentally different from men. They are seen to exhibit a number of gender-specific traits (such as caring and sharing attitudes) that are positive feminine features that make them somehow superior morally to their male counterparts. Alternatively, male traits such as violence and egoism are constant dangers to women individually and collectively. Hence, for many women, the solution is to separate themselves as much as possible from male society, and thus from male domination. As part of this, it is also important to develop and expand a 'female discourse' or construction of the social world that sees things in specifically female gender terms.

## Standpoint feminism

**Standpoint feminism**, also known as anti-racist feminism, developed out of the concern that mainstream feminism represented the realities of white middle-class women's lives. Standpoint feminism argues that different approaches must be taken to end the discrimination that these different groups suffer. Women are not seen as a homogenous group who share common life experiences, but instead are seen as individuals whose reality is shaped by a multitude of factors including race, class, and culture. These differences mean that there are a multiplicity of goals and approaches needed to end the discrimination faced by women and that the lives and experiences of women need to be explored within the context of individual or group. An example of the different realities lived by some women can be found in a Canadian Department of Justice report entitled *Examination of Declining Intimate Partner Homicide Rates: A Literature Review* (2001), which provides an overview of social science research on intimate partner homicide. The report states that while men and women from all walks of life kill and are killed by intimate partners, some groups are more vulnerable. The report goes on to state that females in general—and younger and Aboriginal females in particular—are vulnerable to intimate partner homicide (Department of Justice Canada, 2001).

## Female crime

Each of the feminism perspectives has implications for how we view and respond to female crime. We must further understand that how we respond to 'crime issues' is determined by the way in which the law positions women in society. It is essential here to note that the language adopted within the law is generally male-gendered language, which clearly advances the rights of 'man' but makes little if any mention of the rights of women.

Criminological theorizing did not escape this gender-based critique (see, for example, Allen, 1990). A couple of important observations in that regard can be made:

- There has been sheer neglect of women in criminological thought and enquiry, in part due to the male domination of academic criminology both historically and in the present. This is an important point, since what results is necessarily a male perspective of the world and the selection of issues perceived to be important by males.
- The criminal justice system is also dominated by male personnel—judges, barristers, solicitors, prison officers, and police. Again, it can be argued that the composition of institutional workforces can have a significant impact on how that workforce pursues its tasks in practice.

Hence, in terms of theory and research, as well as at the level of the practitioner, the system is dominated by men; there is obvious male structural domination. This is not to say that there have not been periods where individual men have challenged overtly sexist practices. Judges, magistrates, and barristers have indeed done so, but this has not necessarily produced changes in the overall structural domination (i.e., the way institutional practices themselves are systematically biased against women). Similarly, individual women are directly involved in policing and other justice-agency practices, but in doing so may simply serve to reinforce the conservative views of ideal female sexual behaviour. For example, the policing of the morality and behaviour of female children during the period of the 'child savers' movement at the turn of the nineteenth century was both conservative and spearheaded by women (Platt, 1977). Such practices did not challenge the position of women in society in any way.

The neglect of women within the discipline of criminology is a reflection not only of the composition of the criminal justice system, but also of the picture portrayed by criminal statistics. Women do not appear to be as statistically significant a problem as men. They appear generally to commit fewer crimes, and the crimes they do commit appear to be less serious and less violent than those committed by men. Furthermore, in examining victimization statistics, although there are female-specific categories of victimization such as rape and domestic violence in which women appear over-represented, females do not appear to be victims of homicide to the same extent as males. As a consequence of such observations, investigators within the criminological field have often regarded it as unimportant to look at female offending or female victimization.

When seeking to examine female offending, there has been the additional problem of applying male correlates. Theories of offending have generally been conducted within a male framework and constructed in male terms. Since mainstream criminological theories reflected a male experience, it was difficult to apply them to females; for example, strain theory's concept of opportunity structures and cultural goals (see Naffine, 1987). The limitations of mainstream criminology are discussed further below. For now it is important to acknowledge the need for, and significance of, a perspective that argued that female crime was tied to wider structures of gender and power in society.

## Basic Concepts

The feminist perspectives are based on the premise that women are structurally disadvantaged in the present society (see Table 7.1). That is, male domination and female subordination are an entrenched part of **patriarchy**, which expresses fundamental inequalities between the sexes. Sexual inequality and the disempowerment of women are embodied, as well, in the legal and criminal justice systems.

Feminist criminology defines crime in terms of gender-based and gender-related types of activities. Specifically, a major concern is with the nature of male violence as this impacts upon both female offenders and female victims, and the ways in which forms of gendered inequality and discrimination are institutionalized throughout society. A substantial part of feminist criminology has been directed at exposing the 'hidden' levels of violence against women, and the structural oppressions that they have had to face over long periods of time.

The main focus of analysis, therefore, is the unequal position of women in society, the specific kinds of crimes committed against women as women, and the status of

| Table 7.1 Feminist Perspectives | |
|---|---|
| Definition of crime | • male violence<br>• institutionalized inequality and discrimination |
| Focus of analysis | • unequal position of women in society<br>• victimization of women<br>• victim status of female offenders |
| Cause of crime | • criminality is a function of patriarchy<br>• result of social oppression and economic dependency on men and state |
| Nature of offender | • sexualization of offences and victimization according to gender criteria (e.g., 'femininity') |
| Response to crime | • social empowerment of women<br>• confrontation of institutions of male domination |
| Crime prevention | • economic, social, political power and equality<br>• anti-sexist training programmes for judiciary and other sections of criminal justice system |
| Operation of criminal | • provision of gender-specific services and support systems<br>• justice system within criminal justice (e.g., jails) and welfare spheres (e.g., refuges) |

female offenders in the context of wider social inequalities and gender-based oppressions. Crime against and involving women is seen to be the result of social oppression and economic dependency upon men or the welfare apparatus of the state.

The way in which women, as victims and offenders, are processed by the criminal justice system is described in terms of the sexualization thesis. This refers to the notion that when the criminal justice system and its agents deal with women (in whatever capacity) they do so on the basis of certain gender-related criteria. That is, the behaviour, marital status and appearance of women are constantly linked to particular ideas regarding the preferred forms of 'femininity'. In this way, what is labelled 'criminal' or an act of 'victimization' depends to a large extent upon the perceived sexual behaviour and social status of the woman in question.

It is argued that there is a double standard of morality and power with respect to women in the criminal justice system. Men and women are treated differently on the basis of gendered stereotypes. Furthermore, in many cases this leads to inequitable and unfair treatment of women who present themselves as offenders or victims before the system. One manifestation of this double standard is the fact that the senior members of the police, judiciary, and correctional apparatus are men, and that generally speaking they reflect existing prejudices regarding women's roles, status, and position in society. The history of the Toronto police force provides a good example of the challenges women have faced in policing in Canada. The first female police officer in Toronto was hired in 1913 it was not until 1945 that pay equity between male and female officers was implemented. Female officers did not ride in patrol cars until 1959 and prior to 1972 female officers were required to resign if they had a baby. Additionally, female officers were not allowed to carry firearms until 1974 and at that time they began to carry their revolvers in specially designed handbags. Today female officers make up approximately 12 per cent of the total number of officers on the Toronto police force. While there are high-ranking female police officers on the force there has never been a female police chief.

From the point of view of feminist criminology, there need to be major changes to the existing criminal justice system and to society as a whole. The problem is ultimately seen as one of social empowerment of women as a broad category, and of confronting the negative and restricting nature of male domination as evident in the present institutional set-up. To prevent crimes against women, and to forestall many of the crimes committed by women, it is necessary to have greater economic, social, and political equality. Institutional reforms could include affirmative action policies to advance the position of women within the criminal justice and judicial systems, anti-sexist training for lawyers and judges, and law reforms that recognize and acknowledge the gendered nature of the social world. The criminal justice system needs an overhaul with respect to the provision of gender-specific services and support systems in areas such as detention (e.g., trauma counselling, skills training), and more resources are needed in the wider 'welfare' domain (e.g., rape crisis centres, refuges).

## Historical Development

In the historical development of feminist criminology there are two points to note at the outset. The first is that while female offenders were generally ignored in mainstream analysis, there were instances when they were specifically examined. However, this was a rather small and neglected area of criminological theorizing. Second, the critique offered by feminists was that such theories as did exist were either overtly sexist in nature, or extremely limited in what they could say about the nature of female involvement in the criminal justice system.

When attempting to explain female crime as a distinct and specific social phenomenon, the mainstream theories accepted the narrow, conservative view regarding the place and position of women in society, and more often than not did so on the basis of a form of biological reductionism. This refers to instances where female experiences and behaviour are reduced to the imperatives of biology—the (biological) sex of a person is seen to dictate or determine appropriate social roles and practices in terms of one's gender (social constructions of femininity).

A key contribution of feminist criminology has been to critique one-sided, distorted views of women in the traditional literature that did exist on female offending. The basis of the critique had to do with the conflation of sex and gender (failure to distinguish the biological and the social) in much of the analysis on offer, and the misogynous (women-hating) character of some of the writing. Here we can point to several different theories that have ultimately based their conclusions upon the idea of innate female social characteristics linked to female biology.

## Biological explanations

These explanations view female crime as stemming from biological causes (see, especially, Smart, 1976; Naffine, 1987). Most explanations focus on sex-specific biological differences as the standards by which to compare men and women, and as explanations for particular kinds of activity. They vary in substantive emphasis, but the overall message of biological determinism remains the same:

- Early theories argued that the true, biologically determined nature of women was antithetical to crime. Such views were based upon stereotypical notions of women as being passive, non-aggressive creatures. Criminality was linked to 'maleness' and 'masculine' traits such as aggression and physicality. Therefore the female offender, who was seen as exhibiting male traits, was considered doubly deviant, both socially and biologically—she was an exception to the usual sex of the offender and, as a woman, she went against her biological nature and thus was not fully female.
- Some theories discussed female criminality in terms of the physiological differences between the sexes. In this case, women conceal their offending behaviour (and thus have lower rates of report and detection than males) and use their sexuality to attain (presumed) greater leniency by the police and the courts; they do this because their nature is inherently deceitful and manipulative. This in turn is linked to their physiological make-up, in that women are capable of concealing their sexual arousal (unlike men) and thus in the most intimate human acts they have the opportunity and ability to manipulate those around them.
- In some recent theories, research on hormonal disturbances and social behaviour has tried to establish a link between pre- and post-menstrual activity, and the propensity of women to engage in criminal activity. In a similar vein, it is sometimes argued that post-natal depression is responsible in some instances for infanticide. In other words, as the female body fluctuates in terms of hormonal activity, the woman may engage in a wide variety of antisocial and criminal activity.

## Socialization theories

A common way to explain female crime is to point to differences in the ways in which men and women are, or should be, socialized (Smart, 1976). These types of explanations are generally closely tied to specific notions of appropriate sex roles. The problem is usually seen as inadequate socialization, leading to a violation of the behaviour appropriate for members of the female sex. Again, very often the approaches reduce crime causation to essentially biological factors.

- Some theories see deviancy or delinquency as a form of 'acting out' on the part of young women. It is stated that women have traditionally been socialized to be passive and need affection, and that this explains their lower crime rates. However, if they have been abnormally or poorly socialized, then they may be susceptible to manipulation by men, and this manipulation can result in sex-related deviancy such as prostitution.

- A variation of this theory argues that the key issue is the under-socialization of individual female offenders. The maladjustment of the offender to mainstream social norms manifests itself in the form of sexually inappropriate conduct, such as promiscuous sexual relations. The desire of girls and women for acceptance and approval may result in gratuitous sexual relationships because this is seen as the only way in which the young women can assert themselves (i.e., through their sexuality).

- Some theories begin by arguing that crime is due to the disconnection felt by some women. The psychological absence of love produces instability in these females and this in turn leads to various 'acting out' behaviours of an antisocial or deviant nature. The argument assumes that emotionality is an inherent biological feature of the female sex. Women are said to have a need for dependencies because they are primarily emotional creatures—again a biological reductionist argument.

## Feminist responses

The response of feminist writers to these kinds of biological explanations and socialization arguments is that they represent a 'double standard' in terms of morality and power. Underpinning this double standard is a blurring of the distinction between 'sex' and 'gender'. Females are presumed to have a fixed biological nature, which is indistinguishable from their fixed social role. Any maladjustment to this stereotypical femininity is said to be the consequence of biological defect or inherent biological weaknesses of the female sex. Women's social nature is given naturally by her biological being.

The crucial issue from a feminist perspective is that of relative social power and access to community resources (Alder, 1994). The criminalization process itself is heavily laden with sexist assumptions that reinforce and reproduce structural inequalities of gender in society (Gelsthorpe and Morris, 1990; Comack, 1999; Comack and Balfour, 2004). Sexist assumptions determine how offending behaviour is constructed, and how victims are portrayed (see Table 7.2). The central proposition of much feminist analysis is that women are treated differently in and by the criminal justice system because of the persistence of traditional gender-role expectations regarding 'appropriate' and 'feminine' behaviour for women (and men).

Underpinning this gendered division of the sexes is the question of power; that is, society is male-dominated, and this is reflected in a myriad of social institutions, including the law and the criminal justice system. Thus, feminist jurisprudence has been concerned to demonstrate the gender biases built into the very processes of the law (for example, the 'reasonable man' argument in legal reasoning), as well as specific overt instances of gender inequality (for example, laws that allowed rape in marriage). As discussed in Chapter 1, the status of women as 'property' and as 'rights holders' has been examined historically and as part of an ongoing struggle to assert women's place and position in a patriarchal system and society (Graycar and Morgan, 1990; Naffine, 1990; Schutt, 1990).

### Table 7.2 Women and Crime

| | *Women as offenders* | *Women as victims* |
|---|---|---|
| Nature of | • Sex-specific offences (e.g., prostitution, infanticide)<br>• Sex-related offences (e.g., shoplifting, fraud) | • Sex-specific offences, crimes (e.g., rape, sexual assault)<br>• Sex-related offences, (e.g., consumer rip-offs) |
| Mainstream explanations | • Related to issues of female sexuality (e.g., biological drives) and hormonal activity to men (e.g., married)<br>• Related to notions of gender, e.g., constructions of 'feminine' behaviour, and socialization into these<br>• Categories of 'mad' and 'bad' based upon essentially passive and/or deceitful nature of women and 'provocation' | • Categories of 'deserving' and 'undeserving' victims based upon sexuality and relationship<br>• Related to notion of 'weaker' sex and dominant sex roles and social functions (e.g., housewife)<br>• Sex-specific victimization explained in terms of male biological drives (e.g., rape) |
| Feminist explanations | • Double standard of morality, (e.g., sexualization) of offences for women but not men generally<br>• Prior status of women as victims (e.g., of persistent abuse), of economic dependency<br>• Attempts to control and regulate female behaviour by criminalizing certain offences as sex-specific<br>• Different social opportunities linked to male-dominated institutions and cultures | • Emphasis on women as victims of male violence<br>• Sex-specific victimization linked to patriarchal cultures and institutions<br>• Relative powerlessness of some women to protect themselves from personal and property crime<br>• Traditional gender-role expectations shape victimization process |

The nature of female offending is placed into a wider social, economic, and political context, rather than one that reduces female experience to biological or psychological determinants. Women who commit homicide, for instance, have very often been victims of violence themselves. Similarly, women who commit social security or other minor forms of fraud and theft usually do so, not for themselves, but to support children and dependants. Hence, the generalized violence against women as a social category, and the relative disadvantages they suffer economically, are explored as vital preconditions to any personal or individual offending behaviour.

In the case of victimization, much attention is paid to the ways in which crimes against women have historically either not been considered as crimes (e.g., domestic violence) or are subject to trivialization and sexual bias (e.g., sexual assault trials involving sex workers). It has been argued in some cases that a woman who has been victimized is herself judged in relation to a man, rather than a specific offensive action. For example, a married woman subjected to injury may be seen in terms of a 'serious crime' insofar as it affects her status as her spouse's 'sexual property' or 'homemaker'. The courts may treat an unmarried woman who has a sexual history of multiple partners as having actually provoked a criminal assault. Questions of what is an 'offence' and who is a 'victim' are thus often intertwined with gender stereotypes and biases that reflect a general inequality between the sexes in society. A disturbing example of female victimization that has, for the most part, remained out of the public eye has been the disappearance of dozens of young women—all Aboriginal women except one—along of 720 kilometre stretch of highway in northern British Columbia. Little information has been reported on these disappearances and critics have argued that because of the age and race of the victims, little attention has been focused on solving the crimes. Amnesty International has called on the general public to put pressure on the Canadian government to develop protocols to more effectively deal with missing persons and to address the issue of violence against women.

## Box 7.1  Highway 16

A young girl stands beside Highway 16 with her arm and thumb raised high. A car or truck pulls over, she hops in for a ride, never to be seen alive again. For more than a decade, young women have disappeared or have been found slain long Highway 16 in Northern BC.

Posters bearing their pictures can still be found on hydro poles and laundromat post-it boards. 'Missing', they shout in large letters under a photo of a smiling, unpretentious-looking young woman or teenager.

It's tragic. It's horrific. And it's happening along the quiet 720 kilometres between Prince George and Prince Rupert, a stretch now gruesomely dubbed the Highway of Tears.

A disturbing pattern of disappearances was first noticed between 1988 and 1995. Young girls, mostly Aboriginal in origin and aged 15 to their early twenties, vanished after being seen hitchhiking along the highway.

Some consider the murder of Monica Ignas, 15, to be the first. She disappeared just east of Terrace on 13 December 1974 and was later found lying dead and discarded in a gravel pit. In 1988, Alberta Williams, age 24, was also found murdered a month after disappearing. But it wasn't until 1994 that things really began speeding up at an alarming pace.

The first of the latest series of incidents was Ramona Wilson, 15, who was hitchhiking to a friend's place on 11 June 1994. Her remains were found near the Smither's airport a year later. Five months after that, Roxanne Thiara, also 15, went missing from Prince George only to be found dead—her body 'dumped' near Burns Lake. The slaughter rose to three in a row when the remains of Alishia Germaine, again 15, were discovered on 9 December 1994.

The next six months were event-free until Delphine Nikal, 16, from Telkwa disappeared somewhere between Smithers and her home. She has yet to be found. Lana Derrick, 19, was a forestry student in Terrace who went missing while walking down a street in Terrace in October 1995. She has not been heard from since. Thankfully nothing happened for almost seven years that police know about, or that has been reported. (Was the murderer in jail for a spell?)

Our next casualty was the first Caucasian woman, Nicole Hoar, who disappeared on 21 June 2002. Nicole was a young tree planter hitching her way from Prince George to her sister's home in Smithers. She was hoping to attend the Midsummer Music Festival, but she never arrived. Her family and friends were instrumental in quickly getting the story out to every major news source. A massive poster campaign ensued, rewards were offered, and a fund established to help find the missing dark-haired 26-year-old from Red Deer. The RCMP used aircraft and helicopters, and there were 200 volunteers plus 60+ professional search and rescue members, all to no avail. Nicole Hoar remains on a list of women missing along the Highway of Tears.

On 17 September 2005, a number of ceremonies named "Take Back the Highway" were held in communities between Prince George and Prince Rupert. Activities included marches, minutes of silence, local speakers, and prayers to promote awareness and in protest to the violence against these women.

But four days later Tamara Chipman, 22, went missing somewhere between Prince Rupert and Terrace. Tamara had taken judo for years and was considered able to take care of herself. What happened?

The police have not ruled out the possibility of a serial-killer prowling our highway, although serial-killer profilers and special detectives sent to study the individual cases say there is no evidence of this.

In light of the recent 60+ murders of women by the accused Robert (Willy) Picton near Vancouver, BC, one can only guess what other horrors await us yet to be discovered. Is it scarier to think there is a mass murderer on the loose, or multiple murderers?

Meanwhile, Crystal Lee Okimaw, 24, vanished from Prince George on 16 January and Aielah Saric-Auger, 14, was discovered dead just east of Prince George on 2 February 2006. Guesses as to what sort of person the police might be looking for include a travelling salesman dressed in a suit who would seem like a trustworthy person to catch a ride with. Maybe a hunter who comes to our wildlife-rich area. Maybe a trucker who barrels in, then out of our towns. Or could it be someone who lives here? Someone who always seems to be at the right place to pick up young women.

Amnesty International asks that you write Stockwell Day, the new Minister of Public Safety at the House of Commons, Parliament Buildings, Ottawa, Ontario, K1A 0A6, asking him to implement new protocols for action on missing person cases, particularly along our Highway 16. We need to urge him to help stop the violence against women.

It's unfortunate that hitchhiking is sometimes a necessity for young women living in remote communities. It's time they stopped hitchhiking alone.

I usually never pick up hitchhikers, but recently I gave a young native girl a lift from Granisle to Topley. Not because I wanted the company, but because I feared for what I would have to live with if one day I saw her pretty face on a poster that said, 'Missing'.

From Debi Smith, 'Our Highway of Tears', *Hiway 16 Magazine*. Available at http://www.bcnorth.ca/magazine/pages/Debi/tears/tears1.htm.

A fundamental question assessed by feminist criminology is how various perspectives deal with the sex variable:

- There are theories that ignore the sex variable altogether; the vast majority of traditional criminology appears to do this, since it deals only with male criminality and ignores the specific conditions under which women exist in society; that is, the female experience.
- There are then theories that conflate or blur the distinctions between sex and gender. Females are presumed to have a fixed biological nature and/or role(s), and any maladjustment to this stereotypical femininity is said to be the consequence of biological defect. Women's nature is seen as naturally given by her genitals.
- There are theories that ignore the impact of gender relationships. There is a discussion here of women, but the male/female experience is presented as androgynous. These theories neglect the impact of sex relationships on people.

Feminist criminology explores issues relating to women and looked initially at sex-role differences. Smart (1976) stated that there was a double standard operating in society in relation to morality and power. This was particularly indicated in the nature of offences with which women were charged—primarily sex-specific offences such as infanticide and prostitution (women's crime). The legal framework—both historically, and as revealed by the official statistics—has similarly treated the category of prostitution as relating to women. We know male prostitutes exist, but prostitution is not constructed as a male-specific offence.

There are also sex-related offences such as shoplifting, and of the total number of crimes reported by the official statistics a proportionately higher incidence of shoplifting offences are committed by females. The nature of the goods stolen also appears to be gender-related—for example, perfume, lipstick, and tampons.

In terms of activities pertaining to young offenders, historically men have been picked up for certain 'conventional' violations of the law, while young women were seen as delinquent because of their presumed immorality or promiscuity (see Alder, 1985; Chesney-Lind and Shelden, 1992; Cunneen and White, 2002). It is thus presumed that men are in court because of their criminal offending, while females are there because they have slept around. Clearly, there are double standards operating. Gender is also tied to other offences; for example, passing fraudulent cheques and social security fraud tend to be female offences.

## Contemporary Examples

If we examine contemporary female offending, some interesting pictures emerge:

- A significant proportion of offenders are single parents, of low educational standing, and unemployed; many have been victimized through male violence, such as rape, sexual abuse, incest, etc. There is also an overrepresentation of indigenous women in the system.
- Feminist theorists state that there are obvious double standards operating in terms of how women and men are treated, both as victims and offenders. This can be highlighted once again by referring to the example of prostitution. Why is it that the female service providers are charged with solicitation and offences associated with prostitution, while the male service recipients are not? While there is a dual relationship between servicer and servicee, rarely is the male patron implicated.
- With respect to the offence of rape, again for many years and still today, there are many myths relating to the nature of rapists. The stereotypical rapist has customarily been portrayed as a violent sexual psychopath and serial offender. Thus the individual is disturbed, and/or the victim has been seen to act to arouse the uncontrollable desires of the male attacker (e.g., by wearing inappropriate clothing). This image reduces rape to an individualistic biological problem, disregarding societal explanations that view rape as relating to social power.
- Likewise, in terms of victims, there has been a league table established in relation to the worthiness or otherwise of the victim status; distinctions are made as to who is or is not to be believed. As conveyed in a judge's comments in Victoria, claims of rape made by a nun or married woman are to be believed, while those made by a prostitute are to be treated as dubious. Such distinctions misconstrue the nature of the issue—the exertion of violence and power, and actual evidence of harm.

Feminists explain such double standards of power and morality as a part of the **sexualization theory**; that is, women who deviate from what is construed to be the norms of sexuality and morality are seen to be offenders (see Chesney-Lind, 1974; Smart, 1976).

In particular, when such offenders are young, they are viewed as being immoral or in moral danger. This has been a traditional way of bringing young women into the system; that is, through a category of welfare provision (called 'status offences' in Canada and the US) rather than criminal offence. Hence, they did not necessarily have to have done anything illegal to warrant state intervention. Young women who were considered to be sexually promiscuous (thus 'exposed to moral danger') were incarcerated in juvenile institutions 'for their own welfare'. Historically, intervention was often followed by physical examination and subjection to 'treatment' regimes. Institutionalization aimed to impart necessary instruction in domesticity; adolescent girls were taught to play their 'natural' subservient role as the servers of men. They were released when considered to be 'of a marriageable age'. Men have not been classified, diagnosed, and treated in the same way. Their sexuality has been encouraged, because it is viewed as a 'natural' part of manhood.

The clause in child welfare provisions concerned with 'moral danger' has historically resulted in long periods of incarceration for considerable numbers of young women in Canada (Comack, 1999). It is important to recognize that such provisions were not part of the Canadian criminal law as such, but were part of the child protection legislation. In reality, such treatment regimes translated into harsher penalties than those given for offending behaviour. Such provisions, it should be added, no longer exist, but they form an indelible part of the history of women's involvement with the criminal justice system.

Further, not only the justice system, but psychiatric, welfare, and other relevant establishments all tried to reinforce these conventional boundaries and distinctions. Women who transgressed the boundaries of dominant conceptions of femininity were seen as falling within one of two categories—they were either mad or bad. The policing of female behaviour occurs not only in the legal and medical arena, but also in the wider social community. This is evident, for example, in the examination of the nature of the interactions between men and women in youth centres (Nava, 1984). The policing of females is widespread, with the objective of preserving the good sexual reputations of the women. Derogatory language (e.g., 'slut', 'ho', etc.) is commonly used as a tool to regulate female behaviour.

In recent times, there has been a critique of the sexualization thesis. Carrington (1993) criticizes the sexualization thesis on the grounds that there have been equal proportions of males and females appearing before the courts since the mid-1970s. She discusses the notion of the sexualization of offending, but looks also at the nature of penalties imposed. She examines the notion that young women are prosecuted primarily on the grounds of their immorality and are dealt harsher sentences because of this. She argues instead, however, that when welfare intervention occurs, irrespective of whether the offender is male or female, harsher sentences are received, because the actions are initiated by the welfare-helping professions.

Carrington also challenges the sexualization thesis on another ground. If the sustenance of male patriarchy is the objective of the legal system, then one would expect the system to be dominated by men. She claims we should instead look at the composition of all those seeking to control women's behaviour—welfare workers, youth and community workers, social workers, and so on. If we do, we see that a large proportion of those who are the **gatekeepers** and custodians of female behaviour are women. And among those who wield derogatory and negative labels are young women themselves. Research by Lees (1989), for example, found a liberal use of such terms by adolescent girls within the school ground setting, as well as stereotyped labelling by women teachers of their students.

The impact of 'race' or ethnicity on female offenders is also raised by Carrington as part of the critique of the sexualization thesis. In particular, concern is expressed regarding why working-class and Aboriginal young people are over-represented in the crime statistics. These are the types of questions asked by a number of contemporary feminist criminologists (see Gelsthorpe and Morris, 1990). A more sophisticated and complicated analysis is obviously required: it should focus not just on sex differences, but also on differences of class and ethnicity.

Carrington's rejection of the sexualization thesis has not been entirely convincing, however. In a recent review of Australian feminist criminology, Alder (1994) argues that the sexualization thesis itself should not be oversimplified. While acknowledging differences between women's experiences, Alder argues that the power of the sexualization thesis lies in linking the similarities of women's experiences. Women's offending behaviour, and their subsequent involvement in the criminal justice system, form only one part of their lives. If we were to examine the totality of women's lives, in all their complexities and diversities, both the similarities as argued by the sexualization thesis, and the differences as argued by Carrington, can be supported. Alder goes on to argue that contemporary feminism cannot be oversimplified and parodied any longer as somehow merely advocating a simple relationship between gender and experience. Nonetheless, exploration of the diversity of women's lives reveals consistent themes of surviving, coping, and thriving within patriarchal structures, all of which demand further attention and analysis.

Recent feminist work has tended to focus on two key substantive areas for investigation (Daly and Chesney-Lind, 1996). These are, first, explaining and responding to men's violence towards women (which encompasses issues such as pornography, rape, and prostitution); and second, thinking about the problems associated with equality and difference as these manifest in the legal and criminal justice systems (which encompasses issues such as legal equality, affirmative action, specific needs of female prisoners, and so on). In analyzing these kinds of issues, feminist criminologists have employed a wide array of analytical methods and concepts, as shown in accounts that utilize Foucauldian analysis of knowledge and power relations involving men and women (for example, Carrington, 1993), and those which focus on 'deconstruction', a technique to explore the workings of language—including non-verbal communication—in conveying meaning (see Young, 1990). As suggested by Naffine (1997), contemporary feminist criminology cannot ignore these recent theoretical and methodological insights into the social world, but nor can it ignore the limitations (and strengths) of any one particular perspective or approach. In Canada, Research and Education for Solutions to Violence and Abuse (RESOLVE)—a tri-provincial (Manitoba, Saskatchewan, Alberta) network dedicated to supporting community and university research to assist in uncovering causes of violence and to create and implement strategies to prevent and alleviate violence—is one of five research centres formed in 1992, following the 1989 murder of 14 women at

École Polytechnique in Montreal. These five centres formed an alliance to create a national voice on issues of family violence; the alliance has since expanded in response to a growing understanding of the impact of all violence in society.

RESOLVE creates partnerships between community agencies, governments, and universities across the Prairie Provinces and has undertaken research in such broad areas as child sexual abuse, abuse in institutions, youth in the sex-trade, elder abuse, shelter services, and the treatment of offenders. Further, RESOLVE has published numerous books and research papers based on their activities and the extent of this work, and the growth of their online presence, is indicative of the research contributions of Canadian feminist researchers and scholars made in recent years.

Feminist criminology is diverse, particularly when reviewing the contemporary debate. Feminists focus on the creation and construction of female offending via the sexualization thesis, but they also seek to explore victimology, particularly in relation to the victimization of women. Feminists have long been associated with activism, as well as theoretical debate. In particular, feminist criminologists are concerned to change the law to promote a greater recognition of issues of violence directed against women. This has led many to argue for the harsher enforcement of laws against perpetrators at the operational level, and a call for greater sensitivity of police to these crimes. However, others see limitations to this, and argue that calling for greater use of the criminal law in a patriarchal system to defend and protect women is fraught with problems (Edwards, 1990).

## Critique

Various issues have been the subject of intense discussion and debate within feminist criminology. For example, it has been noted that some feminist approaches do not deal adequately with questions relating to class, ethnicity, and 'race' in discussions of the female offender and the female victim. Yet, as various studies show (e.g., Carrington, 1993), the 'race' of a person is a crucial factor in terms of overall representation of some groups within the criminal justice system. Likewise, the class background of the offender or victim has significant consequences with regard to the actual nature of the criminalization and the victimization process.

A second area that is generating more attention is the notion that feminist criminology needs to do more than provide a woman-centred analysis. It needs to foster a non-sexist criminology that focuses more broadly on gender relations in their entirety. Specifically, it has been suggested that issues of female and male criminality need to be examined in terms of the social constructions of both 'femininity' and 'masculinity', and with regard to the relationship between each of these social constructions (Gelsthorpe and Morris, 1990; Cunneen and White, 2002). Naffine (1997) makes the telling comment that: 'As feminist criminologists have shifted our understanding of women, repudiating the female stereotypes, revealing the differences between women's understandings of their own lives and the orthodox (male) accounts of them, so man (whose meaning is so intimately linked with woman) has been altered too' (91). The idea that women and men need to be understood in terms of their mutual relationship to each other is evident in the literature associated with feminism as such. It is also apparent in the criminological work that has been influenced by feminism but that focuses specifically on men and the male experience (see Messerschmidt, 1986, 1997; Polk, 1994b; Jefferson, 1997). Recent years have seen a burgeoning interest in, and debates over, how best to conceptualize the relationship between men and violence. Work by theorists such as Connell (1995, 2000), Comack (1999), and Comack and Balfour (2004) has consistently pointed to the ways in which certain forms of 'hegemonic masculinity' are played out, and resisted, in specific historical situations. In many instances, how diverse masculinities are positioned in relation to each other (and in relation to various femininities) have been shown to have major implications for youth crime, homophobic violence, violence against women and children, and male-on-male violence (see Connell, 2002; Mason, 2002; Tomsen, 2002).

Generally, as Naffine (1997) argues, the message conveyed in mainstream criminology is that 'feminism is about women, while criminology is about men' (2); but the analytical and political challenges of feminism are nevertheless highly influential throughout the field.

One area where this influence has been greatly felt is in victimology. For example, conventional and some feminist notions of women-as-victims have been subjected to various criticisms. There is the argument that victims should not be viewed merely as passive, but need to be empowered by extending to them the alternative term of 'survivors'. This term is said to imply active response. Hence, debate within the feminist movement has served to push the boundaries as they relate to women, both as victims and as offenders.

More generally, the issue of power, and how this is manifested institutionally, remains an area where more research and discussion are also required. This is particularly so with respect to feminist conceptualizations of the state. Meanwhile, an immediate problem confronting feminist writers and activists is that of the conservative backlash against many of the concepts and issues raised by feminists generally. Feminist criminologists have actively raised the profile of female victims and the dilemmas and inequities surrounding the processing of female offenders. But in the light of contemporary calls for greater 'law and order', there is a fear that such work will be subverted and/or swamped by the simplistic moralizing and simplistic answers of the New Right.

## Conclusion

In summary, the feminist perspectives within criminology challenge the male biases and neglects of mainstream criminology. It is identifiably part of Second Wave feminism, which has been part of the social landscape since the 1960s. Within criminology, criticism is levelled at historical and contemporary examples of the double standards applied to women and men in the criminal justice system. As well, active intervention has been called for in areas such as inappropriate responses to female offenders (e.g., imprisonment), law reform that prevents discrimination against women (e.g., equal employment opportunity), the legal recognition of certain crimes against women (e.g., sexual harassment), and active enforcement of laws to protect women from male violence (e.g., domestic violence, incest, rape).

Feminist criminology cannot be seen, however, as a single theoretical perspective. As outlined in this chapter, there are many strands of feminism, from radical feminism and socialist feminism through to liberal and cultural feminism, each having a distinctive voice within criminology. Taken as a whole, feminist criminology has radically altered the nature of the criminological debate. Challenges highlighted by feminists have influenced debates within left-leaning perspectives such as Left Realism and critical criminology, as well as conservative and liberal theories such as New Right criminology and republican theory. Thus, as well as constituting an identifiable perspective within criminology in its own right, feminist criminology has significantly influenced the wider criminological debate.

## Key Terms and Concepts

- Androgyny
- Autonomy
- Cultural feminism
- Gatekeepers
- Liberal feminism
- Marxist feminism
- Radical feminism
- Sexualization theory
- Socialist feminism
- Social construct
- Standpoint feminism

## Further Reading

A. Calliste and G. Dei, eds, *Anti-Racist Feminism* (Halifax: Fernwood Press, 2000).

K. Carrington, *Offending Girls* (Sydney: Allen & Unwin, 1993).

E. Comack, *Locating Law: Race/Class/Gender Connections* (Halifax: Fernwood Publishing, 1999).

E. Comack and G. Balfour, eds, *The Power to Criminalize: Violence, Inequality and Law* (Halifax: Fernwood Publishing, 2004).

K. Daly, and M. Chesney-Lind, 'Feminism and Criminology', in *Readings in Contemporary Criminological Theory*, P. Cordella and L. Siegal, eds (Boston: Northeastern University Press, 1996).

N. Naffine, *Female Crime: The Construction of Women in Criminology* (Sydney: Allen & Unwin, 1987).

N. Naffine, *Feminism and Criminology* (Sydney: Allen & Unwin, 1997).

J. Scutt, *Women and the Law* (Sydney: Law Book Company, 1990).

C. Smart, *Women, Crime and Criminology: A Feminist Critique* (London: Routledge and Kegan Paul, 1976).

R. Tong, *Feminist Thought: A Comprehensive Introduction* (London: Unwin Hyman, 1987).

## Websites

*www.caveat.org*. Canadians Against Violence Everywhere Advocating its Termination (CAVEAT) is an organization that is concerned with public education and the justice system.

*www.cddc.vt.edu/feminism*. Bibliographies, links, and information for feminist theory in the United States and around the world are provided.

*www.csc-scc.gc.ca*. Correctional Service Canada's website provides the report Patterns of Violent Crime by Women.

*www.umanitoba.ca/resolve*. Research and Education for Solutions to Violence and Abuse is a tri-provincial research network to facilitate active participation of community and university-based researchers committed to producing research useful in policy, practice, and academic settings.

## Films/Documentaries

- *DNA and Dollars* (National Film Board of Canada, 2002)
- *Girls and Aggression* (National Film Board of Canada, 2002)
- *It's a Girl's World* (National Film Board of Canada, 2004)
- *Listening for Something. . .Adreinne Rich and Dionne Brand in Conversation* (National Film Board of Canada, 1996)
- *Monster* (Media 8 Entertainment, 2003)
- *The Masculine Mystique* (National Film Board of Canada, 1984)
- *Widening the Circle* (National Film Board of Canada, 1994)

## Discussion Questions

1. What are the fundamental arguments of feminist criminology? How do they differ from orthodox theories of crime?
2. Which strand of feminist theory do you believe makes the strongest contribution to the study of women and crime? Why? Provide examples to support your position.
3. How has patriarchy influenced the development of criminology?
4. How would a radical feminist perspective explain domestic violence against women? How would this compare to a liberal feminist argument?
5. What do you believe to be the most important contribution feminist criminology has made to the study of crime? Why?

# CHAPTER 8

# New Right Criminology

## Objectives

This chapter will help you develop an understanding of the:

- fundamental concepts found within the new right criminology perspective;
- historical and political contexts in the development of new right criminology;
- influence that new right perspectives have had on the criminal justice system; and
- strengths and weaknesses found with new right perspectives to criminology.

## Introduction

The 1960s and 1970s were broadly characterized by rapid social change and heightened political conflict, which manifested themselves in the rise of radical theories about society in the social sciences, including criminology. By the 1980s, however, a major change in thinking had occurred in society at large. Conservative politicians and political ideologies dominated the electoral landscape across many countries, and 'law and order' emerged as a predominant issue, along with that of high levels of unemployment.

The aim of this chapter is to outline the main currents of New Right criminology. This particular approach or perception of crime has both a populist dimension (related to the political process) and an academic dimension (related to the work of criminologists). The fundamental ideas of New Right criminology are based on two themes: placing responsibility for crime squarely on the individual, and reasserting the importance of punishment in responding to crime.

The chapter makes a broad distinction between 'right-wing libertarian' views and those of **'conservatism'**. These describe essential differences in the political perspectives contained under the New Right criminology umbrella. The chapter also discusses those traditional academic approaches within criminology itself that reflect and are reflected in the general New Right perspective. In particular, the ideas of **'social control theory'** and of 'opportunity-rationality theory' will be discussed.

## Social Context

The phrase 'New Right' refers to a particular political orientation, rather than to a systematic, coherent theory in its own right. A conservative perspective in criminology—directly opposed to the **liberalism** of strain theory and labelling perspectives in particular—arose at a time when the long boom of economic prosperity in the advanced capitalist countries was coming to an end. The mid-1970s saw a world economic recession, followed over the next two decades by periodic, and in some instances devastating, economic slumps.

In these new times there was likely to be an increase in property and personal crime at both corporate and street level. The **alienation** and marginalization of a significant layer of the population, many of them young people, was associated with a range of antisocial and deviant behaviour. For example, 1977 saw the rise of punk rock music and the overt rebellion of many young people against both the commercial music industry for its insipid conformity and slick production values, and the power-brokers and 'respectable' members of society who had done so little to stem the tide of youth unemployment and yet condemned the ripped shirts of the poor.

Politically, by the 1980s there had been a swing to the right at the level of policy formulation and development, regardless of the political party in power. The economic ideas of Margaret Thatcher in the United Kingdom and Ronald Reagan in the United States, the advent of 'Rogernomics' (named after the Treasurer) in New Zealand, and the approach adopted by Bob Hawke and Paul Keating of the Australian Labor Party all signalled an economic rationalist platform for dealing with contemporary issues. The 1984 election of the Conservative Party in Canada heralded similar changes in political policy and the implementation of new trade agreements. These global policies emphasized the notion of 'economic efficiency' above all else in policy development, and in each case led to tax cuts for both individuals and corporations, while at the same time curtailing universal provision in the allocation of the welfare services and benefits. According to the economic rationalists, the wealth created by these measures would benefit both rich and poor. Many argue, however, that the net effect was to exacerbate the growing distance between the rich and the poor in society.

Simultaneously, efforts were made to neutralize any resistance to the economic restructuring that aimed to increase competitiveness and efficiency. Conservative parties in particular made concerted attempts to drastically reduce trade union power. For example, Reagan smashed the air traffic controllers' strike in the US, while Thatcher took on the miners' union in the UK. In Australia, union power was curbed more subtly and, some would argue, more effectively. The Prices and Incomes Accord between the Australian Labor Party and the Australian Council of Trade Unions was used to defuse any possible union militancy. Nonetheless, strong-arm tactics were also used against 'recalcitrant' elements; notably the army was used to break the airline pilots' strike, and the police and courts were used to deregister the Builders Labourers Federation.

The 1980s saw an emphasis on controlling union power and enhancing wealth creation. In the 'decade of greed', much media prominence was given to business entrepreneurs, many of whom gained near folk-hero status. Labour and financial markets were deregulated, and the idea of a 'free economy and a strong state' (Gamble,

1988) was entrenched in places like the UK through the rhetoric of defending the 'people's capitalism'. The Canadian experience, in particular, provides insights into the economic developments taking place globally. Canada experienced a recession in the 1980s that led some politicians and business leaders to argue that the key to Canadian economic prosperity lay not in protectionism, but in free trade. The Conservative Party, elected in 1984 under the leadership of Brian Mulroney, announced their plans to create a free trade partnership with the United States in order to improve and secure access to the American market. A further stated Canadian goal was to strengthen and increase Canadian business competitiveness in the new global market and to further a steady improvement in the standard of living for Canadians.

The two countries began negotiations in May 1986 and by October 1987 the Canada–United States Free Trade Agreement (CUSFTA) was finalized; it was signed in 1988 and came into effect on 1 January 1989. CUSFTA was only the start to even larger trading blocks. On 1 January 1994 CUSFTA was replaced by the North American Free Trade Agreement (NAFTA), which brought Mexico into the trade partnership. This meant that market structures were opened up in order to stimulate greater economic activity. In reality, in most cases it was the strong who stood to benefit most, while the rest would have to work that much harder to gain a share of the societal wealth. State agencies that were seen to impede economic growth were more closely scrutinized. Welfare provisions were often downgraded or targeted at a minority of the most impoverished in society, and those institutions that maintained public order and protected private property, such as the police, were strengthened.

In the context of increasing economic hardship and an ideological swing to the Right, which was supported largely by an economic rationalist mentality, there was a rise in **'law-and-order'** politics, both domestically and internationally. For example, internationally, the former concern with the preservation of 'human rights' propounded by world leaders was quickly transformed into an emphasis on terrorism and the drug trade, and the necessity to combat these 'by any means necessary'.

Domestically, the law-and-order push assumed the tone of a 'war on crime' and an attack on the disorder of society. This translated into a call during the 1980s for increased police personnel, powers, and resources; for longer jail sentences; the provision of more prisons; stronger discipline within families and schools; and a return to more traditional values generally. For young people there was the demand for 'greater responsibility', which translated into more **punitive** attitudes in the area of juvenile justice. The implementation of the 1984 Young Offenders Act in Canada heralded this demand for youth to be held accountable for their behaviour. Whereas the previous Juvenile Delinquents Act was based on a welfare model that suggested negative environmental influences such as poverty, difficulties with schooling and family, and poor moral training significantly influenced juvenile delinquency, the Young Offenders Act adopted a more justice-oriented ideology. Corrado and Markwark (1992) defined this view as a modified justice model. They argued that:

> The major point of departure [for the YOA] from its predecessor [the JDA] is that the former is predicated upon the idea of individual responsibility and accountability for wrongs done, whereas the guiding principle of the Juvenile Delinquents Act was that

responsibility and blame for juvenile misconduct rest fairly and squarely with negligent and deficient parents and with the community at large (1992: 203).

New Right criminology tends to revolve around the individual in society, and to provide a moralistic and punitive approach to issues of crime and criminality (Young, 1981). While academic studies have provided sophisticated defences of these ideas (Tame, 1991; Buchanan and Hartley, 1992), in the public domain the get-tough approach has generally been associated with populist appeals to the public at large. This has proved to be electorally expedient and attractive, even if the consequences of the adoption of such measures leave something to be desired.

Populism is not a political ideology as such, but is a loosely defined mood. It appeals to people on the basis of 'us' versus 'them'. The 'us' is always viewed as virtuous. The 'them', whoever they are, are viewed as being parasites and destructive to the social body. In terms of crime, the essence of populism exaggerates the dangerousness of crime, and the foreign or alien nature of the criminal. The criminal is seen to be outside the society—its networks, institutions, communities, mores, values, methods of income, and ways of life. Insofar as the criminal is not seen to be bound by normal social rules of conduct, so too it is argued that normal rules of order should not necessarily be adhered to if criminals are to be brought to book for their offensive activities.

The rhetoric of populism is one that reduces all crime problems to simple solutions. Offenders are made entirely responsible for their actions, particularly since they exist outside the mainstream institutions of society. They are not seen as members of the 'community' and, indeed, are sometimes presented as not being members of the human race (e.g., they are described as 'animals' or 'savages'). Insofar as this social distancing occurs at the level of rhetoric and policy development, it is not a great leap to encourage ever-more draconian solutions to the crime problem. If the problem is constructed as being one of 'us' against 'them'—as a 'war', which implies violence and destruction—then redemption of the situation is seen to lie in enhanced state power.

One of the recent terms constructed in this war on crime is 'super-predator', which was coined by conservative scholar John DiIulio in the early 1990s to refer to children and young men, mostly of colour, who were cold-blooded and brutal in their violence and who showed no sign of compassion for their victims or remorse for their brutal actions. DiIulio (2001) forecast these super-predators would commit a massive crime wave of unprecedented brutality. The crime wave never happened but the fear that this prediction supported has continued to encourage calls for an increase in the severity and length of punishments for youth involved in criminal activities in both the United States and Canada. Punishment for young persons convicted of a violent crime has been particularly harsh in the United States where thousands of young persons have been sentenced to life in prison without parole for their first offence. Canada's youth justice system has legislated impediments to this kind of treatment for youth but it is continually under attack by conservative policies that lobby to implement more punitive sentences for young offenders.

The 1980s saw populist rhetoric about crime used actively as a major electoral tool. Authoritarian populism refers to a process in which crime is ideologically conveyed in a series of moral panics about 'law-and-order' issues (Hall et al., 1978; Hall, 1980;

## Box 8.1  Conservative Party Election Platform 2006

*A. Serious Crime, Serious Time*

A Conservative government will protect our communities from crime by insisting on tougher sentences for serious and repeat crime and by tightening parole. The drug, gang, and gun-related crimes plaguing our communities must be met by clear mandatory minimum prison sentences and an end to sentences being served at home. Parole must be a privilege to be earned, not a right to be demanded.

*B. More Police On Streets*

Canada needs more front-line law enforcement. According to the Department of Public Safety documents, there is currently a shortage of 1,059 RCMP officers in federal, provincial, and municipal policing roles. In addition, many provincial and municipal police forces are underfunded and overstretched. It is time to reinvest in front-line law enforcement in Canada.

*C. Invest in effective gun control*

When the Liberals first introduced Bill C-68, the federal long gun registry, they said it would cost around $2 million. Today at a cost of almost $2 billion— 1,000 times more than promised—the registry is incomplete, riddled with errors and according to the former Toronto Chief of Police, 'ineffective in helping catch criminals'. Canadians demand more than simple cosmetic reforms to failed programmes. The wasteful long gun registry must end and the money must be redirected to genuine law enforcement policies. Canadians want to see effective gun control that stops crime in our streets.

*D. Get tough with sex offenders*

Families should be able to raise their children without fear of sexual predators in our communities. Women should be able to live without fear in any Canadian city.

*E. Youth at risk*

Too many crime-related problems begin when our youth are not equipped with the necessary life skills to make the right choices, to say 'no' to drugs, gangs, and violence. We need to invest in positive opportunities for young people to say 'yes'.

*F. Strengthen the youth criminal justice act*

The youth criminal justice system must provide effective punishment for adolescents who commit serious crimes, instill a sense of responsibility in young offenders for their behavior, and give young people better opportunities for rehabilitation.

From the Conservative Party of Canada, Policy Declaration. Adopted at the National Policy Convention, Montreal, 19 March 2005. Conservative Party of Canada, *Stand Up for Canada, Federal Election Platform*, 2006.

Taylor, 1981). The extent and seriousness of crime is highlighted (but not necessarily supported by statistical or other research findings) and this, in turn, is used to justify harsher penalties, and the assertion of state authority in more and more spheres of everyday social life. As part of this process, specific groups or categories of people are singled out for special attention: young people, Aboriginals, swelfare recipients, striking workers, and sole parents. Thus, 'we' are protected by having ever-greater state intervention into the affairs of 'them', the most likely candidates for membership of the criminal class. Again, the rationale behind such intrusion is usually a combination of protection of private property and the differential treatment that should be meted out to the moral and immoral in society.

The broad appeal of authoritarian populism is due in part to the pervasive influence of the print and electronic media in conveying particular types of images regarding crime in society (Grabosky and Wilson, 1989; Ericson et al., 1991; Males, 1996). For example, Hogg and Brown (1998) have identified the key assumptions in what they call 'law and order commonsense', many elements of which are perpetuated by the media. The assumptions include:

- crime rates are soaring,
- crime is worse than ever,
- the criminal justice system is 'soft' on crime,
- the criminal justice system is loaded in favour of criminals,
- there should be more police,
- police should have more powers,
- courts should deliver tougher penalties, and
- the greater satisfaction of victims demands more **retribution** through the courts.

These general elements of law-and-order commonsense are seemingly routine aspects of the way in which the electronic and print media portray crime. By and large, crime is sensationalized both in and by the media. The flooding of the media with stories of 'street crime' has, however, real and pertinent effects: heightening the fear of crime, feeding the stereotypes regarding the 'typical offender', exaggerating the extent of extremely violent and serious crimes, and fostering acceptance for policies that appear to 'get something done' about the crime problem. The politically important role of New Right criminology is thus related to the basic electoral appeal of authoritarian populist rhetoric.

## Basic Concepts

The main elements of New Right criminology include a combination of conservative moralizing and free-market competitive ethos. These sometimes contradict each other at the level of specific policies. However, the overriding message is that there is a need to 'get tough on criminals', to hold them responsible for their actions, and to punish the wrongdoer in a consistent manner.

New Right criminology is opposed to perspectives that emphasize 'treatment' and 'reform' rather than punishment. It opposes the views of orthodox positivist criminology, which have a deterministic view or model of the causes of crime; rather, it asserts that people do make choices, and that they therefore must pay for these choices. In a nutshell, the argument is that if you 'do the crime', then you must 'do the time'.

The New Right criminological perspective includes several strands: some deal with more philosophical views regarding the nature of human activity, and some with specific areas of interest such as retributivist concerns with sentencing; the range extends to economic analyses of the causes and social responses to crime. For present purposes, however, we will illustrate the broad orientation of these kinds of perspectives by examining two general views on the nature of crime and crime control—right-wing libertarianism and traditionalist conservatism. Each is concerned with the punishment and disciplining of offenders, but the overall analysis of crime in society does nevertheless differ.

## Right-wing libertarianism

The right-wing libertarian perspective harkens back to the days of classical liberalism, characterized by competitive free-market capitalism and minimal state intervention, including welfare provision (see Table 8.1). In this approach, human beings are conceived of as rational entities with free will. It is based upon a moral philosophy of egoism (selfishness), in which the only constraints on behaviour are that there should be a duty not to initiate force over others.

The notion of a competitive ethos pervades this perspective. This is usually tied to the idea of rights to private property as being the first virtue of the legal and criminal justice system. Accordingly, crime is defined in terms of the infringement of private property, including infringements of one's physical self. Generally this approach defines crime in restrictive terms, as only those acts that violate the 'natural rights' of others.

**Table 8.1   Right-wing Libertarianism**

| | |
|---|---|
| Definition of crime | • (restrictive) only those acts that violate the 'natural rights' of others |
| Focus of analysis | • individual liberty and protection of private property rights |
| Cause of crime | • matter or rational choices involving incentives and disincentives |
| Nature of offender | • fully responsible for their own actions |
| Response to crime | • retribution, deterrence, incapacitation, and punishment insofar as the individual held responsible |
| Crime prevention | • decriminalization, minimal state intervention, moral call for taking personal responsibility and self-control |
| Operation of criminal justice system | • reduction in number of laws relating to 'victimless crime'<br>• greater use of incarceration and detention<br>• use of restitution to compensate victims<br>• support for privatization of security, law enforcement, and prisons |

From this perspective, human nature is conceived of as being possessive and individualistic, and since crime is conceived mainly in terms of private property, then the role of the state should be restricted to those instances where other people actually come to harm by one's social actions. In other words, there should be minimal state intervention in one's life. What intervention there is should be tightly focused on enhancing and protecting individual liberty and protecting private property.

The cause of crime is seen to lie with the individual. In reinforcing notions of individual selfishness, rights, and individuality, this perspective simultaneously asserts that criminological theorizing of the recent past has made excuses for individuals, by taking away people's responsibilities for their actions. It is argued, for example, that to speak of biological drives or social determinants such as poverty takes away any notion of choice in the selection of behaviour and activity.

Thus, individuals should be held fully responsible for their actions. Crime is seen fundamentally as a matter of rational choice, involving various incentives and disincentives. Since individual liberty is highly valued, however, the perspective believes that so-called 'victimless crimes' should be decriminalized insofar as they do not directly affect those beyond oneself. In other words, anything goes—people should have complete liberty to do as they want, as long as they do not infringe upon the property or person of others in an illegal way.

Where harm to another individual does occur, as in the case of the commission of an offence, then the offender should be punished. The perspective generally favours the promotion of retribution, deterrence, incapacitation, and punishment in its response to crime. It is informed by a just deserts philosophy, whereby punishment should be proportional to the crime. Furthermore, it favours the enforcement of restitutive measures with respect to the victims of crime; that is, the offender should pay compensation to the victim for any harm that he or she may have caused in the course of the offence.

In response to perspectives that see behaviour mainly in terms of psychological or social influences, this approach calls for a moralizing of society. Morality is seen in this context to be rooted in the individualistic ethos of personal responsibility and self-control. In return for minimal state intervention, it is essential that people use their liberty in accordance with the law. Where this is not so, then they should have to shoulder the penalty themselves.

In line with a general libertarian philosophy that de-emphasizes the state, this approach also supports the idea that security, law enforcement, and prisons should be private rather than public institutions. This reflects a broad ideological commitment to the so-called free market as the best and most efficient avenue for the provision of social services. Canada, to date, has had minimal involvement with prison privatization. There were discussions in the mid-1990s around the idea of the privatization of prisons in Alberta, Nova Scotia, and Ontario, but only Ontario moved forward with the concept; the first privately run prison in Canada—the Central North Correctional Centre (CNNC)—opened in Penetanquishene, Ontario in November 2001. This prison operated under a five-year contract with the Management and Training Corporation of Utah. The CNNC was a 1200-bed, multi-purpose facility for offenders serving sentences of up to two-years less a day, and it was created to allow the province to close several smaller and older regional jails. This 'super jail' was returned to public sector management at the end of the five-year contract with high operating costs and poor performance sited as reasons for its unsustainability.

## Traditionalist conservative

The traditionalist conservative perspective on what constitutes a crime takes a broader view than the right-wing libertarian one (see Table 8.2). The conservative view of crime includes not only that activity which endangers property or the person, but also that which offends morality. Hence, attacks on certain traditional values and people's general respect for authority may be viewed as criminal.

From this point of view, crime is not only a matter of 'free choice' but also is linked to certain intrinsic aspects of humanity. In particular, people are seen to possess certain 'natural urges' that go against the more civilized or divine purposes of society. Whether it is the concept of 'original sin' or a secular theory of human nature that sees people in a negative light, the idea is that all people are somehow inherently evil or flawed.

In order to constrain the 'natural' urges to do wrong, it is necessary to establish a strong order based upon personal sacrifice, self-discipline, and submission to authority. Order must take precedence over all else, including justice. Crime is said to be caused by the unwillingness of people to accept discipline, the undermining of traditional loyalties—such as to the (patriarchal) family—and the pursuit of immediate individual gratification without appropriate hard work.

According to this approach, punishment is an essential part of deterrence. This is not only because it establishes personal responsibility for one's actions, but also because it has an important symbolic impact on society as a whole. In other words,

### Table 8.2  Conservatism

| | |
|---|---|
| Definition of crime | • (expansive) violations of law, and acts that offend morality as well |
| Focus of analysis | • personal discipline and self-control |
| Cause of crime | • lack of self-discipline, undermining of traditional loyalties, lack of respect for authority |
| Nature of offender | • inherently 'evil' or flawed |
| Response to crime | • need for strong coercion, general deterrence strategies, assertion of authority |
| Crime prevention | • importance of traditional morality in maintenance of social authority, emphasis on self-discipline and submission to authority |
| Operation of criminal justice system | • expansion of laws relating to 'moral' issues such as pornography<br>• harsher penalties to enforce the legal and moral code<br>• order to take priority over justice<br>• emphasis on conformity to established traditions and social roles |

punishment has to be seen in terms of its effect on the establishment of moral solidarity through stigmatization. Punishment is, in effect, a form of social retribution, and may thus represent a response that is not proportional to the offence (in fact it may be much greater) due to the important symbolic role of punishment in bonding community members together.

Strong emphasis is placed upon the importance of morality in the maintenance of social authority. Thus, if someone does something deemed to be wrong or harmful, then they must be punished swiftly and appropriately in order to set the moral standard. Simultaneously, it is important to set clear moral standards and guidelines to conduct.

The traditionalist conservatives generally possess anti-libertarian views with respect to pornography, sexual behaviour, drug use, and abortion; that is, they favour intervention in areas regarded as victimless crimes. Indeed, the conservative point of view often favours increased state intervention in everyday social life because it is felt that only strong coercive measures will ultimately keep people in line and teach them the discipline they require to live as members of a civilized community.

## Historical Development

The New Right perspective has historical links with several different traditions within criminology. The right-wing libertarian approach is clearly identified with a classical criminological perspective. The emphasis on individual choice and responsibility, punishment and proportionality, and protection of liberty and property all have their echoes in the previous discussions of the social contract.

The traditionalist conservative approach has also been reflected in sociological and criminological theorizing. For example, the emphasis on punishment as a means of reinforcing moral boundaries echoes aspects of Durkheim's work. As Garland (1990) puts it, Durkheim saw punishment as a social institution intimately concerned with morality and social solidarity: 'The existence of strong bonds of moral solidarity are the conditions which cause punishments to come about, and, in their turn, punishments result in the reaffirmation and strengthening of these same social bonds' (28). Durkheim was, therefore, concerned with exploring conceptually the nature of punishment, particularly in relation to the ideas of the 'collective conscience' and the role of passion and sentiment in social life. However, unlike Durkheim, conservative traditionalists promote a single moral 'rightness' that pertains to society as a whole, whereas Durkheim was at pains to point out that morality varied between different societies.

More recent work has elements of both descriptive and proscriptive analysis. The emphasis on discipline, coercion, and self-control in the traditionalist conservative approach, for instance, is mirrored in the concerns of control theory. Whether it emphasizes bio-social processes (as in Hans Eysenck's work) or socialization processes (see Nettler, 1984), a social control perspective argues that the nature of crime is intertwined with the connection between individual and society.

Control theory as formulated by Hirschi (1969), for example, is premised upon the idea that it is an individual's bond to society that makes the difference in terms of whether or not they abide by society's general rules and values. From this perspective, all people are inherently antisocial, and thus all people would commit crime if they so dared. It is the nature of the bond that children have with their society that ultimately determines their behaviour (Empey, 1982; Nettler, 1984).

Hirschi (1969) theorized that the social bond is made up of four major elements:

- *Attachment*: the ties of affection and respect to significant others in one's life, and more generally a sensitivity to the opinion of others.
- *Commitment*: the investment of time and energy to activities such as school and various conventional and unconventional means and goals.
- *Involvement*: the patterns of living that shape immediate and long-term opportunities; for example, the idea that keeping busy doing conventional things will reduce the exposure of young people to illegal opportunities.
- *Belief*: the degree to which young people agree with the rightness of legal rules, which are seen to reflect a general moral consensus in society.

It is the combination of attachment, commitment, involvement, and belief that shapes the life world of the young person, and that essentially dictates whether or not they will take advantage of conventional means and goals of social advancement, or whether they will pursue illegal pathways to self-gratification.

It is up to society, and its agents, to step in and ensure that its younger members are imbued with the right bonds. In other words, there is a high degree of intervention necessary if children and young people are to be guided the right way, and if they are to follow paths that uphold social values, but that ultimately go against their essential antisocial nature. Without adequate socialization—a strong social control presence of some kind—criminal behaviour would be common.

## Contemporary Examples

In related and more recent work, Gottfredson and Hirschi (1990) argue that the central issue in explaining crime is that of self-control; that is, people differ in the extent to which they are restrained from criminal acts (see also Wilson and Herrnstein, 1985). This, in turn, is linked to the question of social bonding, and especially the problem of ineffective child rearing. The theory incorporates elements of other theories and perspectives: classical theory, in its acceptance of the idea that people are basically self-seeking; bio-social positivism, in its focus on the importance of proper 'conditioning' or training of the young; and sociological perspectives, which look to the nature of the family as a key variable in the development of self-control.

The theory does not analyze specific social divisions (e.g., class, gender, ethnicity), but rests upon a conception of human nature that sees all people as essentially driven by the same kinds of 'universal tendency to enhance their own pleasure'. Given this, the crucial issue is then one of how best to socialize all people to conform to society's values and to engage in conventional law-abiding behaviour.

In policy terms, the answer to juvenile crime lies in redressing the defective social training, which characterizes offenders who have in some way 'lost control'. In other words, the emphasis from a practitioner's perspective will be to reattach the young people to some kind of family, to recommit them to long-range conventional goals, to involve them in school and other constructive activities, and to have them acquire beliefs in the morality of law (Empey, 1982: 269).

Importantly, the control perspective is premised upon the idea that 'deviancy' stems from lack of self-control, and that this is fundamentally a matter related to the processes of socialization. Whereas Gottfredson and Hirschi emphasized the significance of relationships within the family, other contemporary criminologists have concentrated on making changes to the costs and benefits of crime.

Much work, for example, has been done in the general area of opportunity-rationality theory. This approach reflects the libertarian emphasis on choice and responsibility for one's actions. It is postulated that crime cannot be understood apart from the nature and distribution of opportunities for both crime and non-criminal behaviour. Thus, when people find themselves in situations in which they have opportunities to commit crime, the decision to do so or not to do so is a rational one (see Barlow, 1993).

In fact, from the point of view of **rational choice theory** we need to assume that most 'criminals' are rational agents who can be deterred from committing additional crimes by an increase in the punishment they might expect to receive (Buchanan and Hartley, 1992). In economic terms, the idea here is that individuals will always act in such a way as to maximize their own benefit. They are responsive to incentives and disincentives. From an economic rationalist position, therefore, the best criminal justice policy is one that prevents the commission of crime at the least financial cost. For example, according to the advocates of this approach, the most economically efficient way in which to manage the crime problem is to privatize institutions such as prisons, and to increase the probability of detection and conviction of offenders.

The broad philosophical orientation of rational choice theory is also closely related to the adoption of crime prevention techniques directed primarily at opportunity reduction (see Felson, 1994), rather than the structural reasons for offending behaviour or the criminalization process itself. Analysis of particular activities and locations can form the basis of a strategy designed to change the risks and costs associated with certain behaviours. In this way, the potential offender is deterred from making the decision to commit crime in certain areas, against certain targets.

A third perspective identified with New Right criminology is that of underclass explanations (Murray, 1990; Herrnstein and Murray, 1994). In this view, the problem resides in the behaviour of certain population groups, particularly the poor, the homeless, single mothers, and, in the United States, African-Americans (see Fraser, 1995; Mooney, 1998). The problem of crime and deviancy is thus seen to lie within the identified populations themselves. The 'underclass' comprises those sections of the poverty-stricken who, through their own volition or choice, or by genetic default, engage in criminal activity, substance abuse, illegitimate births, and deliberate non-participation in paid employment. Essentially, the so-called underclass is presented here as a 'moral' category, given that the emphasis is on behaviour (rather than structural conditions such as a lack of jobs) and disapproval (rather than understanding of social hardship).

Lind (1995) provides a summary of the common themes in New Right writings on the underclass. The nature of the problem, from a right-wing perspective, is a combination of lack of economic incentives (e.g., welfare dependency), a culture of poverty (e.g., familial breakdown and inappropriate role models), intellectual deficiencies (e.g., hereditary genetic inferiority), and low standards of morality (e.g., illegitimacy via sole parenting). The proposed solution is to make members of the 'underclass' more responsible and accountable for their own welfare and lifestyle choices. In effect, the demand is for the withdrawal of government support for the disadvantaged, coupled with efforts to resocialize people into new value and moral systems.

Whatever the specific theories that have been developed over the years, it appears that many writers have adopted a New Right criminological position simply due to the perception that 'nothing else has worked'. The so-called new realists, for example, have observed the deficiencies of a system partly built upon 'treatment' and positivistic assumptions, and concluded that it is time to reassert order and authority across our social institutions (see Wilson, 1975; Tame, 1991). Given the trends towards economic and social polarization, and given the apparent electoral appeal of law-and-order scapegoating, it is also the case that New Right criminology dovetails with New Right politics generally.

From the point of view of crime control and public order, the direction of policing and punishment fostered by New Right criminology is towards more active containment of, and control over, what are seen to be criminogenic populations—the 'dangerous classes' of the late modern era. The practical implementation of criminal justice policy is based upon the regulation of those population groups most closely identified with the 'underclass'. For instance, intervention is increasingly concerned with identifying, classifying, and managing groups in the community that are assessed on the basis of 'risk' and 'dangerousness' (see Feeley and Simon, 1994). This is associated with various kinds of pre-emptive action and incapacitation strategies, such as 'zero tolerance' policing and 'three strikes and you're out' punishment. The emphasis is on attacking the 'signs of disorder' through confrontational policing strategies (in which any behaviour, activity, or group deemed to be antisocial is not to be tolerated by authorities), and by locking up those who transgress the criminal and moral norms of society (through committing them to long prison terms). Getting 'tough on crime' is part of a generalized escalation in the punishment ethos. Both this punishment ethos and the references to an 'underclass' can be found a speech given by John Tory, the Leader of the Progressive Conservative Party of Canada, to the Ontario Convenience Store Association in February 2006. Mr Tory, while discussing the fear of crime felt by many convenience store workers made the following statements:

> This speaks to a wider issue of violent crime. . .and the forces that provoke it. . .Most of the media attention has centred on the rash of gun violence—in particular the more than 50 senseless gun-related killings we've seen over 2005 and 2006. These shootings are unquestionably tragic. However, they are also the tip of the iceberg when it comes to violent crime and the tragic consequences of that lethal combination of guns, gangs, drugs, and criminals. . .a vicious spiral the snares too many of our province's youth. The growth of a gang culture that glorifies violence and lacks any respect for authority takes its toll on our communities in a number of ways. It might start with incidents of vandalism, harassment or petty theft. . .but you do not have to be a criminologist to see how such a culture can grow to include armed robbery, assault, and

other violent crimes. If we live in a world where convenience store break-ins and robbers are up close to thirty per cent. . .the spiral is very real. . .I went into some of our most troubled neighbourhoods to hear first hand people's concerns. Our caucus also met with social workers, law enforcement and other community leaders. Last fall we were proud to release a comprehensive report of our findings. In short—our report calls for fighting crime by fighting the criminal culture that encourages it. That means getting more police on our streets. Ending lax sentencing practices and ensuring violent offenders serve real time behind bars. And partnering with the private sector so at-risk youth can find mentorships. . .internships. . .education and employment opportunities and break the gangs and guns cycle (Tory, 2006).

For all the criminological talk about 'rationality', it would appear that, increasingly, criminal justice policy is marked by sensationalist hyperbole and, indeed, a high degree of irrationality about crime and what to do about it.

## Critique

A critique of New Right criminology stems from the way in which theories within this perspective ignore issues of power in their assertion of choice and free will. In this way the critique of New Right criminology mirrors, to some extent at least, criticisms of classical criminology. On 'rational' criteria, there is much to criticize in New Right criminology, particularly in its populist political guise.

On a theoretical level New Right criminology does not analyze the nature of choice within a society that is characterized by inequality, as opposed to equality. It does not address concerns about the ethnic and 'racial' divisions in society, and the way in which certain groups, such as indigenous people, are systematically over-represented in the criminal justice system. The explanation that such over-representation can be explained purely by a 'choice' to offend does not seem to take us very far. Much New Right criminology simply ignores issues of 'race', ethnicity, gender, and class by prioritizing the individual, along with individual choice and individual values.

Where levels of analysis other than that of the individual are evident, it is clear that they rest on a particular set of values that does not include significant sectors of society. For example, control theory talks unproblematically about inculcating majority values, expressed through belief in the rightness of legal rules that are seen to reflect a general moral consensus in society. The interdependence of individuals that prevents criminal behaviour is premised upon adherence to the moral consensus. Non-adherence predisposes an individual to criminal offending. Within multicultural societies such as Australia, Canada, the US, and the UK, there are major problems if the notion of consensus is defined in the narrow terms that traditional conservatives tend to use.

Many of the policies proposed by New Right theories have themselves been discredited. In particular, the capacity of harsh, or even proportional, punishment to deter individuals from reoffending has been the subject of long debate. There is substantial evidence that imprisonment in particular is counterproductive, and serves only to exacerbate, not diminish, rates of offending. Prison (and the 'big stick' in general) is both ineffective and expensive.

Furthermore, the debate concerning the need for harsher penalties has negative consequences in and of itself. For example, it engenders a fear of crime, which is out of all proportion to the realistic possibility of victimization. The problem of how to deal with the fear of crime—independent of how to deal with crime per se—is an urgent issue facing many people today.

Finally, crime itself is defined narrowly. For the majority of New Right theorists, the major concern is with 'street crime'. Crimes of the powerful and crimes of the state are hardly mentioned. Where they are mentioned, the state is seen as able to deal adequately with the problem, since there is no conception that the state itself may favour the powerful over the powerless.

The popularity of the law-and-order debate, and with it the popularity of New Right criminology in general, cannot be accounted for adequately by reference to a rational 'scientific' debate. It is best explained by the need of societies for symbolic assurances of certainty in the face of growing economic uncertainty. The symbolic and political nature of the crime debate is well evidenced through the popularity of New Right criminology. It provides government with a justification to capture the emotional needs of an electorate within a capitalist democracy. The potency of the symbol of 'law and order' is not lost on governments increasingly at the mercy of unpleasant financial and employment trends in the economic sphere.

A further, and worrying, aspect of the authoritarian strand within New Right circles is the merging of global and international developments with national and domestic concerns. This is most evident in the ways in which the so called 'war on terrorism' has seen even greater collaboration between military, police, and secret services; a greater propensity to do away with long-established human rights and civil rights protections (in the name of homeland security); and the putting into place of informal and formal sanctions designed to ensure public 'unity' in support of war efforts (both within and without national borders). Politically, the pursuit of 'security' has been accompanied in the United States by what has been called 'prescriptive patriotism', an orchestrated patriotism that is 'aimed at closing down debate and dissent through the imposition of a prescribed allegiance' (O'Leary and Platt, 2001: 42). Crime and deviance is thus defined almost exclusively in terms dictated by ruling elites, who mobilize public opinion in ways that allow for the silencing of dissent, the imprisonment of those who have not been formally charged with a crime, and the vilification of minority groups.

Similar types of processes are also apparent with regard to immigration controls and border protection. Once again, the treatment of asylum seekers, especially in countries such as Australia, has frequently been characterized by systematic denial of human and legal rights, an emphasis on illegality of entry, the selective rejection of refugees by possible host nations, and the enforced detention of those who survive the journey to new lands (see Pickering and Lambert, 2001; Weber, 2002). The symbols of the New Right are basically constructed around notions of social difference, which are in turn interpreted as evidence of social deviance. This applies to 'deviants' inside a country, as well as those outside.

Despite the negative aspects of New Right criminology, there are elements that are of importance to the criminological debate. While it asserts issues of individual responsibility, it also highlights individual rights and, in particular, the right to feel safe and secure. The rights of victims, which had been ignored by the majority of criminologists, are brought to the fore within this perspective. Victims' rights and needs can no longer be ignored within criminological theory. Finally, the phenomenon of New Right criminology is a timely reminder of the political nature of crime and crime policy. Criminological theory has to come to grips with political realities if its policy proposals and strategic plans of action are to go beyond mere conjecture.

## Conclusion

New Right criminology refers to a particular political orientation, rather than to a systematic, coherent theory in its own right. For this reason there is a broad range of theoretical perspectives that are brought together in this chapter, from authoritarian populism and right-wing libertarian perspectives through to traditionalist conservatism and control theory. Despite the differences of these approaches, all can be characterized by a focus on the rights, responsibilities, and free will of the individual who offends. Each has a particular moral stance that upholds the status quo of society and the right of those with power to dictate what constitutes the moral consensus.

Each strand of New Right thinking also tends to see human nature as ultimately depraved. Without sufficient deterrent measures put in place by the state, or strong social bonds as defined by control theory, human nature would automatically lead to antisocial and criminal behaviour. Overlaid on this perspective of human nature is the need for society to clearly define right from wrong, to reward the right, and, more importantly, to punish the wrong. Without such an approach, a general breakdown in law and order would result.

Like many criminological theories, the popularity of New Right criminology cannot be divorced from the broader political environment. The political popularity of the law-and-order debate and calls for tougher punishment on a political level are legitimized through many of the perspectives outlined above. The prominence of the law-and-order debate, as fostered by New Right ideas, led directly to the emergence of a new theoretical perspective on the left, namely Left Realism. It was the success of the New Right at a popular level that led sections of the Left to 'take crime seriously'. To do so they recognized that issues such as victims' rights and the popularity of a strong response to criminal behaviour resonated with community concerns, and were thus important.

### Key Terms and Concepts

- Conservatism
- Rational choice theory
- Retribution
- Right-wing liberalism
- Social control theory

### Further Reading

C. Buchanan and P. Hartley, *Criminal Choice: The Economic Theory of Crime and Its Implications for Crime Control* (Sydney: Centre for Independent Studies, 1992).

Dilulio, J. Jr, R.P. George, and T.L. Simmons, *The Clash of Orthodoxies: Law, Religion, and Morality in Crisis* (New York: ISI Publishers, 2001).

P. Elikann, *Superpredators: Demoralization of our Children by the Law* (New York: Plenum, 1999).

M. Feeley and J. Simon, 'Actuarial Justice: The Emerging New Criminal Law', in *The Futures of Criminology*, D. Nelken, ed. (London: Sage, 1994).

M. Gottfredson and T. Hirschi, *A General Theory of Crime* (Stanford: Stanford University Press, 1990).

R. Herrnstein and C. Murray, *The Bell Curve* (New York: Basic Books, 1990).

M. Lind, 'Brave New Right', in *The Bell Curve Wars: Race, Intelligence and the Future of America*, S. Fraser, ed. (New York: Basic Books, 1995).

C. Murray, *The Emerging Underclass* (London: Institute of Economic Affairs, 1990).

G. Nettler, *Explaining Crime* (New York: McGraw-Hill, 1984).

R. Surrette, *Media, Crime, and Criminal Justice: Images and Realities* (Belmont, CA: West/Wadsworth, 1998).

C. Tame, 'Freedom, Responsibility and Justice: The Criminology of the "New Right"', in *The Politics of Crime Control*, K. Stenson and D. Cowell, eds (London: Sage, 1991).

## Websites

*www.canada.justice.gc.ca.* The Canadian Department of Justice's website provides general information about Canada's criminal justice system.

*www.conservative.ca.* This website makes the latest news and information from the Conservative Party of Canada easily available.

*www.crime-prevention.org.* The National Crime Prevention Council of Canada's website provides information on federal government crime-prevention initiatives.

*www.statcan.ca.* Statistics Canada provides current statistics on crime in Canada.

## Films/Documentaries

- *Cell 16* (National Film Board of Canada, 1971)
- *Damage Done: The Drug War Odyssey* (National Film Board of Canada, 2006)
- *Doing Time* (National Film Board of Canada, 2002)
- *High Risk Offender* (National Film Board of Canada, 1998)
- *Justice Denied* (National Film Board of Canada, 1989)
- *Law and Disorder* (National Film Board of Canada, 2003)

## Discussion Questions

1. According to new right criminology, what is the cause of crime?
2. What is meant by the term 'super-predator' and what impact has this term had on youth justice policies?
3. Do you believe that increasing the number of police on the streets would effectively reduce crime rates? Why or why not?
4. Travis Hirschi argued that young people commit crimes when they lack strong social bonds. What four elements made up Hirchi's social bond theory and how did they interact to effectively control the behaviour of the individual?
5. What, in your opinion, are the strongest contributions to the study of crime and criminal behaviours made by new right criminology? What are the weakest contributions? Provide examples to support your position.

# CHAPTER 9

# Left Realism

## Objectives

This chapter will help you develop an understanding of the:

- fundamental concepts found within the **left realist criminology** perspective;
- historical and political contexts in the development of left realist criminology;
- influence that the left realist perspective has had on the criminal justice system; and
- strengths and weaknesses found within a left realist perspective to criminology.

## Introduction

Left Realism is best seen as a response to two conflicting perspectives on crime that emerged strongly in the mid 1980s: **New Right criminology** and **Marxist criminology**. The previous chapter outlined the political popularity of the conservative political perspective with its strong emphasis on 'law and order'. Left Realism was concerned that the political debate was being dominated by the right wing, which had a destructive impact on the lives of the working class. It attempted to capture the political debate by focusing, like the conservatives, on the victims of so-called street crime. However, Left Realists wanted to highlight the fact that the majority of victims of street crimes were from the working class, not the middle and upper classes. In doing so, Left Realism wanted to reorient the law-and-order debate away from the middle-class fear of the working class and towards a consideration of how the working class itself suffers from crime.

Left Realism saw radical criminology as unable or unwilling to ameliorate this suffering of the working class because it failed to take crime seriously. This failure further meant that such criminological analysis was unable to provide the antidote to the conservative 'law-and-order' politics that dominated crime policy. Left Realists contrasted the political popularity of the conservative Thatcher government in Britain with the political marginalization of the radical perspective, or 'left idealist' view (as it was labelled by the Left Realists). The reason for such marginalization, they suggested, was the lack of practical suggestions put forward by Marxist criminology to deal with crime in the inner city.

This chapter will outline the origins of Left Realism and the nature of the response it made to 'law-and-order' politics from a left perspective. It has received considerable criticism, mainly from the left, and has undergone considerable revision. The major revisions within Left Realism will also be outlined in this chapter. What is central to the Left Realist endeavour, and common to all permutations of the theory, is its pragmatic core. Left Realism sees itself as both a reasonable and practical response to the problem of crime in inner-city communities.

## Social Context

In terms of social context, Left Realism can be seen as a concern within (initially) British criminology with the policies of neo-conservatism in general and the Thatcher government in particular. It was avowedly political in that it saw itself as a political response to the law-and-order agenda of the right. It was this response to the law-and-order debates of the early 1980s that galvanized the thinking of Left Realists. Prior to this time they had been writing as predominantly Marxist or radical criminologists debating with other radical criminologists from within the same essential paradigm.

In attempting to enter into the political discussions of law and order, the Left Realists joined in the conservative debate about crime control, which was less concerned about the causes of crime. In doing so, they confirmed that conservative politics had successfully defined the crime problem as one where there were clear distinctions between those who were criminal and those who were not. In this conception, crime was a unitary phenomenon defined by common sense. With this in mind, crime policy was properly concerned with controlling crime, not with reducing conditions that might give rise to criminal behaviour, such as inequality and unemployment.

This emphasis on controlling crime, rather than on dealing with the causes of crime, could be seen clearly in the contribution Left Realist writers made in response to the riots experienced in Britain in 1981. These riots occurred in areas of poverty and high levels of unemployment, such as Brixton, but it was not this unemployment and deprivation per se that captured the imagination of the Left Realists. These theorists argued that while poverty and deprivation were a precondition of riots, and more generally of increases in crime, they were not a sufficient cause. Poverty and unemployment could be associated with quiescent fatalism and the acceptance of adversity, as much as with rebellion and violence (Lea and Young, 1982). Left Realists argued that the riots had their genesis in three factors: West Indian **counterculture**; the political marginalization of the inner city; and, crucially, the police methods of dealing with people who lived in deprived neighbourhoods.

The explanations by the realists for the existence of a violent and aggressive counterculture are similar to the explanations of the strain theorists, which were outlined in Chapter 4. Left Realists argued that countercultures thrive where the expectations of material rewards engendered by the education system and the mass media are manifestly not available to certain sectors of society. In particular, successive generations of West Indian immigrants in the UK saw themselves as discriminated against and alienated from the mainstream culture. In the face of this lack of opportunity, a counterculture developed—based on a 'hustling' mentality and street culture—that was competitive, disorganized, and antisocial. Along with poverty and unemployment, the existence of this counterculture produced extremely high rates of inner-city crime. In opposition to Marxist criminologists, who downplayed or denied the existence of rising rates of street crime, Left Realists argued that street crime was much higher than police figures suggested.

Those who lived in the decaying inner city lacked access to an effective voice within the political process; this exacerbated the alienation that people in those neighbourhoods experienced, and spawned the counterculture. Those marginalized within the inner city had no access to traditional centres of power within society, such as those controlling capital or the trade unions. Such people were locked out of the world of production and, with this, access to the political system was also denied. Left Realism suggested that the return to violence, epitomized by the riots, was the politics of last resort. Economic marginalization exacerbated political marginalization.

Government or state agencies did not address the marginalization felt by people in these neighbourhoods. Rather, the methods used by the arm of the state that had the greatest impact in the area, namely the police, were disastrous. Left Realists argued that in deprived neighbourhoods police deliberately shifted away from 'consensus' policing (policing for the community), which might have at least gone some way to reducing alienation in these communities. Instead, police used military tactics, 'swamp' procedures, and 'stop and search' provisions that allowed on-the-street searching of any suspicious-looking person. These tactics had the effect of blurring the distinction between offender and non-offender to a point where, Left Realists argued, any action by police became perceived as a symbolic attack on the community as a whole. It is at this point that any consensual relationship that existed between the police and the public breaks down, and actions by police can trigger rioting (Lea and Young, 1982).

The analysis of the riots in the UK set the scene for the early formulations of Left Realism, and defined the theory as one primarily concerned with the control of crime, rather than amelioration of the preconditions of crime. Relief of the preconditions of the counterculture, for example, was not the primary policy goal of the theorists. Rather, they took as central planks the second and third strands of analysis outlined above—political marginalization and policing reform. The political dimension was addressed by alignment with the British Labour Party and the production of policies with which the left could intervene effectively in the law-and-order debate (Lea and Young, 1984). The substance of the policies provided by Left Realism predominantly addressed the third strand of analysis, that of policing reform, and the creation of consensus-style policing within inner urban areas.

The focus on policing was seen as justified because of perceived omissions by Marxist criminology concerning the reality of crime in working-class areas. The theory argues that the major concern of the working class and marginalized poor in the city was not the crimes of the powerful, as suggested by Marxist criminology, but the property offences, robbery, and domestic violence that were experienced as an everyday reality. The victims of such crimes, as well as the perpetrators, were predominantly the poor and vulnerable sections of society. The radical criminological focus on crimes of the powerful and crimes of the state 'missed the point' and failed to accurately represent the needs of the working class. Furthermore, when 'street crime' was mentioned by radical criminology it was too often romanticized: street criminals were characterized as 'latter-day Robin Hoods' rather than as perpetrators of criminal behaviour that was seriously antisocial and destructive. So, for Left realists it was the street crime of inner-city neighbourhoods that should form the predominant focus of criminology.

## Basic Concepts

Left Realist criminology is characterized by its pragmatic focus on crime control (see Table 9.1). Because of this, it is not concerned with lengthy analyses of what crime actually is. Rather, it is content to define crime as that contained in the legal code. This can be seen as partly a result of the major means of data collection used by the Left Realists—namely, local crime victim surveys (see for example Jones et al., 1986). Local crime victim surveys target specific inner-city locations, and ask residents about their victimization from criminal activity, and what residents would like done about it. As a result, the definition of crime is driven by the definitions of crime that are reported on the survey. Local residents are more likely to see crime as defined in traditional terms, and so Left Realism itself defines crime in traditional terms.

**Table 9.1 Left Realist Perspectives**

| | |
|---|---|
| Definition of crime | • as contained in legal code, with main focus on street crime |
| Focus of analysis | • crime by and against working class, with working-class as both offender and victim<br>• use of crime victim surveys |
| Cause of crime | • **relative deprivation**<br>• ineffective methods of policing |
| Nature of offender | • most crime is intra-class<br>• offenders must be held responsible to a degree for their own actions |
| Response to crime | • develop more effective policing, and greater community control over criminal justice agencies |
| Crime prevention | • reduce alienation of community from the criminal justice system<br>• adopt problem-solving approaches<br>• take crime seriously |
| Operation of criminal justice system | • active cooperation between police and community members<br>• meeting of victim needs<br>• crime prevention programmes |

The local crime victim survey is the major tool of analysis of Left Realists. Because the emphasis is on addressing the concerns expressed by inner-city populations, analysis is directed towards concerns raised about crime in local areas as expressed through the crime surveys. In particular, this perspective is noted for concern about intra-class crime; that is, criminal behaviour by the working class against the working class.

More recent analysis has focused on the '**square of crime**'. This consists of two dyads. One is concerned with the criminal act, which comprises offender and victim. The other is concerned with social control, which comprises social action (e.g., the actions of police and 'multi-agencies') and social reaction (e.g., the reaction of the public). A complete analysis of crime, according to Left Realists, should focus on both dyads (Young, 1991).

The causes of crime as perceived by the Left Realists span both the conditions endemic to inner-city working-class areas, such as poor facilities and lack of jobs, and the response by the criminal justice agencies, notably the police, which exacerbate the problem of crime by their heavy-handed responses. The cause of crime, according to Left Realism, results from the amalgamation of three aspects: the relative deprivation of those in working-class areas, which gives rise to countercultures; the lack of access to the political sphere, which spawns feelings of powerlessness; and dissent and police responses that antagonize local populations and cause further breakdown in these communities. This leads to rising crime rates in these areas. The level of crime, according to Left Realists, is higher than that in official figures, and is rising in areas of high social breakdown (Young, 1991).

Concern with the suffering of the victims of crime has led Left Realism to adopt a less-than-sympathetic view of the offender. Offenders are responsible for their behaviour, which is antisocial and destructive, and causes great hardship within already impoverished areas of society. However, unlike New Right criminology, Left Realists do not see offenders or offending totally as a result of free will. The motivation to offend springs from the relative deprivation in these areas. Young people and ethnic minorities are led by the broader culture to expect material reward, yet their situation within the social order prevents them achieving that reward. Further to this, social cohesion in these areas has broken down. Left Realists argue that in other times of great hardship, such as the depression of the 1930s, there was a working-class solidarity and working-class culture that saw people pull together. Today inner-city areas with a high crime rate lack social solidarity that could insulate against feelings of deprivation. The result is anger and frustration, particularly in young people.

Recently there has been much media coverage about gun violence in Toronto, where 1,193 people were victims of violent gun-related offences in 2006 (Statistics Canada, 2008). In 2005, more than 50 people were killed in gun violence, the majority of which appears to be gang-related. This has created a clear and compelling example of the type of intra-class violence fueled by the discontent, frustration, and deprivation felt by many of today's young people. The 21 July 2007 death of Ephraim Brown, an 11-year-old Toronto boy, is one example of not only the impact of this frustration and alienation, but also of how the community and the police must work together to both solve crime and to find and implement solutions to the social causes of such violence. Brown was attending a birthday party in the northwest end of

Toronto when he was caught in the crossfire of a gang shooting. At a press conference held the next day, Ephraim's two sisters pleaded with the community to come forward and assist the police in solving the murder of their brother. Police representatives also urged the community not to take retaliatory action but to trust and work with police. Police Chief Bill Blair recognized the need for police to help change the circumstances that foster such violence and to work with the community to provide opportunities for positive choices for young people.

## Box 9.1  Cooperation Urged by Family of Slain Boy

The sisters of an 11-year-old boy killed in the crossfire of a fight between two rival gangs called for their troubled community to take action and ensure that no more innocent lives are lost.

Speaking at a news conference Sunday, 15-year-old Camisha Brown tearfully mourned the loss of her brother Ephraim who died early Saturday after attending a birthday party.

'Ephraim was only in grade six, 11 yeas old,' she said. 'He didn't need to get his life taken away. . .I just don't understand how many young, innocent lives you guys need to take in order for the community to step up, take charge and take action.'

Ephraim's other sister, Amanda Taylor pleaded with community members to come forward and assist police, adding that 'somebody out there knows something.'

'Just have the courage to come out and do what is right, because enough is enough. These kids need to stop dying, and it really just has to stop with my brother,' Taylor said.

City police are urging members of the community to 'not engage in retaliation' as they cope with the death of another youth. 'I would ask the community to trust us, work with us, and allow us to identify the people that are responsible for this and not engage in retaliation,' Toronto Police Chief Bill Blair said. 'That will not bring the young boy back.'

Investigators plain identified gang violence as the cause of the 11-year-old's death. 'It's clear, in the early stages of the investigation, that the 11-year-old was caught in between two rival gangs that were shooting at each other in this particular housing complex,' homicide squad Det. Gerry Giroux said.

Blair compared the incident to the 2005 shooting death of 15-year-old Jane Creba, who died on a downtown Toronto street when she was hit while rival gangs fired at each other through a crowd of Boxing Day shoppers.

Blair said the investigation was progressing well, although he declined to comment on whether there were any suspects. Both the Toronto police Guns and Gangs Unit and the Organized Crime Unit are investigating the case.

Another 21-year-old, whose name was not released, was wounded in the shooting and is in the hospital. Blair said the person was known to the police but was not cooperating in the investigation. The 21-year-old is not a suspect at this point, he added.

Toronto Mayor David Miller and Ontario Attorney General Michael Bryant have committed 'anything and everything that is required to successfully resolve this matter,' Blair said, adding that his force will do all that is required 'to bring those responsible to justice.'

'We must do everything we can to change the neighborhood, to change the circumstances that give rise to this violence and these senseless killings, to work with the people of this community to give our young people positive choices,' Blair said.

From Lisa Abel, 'Stop the violence, sisters of slain boy plead', *Toronto Star*, 22 July 2007.

So, how do Left Realists see effective responses to these problems? The primary response has been in the area of police and policing. Crime can be controlled by a police force that is responsive to the needs of the local community (Kinsey et al., 1986). Furthermore, the community needs to be in control of the police force: police should respond to local city councils rather than a distant bureaucracy at the state or national level. Local communities need effective political responses to their concerns, which can be brought about by giving greater power to local councils to control criminal justice agencies. More recent writing in the area of Left Realism has dealt with what to do once offenders are apprehended. However, in areas such as penology (the study of corrections), Left Realism has largely 'borrowed' from the liberal analysis, which emphasizes the need for community-based corrections.

Crime prevention, then, will be achieved by reducing the alienation of the community from the criminal justice system. This will not be achieved, though, by the agencies themselves deciding what is in the best interests of these high-crime areas. Policies are needed that will reduce the alienation of the community from the criminal justice system. These policies will give the local communities an active voice in how the police, in particular, go about dealing with people in local areas. Local communities should be able to decide what the problems are that the police should tackle, and then should be able to work cooperatively with police to solve these problems.

The criminal justice system under a Left Realist policy agenda would involve active cooperation between community members and police. The system would be geared towards the concerns of local communities rather than driven by a broader, and more partisan, political agenda. The law-and-order debate would then be immune from capture by political concerns aimed at providing a 'quick fix', such as military-style policing, which is ultimately a symbolic and destructive solution.

# Historical Development

The historical development of Left Realism can be seen as two 'waves'. The first came out of the analysis of the Thatcher years by Left Realists in the mid 1980s; the second, more comprehensive theory arose in response to a critique of early formulations of the theory, mainly from the so-called left idealists. Before describing these two waves, it is important to describe the way in which data is gathered for analysis and theorizing under a Left Realist perspective. Left Realism prides itself not only on development of a paradigm with which to understand the problem of crime and criminality, but also on development of the research instrument that underpins this theorizing—the local crime victim surveys.

Local crime victim surveys can be differentiated from broad-based crime victim surveys undertaken at state or national levels. The aim of these local surveys is to understand the problem of crime and victimization within specific locations. These locations are the poorest and most marginalized. In the UK, for example, the first survey was undertaken in Islington, a predominantly Black working-class area in London. The aim of the surveys is to monitor people's needs concerning crime, and then develop policies that accurately reflect those needs. Questions in the surveys concern themselves broadly with issues of victimization and relationship with criminal justice agencies. The surveys purport to measure some 550 variables (MacLean, 1993).

Importantly, the surveys are seen as a complete method in themselves of obtaining the necessary information on which to base theory and policy. This can be contrasted with the traditional methods of radical research—case studies and ethnographies (interview and participant observation). Left Realists claim that the victim surveys generate better empirical data, which is then more authoritative in the public sphere.

There are, however, significant shortcomings in victim survey data. Among these shortcomings is the problem of reporting only on those crimes that are included on the survey; white-collar crimes, for example, were omitted from early studies. Furthermore, other crimes, such as domestic violence, pose problems for those using a survey format due to the sensitivity of the material. In addition, the surveys were not used to explore the various meanings of the label 'criminal', and terms such as 'violence', 'vandalism', and 'sexual assault'. While there may be consensus regarding their seriousness, there may be little agreement concerning what these terms actually mean (Hogg, 1988). Finally, asking about what people want done about crime may not elicit the most useful response. Organized burglaries may result from the influence of the receiver of stolen goods, not the actual burglar. Arresting one burglar is unlikely to stop burglaries from happening if it is the receiver of stolen goods who provides the primary influence for the offending (Hogg, 1988).

Left Realism has attempted to deal with some of these criticisms, primarily through redesigning the survey instrument. Successive waves of victim surveys have resulted in successive refining of the theory itself. It is to the major developments that we now turn.

### Early versions of Left Realism

The first formulation of Left Realism was well summarized by Russell Hogg (1988), and is substantially reproduced here. The main points are outlined below, in each case pointing to the similarities to, and differences from, mainstream radical criminology.

- *Crime is a major problem, especially personal violence and property crime, and is a problem of growing proportions.* By denoting 'crime' as the major focus, Left Realists were reasserting the centrality of 'crime' as a unifying focus for criminology. Although Marxist criminology, as well as labelling theory, had gone to great lengths to highlight the contextual nature of labelling an event 'criminal', Left Realists saw crime as a unitary concept, something 'out there' and measurable. Furthermore, unlike Marxist criminology, Left Realism emphasized 'street crime' and played down white-collar and state offences. Finally, this differed from Marxist criminology in that it saw crime as increasing. Some Marxist criminologists are less convinced of an increase, and see the rise shown by statistics as more likely a result of a 'law-and-order' panic, than any real increase in the rate of offending.
- *Official crime statistics considerably underestimate the problem due to the levels of unreported crime, which is in large part a result of public alienation and frustration with the ineffectiveness of criminal justice agencies, particularly the police.* Here Left Realism is somewhat similar to mainstream radical theory in that it asserts that the community is alienated from the criminal justice system (in this case, the police). However, unlike radical criminology, Left Realism argues that there is even more crime, defined in traditional terms, than suggested by police statistics.
- *Most personal crime (robbery, assault, burglary, etc.) is intra-class and disproportionately afflicts the poor and their neighbourhoods, thus compounding the inequalities and exploitations they already suffer.* The similarity with mainstream radical theory here is that it is the working class that primarily suffers exploitation and hardship. However, unlike some Marxists, Left Realists argue that the victimization is primarily intra-class: that is, the working class preys on the working class. This is a marked diversion from traditional Marxist criminology, which emphasizes that the ruling class preys on the working class.
- *The police are both extremely inefficient at dealing with inner-city crime and are endemically hostile and discriminatory with regard to the inner-city populace (especially youth and ethnic minorities).* Much of this resonates with a traditional radical view with respect to the endemic hostility between police and the working class. Unlike traditional Marxists, who see police as an instrument of class control and maintenance of the status quo, Left Realism sees possible positive roles for police. Police might well be useful, if only they were more effective.
- *The mutual antagonism between police and local communities sets in train a vicious circle of non-cooperation whereby the alienated community does not report crime to the police, and the police respond by heavier proactive and discriminatory police strategies, which alienates the community further.* This elaborates on why the police are ineffective, and underscores the futility of current policing methods in attempting effective control of crime. Marxist criminologists would argue, however, that the purpose of discriminatory policing is not crime control, but control of the

working class. For Marxists, then, such discriminatory policing is fulfilling its purpose if it is effective in 'quieting the masses'.

* *Inner-city working-class communities are deeply concerned about local crime, want effective policies to control it, and see the police as central to crime control.* This is crucial to the Left Realist position. Left Realism takes the working-class communities' opinion at face value and reasserts the position that the communities themselves see police and police response as key elements of crime control in inner-city areas. Left Realists argue that these sentiments must be listened to, and acted on, if radicals are to claim any credibility in attempting to help these communities. If the communities say police are potentially useful, the task for criminology is to assist in making police more responsive to the communities' needs—not to decry the police existence.

* *Effective policing requires that police concentrate on those crimes that the public perceive as most serious, that they cease alienating the public by heavy-handed intrusive strategies, and that they be brought under local democratic control through elected police authorities.* This is the last major argument of the early formulations of Left Realism. It argues that crime can be controlled within working-class communities to some extent. This must be achieved through active cooperation between the police and the policed. This differs from the general thrust of Marxist criminology, since it places prime emphasis on the possibility of reform within the capitalist system that would benefit the working class in the long term, and also argues that reform of police is possible.

The development and adoption of the community-policing model in Canada provides an example of the type of policing advocated by Left Realists and outlined briefly in the points above. The goals of this model are to encourage public safety and confidence through the reduction of the fear of crime held by individuals in the community and to encourage citizen involvement. There is an acknowledgment that in order for these goals to be reached, police must include community groups, business people, schoolteachers, and residents as 'key partners. . .in the creation of safe and secure communities. The success of the police depends not only on the development of their own skills and capabilities, but also on the creation of competent communities' (Moore and Trojanowicz, 1988). The Edmonton Police Force was the first to adopt this philosophy in 1984, and since then the community-policing model has become the standard model of delivery for the majority of Canadian police forces.

This early version of Left Realism caused much debate. It became clear that the theory was too narrow, and too fixed on issues of policing. The key criticisms of this first attempt hinged around four major areas, and arose in part from weaknesses in the research instrument, the local crime victim survey.

The first criticism concerned the problem of using 'crime' as the unifying focus. While Left Realists asserted the need to 'take crime seriously', critics asked which crime should be the major focus and, more importantly, what was meant by the term 'crime'. Critics argued that the theory treated definitions of crime as if they had common meanings that were universally accepted. Such an assumption is anathema to many on the left who assert that the term 'crime' has no common meaning. Further, popular definitions of crime are too heavily influenced by the state to be of constructive use. Terms such as 'vandalism' and 'graffiti' are used in the political sphere for political ends. The theory failed to take account of the political dimension of terms concerned with crime and criminality.

Furthermore, the use of politically tainted terms allows popular misconceptions of crime and criminality to continue. In particular it exacerbates the problem of stereotypical impressions of who 'we' are (the goodies), as opposed to 'them' (the baddies). Critics argued that Left Realism tended to treat the results of the victim surveys as if they represented a true picture of crime, and what crime is. Public concern must be understood as the result of a political process, and in particular a result of the active influence of the police and the media in shaping popular conceptions of crime and criminality.

Besides the problems of the definition and meaning of the term 'crime', critics also pointed to the narrow scope of victimization covered by Left Realism. Concern was expressed that only certain forms of victimization were considered as important. The most notable omissions were in the area of white-collar crime. Certain forms of white-collar crime also disproportionately affect the working class, most notably industrial pollution and negligence, loan sharking, and false advertising.

Great criticism was also levelled at the narrowness concerning effective responses, notably the almost exclusive focus on policing. This partly resulted from the emphasis of the surveys themselves. Early surveys placed a great weight on what the victims felt should be done about crime. Critics argued that this allowed the assumption to remain unchallenged that in order to reduce crime one must necessarily focus on police action. Effective reduction strategies may mean something else entirely: in particular, solutions may lie outside the criminal justice system. A good example of this arises within Canada. Aboriginal communities recognize that the problem of violence within their communities is a result, in part, of the availability of alcohol. Some of these communities have taken action to limit the availability of alcohol, in some cases restricting sales on reserves, such as in Old Crow, a community in the Yukon that banned alcohol in the early 1990s. Another successful 'dry' aboriginal community is Alkali Lake in British Columbia, which banned alcohol in 1972. The history of Alkali Lake's transition to a dry community has been documented in a 1992 film entitled *The Honor of Al: The Story of Alkali Lake.* This approach is seen to be far more effective than direct police action. Police action, however well intentioned, may simply exacerbate the violence, since the cause lies outside police control.

Critics also argue for greater attention to the possible consequences of increased cooperation between the public and the police. Police responding to complaints may be ineffective in solving burglary, as mentioned above, if the primary problem is one of receiving stolen goods. Left Realists argue that changes in policing style—so that it is reactive, cooperative, and accountable—will increase the flow of information to police and dramatically improve clear-up rates. However, the opposite might occur if, for example, clear-up rates were substantially boosted by 'verballing' (i.e., untrue police testimony).

If policing strategies did lead to a greater number of arrests, Left Realism had also left open the question of what to do with offenders once they had been apprehended. They had not considered what was appropriate in dealing with offenders in terms of a humane penal policy. Furthermore, penal policy—in particular, the greater use of jails—is very expensive, and Left Realism had not come to terms with methods of funding an increase in the size of the system. There were fears that this vacuum in theorizing would result in the familiar conservative plea for harsher penalties.

## The second wave of Left Realism

Left Realism has made attempts to come to terms with the criticisms levelled at the theory as it was initially expressed. In collection of data, analysis, and policy-making there has been considerable revision of the original theory.

In terms of data collection, Left Realists have undertaken a second wave of surveys. They argue that the notion of 'victim surveys' is a misnomer, since they now attempt to deal with a far broader range of issues. Among the new questions considered are those concerning self-report data, public evaluation of police service deliveries, police public encounters, public attitudes to adequate punishment, and avoidance behaviour with respect to some crimes. Left Realists have also retreated from seeing the survey as the sole focus of data collection. They now argue that, while these surveys are important, it is necessary to supplement the data gathered in this manner with other forms of empirical inquiry. Positivist methods of data collection (such as psychological testing, for example) are seen as relevant, along with traditional radical research methods such as case studies and ethnography.

In theory at least, Left Realism has widened the focus beyond exclusive concentration on the offender towards a broader emphasis, which they conceptualize as the square of crime. The square of crime, as we have seen, involves two dyads. The first concerns social control, and comprises police and other agencies of social control on the one hand, and the public on the other. The second concerns the criminal act, and comprises the offender and the victim. The current aim of Left Realism is to address all parts of the square, in that all aspects need to be addressed in theory, research, and policy. Further to this, each aspect should not be taken as a separate entity, as the interaction between each element is crucial to understanding crime and crime control. Crime rates are, according to Left Realists, a product of the four aspects of the square of crime (Young, 1991).

This proposal by Left Realists of the centrality of the 'square of crime' directs attention to the criminal act and its context by its emphasis on four separate but interrelated dimensions: the police, the public, the victim, and the offender. They argue there needs to be analysis of the state and the problems of defining crime within a political system, as the left argues, but there also needs to be realistic account taken of the 'reality' of crime and the offender–victim dyad. This means researching appropriate responses that can address the needs of victims, as well as supporting programmes and policies that both reduce offending before it occurs (crime prevention), and respond effectively when offences do occur.

Left Realism has also broadened its focus in terms of the crimes that are considered of major concern. Recent volumes contain analyses of white-collar offending and issues of gender that are more explicitly brought into the Left Realist fold (Lowman and MacLean, 1992). Importantly, Left Realism has also acknowledged the need to discuss penal reform.

However, much of this writing has not come from the Left Realists themselves, but from authors with particular research interests that are used to 'fill the gaps' of earlier versions of the theory. In addition, those readily identified with Left Realism, such as Roger Matthews (1989) in the case of penal reform, undertake theorizing the suggestions that are mooted do not differ significantly from liberal suggestions in the same area.

Left Realism has then shifted ground from identifying with radical or Marxist criminology to a position that is more easily described as social democratic or liberal. That is, it is more concerned with a reform agenda that deals with the issues of crime and crime control within the current social system than with suggesting that the system itself is the root of the problem and should be changed. In doing so, it borrows heavily from theories and research that are characteristic of the middle ground, such as strain theory, labelling, and certain strands of radical criminology. By shifting ground in this way, Left Realism loses some of its identity and at times becomes indistinguishable from the theories it replaces, or purports to supersede.

## Contemporary Examples

While this section will examine Left Realism in North America, it is important to point out that Left Realism, per se, does not exist as an independent entity within Canada and the United States. Nevertheless, a group of researchers and academics have explored and questioned many of the Left Realist ideas (see DeKeseredy, MacLean, and Schwartz, 1997; Schwartz and DeKeseredy, 1998; DeKeseredy and Schwartz, 2005; DeKeseredy, Schwartz, and Alvi, 2006). Through an exploration of the development of victims' rights advocacy groups, it is possible to see how the main concepts found within Left Realism have developed within North American political policies.

During the 1970s, the women's movement had been instrumental in the emergence of shelters for victims of domestic violence throughout Canada. However, there was still little public or political recognition of the needs of victims of crime. One of the first groups of this type was formed in July 1981 in response to a series of child murders committed by Clifford Olson. Parents of murder victim Daryn Rosenfeldt formed a support group—Parents of BC Murder Victims—to provide a service that was not available to them on any government or community level. This group provided the families with support and gave them an opportunity share their grief and frustrations with the legal process. In September 1981, in response to the murder of a 15-year-old girl in Duncan BC, local residents and politicians formed Citizens United for Safety and Justice. In 1984 the Rosenfeldts took their advocacy campaign for victims' rights to the national level and registered the group Victims of Violence as a national charitable organization.

The movement for victims' rights continued to gain strength throughout Canada during this time. Some groups advocated for legislative changes to reform the parole system while others concentrated on victim impact statements and sentencing reforms. Still other groups turned their attention to the need to provide emotional, practical, and financial support to victims of crime. Concerned citizens, politicians, researchers, and academics were all involved in the victim rights movement. For example, in 1984

Renée Collette, a professor of criminology and former parole officer, along with Micheline Ball, worked with members of various sectors to form the Association Québecois Plaidoyer-Victimes to train Quebec police officers on how best to work with rape victims. They also worked with the Quebec Health and Social Services Department to support victims and to collect data about the needs of victims. This pilot project resulted in the creation of Quebec's Centre d'Aide au Victimes Criminales, a community-based approach to assisting victims (Government of Canada, 2007b).

The movement for victims' rights gained momentum during the 1980s and contributed to the creation and implementation of amendments to the Criminal Code regarding sexual assault, child abduction (which became law on 4 January 1983), and child sexual abuse (which became law on 1 January 1988).

From a Left Realist perspective, it is also important to note that 1982 saw the delivery of *The Canadian Urban Victimization Survey* by the Ministry of the Attorney General. This victimization survey—the first major survey of this nature undertaken in urban Canada—studied the nature and scope of victimization in relation to eight categories of property and personal crime. The Victims Assistance Fund was established in 1987 by the Department of Justice, which allowed all territories and provinces in Canada to develop information, education, and training programmes to improve the delivery of victim services and activities.

Canadians Against Violence Everywhere Advocating its Termination (CAVEAT) was created in the early 1990s with a mandate to focus on education and violence prevention, on victim's rights, and on changes to legislation. This organization was instrumental in increasing national awareness around issues of victims' rights and bringing advocacy organizations together with policy makers and police (Government of Canada, 2007b). CAVEAT hosted two Safety Net conferences with the Canadian Police Association (1994 and 1995); the drafting of recommendations for legislative reforms for all levels of government was one outcome of the conferences. Included in the recommendations were calls for 'truth in sentencing' provisions, tougher sentences for offenders, and increased services for victims of crime.

A successful example of the recommendation for increased services for victims is the 1993 creation of the Canadian Resource Centre for Victims of Crime. The Centre is a non-profit organization supported by the Canadian Professional Police Association, other police organizations, and donors, and it acts as an advocate for victims and survivors of violent crime. The Centre also conducts research and lobbies all levels of governments for changes in legislature and services in this area.

The development of victims' rights advocacy groups provides an example of how Left Realists seek to place 'crime' on the political and academic agenda in a way that recognizes the social and political motives of crime and crime policy. They seek to engage governments in dialogues about reforms in order to reduce the victimization of vulnerable groups.

Interestingly, there is some question as to which political debate needs to be captured. In recent years there has been a re-evaluation of the split between 'left idealism' and 'left realism', in which some argue that the debate was from the beginning fraught with inaccuracies and misleading characterizations (Cottee, 2002; for a response see Cohen and Young, 2004). Similar concerns about accuracy and representation also have been seen in discussions of law-and-order politics and policy in Canada, the United States, and Australia. The political debate in this instance is within criminology itself, and those on the receiving end are the Left Realists. For example, Weatherburn (2002) has argued that researchers such as Brown and Hogg, who are closely identified with Left Realist concerns in Australia, have not taken crime seriously enough and that they do not appreciate fully the seriousness of the crime problem. The latter writers, who have been accused of lack of methodological rigour and political disinterest, have responded with a spirited defence of their empirical work. They also have distanced themselves from a purely 'evidence-driven' policy formation approach, and reaffirmed their commitment to examination of the normative and political nature of law-and-order politics (Indermaur et al., 2002). How debate is carried out is perhaps one of the more salient lessons from our review of Left Realism as a criminological development. The review also highlights the continuing commitment of those willing to translate their concerns about crime into practical forums without necessarily compromising political critique.

## Critique

An adequate critique of Left Realism must encompass both early and later versions in order to get a clear picture of the strengths and weaknesses of the theory as a whole.

It will be remembered that the criticisms of early versions of Left Realism were as follows:

- The theory treated definitions of crime as if they had factual, uncontested meanings.
- The scope of victimization covered by Left Realism was very narrow. It omitted certain offences, most notably white-collar offences, and then presented the results as if this gave a total picture of crime.
- The focus of response was very narrow. The theory was almost exclusively concerned with issues of police and policing style.
- There was a lack of any realistic penal policy. The theory had not considered to any degree how to deal with offenders once they were apprehended.
- Finally, there were concerns, mainly expressed by radical criminologists, that Left Realists accepted the notion that the criminal law could be liberating. Critics argued that the problem in working-class areas was not crime, but community breakdown. This being the case, the criminal law could only exacerbate problems, not ameliorate them.

As stated, Left Realists made a concerted effort to address these problems. In particular, they broadened the scope of their analysis to include white-collar offences in their victim surveys. They also began to look at the issues surrounding an adequate penal policy. Rather than being a narrow, single-issue theory, Left Realism now attempts to look at what it calls the 'square of crime' concerned with both social control and the criminal act, as outlined above—but how successful has this been?

In broadening its focus Left Realism could be said to have lost its defining parameters, and with them any claims for being a separate theoretical entity. Many elements of Left Realism appear in similar form elsewhere: for example, elements of strain theory deal with the formation of antisocial cultures; and liberal forms of criminology also seek to redress the inequities of the system here and now. Left Realism is an eclectic mix of criminological theory of a generally liberal nature, which sees society as based on conflicting, but ultimately not irreconcilable, differences.

There is nothing wrong with an eclectic theory or one based on 'multifactorial explanations'. However, when a theoretical perspective draws together theoretical insights from diverse traditions, the question of compatibility of ideas arises. Left Realism identifies itself with a Marxist tradition; however, this tradition sees attempts to democratize sections of the state apparatus, such as the police, as being linked to wider political strategies that go directly to the heart of who controls production and government in a capitalist society. Indeed, attempts to democratize the police through local councils in the UK kindled the ire of the conservative national government; it responded by substantially reducing the power of local government in that country, effectively neutralizing police reforms. The point is that eclecticism is acceptable if the theory links diverse traditions in a way that is ultimately productive and without irretrievable conflict.

Some would argue that Left Realism has failed to do this. It retains a notion of consensus concerning crime that many would argue is not sustainable. Furthermore, the aims of the theory itself may be incompatible. For example, to enlist the cooperation of police in 'fighting crime' while at the same time attempting an adequate critique of the role of the state in perpetuating crime would be seen by many as a contradiction in terms.

It is notable, therefore, that one of the leading proponents of Left Realism in the UK has in more recent years turned his attention to structural issues rather than those relating to policy implementation as such. Jock Young (1999) appears to have abandoned the quest for pragmatic criminal justice responses in favour of a more sustained analysis and critique in which the dynamics of social exclusion, antagonism, and conflict once again become central. In doing so, Young is also challenging previous approaches that fail to take into account the existential and experiential dimensions of crime. In other words, cultural criminology is accorded an important place in the new understandings of social division, and the world of crime is interpreted in the light of emotional and structural factors (Young, 2003). If this is Left Realism, it is now Left Realism with 'attitude'.

Left Realism correctly identifies the central place of crime in society. People are concerned about crime. Perhaps what this perspective has ignored, though, is the multifaceted nature of that concern. Drawing from Durkheim, it would be possible to argue that this concern reflected, at least in part, anxiety about the state of our society as well as anxiety about the actual chances of victimization. Further, it is this concern that is most amenable to manipulation for political ends. Fears and insecurities about jobs, education, and so on, can be allayed (at least in part) by governments espousing strong law-and-order rhetoric in order to secure their political popularity. This tactic is well illustrated in Australia, as well as in the US and the UK, in recent years.

Nonetheless, Left Realism has contributed positively to the criminological debate. It has reasserted the need to take account of those most affected by crime—the marginalized and the working class. It has sought to take the views of these people seriously and to translate their views into a workable policy agenda. This has been particularly important at a time when 'law-and-order' policies dominate the political debate.

## Conclusion

Left Realism can be seen as a left-wing response to the law-and-order debate dominated predominantly by the Right in politics. As such, it sees itself in contrast to that criminology which sees the discipline as a value-free and neutral exercise. Left Realism identifies itself as part of a socialist strategy to democratize the state apparatus and other areas of social and economic life. Responding to crime is a political process, not a neutral research exercise. However, Left Realists argue that doing something practical in the current environment means much more than simply raising class-consciousness or working for 'the revolution' some time in the future.

Left Realism has stimulated much debate, with most of it from other radical traditions. The response to the criticisms has been for Left Realism to broaden its focus, use a wide range of empirical research, and borrow from other theoretical perspectives in order to 'fill the gaps' of its initially narrow focus. There have been some successes in this attempt, and it has spawned useful debate in the Australian context with the work of the Campaign for Criminal Justice.

In the next chapter we focus on another recent theory that is generally eclectic in nature. In this case, however, the theory starts from a very different philosophical base, that of republicanism.

### Key Terms and Concepts

- Counterculture
- Law-and-order
- Left Realist criminology
- Relative deprivation
- Square of crime
- Victim surveys

### Further Reading

W.S. DeKeseredy, M.D. Schwartz, and S. Alvi, 'Left Realism', in *Current Issues in Critical Criminology*, W.S. DeKeseredy and B. Perry, eds (Lanham, MD: Lexicon Books, 2006).

W.S. DeKeseredy, B.D. MacLean, and M.D. Schwartz, 'Thinking Critically about Left Realism', in *Thinking Critically About Crime*, pp. 19–27, B.D. MacLean and D. Milovanovic, eds (Vancouver, BC: Collective Press, 1997).

R. Hogg, 'Taking Crime Seriously: Left Realism and Australian Criminology', in *Understanding Crime and Criminal Justice*, M. Findlay and R. Hogg, eds, (Sydney: Law Book Company, 1988).

J. Lea, and J. Young, *What Is to Be Done about Law and Order?* (London: Penguin, 1984).

T. O'Reilly-Fleming, ed., *Post-Critical Criminology* (Toronto: Prentice-Hall Canada Inc., 1996).

J. Young, 'The Failure of Criminology: The Need for a Radical Realism', in *Confronting Crime*, R. Matthews and J. Young, eds (London: Sage, 1986).

J. Young, 'Left Realism and the Priorities of Crime Control', in *The Politics of Crime Control*, K. Stenson and D. Cowell, eds (London: Sage, 1991).

J. Young, 'Realist Research as a Basis for Local Criminal Justice Policy', in *Realist Criminology: Crime Control and Policing in the 1990s*, J. Lowman and B. MacLean, eds (Toronto: University of Toronto Press, 1992).

J. Young, *The Exclusive Society: Social Exclusion, Crime and Difference in Late Modernity* (London: Sage, 1999).

## Websites

*www.acjnet.org/victims.* The Victims of Crime website provides a source of information about dealing with the consequences of becoming a victim.

*www.crcvc.ca.* The Canadian Resource Centre for Victims of Crime advocates for individuals and families who were victims of crime.

*www.justice.gc.ca/en/ps/voc.* Policy Centre for Victim Issues is a Department of Justice website with information on federal programmes and initiatives dealing with victims of violence.

*www.raggedclaws.com/criticalrealism.* An independent website for the study and promotion of critical realism.

*www.statcan.ca.* A government website that provides statistical information on a variety of topics including crime rates and types of crime.

## Films/Documentaries

- *Cottonland* (National Film Board of Canada, 2006)
- *Donna's Story* (National Film Board of Canada, 2001)
- *Fix: The Story of an Addicted City* (National Film Board of Canada, 2002)
- *Learning Peace: A Big School with a Big Heart* (National Film Board of Canada, 2001)
- *The Honour of All: The Story of Alkali Lake* (The Four Worlds Development Project and Phil Lucas Productions, 1986)
- *Zero Tolerance* (National Film Board of Canada, 2006)

## Discussion Questions

1. What are the main concepts found within a Left Realist perspective? How are these different from Marxist criminological understandings of causes of crime?
2. What is meant by the term 'relative deprivation'? Can you come up with examples to explain what is meant by this term and how it might impact criminal activity?
3. In your opinion, has Left Realism contributed to our understanding of the need for victim support after a crime has been committed? If yes, how has it contributed? If no, where has Left Realism failed?
4. What contributions has Left Realism made to the field of criminology? Provide examples to support your answers.
5. What is meant by the square of crime? How has this concept impacted how crime is viewed? Provide examples to support your answer.

# CHAPTER 10

# Restorative Justice

## Objectives

This chapter will help you develop an understanding of the:

- fundamental concepts found within **restorative justice** approaches;
- historical and political contexts in the development of restorative justice approaches;
- influence that restorative justice approaches have had on the criminal justice system;
- fundamental concepts found within peacekeeping criminology; and
- strengths and weaknesses found within restorative justice approaches, including peacekeeping criminology.

## Introduction

This chapter discusses the restorative justice perspective of criminal justice. As a relatively new theoretical perspective, restorative justice draws upon a wide range of concepts and trends that we have previously examined. The strength of a restorative justice perspective is that it provides a holistic view of crime and society. With respect to this view, the theory seeks to move away from a punitive model of justice and to reform or reshape our ways of thinking about crime in accordance with the ideals of individual and community healing and the restoration of peace and harmony.

## Social Context

Some criminological theories commence with a broad conception of the society we live in and what the society as a whole should be striving to achieve. Such theories usually begin with a theory of society, and a vision of 'the good'. Within the radical framework (Marxist and feminist theory), for example, society is characterized by profound inequalities, such as poverty, racism, sexism, and other exploitative situations created by imbalances of power. The solution sought is for a revolutionary change in the core structures and nature of society generally, requiring collective mobilization for change. There is an attempt to raise the consciousness of those most affected by the discriminatory actions of the capitalist state, to expose the evils and injustices built into the system, and to expand democratic participation and economic redistribution.

Conservative theories (New Right and other populist versions of this) also start with a conception of society as a whole. Here society is characterized as comprising self-interested individuals, some of whom are particularly evil or bad. This perspective asserts that crime results as a consequence of the disorder in society. It therefore seeks to re-establish discipline, order, and authority. The aim is to restore society to the way things used to be; in this sense, it often appeals to a mythical 'golden age'. The theories argue that the society requires a strong state that will assert its authority in a moral way, in order to maintain the free economy. In this system, law and order must take precedence over justice. The focus is on 'street crime' and crimes committed by the less powerful; for example, social security fraud. Crime is seen to result from a breakdown in the societal moral fibre, hence the stress on morality, liberty, and authority.

As we saw, Left Realism emerged as a response to the conservative backlash of the 1980s. This perspective has tended, however, to move away from a theory of society per se (i.e., based upon socialist principles) to focus specifically on crime, which is viewed as a problem that needs to be taken seriously. There has been a consequent shift away from the big picture (that is, structural causes) to focus on specific issues, such as the victims of crime and the effects of crime on the less powerful—the working class, the poor, Blacks, females, etc. It is argued that because the community is concerned about crime, the focus should be on fighting crime at the local level, and the main concern is with developing an effective form of policing that is responsible, responsive, and democratic.

The conservative push to get tough on offenders through concerted law-and-order campaigns spurred the particular response adopted by the Left Realists. Restorative justice, likewise, is a response to the conservative push of the last two decades (see Braithwaite and Pettit, 1990). Many conservatives were critical of the crime prevention strategies of treatment and **rehabilitation** being pursued by the positivists in dealing with offenders. The retributivists claimed treatment, rehabilitation, and preventive measures had not worked, and had in some instances been grossly unjust. They pointed to cases where indeterminate sentences had been wrongly applied (e.g., in the US, a juvenile offender making obscene phone calls was put into detention for six years). They highlighted the injustice and futility of strategies adopted by the preventivists, who sought to rehabilitate and deter offenders through incapacitation. The retributivists called for punishment of the offender in accordance with their 'just deserts' —that is, offenders should get what they deserve in proportion to the gravity of the offence and the culpability of the offender.

Retributivists have tended to focus on sentencing. The notion is that we must change the way in which we sentence people, because treatment is not working. Braithwaite and Pettit (1990) challenged the retributivist perspective on a variety of levels. They argued that a theory of criminal justice must cover a broad range of issues. A comprehensive theory is required to cover such things as what should be criminalized, what guidelines should cover police surveillance, what initiatives should be possible in the pursuit of offenders, what procedures should be followed in prosecution and adjudication, and what the sentences imposed for given offences should be.

Braithwaite and Pettit (1990) argued that the retributivist theory does not address these questions adequately and, instead, focuses solely on sub-questions. They argue that if a theory deals only with questions of sentencing, as the retributivist theory does, then any initiatives taken in respect to this area of the justice system are likely to flow on and affect other parts of the system. Hence, they argue that we cannot simply tinker with only one part of the system: we need to look at the system as a whole.

They are critical as well of other goal-oriented approaches such as utilitarianism—a system that suggests we should promote the greatest good for the greatest number, because injustices can lead to good for the greatest number. They are also critical of the sole goal of the criminal justice system being that of crime prevention, because this can lead to increased intrusiveness, such as holding parents totally responsible for their children's actions.

The alternative theory proposed by Pettit and Braithwaite is known as **republican theory** and may be considered a particular model of restorative justice (Braithwaite and Pettit, 1990; Pettit and Braithwaite, 1993). From a republican point of view, the causes of crime lie in a combination of social and psychological factors. Part of the problem is the lack of a self-sanctioning conscience. This is where an individual has not learned adequately the interpretation and acceptance of societal norms as being right and just. One of the results of a punitive and stigmatizing system is that it propels people into associating with other similarly ostracized individuals (for instance, in a criminal subculture) who individually and collectively do not develop this conscience.

The response to crime in a specific sense is to utilize the least restrictive measures possible, and to undo the wrong that has been committed. The republican theory of criminal justice is intended to deal with the victim so they can once again exercise public dominion and the community can be reassured. The focus is on maximizing personal dominion for the victim. However, there is also the assumption that the offender should be reintegrated so that their dominion also can be reinstated. The theory seeks a minimalist response on the part of the state to the offender. A reintegrative equilibrium needs to be established where the victim, the community, and the offender are considered.

The republican response to crime therefore bases itself on the concept of **reintegrative shaming**. This involves a process in which the offender is shamed for their action, but is not 'cast out' as a person. It describes a process whereby the offender is publicly rebuked for the harm they have caused, but is then forgiven and reintegrated into the mainstream of society. As part of the reintegrative shaming process, the victim is directly involved in proceedings and is able to be compensated in some way for the harm done. As Braithwaite states:

> Shaming is more pregnant with symbolic content than punishment. Punishment is a denial of confidence in the morality of the offender by reducing norm compliance to a crude cost-benefit calculation; shaming can be a reaffirmation of the morality of the offender by expressing personal disappointment that the offender should do something so out of character, and, if the shaming is reintegrative, by expressing personal satisfaction in seeing the character of the offender restored. Punishment erects barriers between the offender and punisher through transforming the relationship into one of power assertion and injury; shaming produces a greater interconnectedness between the parties, albeit a painful one, and interconnectedness which can produce the repulsion of stigmatization or the establishment of a potentially more positive relationship following reintegration (in Van Ness and Strong, 1997: 117).

From a crime prevention perspective, steps should be taken to promote valued norms (which, in turn, become the basis for the formation of a self-sanctioning conscience) and to foster greater communitarianism by enhancing educational, work, and social opportunities. The criminal justice system ought to incorporate a broad range of informal and more formal institutional arrangements, such as conferences of the offender and victims, and be oriented towards the least intrusive kind of intervention possible.

## Historical Development

The historical development of restorative justice approaches in Canada has strong roots to both the Aboriginal community and to the social changes that occurred in Canada during the 1970 and 1980s. During this time period there was considerable academic, public, and political debate about whether the adversarial model did, or could, lead to lower crime rates and increased public safety. Critics argued that the justice system had not succeeded in either endeavour and pointed to high crime rates and high rates of incarceration as clear indicators of the continued failure of an adversarial system of justice to bring about positive change (Garland, 2001).

Critics also pointed to the significant over-representation of Aboriginals in the prison system as another failure and argued that the limits of the justice system were particularly acute for Aboriginal peoples. Aboriginal leaders began to create and implement restorative justice initiatives in an attempt to deal with a significant need for spiritual and emotional healing within their communities. These initiatives often reinforce and extend the influence of traditional healing and spiritual practices for the community (Solicitor General of Canada, 2002).

A crime against an individual has an impact on the whole community because everyone is connected through relationships and through belief and value systems based on connections with land, animals, and spirits. In some communities, the extended family or clan must repair a crime committed by an individual, and amends must be made to all other families or clans (Law Commission of Canada, 2003: 28).

The development of victims' rights organizations also contributed to the debate on the viability of an adversarial justice system. These organizations voiced concerns that victims were excluded from the court process, had little or no input into decisions regarding how their cases were processed, and lacked access to information about what happened to offenders as they progressed through the correctional system (Law Commission of Canada, 1999). In response to these concerns, legislative changes were made to the justice system to meet the needs of victims of crime and to allow them greater participation in the criminal justice system (Roach, 2000). In the words of Wilma Derksen (2002):

As victims we know the power of truth to hold the offender accountable. We know we have the right to feel angry and to give the person who has hurt us a piece of our mind. . .We need to remember that justice isn't only about giving a stolen five-dollar bill back to the person from whom it was stolen. It is about mending the broken relationship and restoring trust. Violent crime is about hurting someone physically, spiritually, and emotionally. Crime steals from us our safety, our dignity, and our trust. Therefore to do real justice, it is more than simply establishing who did the crime and compensating the victim; it is about restoring the safety, dignity and trust (103).

The development of a social movement that advocated the return to local decision-making and the use of community justice also contributed to the move towards restorative justice initiatives to deal with criminal behaviour. Advocates of community-based justice posited that a reform of the criminal justice system could not ameliorate the shortcomings of an adversarial system that treated everyone as equal and homogenous and that did not recognize the reality of diversity and power differences (Shonholtz, 1984). According to advocates of community justice, the state views conflict as negative and as something that needs to be controlled; this negates the opportunity to dialogue freely about conflicting values that are often at the core of conflicts. Advocates claim that community-based justice initiatives may encourage a peaceful expression of conflict while building respect for community and encouraging the community to take responsibility for problem-solving (Christie, 1993).

Debate was also occurring in the political arena during this time. The Canadian Sentencing Commission undertook an exploration of the criminal sentencing process in Canada in the 1980s, and as a result of this study, the Commission recommended that the Canadian government implement a two-prong reform strategy in which the first step was to adopt a 'just deserts' model of sentencing. A strict system of guidelines would also be created with offences ranked according to severity with each offence having a presumptive sentence attached. According to the Canadian Sentencing Commission, this approach would create a system of sentencing based on proportionality and the most important factor would be the gravity of the offence. Under this model, proportional punishment is viewed as the measure of true justice (Law Commission of Canada, 2003).

However, unlike many countries, Canada did not fully embrace or adopt the 'just deserts' model. A parliamentary committee, headed by MP David Daubnesy, was mandated to address the recommendations put forward by the Canadian Sentencing Commission. Instead of embracing the recommendations, Daubnesy's committee encouraged Parliament to explore alternatives to imprisonment. Importantly, these alternatives included the use of restorative justice.

Therefore, restorative justice approaches aim to integrate the needs of both victims and offenders within the same system and to develop policies whereby the offender makes reparations for wrongdoing, and in doing so restores both the victim's and the general population's faith in society. Conceptually, restorative justice sees crime, fundamentally, as a violation of people and interpersonal relationships, and the point of action is to seek to heal and put right the wrongs (Zehr, 1990). The justice process, in this framework, is seen rightly to belong to the community, rather than exclusively to the state. The emphasis is on reparation of harm to victims, addressing the offender's needs and competencies, and sending offenders a message of disapproval about the impact of the crime (Bazemore, 1997).

Translated into specific assumptions and principles, the restorative justice lens can be usefully summarized as being based upon three interrelated propositions (Zehr and Mika, 1998):

- *Crime is fundamentally a violation of people and interpersonal relationships.* The key issue is that victims and the community have been harmed and are in need of restoration. Importantly, victims, offenders, and the affected communities are seen as the key stakeholders in justice and, as such, ought to be directly involved in the justice process.
- *Violations create obligations and liabilities.* It is felt that the offenders' obligations are to make things right as much as possible for the harm they have caused. However, it is also argued that the community's obligations are to victims, to offenders, and for the general welfare of its members. Obligations are thus both individual and collective in nature.
- *Restorative justice seeks to heal and put right the wrong.* The starting point for justice is the need of victims for information, validation, vindication, **restitution**, testimony, safety, and support. The process of justice ought to maximize the opportunities for exchange of information, participation, dialogue, and mutual consent between victim and offender, and the justice process ought to belong to the community. The offenders' needs and competencies also are to be addressed. In the end, justice needs to be mindful of the outcomes, intended and unintended, of its responses to crime and victimization.

## Box 10.1 Objectives and Values of Restorative Justice

| The Objectives of Restorative Justice | The Values of Restorative Justice |
| --- | --- |
| The Commission believes there are five objectives that restorative justice processes ought to strive for: | The Commission believes there are five values that restorative justice processes possess: |
| <ul><li>delineating and denunciating unacceptable behaviours,</li><li>supporting victims,</li><li>reforming individual offenders through active responsibility-taking,</li><li>restoring community order and peace, and</li><li>identifying restorative, forward-looking outcomes.</li></ul> | <ul><li>participation,</li><li>respect for all participants,</li><li>community empowerment,</li><li>commitment to agreed outcomes, and</li><li>flexibility and responsiveness of process and outcomes.</li></ul> |

From *Transforming Relationships Through Participatory Justice* (Ottawa, ON: Law Commission of Canada, 2003).

There are various specific models of restorative justice, ranging from, for example, circle sentencing, family group conferencing, and reparative probation through to victim–offender mediation, which will be discussed in detail later in this chapter (see

Bazemore, 1997, 1998; Wright, 1991). Each model has different key objectives—from citizen involvement to meeting victims' needs—each shaping the manner in which restorative justice is institutionalized in practice. Generally speaking, however, each programme or model tends to focus on the 'victim', the 'offender', and the 'community', and each attempts to respond to the immediate harm, and to the specific situation and individuals that are linked by a particular criminal harm. Some approaches are based upon moral categories (e.g., reintegrative shaming) where the aim is to shame the offence, while offering forgiveness to the offender (Braithwaite, 1989). Others are based upon strategic assessments of offenders and events (e.g., balanced restorative approach), in which case the aim is to design interventions that best address issues of offender accountability, competency development, and community safety (Bazemore, 1991; Bilchik, 1998). Some approaches focus almost exclusively on meeting victim needs (usually via some method of restitution or compensation involving the offender); others place emphasis on widespread community engagement in dealing with underlying problems and issues, of which specific offending is but one manifestation.

## Contemporary Examples

As previously discussed, the failure of the adversarial justice system to lower crime rates and alleviate public fears, combined with a growing concern about the over-representation of Aboriginals in the criminal justice system, and the rise of victims' rights organizations and community-based justice initiatives contributed to the development of restorative justice in Canada. Initially many of the initiatives were developed outside of any precise legislative framework. However, in the last three decades, a series of court decisions and legislative initiatives have provided parameters for the inclusion of restorative justice initiatives in the criminal justice system.

The most commonly used forms of restorative justice within Canada can be classified under four different types. However, it is important to recognize that overlap does occur between these types and that many organizations involved in restorative justice initiatives incorporate more than one type of initiative in their programmes.

### Victim-offender mediation (VOM) and Victim-offender reconciliation programmes (VORPs)

These two models of restorative justice are among the earliest initiatives undertaken in Canada and they share the common characteristic of bringing the victim and offender together, in the presence of a trained mediator, to give both parties the opportunity to determine the best way of responding to the harm done by the conflict. Referrals to mediation may take place at any of the four points in the processing of a criminal event: (1) pre-charge, or the police-entry point; (2) post-charge but pre-trial, or the Crown-entry point; (3) at the sentencing stage, or the court-entry point; or lastly (4) following incarceration and before release, or the corrections-entry point.

The Fraser Region Community Justice Initiative Association provides an example of an organization that provides restorative justice initiatives to individuals involved with the criminal justice system. The Association, created in 1985, is a multi-programme organization that works with the criminal justice system, educational institutions, businesses, and community centres to provide mediation training within a framework that includes material development and a practicum-based curriculum. The Association also began, in 1990, to provide a post-incarceration victim–offender mediation programme that focuses on accountability, healing, and closure issues for those involved in criminal offences. One of the oldest and most successful programmes offered by the Fraser Region Community Justice Initiative Association, the victim–offender reconciliation programme, was suspended in 2004 because of a lack of funding.

Community and family group conferencing, which was created and implemented in New Zealand to originally deal with youth justice processes, are now extensively used in Canada. The focus for this form of restorative justice is usually broader than that found in victim–offender mediation or victim–offender reconciliation programmes. Within this model, a trained coordinator invites family and/or friends of both the victim and offender to meet and discuss appropriate ways of addressing the offending behaviour, to determine the desired outcomes for the families or community, and to identify reparative elements that may be needed. The group then also develops a plan for how to monitor the future behaviour of the offender.

An example of this type of initiative is the Calgary Community Conferencing programme, which began in 1998 as a part-time initiative of Calgary's Youth Probation Services. It has since developed into a partnership with Calgary Family Services, Calgary Police Services, John Howard Society, Mennonite Central Committee, and the Calgary Board of Education. The mandate of Calgary Community Conferencing is to bring together youth and their family and/or supporters, with anyone who has been affected the young person's wrongful act. Preparatory meetings are held with each member affected and by working together an agreement is developed and implemented on how to best deal with the situation. The number of youth referred to Calgary Community Conferencing continues to grow.

Sentencing circles operate within many Canadian communities and allow a multitude of individuals to participate in a healing process for the victim, the offender, and the community. Victims, offenders, community elders, court officials, and other community members meet to discuss the consequences of the offence and to explore ways of resolving the conflict. Restitution to the victim and the **reintegration** of the offender into the community are high priorities for sentencing circles. Some circles operate within the formal justice system and provide an alternative to conventional processes while others are used if cases are diverted from the justice system into alternative measure programmes (Law Commission of Canada, 2003).

The Community Council Program hosted by the Aboriginal Legal Services of Toronto provides offenders an opportunity to participate in this kind of restorative justice initiative. The Aboriginal Legal Services of Toronto was formed in 1990 to 'strengthen the capacity of the Aboriginal community and its citizens to deals with justice issues and provide Aboriginal controlled and culturally based justice alternatives' (Aboriginal Legal Services of Toronto, 2007). Programmes that the Aboriginal Legal Services of Toronto are involved with include a court worker programme, a legal clinic, Gladue court, victim's rights, and law reform and advocacy for Aboriginal peoples.

## Box 10.2  Mandate of Aboriginal Legal Services of Toronto's Community Council Program.

The Community Council is a project that allows the Aboriginal community of Toronto to take a measure of control over the manner that the criminal justice system deals with Aboriginal offenders. It is a variation on the diversion concept in use with young offenders. With a diversion, an accused person who admits responsibility with respect to the charge(s) they face does not go to court or get a criminal record for the particular offence(s). Rather they receive an alternative type disposition such as counselling, treatment, restitution etc.

The Community Council Program takes the diversion concept and applies it to adult criminal offenders. The system works as follows: the ALST Criminal Court Workers, the Coordinator or Director approach a Senior Crown Attorney when they see a Aboriginal accused that may be an appropriate candidate for the Community Council. Referrals come from defense/duty counsel, Aboriginal and non-Aboriginal agencies, clients and their families and many other sources. The decision on whether a person can be helped by the Council depends solely on the resources available in the community—not on any particular character-istic of the offence.

The Crown reviews the facts of the case and decides whether it is appro-priate that the case goes before the Council. Decisions by the Crown are made on a case-by-case basis but the fact that the accused person might go to jail if convicted will not prevent the matter from being diverted. In fact, individuals who have already been to jail are one of the Council's target groups and make up most of those diverted.

If the Crown consents to the diversion, the offender is approached and asked if they wish to go before the Council. Since the Council cannot decide guilt or innocence, the accused person must first admit that they are responsible, to some degree, for their charge(s). Before the individual decides whether they wish to go before the Council, they are required to consult with defense/duty coun-sel. Counsel will explain the Community Council process, including potential dis-positions the individual may face at a Council hearing and the penalties for not complying with a Council decision. Counsel will also stress to individuals that if they feel they are not guilty of the offence then they should try for an acquittal in court. If the accused person agrees to go before the Council, the charge(s) against him or her are stayed or withdrawn by the Crown Attorney.

A Council hearing will usually have three people serving. The Council will reach its decision by consensus and only the individuals involved with the offence themselves discuss their cases with the Council. Where the offence involves a victim, every effort is made to encourage victim participation in the hearing.

The role of the Community Council is to begin the healing process necessary to reintegrate the individual into the community. In deciding how best to accomplish this healing, the Council will make a decision requiring the individual to do certain things. Any option, except jail, is available to them in making this decision. Some options include counselling, restitution, community service, treatment suggestions or a combination of the above. If an individual does not comply with the decision of the Council they are required to reappear before the Council to explain their lack of action. In addition, a person who fails to comply with a Council decision is not allowed into the Community Council if they are arrested again. The charge(s) are not relaid if a person does not comply with a Council decision other than in exceptional circumstances. The charge(s) can be brought back by the Crown Attorney if the individual fails to appear for the Council hearing itself.

The concept of the Community Council is not new. This is the way justice was delivered in Aboriginal communities in Central and Eastern Canada for centuries before the arrival of Europeans to North America. It is also the way that disputes continue to be informally resolved in many reserve communities across the country. The idea behind the Community Council Program is that the Aboriginal community best know how to reach Aboriginal offenders. We know that the dominant justice system does nothing but provide a revolving door from the street to the jail and back again for most Aboriginal accused. The programme has been operational since March of 1992 and our experience is that the Community Council process is more relevant and meaningful to offenders. It is our hope that the Council can serve to reduce the recidivism rate among Aboriginal offenders.

From Aboriginal Legal Services of Toronto, *Mandate of Aboriginal Legal Services of Toronto's Community Council Program*. 2007. Available at http://www.aboriginallegal.ca/program.

Community boards or panels are comprised of volunteers from the community who meet formally with victims and offenders with the goal of facilitating a discussion on the appropriate outcomes for a successful resolution of conflict. These boards or panels may be used as a pre-charge diversion from the formal criminal justice system, or after a guilty plea has been entered as an alternative means of determining an appropriate sentence.

The Whitehorse Youth Justice Panel, the first of its kind, was implemented in 2001 and is a post-charge interagency screening programme for young offenders. The goals of the Panel are embodied in the restorative justice principles of the Youth Criminal Justice Act and include increasing the number of referrals of youth to extra-judicial measures, reducing court-processing times, reducing custody committals, and building partnerships in an effort to enhance family and community capacity to repair harm (Stuart and Eakins, 2003).

Restorative justice programmes also take place in prison and work with incarcerated individuals to prepare them for reintegration and participation in society upon their release. Examples include the establishment of a Restorative Justice and Dispute Resolution Branch created by Correctional Services of Canada to provide advice and support in the coordination of restorative justice and dispute resolution processes. Several penitentiaries have also incorporated restorative justice initiatives into their programming and have worked with inmates, community members, and staff to create Restorative Justice Coalitions to provide educational initiatives to inmates.

It is also interesting to note how collaboration between the Mennonite Central Committee and Correctional Services Canada provides a strong example of how faith communities have become involved in the implementation of restorative justice initiatives. This collaboration a resulted in the creation of Circles of Support and Accountability, a programme that provides high-risk sexual offenders with circle support from small groups of community volunteers. The goal of this programme includes recognition of the need to help communities respond to the needs of high-risk sex offenders who are released at the end of their sentence.

As we can see, there are differences under the restorative justice umbrella between those who see restorative justice as, essentially, a form of diversion from the formal criminal justice system, and those who view it as a potential alternative to that system and thus as something that could supplant the existing system in total (Bazemore and Walgrave, 1999). Whatever the specific differences, it appears that the central thread underlying restorative justice is the spirit within which 'justice' is undertaken—the intent and outcomes of the process are meant to be primarily oriented towards repairing harm that has been caused by a crime, and this means working to heal victims, offenders and communities that have been directly injured by the crime (Zehr and Mika, 1998; Bazemore and Walgrave, 1999; Zehr and Toews, 2004).

In recent years a new way of examining issues of crime, violence, and victimization based on the principles of restoration and reparation has emerged and is known as **peacemaking criminology**. This perspective challenges the historical focus of the criminal justice system comprised of police, courts, and corrections, and their concentration on the detection and control of individuals or groups engaged in criminal activity. This model of crime control is reflected in an adversarial position where only one side—either crime control or crime itself—can emerge victorious. Recently however, peacemaking criminology has emerged to provide a new way of looking at crime and the criminal justice system.

It is argued in the peacekeeping criminology perspective that the criminal justice system fails at every level. The criminal justice system represents a state-sanctioned means of inflicting pain under the guise of reducing criminal activity and, yet, the imposition of punishment and repression never solves—and never will solve—social problems. The basic philosophy is that society cannot solve violence or human suffering with more violence and more human suffering. Instead, it is argued that humanistic and restorative principles need to be adopted at the level of dealing with the offender, and in dealing with wider social conflicts as well. The emphasis is on transformative strategies that are themselves premised upon participatory forms of conflict resolution. As John Fuller (1998) states:

From a peacemaking perspective, this involvement of the offenders and the victims in the process can do much toward revitalizing the trust citizens have in their ability to govern themselves. When the victim and offender are pawns in the games played by the courtroom work group they become disenfranchised. When mandatory sentences are decided by the legislature, the criminal justice practitioners also become distanced and alienated from the process. In our rush to remove discretion from the criminal court system, we have also removed the attachments that bond individuals to the process and the outcomes. From a peacemaking perspective, what is needed is a way to bring people back into the system (121).

Drawing upon various peacemaking traditions—such as religious, humanistic, and feminist approaches to understanding and responding to violence—peacemaking criminology criticizes models of interaction based upon the idea of winners and losers. Instead, and in contrast, the approach speaks about openness, trust, and cooperation (Moyer, 2001). In many cases, it is argued that, literally, peace begins at home; that is, it is important that each individual lives their everyday life based upon love, forgiveness, kindness, and hope (see, for example, Quinney, 1991). These principles and concepts are also pertinent to developing a critique of a society that is class-divided, racist, and sexist, and that predominantly operates on the basis of power, domination, exploitation, and control over others. Richard Quinney and John Wildeman (1991) provide a succinct summary of the foundation of peacemaking criminology with these words:

> (1) thought of the Western rational mode is conditional, limiting knowledge primarily to what is already known; (2) each life is a spiritual journey into the unknown and the unknowable, beyond the ego-centered self; (3) human existence is characterized by suffering; crime is suffering; and the sources of suffering are within each of us; (4) through love and compassion, beyond the ego-centered self, we can end suffering and live in peace, personally and collectively; (5) crime can be ended only with the ending of suffering, only when there is peace and social justice; and (6) understanding, service, justice—all these—flow naturally from love and compassion, from mindful attention to the reality of all that is, here and now. A criminology of peacemaking —a non-violent criminology of compassion and service—seeks to end suffering and thereby eliminate crime (31).

Peacemaking criminologists propose that the solution to social problems, including crime, rests on as series of undertakings that include the creation of communities of caring people, the creation and implementation of universal social justice, and the reduction of hierarchical structures. Particular prominence is given to the importance of human transformations and the need for spiritual rejuvenation and inner peace that will allow people to both practice empathy to others less fortunate and to respond to the needs of others. Peacemaking criminology posits that this human transformation must occur in both the economic and authority structures. People must not only become more connected with the well-being of others, but social institutions must also be modified to emphasize the same concerns (Williams, III and McShane, 2004).

Additionally, the composition of the economic structure has to be modified in such a way that it discourages competition and a focus on individual gains. People must cooperate and work together, instead of against each other. As members of a community develop the capacity to work together and cooperate to meet each other's needs, peacemaking criminologists contend that an even greater level of understanding and compassion will develop in the community. This, in turn, will facilitate the development of interpersonal cohesion that will serve to limit and control violence. In relation to the development of community cohesion, peacemaking theorists also believe that the criminal justice system (police, courts, and corrections) must undergo a transformation that will allow for much greater community involvement. An example of this transformation at work is the development of a community-policing orientation that has been implemented in police departments across Canada and the United States. Community policing provides a method for bringing police and citizens together to manage conflict and defend against violence and crime. Peacemaking practitioners maintain that this approach facilitates an opportunity for citizens and police to work together to ensure that citizens have greater input and control over how interpersonal disputes are handled.

Rather than using punishment, peacemaking criminologists advocate the use of mediation and conflict resolution when dealing with criminal justice issues. New Age principles may also be utilized as a means of encouraging human transformations. In 'Correctional Treatment, Peacemaking, and the New Age Movement' Bartollas and Braswell (1993) apply New Age principles to correctional treatments. They argue that most offenders have suffered from abusive, deprived childhoods and

> [t]reatment that focuses on the inner child and such qualities as forgiveness and self-esteem could benefit offenders. Some New Age teachings tempered by the ancient spiritual traditions may offer offenders the hope they can create a future that brings greater fulfillment than their past. This changed future may include growing out of the fear of victimization, becoming more positive and open to possibilities, viewing one's self with more confidence and humility, understanding the futility of violence, and attaining emotional and financial sufficiency (52).

In essence, peacemaking criminologists posit that is essential for people to first transform themselves before they can enact world transformation. Lozoff and Braswell (1989) express the same sentiments: 'And the message is clear: without peace, within us and in our actions, there can be no peace in our results. Peace is the way' (11).

One of the key challenges of peacemaking criminology has been to translate a philosophy of 'being nice' into the practical realities of actual conflicts and instances in which social harm is occurring. To put it differently, how does one move beyond expressing the sentiments of compassion and empathy to concretely addressing real sites of conflict? The recent work of McEvoy (2003) provides an answer for part of this question. Based upon grounded interventions with paramilitary groups in Northern Ireland, McEvoy (2003) argues that a 'new' peacemaking criminology might include:

- an explicit focus on jurisdictions where actual political or ethnic conflicts are occurring;
- a recognition of the idea that political engagement is necessary and that conflict transformation be based upon the objective of trying to make a difference;
- a substantive engagement with human rights discourses, particularly as a counter-weight to those sorts of moral relativism that can impede practical intervention; and
- a reframing of the evaluation of 'what works' into a political rather than a technical exercise, thereby acknowledging the profound transformations in individuals, groups, and communities that peacemaking criminology, somewhat ambitiously, wishes to make manifest (2003).

An important observation of peacemaking criminology, generally, is that very often war and the war on crime are interlinked and share many of the same attributes and institutional dynamics. Philosophically, and increasingly at a practical level of intervention, peacemaking criminologists wish to challenge violence, repression, and humiliation as preferred modes of conflict resolution—whether this be at the level of individuals, groups, families, communities, or nation-states. Conversely, drawing upon human rights discourses and restorative justice activities, such as community mediation, and by stressing the positive value of non-violent alternatives and the vital need to address the material reasons for social differences, peacemaking criminology aims to transform social settings in more profound ways than traditional criminal justice approaches. Peacemaking criminology suggests the possibilities of both a normative theory of crime, war, and violence, and the potential practices that might reflect and reinforce the restorative justice ethos.

## Critique

A number of criticisms can be levelled at restorative justice. One weakness of the theory is that it does not really look at the causes of crime. What it does do is provide a whole range of variables that are associated with crime, at the level of both the individual (interdependency) and society (communitarianism). The theory thus provides a description of 'background' characteristics of the 'typical offender' (e.g., young, unemployed, male, transient) without really exploring how these factors interact with the given environment that leads to offending.

It is one thing to link variables by way of association to an underlying construct, but it is quite another to map out, in any given society, how each is ordered, and what the 'flow' of the variables is. It is important to do this in order to explain why some parts of society are more vulnerable to crime, and in particular to locate the individual offender within society in a way that provides a meaningful explanation for the pressures to offend. Thus far restorative justice perspectives, including republican theory have tended to remain at the level of description when dealing with the way the world actually is, with the theory outlined in its fullest extent with respect to some notion of an ideal society.

When dealing with a less than ideal society, further problems arise. The notion of exercising self-control and the concept of the self-sanctioning conscience raise a number of questions when they are applied to a society that has a great divide between rich and poor. The theory assumes that individuals make incorrect choices that ultimately lead to their criminal behaviour. However, if the social and economic world of the individual is falling apart, the offender is obviously in a difficult situation. The theory has little to say about the structural characteristics of the young offenders being targeted. How does the family group conference or other arenas that flow from restorative justice aim to take account of these issues? The policies that have been suggested thus far appear unable to deal with real clashes of interest between wealth and poverty, issues of racism, and the wider issues of class structure. The policies emanating from the theory do not address the degree to which young people may be brought into the system because of institutional biases, such as police bias, or bias in the decision-making of the courts.

These problems arise partly because the theory works on the idea of a presumed consensus within society. In particular, there is a consensus concerning the nature of criminal activity: crimes are those predatory acts that are accepted by all as criminal. From previous chapters we have seen that many would argue with this. The concern is that the definition of crime and the application of criminal law are subject to political interests; as a result, both the definition and the application are biased. The theory does not take adequate account of these biases within the system itself.

The translation of theory into practice, and of understanding into action, is more transparent and integral to republican theory than has been, to date, generally demonstrated in peacemaking criminology. However, in the case of republican theory the notion of reintegrative shaming also raises a number of issues. It is not clear from the model which element comes first: effective shaming or low crime rates. It may be that low crime rates are a precondition for the success of a criminal justice process that relies on shaming a transgressor so they do not reoffend. Following on from this, it is possible to argue that it may not be possible to shame successfully in a society that is low on communitarianism. Put another way, if an offender was never integrated into society in the first place, it makes no sense to 'reintegrate' that person. Reintegrative shaming loses its meaning when faced with someone who is marginalized from society and not repentant in the least.

The difficulties of trying to 'repair the harm' in the context of social disintegration and inequality have been implicitly acknowledged in other types of restorative justice approaches. For instance, rather than being based upon a concept of 'shaming', the balanced restorative approach is based upon a 'balanced' assessment of the offender's needs and competencies (Bazemore, 1991). This approach relies not so much on what is essentially a moral category (shaming), but rather on situational assessment (involving close scrutiny of offender capabilities). As such, it attempts to explore the specific requirements related to each case of offending and to variably respond to each offender in terms of their immediate situation and capacities. Such an approach appears to offer more scope in dealing with issues relating to the marginalization and alienation experienced by young offenders in particular.

Problems also arise with the way shaming works in practice. For example how, in practice, do we distinguish between reintegrative shaming and stigmatization? It may be that a wider form of stigmatization occurs because so many more people are involved in situations such as the juvenile conference. There are further problems with the concept of shaming and compliance, in that there is a need to distinguish between compliance with what the group wants, which is not internalized, and conformity, which is internalized (Potter, 1992). Presumably, the ideal is for shaming to lead to changes internal to the individual that will reduce the chance of future offending. Shaming, then, is ultimately a concept that is internal to the individual, and yet the theory does not detail how successful shaming is to be measured, so that we can avoid stigmatization or mere external compliance, both of which may lead to future offending.

Furthermore, the notion of shaming is used with certain types of offenders, mainly young people. There is little discussion regarding the success or otherwise of reintegrative shaming as it might be applied to white-collar offenders. There are yet other crimes, state crimes for example, that do not lend themselves easily to the concept of reintegrative shaming, which focuses on individual transgressions.

It can also be argued that the practical examples of restorative justice, such as juvenile conferencing, involve a denial of due process. If guilt is not admitted by those who are the subject of these programmes, such programmes can be seen to be attempting to shame someone before they admit to offending, which is problematic. In practice, then, those accused of offending who participate in such programmes either need to plead guilty, or to have their guilt assumed before they participate. This can be seen as a denial of due process of the law, which presumes people are innocent until proven guilty. Many pre-court processes come up against this difficulty. The problem is that, if a given body is granted the power to punish an individual, the state has to be satisfied that the individual in question really committed the offence. The traditional way for this to happen is for the case to be tried in a court. However, these programmes try to avoid the court process, because it is seen as stigmatizing and also expensive, but in doing so they deny the accused the right to have their case proved in the appropriate manner in open court.

Without the mechanism of the court ensuring those who receive punishment are really guilty, it can be argued that reintegrative shaming is potentially nothing more than a net-widening process of social control, without reducing the number of people subject to punitive sanctions of the state. If the aim of the criminal justice system is to reduce the number of people being caught up in the system, programmes set up to 'reintegratively shame' people as an alternative to court may simply make the overall system larger, without any positive effect in terms of reduction of crime. It can be argued that the programme represents an extension of power into civil society in the process of shaming. Some would argue that there should be a clear distinction between a process that is based in the criminal justice system, and one that properly resides within the community. The concept of reintegrative shaming blurs this distinction.

Peacemaking criminology has been criticized for providing little more than a utopian vision of society, and that, in the end, it does not provide for an adequate empirical and theoretical understanding of crime and crime control. As Akers (1997:

183, quoted in Moyer, 2001) puts it: 'This is a highly laudable philosophy of criminal justice, but it does not offer an explanation of why the system operates as it does or why offenders commit crime.' Similar types of criticism have also been noted among supporters of peacemaking criminology. For example, McEvoy (2003) is highly conscious of the fact that too often the tendency in peacemaking criminology is to stimulate interest in the perspective but to pay much less attention to practical application. The perspective is pitched at a level of abstraction and philosophical reflection that offers a different way of framing and thinking about crime and criminality. But, as an emerging form of criminological theory, it has some way to go in providing more specific, grounded analyses of relevant issues and trends.

Moreover, big questions remain with respect to the analysis of different types of violence, whether and under what conditions violence can be seen as liberating or repressive, the legitimacy of violence that enables the state or community to wield authority and to enforce collective decisions, and the moral basis upon which to condemn (or support) those who utilize violence to achieve social goals. Resolution of these practical and conceptual issues is most likely through specific case studies and strategic interventions as illustrated, for example, in McEvoy (2003). Lastly, critics argue that many victims do not expect to achieve peace with their victimizers and, indeed, may be re-victimized in the process. Defenders of peacemaking criminology counter by claiming that this criticism is improperly directed towards a level of analysis that peacemaking criminologists do not presuppose. The focus for peacemaking criminologists, while involved with individual offenders, visualizes positive transformations at the societal and institutional level and does not advocate that victims take on the task of effecting personal change in the offender (Schmalleger and Volk, 2005).

Despite these problems, restorative justice, including republican theory, has some clear strengths. First, it provides a more holistic account of crime and crime prevention, as distinct from individualistic and 'bad apple' approaches. It attempts to provide an overall view of society, and then locate criminal justice policy within this broader framework. As such, it can be seen as a comprehensive theory that provides an integrated view of all parts of the criminal justice system.

Finally, restorative justice is politically attractive. It provides justification for building a new type of consensus in society and has an emphasis on restorative justice that is positive. Furthermore, the method of achieving lower crime rates is relatively inexpensive in that it is based on minimal intervention. In addition, it captures many of the political concerns of the day, such as the need to take account of the victim, and the emphasis on family as the basic unit in society.

## Conclusion

The rise in popularity of restorative justice and peacekeeping criminology needs to be considered. The political directions of crime in recent years have seen a concentration on individual responsibility for one's actions, with the retributivists arguing that the individual who has committed the action must be punished. Restorative justice perspectives agree that people should be responsible for their actions, but argues that our response to those actions should be constructive.

Economic directions of criminal justice can, in part, explain the attraction of the theory. Fiscal crises in various jurisdictions have seen governments increasingly worried about how to best constrain expenditure in order to curb state debt. In this climate, prisons are viewed as expensive, and the legal aid crisis is seen as a problem arising out of the lengthy, and hence costly, formal court process. Hence, from a strictly economic viewpoint it makes sense to look at alternative cost-effective and efficient measures of crime control.

Another attraction of the republican theory and restorative justice approaches is that they offer a perspective on conflict and conflict resolution that is intrinsically humane and socially positive. As such, they provide a refreshing change from traditional law-and-order discourses. They offer messages of hope, and redemption, in a world seemingly driven by hatred and intractable social differences. Combining powerful moral critiques and practical methods of intervention, they demonstrate that alternatives are, indeed, possible and desirable.

## Key Concepts

- Community boards or panels
- Community and family conferencing
- Conservatism
- Just deserts
- Law-and-order
- Left Realist criminology
- Marxist criminology
- New Right criminology

- Peacemaking criminology
- Reintegrative shaming
- Republican theory
- Restorative justice
- Sentencing circles
- Victim-offender mediation programmes
- Victim-offender reconciliation programmes

## Further Reading

G. Bazemore, 'The "Community" in Community Justice: Issues, Themes, and Questions for the New Neighbourhood Sanctioning Models', *Justice System Journal* 19.2 (1997): 193–227.

J. Braithwaite, *Crime, Shame and Reintegration* (Cambridge: Cambridge University Press, 1989).

J. Braithwaite, and P. Pettit, *Not Just Deserts: A Republican Theory of Criminal Justice* (Oxford: Clarendon Press, 1990).

Canadian Centre for Justice Statistics. *The Juristat Reader: A Statistical Overview of the Canadian Justice System* (Toronto: Nelson, 1999).

Law Commission of Canada, *From Restorative Justice to Transformative Justice* (Ottawa, ON: Law Commission of Canada, 1999).

Law Commission of Canada, *Transforming Relationships Through Participatory Justice* (Ottawa, ON: Law Commission of Canada, 2003).

J.J. Llewellyn, and R. Howse, *Restorative Justice: A Conceptual Framework* (Ottawa, ON: Law Commission of Canada, 1999).

P. Pettit, and J. Braithwaite, 'Not Just Deserts, Even in Sentencing', *Current Issues in Criminal Justice* 4.3 (1993): 225–39.

H. Zehr, *Changing Lenses: A New Focus for Crime and Justice* (Scotsdale, AZ: Herald Press, 1990).

## Websites

*www.aboriginallegal.ca*. This website provides information on a programme that seeks to strengthen the capacity of the Aboriginal community and its citizens to deals with justice issues and provide Aboriginal controlled and culturally based justice alternatives.

*www.acjnet.org*. A comprehensive Canadian website dealing with law and justice. The site contains extensive links to other Canadian and United States criminal justice sites.

*www.ammnesty.org*. Amnesty International is a worldwide movement that campaigns to promote human rights.

*www.calgarycommunityconferencing.com*. This website provides information on a programme that brings together a young person and their victim(s), their respective families and supporters, other key people affected by the conflict, and relevant community members to address what's happened and find solutions beneficial to all.

*www.crimetheory.com*. A website that provides teaching resources offered through the University of Washington.

*www.johnhoward.ca*. The John Howard Society of Canada is an organization of provincial and territorial societies comprised of and governed by people whose goal is to understand and respond to problems of crime and the criminal justice system.

*www.justicecanada.ca/en/ps/ajs/*. The Aboriginal Justice Strategy (AJS) is composed of community-based justice programmes that are cost-shared with provincial and territorial governments, and self-government negotiations in the field of administration of justice.

*www.sfu.ca/crj/*. This website contains resources, full text articles, materials for teaching, and much more information about restorative justice.

## Films/Documentaries

- *Circles* (National Film Board of Canada, 1997)
- *Communities and the Challenge of Conflict: Perspectives on Restorative Justice* (Law Commission of Canada, 2000)
- *Community Mediation: Two Real-Life Experiences* (National Film Board of Canada, 2003)
- *Hollow Water* (National Film Board of Canada, 2000)
- *Is the Crown at War with Us?* (National Film Board of Canada, 2002)
- *No Turning Back* (National Film Board of Canada, 1996)
- *Story of a Mediation* (National Film Board of Canada, 2006)
- *The Green Mile* (Castle Rock Entertainment, 1999)

## Discussion Questions

1. The authors posit that restorative justice approaches are based upon three interrelated propositions. What are these and how do these work together to create a new way of looking at ways to deal with crime?
2. Do you believe that a restorative justice approach is a viable alternative to the traditional adversarial approach to justice? Why or why not?
3. Define and discuss the importance of community to the idea of restorative justice. Provide examples to support your discussion.

4. What, in your opinion, are the strongest contribution(s) that restorative justice approaches offers to both victims and offenders involved in the criminal justice system? What are the drawbacks to such an approach? Create scenarios or give examples to support your answers.
5. Where did the principles found within peacemaking criminology come from?
6. How do peacemaking criminologists believe to be the root causes of crime? How do they propose to deal with them?
7. What are the strengths and weaknesses of a peacemaking approach?

# CHAPTER 11

# Critical Criminology

## Objectives

This chapter will help you develop an understanding of:

- the fundamental concepts found within critical criminological theories;
- the historical and political contexts in the development of critical criminology;
- how the concept of power and the allocation of resources influenced the development and direction of critical criminology;
- the fundamental concepts found within both structural and **postmodern critical criminology**; and
- the strengths and weaknesses found within critical criminology.

## Introduction

The aim of this chapter is to discuss the main ideas and concepts of critical criminology. This perspective combines a wide range of concerns from across the more radical approaches, such as Marxism and feminism, and attempts to develop a type of left-wing criminology that is relevant and appropriate for contemporary society.

As with many of the perspectives in criminology, critical criminology incorporates a wide number of ideas and analytical strands. A distinguishing characteristic of critical criminology is that it is generally associated with an oppositional position in relation to much of the work of conventional criminology, and also to many contemporary policy developments in the field of criminal justice (see Carrington and Hogg, 2002; Schissel and Brooks, 2002).

Critical criminology nevertheless exhibits a number of elements that make it a natural intellectual and strategic partner of both the Left Realist and restorative approaches. As will be demonstrated in this chapter, however, politically the perspective retains a strong socialist (rather than liberal-reformist) orientation. Its analytical focus emphasizes the causal significance of capitalism in the generation of and responses to 'crime' (rather than relying on multifactorial descriptions).

## Social Context

As much as anything, critical criminology represents a further development of the broad radical strands within criminology. In particular, it builds upon the basic concepts and strategic concerns of the Marxist and feminist perspectives. Generally speaking, it does so from the point of view of a broadly anti-capitalist position, which incorporates the ideas of creating a social and natural environment that is not associated with heterosexist, racist, and destructive practices of production and consumption.

There is some confusion and debate surrounding the term 'critical' criminology. A wide range of writers have used it to describe a wide range of theoretical and political positions, and in some discussions, Left Realism is regarded as part of the critical criminology perspective while in others it is not. In some instances, any critique of the existing criminal justice system from any political position other than conservative has been associated with critical criminology. This simply equates 'critical' with specific criticisms, rather than using the term to identify a particular analytical framework.

Both liberal and radical approaches may call for change to existing criminal justice practices, and they may overlap on a range of conceptual and strategic issues (e.g., that unequal distribution of societal resources underpins much working-class crime). However, fundamental differences in ideology and ultimate goals remain, and these must be acknowledged as they have significant implications for criminological theory and practice.

The difficulties and lack of clarity in the use of the term 'critical' are due to the blurring of boundaries between liberal and radical kinds of analysis and intervention. They are also a reflection of other changes occurring in society that have had a major impact upon prevailing attitudes and ideologies. The 1980s was a period of highly volatile politics on a world scale. The demise of Stalinism in the former Soviet Union and Eastern Europe represented not only the end of the Cold War, but also part of a general rethinking of politics and ideology around the world.

The notions of glasnost (openness) and perestroika (restructuring) signalled a far-reaching process of change, reform, and transformation in the non-capitalist countries. Meanwhile, the world economy was steadily and rapidly being internationalized and globalized. Production, consumption, finance, culture, employment, debt, sport—everything was subject to processes that universalized certain ways of doing things, seeing things, and engaging in things. Simultaneously, people became aware of the increasing fragmentation of their lives, as previous loyalties, communities, and affiliations (e.g., links to a sporting club, to a neighbourhood, to a job) were no longer relevant or appreciated.

An age of profound uncertainty had been broached. By the late 1980s, it was clear that the world would never be the same again—politically, in terms of traditional capitalist versus communist ideologies; economically, in terms of employment and distribution of wealth; environmentally, in terms of ecological imbalance and degradation; or socially, in terms of how people relate to each other across many types of interactions. The hallmark of this period has been rapid change, often associated with technological innovation (in the form of the computer microchip) and the concentration of wealth and power into fewer and fewer hands on a global scale.

The world was not only an uncertain place, but also increasingly an unequal one. In trying to understand the nature of the processes of inequality, the concept of difference was highlighted in social analysis and reflected in the ongoing presence of the 'new social movements'. Gay and lesbian rights groups, environmental and conservation movements, pro-choice and broad women's rights organizations, animal rights activists, Third World solidarity action groups, human rights advocates, anti-racist groups, and so on were raising the issues, and voices, of those who had not previously been heard in mainstream political or academic circles.

The world outside criminology obviously has an impact upon what occurs within the discipline. Not surprisingly, then, a number of new strands of thought began to emerge alongside the established approaches such as those we have explored in this book so far. For example, the fascination with meaning, social difference, and discourse analysis was manifest in so-called postmodern analysis. This describes the use of certain analytical tools to 'deconstruct' or decode the language and meaning of law and order, and of the criminal justice system, especially 'the law'. Thus, for example, feminist **jurisprudence** emphasized the inbuilt biases against women in a legal system premised upon certain conceptions of the 'reasonable man' (see Naffine, 1990). This type of analysis uncovers the 'hidden' text of **oppression** as this pertains to women, ethnic minority groups, working-class people, and so on.

In some cases, the method of the postmodern was elevated to the level of social theory. Thus, all meaning—every association between subject (you) and object (the world around you)—is entirely an artefact of language (e.g., signs and symbols), and language, in turn, is relative to and determined by your particular perspective. In other words, there is no 'objective' world that is not constructed 'subjectively' by the author of a particular 'text'. There can be no privileged interpretation of reality. For some, this also means the adoption of a new neutrality that favours no particular politics (not conservative, liberal, or radical) and that ultimately may reject the idea that there are certain dominant structures of power. Such a perspective makes it difficult to speak about and act upon oppression as a structural phenomenon (see Thompson, 1992).

The term postmodernism is used in a number of different ways, some of which appear to be contradictory. Some care, therefore, has to be taken to clarify its meaning in any particular instance. For example, it has been used in reference to:

- analysis of postmodern trends (e.g., the social impact of new communication and information technology; the commodification of symbols, especially as this relates to consumption);
- the idea of a postmodern society as distinct from 'modernity' (e.g., one that exhibits high degrees of social differentiation, individuation, and diverse forms and constructions of subjectivity or personal identity);
- postmodern techniques (e.g., methods of analysis, which centre on the nature and dynamics of language);
- postmodern theory (e.g., the universalization of its method to consider knowledge and power relations across a broad spectrum of social life); and
- postmodern epistemology (e.g., a philosophical stance on the central place of language in the relationship between the 'knower' and what is 'known', which makes problematic any assigning of 'truth' to statements about the world around us).

The postmodern approaches have also gone under different names, such as 'constitutive criminology' or a 'social constructionist' paradigm (Henry and Milovanovic, 1994; Arrigo and Bernard, 1997).

If some of the new types of analysis stressed 'difference' and the relative rather than absolute nature of the social world, others emphasized 'commonality' and shared experience as the basis for criminological work. The idea of peacemaking criminology (discussed in the previous chapter) asks that we recognize our 'oneness' with the world around us. It views crime as essentially a consequence of a general violence towards and separation from people due to the ways in which society responds to offenders. Its main themes include 'connectedness', 'caring', and 'mindfulness' (Friedrichs, 1991).

The relationship of increasingly fragmented societies, and pluralized modes of government, to other more homogenizing social processes is also subject to criminological attention. For example, the concept of a **'risk society'** (Beck, 1992) has been used to describe new forms of risk related to accelerating technological change and globalization of economic, political, and social relationships. In this framework, there are a series of threats to human life that are increasingly shared by the inhabitants of the planet, such as pollution, global warming, crime, and so on. These phenomena do not respect national borders, and nor do they necessarily privilege any particular 'victim' above another. The risks, in one sense, transcend the ordinary social differences of late modernity. Another related idea is that of 'ontological insecurity' (Giddens, 1990, 1991), which describes the feeling of being physically and psychologically at risk in an unstable and rapidly changing world. The direct result of the collapse of traditional social structures, and the limitations of those that are meant to provide security and predictability (such as the family, school, work), results in a process of **'individualization'** (see Beck and Beck-Gernsheim, 2002). This refers both to the process whereby individuals are institutionally made more responsible for their well-being and less reliant upon state or collective support, and to the cultural and ideological prominence given to the 'project of the self' in self-managing one's choices and action.

While not unproblematic, these conceptualizations of risk, of uncertainty, of individualization, and of risk management have nevertheless spurred considerable interest and application in the specific area of crime and crime control. From a criminological perspective, attention has been directed at the ways in which governments have attempted to manage crime-related risk, in a context in which inequalities have increased and other social ills have grown. It is argued that many Western states have responded to this by devolving responsibility for personal security on to individuals, while simultaneously adopting more draconian methods of responding to crime (see Stenson and Sullivan, 2001). The individualization of responsibility in fact masks the social differences in capacity to deal with personal risk; it also ignores the social patterning of both victimization and offending behaviour.

The various critical criminology perspectives reflect, in many ways, the uncertainties and the hopes of the current age. Their development has been intertwined with radically altered material circumstances, and the emergence of the new social movements as political forces in society. The ideas of these perspectives have been drawn upon to varying degrees in contemporary criminological work.

## Basic Concepts

What distinguishes critical criminology per se is its concern with structures of power. These are seen to be institutionalized in particular ways, and to reflect social interests that oppress specific categories of people. How power is conceptualized, however, marks out one of the main differences of approach within critical criminology.

Critical criminologists more or less agree that the present operation of the criminal justice system is unfair, biased, and operates in ways that advantage certain groups or classes above others. The primary task of the critical criminologist is to expose the nature of the underlying power relations that shape how different groups are treated in, and by, the criminal justice system. In many cases, the task is also seen as trying to initiate action and to develop strategies that will transform the present social order, including the criminal justice system.

The focal point of critique within this perspective is how power is mobilized within the broad sphere of criminal justice. There is a range of differing approaches within critical criminology, providing many different methods, empirical studies, and theoretical insights. For present purposes, we can identify two general trends in the critical criminological literature. The 'structuralist' approach tends to focus on power as something that is ingrained in social structures, and that manifests itself in the form of the action of institutions and the activities of sectional interest groups (see Scraton and Chadwick, 1991). The 'postmodern' approach, on the other hand, sees power in terms of language, and the ways in which knowledge production shapes human experience while simultaneously engendering conflict over meaning (see Arrigo and Bernard, 1997; Lea, 1998). The differences between these approaches are seen by some writers to be so great as to warrant treatment as distinct models of social inquiry (Arrigo and Bernard, 1997; Russell, 1997). Others do not necessarily share this view or are less definitive about the 'break' between the two perspectives (Henry and Milovanovic, 1994; Einstadter and Henry, 1995).

Part of the complexity, and to some extent the confusion, in the area of postmodern criminology arises because this form of theorizing has expanded the range of disciplines from which criminology draws theoretical insight. Disciplines, each with their own separate history, may use the same term to mean very different things. There are a number of examples of this and, not surprisingly, we must clarify our meaning of one of these 'contested terms'—namely, structuralism. Within sociology, the term structuralism has meant a theoretical perspective that places an emphasis on the way economic, political, and social structures shape individual behaviour and, in the case of criminology, the definition of crime. This is this definition of the term that is used in this chapter. For some postmodernists (perhaps, more accurately, post-structuralists) the term structuralism means something quite different. In this case, structuralism generally makes some reference to the work of Ferdinand de Saussure, a French linguist. Saussure's theory (labelled 'structuralism') argued that language was a self-referential system of meaning whereby a word was given meaning not because it related to a 'thing' (such as a flower) but primarily because the giving of meaning enabled some **discrimination** in meaning from another word (such as 'grass') within the language system itself. Language was thus 'structured' in terms of a substantially closed, formal system of meaning. The meaning and existence of words could be explained most fully by way of understanding the structure of a particular language itself, not by reference to anything outside that language. Post-structuralism, as a theoretical perspective, draws heavily from linguistics; as such it tends to build, critically, upon the Saussurean meaning of the term structuralism, as opposed to the sociological meaning of the term.

## Structuralism

While there are a number of different strands to **structural critical criminology**, in general it can be said that crime is defined in terms of oppression (see Table 11.1). Some groups are particularly vulnerable to oppression. Members of the working class (especially its more powerless sections, including the 'underclass'), women (especially those who are poor, who are sole parents, and who are socially isolated), ethnic minority groups (especially those from non-English-speaking backgrounds and refugees), and indigenous people (especially those worst-affected by long-term colonization processes and institutional disadvantage) are those most likely to suffer from the weight of oppressive social relations based upon class division, sexism, and racism.

The focus of analysis for structuralist criminology is both the crimes of the powerful and the crimes of the less powerful. In examining the crimes of the powerful, attention is directed at issues relating to ideology (e.g., the nature of 'law-and-order' politics), political economy (e.g., social impacts of privatization), and the state (e.g., managerial rather than democratic modes of rule). The structural context of crime

### Table 11.1   Structuralist Criminology

| | |
|---|---|
| Definition of crime | • structural forms of oppression (class, gender, 'race') |
| Focus of analysis | • crimes of the powerful (the state, **political economy,** ideology) <br> • crimes of the less powerful (specific class, gender, ethnic, 'race' groups) |
| Cause of crime | • marginalization, criminalization (e.g., racialization of crime) |
| Nature of offender | • structurally determined context, process of homogenization, **legitimation** crisis |
| Response to crime | • social empowerment, redistribution of social resources, participatory democracy |
| Crime prevention | • anti-racist campaigns, human rights emphasis, public ownership under community control |
| Operation of criminal justice system | • emphasis on restorative justice, self-determination at community level, employment orientation, open and public accountability of state officials |

vis-à-vis capitalist development and institutional pressures is viewed as central to any explanation of crimes of the powerful.

The crimes of the less powerful are examined from the point of view of the specific experiences of particular sections of the population. Different forms of criminality are thus linked to specific layers of the working class, particular categories of women and men, certain ethnic minority groups, and indigenous people in a variety of rural and urban settings. There is a twofold emphasis: on the specificity of crime and criminal involvement (i.e., specific groups, specific kinds of activity); and on the generalist features that unite the disparate groups (i.e., shared economic, social, and political circumstances).

Crime is seen to be associated with broad processes of political economy that affect the powerful and the less powerful in quite different ways. For the powerful, there are pressures associated with the securing and maintenance of state power and specific sectional interests in the global context of international trade and transnational corporate monopolization. For the less powerful, the cause of crime is seen to lie in the interplay between marginalization (separation from mainstream institutions) and criminalization (intervention by state authorities). Of particular note is the increasing racialization of crime, in which certain communities are targeted for media and police attention in the 'war against crime' and 'public disorder'.

Offending behaviour is thus linked to a social context that is structurally determined by the general allocation of societal resources and by the specific nature of police intervention in people's lives. There is a process of homogenization, in which the least powerful and most vulnerable in society—the poor, the less educated, the unemployed—are filtered through the system until they constitute a disproportionate number of repeat offenders and/or recidivist prisoners.

The growing disparities between rich and poor, and the expansion in the sheer number of the poor, constitute a legitimation crisis for the system as a whole. One response is the swing towards 'law-and-order' politics that entrenches and exacerbates the homogenizing process of identifying and punishing offenders. A particular area of concern is the repressive nature of the state in relation to particular layers of the working class and in regard to particular communities.

For structuralist criminology, a response to crime must be built upon a strategy of social empowerment. This means involving people directly in decisions about their future through direct participatory democracy. It also requires a redistribution of social resources to communities on the basis of social need and equity.

To counter crimes committed by the powerful, there must be open and public accountability of all state officials. Further, as part of wealth redistribution, there has to be a transfer of wealth from private hands to public ownership under community control.

As a general crime-prevention measure, and to diminish the prevalence of certain crimes, there needs to be anti-racist and anti-sexist campaigns (including re-education and retraining of state officials such as the police). Strong emphasis is given to extending and protecting basic human rights (which include economic, social, cultural, and political rights), and institutionalizing these by means of watchdog agencies (e.g., Children's Commissioner, Human Rights Commissioners) and developmental policies.

The criminal justice system should be based upon a model of restorative justice, rather than retribution and punishment. The state should not be repressive in orientation, but coercion may be required as part of the redistribution of community resources from the advantaged sectors of the population to the less advantaged. Moreover, the criminal justice system should operate openly, publicly, and with full community accountability. As far as possible, its functions should reflect self-determination at the community level, within the boundaries of human rights.

## Poststructuralism/Postmodernism

The terms poststructuralist and postmodernist are often used interchangeably to mean theories that explore the creation and use of dominant modes of expression in a society. They argue that the dominant discourses of any society are tools are both created and used by the dominant group to facilitate conformity to their visions of how society should operate. Poststructuralists—Mikhail Kakhtin, Pierre Bourdieu, and Michel Foucault are often referred to as poststructuralists—challenge the notion that discourse develops simply as a tool of communication. Instead, they argue that communication and language are tools of social control created by those in power to create conformity (Brooks, in Schissel and Brooks, 2002).

The starting point for a postmodern (or social constructionist) approach to critical criminology is the idea that language structures thought. Language is seen as the crucial intervening variable between social relationships and institutions, and all methods of knowing the social world. Crime is thus defined in terms of linguistic production, and relationships of power that shape the nature of this production (see Table 11.2). The social world is effectively limited to, and constituted by, the collective reality of language. In other words, there is no necessary logical connection between the use of language and what it purports to describe—there are no 'objective truths', only different ways of speaking about and describing social reality.

Accordingly, social constructionists tend to reject the idea of any 'grand narrative' (e.g., technological revolution, enlightened social progress) as providing a foundation for understanding the world. This is because the social world is viewed as inherently chaotic and based upon contingency, rather than as a coherent system that is regulated in terms of some central steering mechanism (e.g., class struggle, social solidarity). Society is characterized as being in constant flux and change, and the emphasis is on fragmentation, diversity, and ambiguity. As such, reality cannot be understood, depicted, or changed as a whole; there is not one 'truth' but 'many truths', and these, in turn, are constantly changing.

The only real universal feature of social life is the way in which individuals seek power over others by gaining knowledge of them. The focus, therefore, is on power as a ubiquitous feature of social life. The point of analysis is to explore the 'micro-processes' of power, which operate in institutions such as police, courts, and prisons, in order to reveal how power is exercised and how the exercise of power engenders resistance.

Those who control the means of expression are seen to hold the key to controlling and exercising power over others. Simultaneously, however, it is acknowledged that where there is power (in any social relationship), there is also resistance to this power. Language and meaning are contested, and there is always a dynamic tension between

| Table 11.2 Postmodernism | |
|---|---|
| Definition of crime | • not absolute<br>• continuous struggle over control of linguistic production |
| Focus of analysis | • human subject<br>• conflicts over 'existence' or 'reality' as expressed in and through language |
| Cause of crime | • hegemony of dominant discourse<br>• suppression of alternatives |
| Nature of offender | • discursively constituted through dominant discourses<br>• relationships of resistance/power |
| Response to crime | • replacement discourses<br>• no action |
| Crime prevention | • conflicts over discursive frames<br>• new voices and listening<br>• no action |
| Operation of criminal justice system | • localism, plurality<br>• deconstruction and critique<br>• acknowledgement of diverse 'discursive subject positions' |

dominant social voices and those that are silenced or expelled by the dominant modes of expression.

The key to social transformation, therefore, lies in analyzing the languages that construct social relationships in a particular way, to the advantage of some and to the disadvantage of others. Exposing the discourses (i.e., modes of speech, knowledge, categorization of the social world) of everyday life opens the door to other expressions of reality that have been submerged by the dominant or hegemonic discourse. The main method of the social constructionist is that of discourse analysis, which examines how meaning and sense are constructed in everyday language. This involves a process of **deconstruction** of meaning to reveal the hidden and suppressed meanings embodied in certain social relationships.

An important part of this deconstruction of meaning is to examine the discursive subject positions that inform the way in which people speak and think. For example, in the field of criminal justice there are a number of activities and social roles or positions. These include, for instance, offending (the offender), lawyering (the lawyer), policing (the police officer), and judging (the judge or magistrate). It is argued by postmodern writers that the people (subjects) who assume these positions speak, think, feel, and know through the language that is embodied in these structures. Thus, the person who assumes the discursive subject position of police officer, who engages thereby in 'policing', does so in a manner that reflects and embodies what it is to 'be a police officer' (rather than, say, a husband, mother, lover, or football player). Insofar as this is the case, then these subjects can be described as being decentred, in the sense of not being entirely in control of their own thoughts. They act and think like a 'police officer' from the moment that they assume or take on the policing discursive subject position.

The big question for the social constructionist is how the dominant linguistic regime (e.g., legal jargon and categories) in the criminal justice system dismisses particular languages (e.g., the emotional experiences of rape victims) that express a different view and experience of the social world. The 'languaging' of reality is demonstrated in the legitimacy found in the acceptance of certain discursive subject positions (e.g., the judge as rational), but not others (e.g., the victim as not rational). It is argued that: 'By dismissing these oppositional languages, certain versions of how to think, act, feel and be are indirectly de-valued' (Arrigo and Bernard, 1997: 44). The task, therefore, is to expose the different ways in which criminal justice is languaged, and to offer a voice to those who have been silenced by the dominant discourses of the law.

Given the central importance of language, and the study of language, it is understandable that social constructionists tend to reject causal explanations of crime that portray crime as part of a 'grand narrative' (e.g., strains, biological factors). Rather, attention is drawn to how those who control the means of linguistic production also control the prevailing and official definitions of crime. The key question is 'whose "languaged" (and therefore social) interests are valued and de-valued in the prevailing (or alternative) definitions of crime' (Arrigo and Bernard, 1997: 48).

In another sense, the 'cause' of crime is seen to lie in linguistic domination itself. That is, the linguistic domination varyingly 'criminalizes' that speech, thought, and behaviour that resists, de-legitimizes, or opposes the potency of the discourse in effect. The solution to this dilemma is to develop replacement discourses that will neutralize the power of the dominant languages that regulate and discipline the lives of alienated collectivities (especially ethnic minority people, indigenous people, women, and gay men and lesbians). The emphasis, therefore, is on social inclusiveness, diverse modes of communication, and a pluralistic culture. To undercut the dominance of the hegemonic discourses, and to acknowledge the specificity of different 'voices', the main focus for action (if any) is at the local level and through decentralized means of social control and interaction. For some writers, however, any attempt to establish a replacement discourse is itself a form of linguistic imposition (Morrison, 1994; Lea, 1998). For these people, we can deconstruct meaning, but the construction of alternative discursive frames is simply not on the agenda (as to do so implies new conflicts revolving around knowledge, power, and resistance).

## Historical Development

Critical criminology is part of an important tradition of struggle and political conflict to win or defend social and human rights within a class-divided, sexist, and racist social structure.

Ideologically, the perspective is most closely identified with the socialist tradition, and its emphasis on power relations, social conflict, and change as a result of contest over resources. The guiding rhetoric is that of social justice and the importance of empowering the less powerful. The critical criminology perspective is relatively new, although as a particular theoretical model within criminology it has continuity with both the Marxist and feminist approaches.

The initial development of critical criminology as a bona fide current within the mainstream of the discipline began with the coming to prominence of labelling theory. Sometimes referred to as 'new deviancy theorists', writers who spoke about crime as a social process challenged the discipline's conventional conceptions of, and means of dealing with, criminal justice issues. As we saw in Chapter 5, the combination of labelling and the power to label was seen to have a dramatic impact upon the person so labelled. Importantly, this perspective focused attention upon the institutions and forces of 'social reaction' and how through professional practices the process of crime actually occurred.

Left-wing critics of labelling theory argued that analysis of the processes and situations within which labelling took place was not enough. It was also essential to examine the structural relations of power in society, and to view crime in the context of the social relations, state institutions, and political economy of advanced capitalism (Scraton and Chadwick, 1991). It was at this point that much work was done from a Marxist perspective to identify the causal basis of crime, and to make the link between dominant institutions and ruling-class interests. However, there was a tendency at times either to romanticize crime (as acts of rebellion or resistance) or to see crime solely in economic terms (as always reducible to material necessity). Later work was to explore in more detail the specific contexts and lived experiences of people involved with the criminal justice system (Hall and Scraton, 1981).

The issues of racism, sexism, and heterosexism were by and large ignored or insufficiently explained in much of the Marxist writing. This was not simply an analytical problem; it was immediately relevant from a political point of view as well.

The diminished popularity of academic Marxism in the 1980s demanded a response that could speak to a wider range of people than a more restrictive, narrowly conceived approach. Furthermore, the rise of the New Right in the West, the tearing down of Stalinist institutions in the former communist nations according to capitalist free-market criteria, and the political mobilization of the new social movements had implications for Left criminology generally.

The acknowledgement of differences (in terms of specific needs, experiences, and histories) and recognition of commonalities (in relation to marginalization and criminalization processes) was translated into a concern with all forms of oppression within the critical criminology framework. Issues of class, gender, and ethnicity were seen to be interrelated, and to reflect the general institutional processes of capitalism.

At the other end of the spectrum, there was a need to keep the focus on the actions of those in power, not only in relation to those marginalized in society, but also more generally in the area of what has come to be known as white-collar crime. Edwin Sutherland (1983) was the first to coin this phrase in 1939, when he led a blistering attack on the actions of the respectable in society; actions that in a different context would be labelled as criminal and dealt with accordingly. Sutherland saw a need to address the inequalities in treatment of people who engaged in harmful behaviour between those with power and those without power.

This led to a steady stream of research and writing, initially in the United States and then gradually spreading worldwide, on the topic of white-collar crime (Geis and Goff, 1983). The philosophical orientation of such work was not, however, Marxist. Rather it came from Sutherland's own theorizing, that of **differential association theory** (outlined in Chapter 4). Critical criminology can be seen as continuing the focus on white-collar crime, with a clearer focus on the impact of contemporary capitalism in providing opportunities for corporate criminality, and providing the justification for the lack of enforcement in the area. As such, it shares a stronger legacy with Marxism than with Sutherland and his contemporaries.

The conceptual legacy of Marxism was to establish a firm interest in examining questions relating to the nature and exercise of state power. In a similar vein, and reinforced by feminist studies on the cultural and psychological basis of oppression, research was directed at the role of ideology in shaping lived experience. Racism, sexism, and individualism are all bound up with certain ways in which the world is described and categorized—the definition of who is 'dangerous' and who is not, for example. The task of critical criminology was to expose the processes whereby certain groups and categories of people are deemed to be worthy of social exclusion, and to develop strategies that could open the door to a more humane and equal society.

## Contemporary Examples

One of the hallmarks of critical criminology is its association with direct interventions in various law-and-order and criminal justice debates. Indeed, more than this, one of the main contributions of this strand of criminological activity has been to raise for public discussion a series of important social issues. For example, the work of critical criminologists has been crucial to ongoing critiques of the prison system and of developments relating to the privatization of punishment (see Mathiesen, 1990; Christie, 1993; Moyle, 1994). Much of this type of research, scholarship, and commentary has been informed by a concern to publicize existing injustices, and potential abuses, of criminal justice institutions (Carrington and Hogg, 2002; Schissel and Brooks, 2002).

A key feature of critical criminology is that it is one of the few perspectives to focus specifically on issues of racism and crime. New Right criminology tends to attribute 'blame' for crime, poverty, and unemployment to particular ethnic minority communities themselves. In the conservative framework the emphasis is on the 'bad behaviour' of community members, and the 'choices' they make to be the way they are and to do the things they do. The mainstream perspectives—such as labelling, strain, and republican theories—have a more explicit concern with issues relating to racism. Here, however, the solution is often seen simply in terms of making criminal justice processes and procedures as fair and unbiased as possible. The idea is that high rates of incarceration and contact involving certain social groups are due mainly to 'discrimination' and improper use of discretion (see Cook and Hudson, 1993).

From a critical criminological perspective, the main issue is one of structural inequality. Very often this inequality has been institutionalized in a racist fashion (see Cunneen and White, 2002; Schissel and Brooks, 2002). In such circumstances, insensitive and coercive policing, for instance, cannot be reduced to 'bad attitudes' on the part of the police; it stems from the structural role of the police in regulating the most marginalized sectors of a class-divided society. These divisions may, in turn, be associated with particular ethnic and 'race' groupings (e.g., indigenous people, non-English-speaking immigrants from South-East Asia). Issues of under-policing and over-policing are seen as flowing from broader societal pressures and divisions that have had a particularly negative impact on indigenous people and those from ethnic minority communities.

In recent years Saskatoon Police Services has come under harsh criticism for the treatment of Aboriginals in contact with police officers. In the winter of 2001 the frozen body of an Aboriginal man was found near a power plant located at the edge of the City of Saskatoon. Four days later the body of a second Aboriginal man was discovered in the same area. Rumors circulated that the men had been taken on what was known in Aboriginal circles for years as a 'starlight tour': police driving drunk Aboriginals out of the city and leaving them to walk home and sober up (CBC, 2004). The starlight tours may have remained an urban legend except that another Aboriginal man came forward to accuse two police officers of taking him to the edge of the city and abandoning him in the same area where the two bodies were found. After a lengthy investigation two Saskatoon police officers were charged with unlawful confinement in the case. The officers were tried, convicted, and sentenced to eight months in jail. While Darrell Night survived, his complaint against the Saskatoon City police casts suspicion on at least five deaths of Aboriginal men in Saskatoon over the past decade (Amnesty International, 2002).

More generally, the work of critical criminologists has been instrumental in exposing and illuminating a wide range of issues pertaining to the less powerful groups in society. The victimization, and empowerment, of indigenous people, immigrant communities, refugees, gay men and lesbians, working-class young people, and so on have

## Box 11.1  Discriminatory Attitudes and Practices of Police

In September 2001, two police Saskatoon City police officers, Ken Munson and Dan Hatchen, were convicted of the Criminal Code offence of unlawful confinement for forcibly abandoning an Aboriginal man, Darrell Night, on the outskirts of the city in freezing temperatures on a night in late January 2000. Darrell Night survived the incident. But his complaint against the Saskatoon City police casts suspicion on at least five deaths of Aboriginal men in Saskatoon over the past decade. In the most recent cases, the frozen bodies of Rodney Naistus and Lawrence Wegner were found on 29 January and 3 February 2000, near the location where Night was abandoned. Royal Canadian Mounted Police (RCMP) investigations and coroner's inquests into these cases have been inconclusive.

Amnesty International is deeply concerned by allegations that some Saskatoon City police officers have routinely dealt with Aboriginal people perceived as being intoxicated or troublesome by taking them into custody and then forcibly abandoning them outside the city without regard for their safety and well-being. The practice is allegedly so widespread that a euphemism, 'the starlight tour', has been developed to describe it. Writing in a column about police life that appeared in the Saskatoon Sun in 1997, a city police officer described police officers abandoning an Aboriginal man at the power plant outside the city, the same location where two bodies were found in the winter of 2001. All this raises the possibility that the practice, even if restricted to a few officers, may have been at least tacitly condoned by colleagues and superiors. This also raises the concern that investigations into the freezing deaths may have been thwarted by solidarity within police ranks.

Amnesty International welcomed the announcement in the latter part of 2001 by the Saskatchewan government that a commission of inquiry will be established to look into issues of Aboriginal peoples and the justice system. It is our hope that this commission will provide an opportunity to reexamine the Saskatoon freezing deaths and the degree to which discrimination may have been a factor in those cases. Amnesty International also believes that the conviction of officers Munson and Hatchen, and the allegations of similar abuses that have been raised, point to an urgent need for human rights training for Canadian police officers, that should not wait for the outcome of the recent commission.

Amnesty International urges the Canadian government:

- to press the government of Saskatchewan to ensure that the Saskatoon freezing deaths are given full attention in the course of the current commission of inquiry, with particular attention to the possible role that discrimination may have played in those cases; and
- press for enhanced human rights training, including anti-discrimination training, for police forces across Canada.

From Amnesty International, *Without Discrimination: The Fundamental Right of All Canadians to Human Rights Protection.* Brief to the UN Committee on the Elimination of Racial Discrimination on the Occasion of the Examination of the Thirteenth and Fourteenth Periodic Reports Submitted by Canada, July 2002. Amnesty International, Canadian Section (English-speaking).

been the subject of probing analysis and insightful discussion (see Brown and Hogg, 1992; Carrington and Hogg, 2002). One feature of this work has been its emphasis on explaining the specific empirical aspects of a particular phenomenon, without attempting to say that 'all crime is the same' or trying to deal with 'crime in general'. Nevertheless, the discussions of specific groups (e.g., indigenous people, female prisoners) and particular institutions (e.g., special police tactical response units, private prisons) are usually framed within a general perspective that views the state and powerful social interests (e.g., corporate sector) as problematic.

Convict criminology provides an example of how critical criminology seeks to give voice to less powerful groups in society. It is a relatively new field of study that has been primarily undertaken by convicts or ex-convicts who have either completed a PhD or who are pursuing post-secondary education. It is comprised of empirical research and essays, although established academics have also contributed to its creation. The primary goal of convict criminology is two-fold. The first goal is focused on ways in which research on prisons is done, while the second goal is to continue to encourage professional associations to create and communicate policy reforms that will facilitate the creation of a more humane criminal justice system.

There was a growing awareness among criminologists during the 1960s and 1970s that the voices and experiences of victims were very seldom considered when examining criminal justice processes and outcomes (Karmen, 2001). This, along with a newly developing victim's rights movement, led to the development of a subdiscipline within criminology known as 'victimology'. Victimology focuses on the awareness that researchers must consider the voices and experiences of those oppressed through their experiences with the criminal justice system (Henry and Milovanovic, 1996; Milovanovic, 1996; Richards and Jones, 1997; Richards, 1998). At its core, the perspective argues that understanding the voices and experiences of those incarcerated has been absent but must not continue to be overlooked; or in the words of Gaucher (1998), 'Perhaps in the new millennium, criminologists and other social scientists might also realize that convict voices, in many instances, have been forgotten, marginalized, or simply ignored' (14).

To date, literature providing an inside perspective on crime and on convicts has emerged from a variety of sources, including political activists, journalists, lawyers, academics, ex-convicts, and convicts (see Burton-Rose, with Pens and Wright, 1998, Parenti, 1999; Conover, 2000; Hallinan, 2001; Abramsky, 2002). Some ex-convicts and convicts are academics who have been incarcerated and are able to combine their academic abilities with their life experiences to provide new insights into the operations of the criminal justice system and the experiences of those involved. The types of literature created through convict criminology is also varied and includes journalistic accounts of life inside prison; monographs about prison life written by convicts; prison journalism, written by convicts and published in prison newspapers or in academic journals such as *The Journal of Prisoners on Prison*; edited collections of works by convicts; and sole-authored or edited books by academics who have done research in the area of offenders and convicts (see Cleaver, 1968; Jackson, 1970, 1972; Abbot, 1991; Rideau and Wikberg, 1992; Abu-Jamal, 1995; Hassine, 1996; Peltier, 1999; Ross and Richards, 2003).

**Ethnographic methods** have been used in a variety of criminological research endeavors in an attempt to develop a deep, detailed understanding of their subject matter. Convict criminologists stress the importance of ethnographies in their work and have successfully used this methodology in a variety of ways. For example, Irwin (1970, 1980) called upon his own experiences in prison to assist him in interviewing prisoners and to help explain the subtle processes that occur in prison (see Irwin and Cressey, 1962; Newbold, 1982, 1985; Ferrell and Hamm, 1998; Austin and Irwin, 2001).

Convict criminology also points out that in recent years significant attention has been brought to the failure of prisons to rehabilitate incarcerated individuals and to reduce rates of recidivism. Instead, as Johnson (1996) states: 'prisoners serve hard time, as they are meant to. . . . They adapt to prison in immature and often destructive ways. As a result they leave prison not better, and sometimes considerably worse, than when they went in' (xi). Prison systems function as vast depositories for drug offenders, minorities, and petty offenders, rather than as rehabilitation centres (Miller, 1996; Austin and Irwin, 2001). Convict criminologists have also levelled criticism at the criminal justice system for the dramatic increase in the number of individuals incarcerated within both provincial and federal prisons. A large percentage of this population, although they have been convicted of a criminal offence, is not violent and poses little or no threat to society. Critics also argue that prisons hold people for greater lengths of time than is necessary. According to Austin and Irwin (2001), 'it is not just about hard time, it is about time. . .a long time, and repeated time in prison' (46).

The development of prisoner's rights movements has also impacted the development of convict criminology. Historically, individuals and organizations such as the Canadian Civil Liberties Association, Human Rights Watch, and Amnesty International have advocated for changes and improvements in prison conditions in Canada, the United States, and around the world. Michael Welch (1994) claims that the development of a prisoners' rights movement has meant that

> correctional institutions have been forced to rely less on coercive mechanisms to control inmates and to resort to bureaucratic measures instead. Today, prison officials must formally respond to grievances and lawsuits by producing their own reports concerning alleged violations (370).

In addition to the work done by these organizations to promote constitutional and civil rights for incarcerated individuals, inmates have become more aware of their constitutional rights and have developed an increased level of legal and political consciousness (Welch, 1996).

In summary, these factors have facilitated the development of a new criminological perspective that actively seeks to further our understandings of criminal justice issues through the use of ethnographic research methods. Additionally, convict criminology seeks to give voice to a group of marginalized and disempowered individuals—convicts—in an attempt to create and implement a more humane criminal justice system.

Beyond focusing on the powerless, critical criminology has also been concerned with the harm directly perpetrated by those in positions of power. Studies of white-collar crime and corporate crime (crime specifically resulting from the action of organizations) have pointed to the enormity of harm perpetrated in the white-collar sphere. A consistent focus of this research has been to label such acts criminal, and to call for their inclusion as quintessentially criminal acts to be dealt with accordingly (see, for examples, Pearce and Tombs, 1990; Friedrichs, 1996; Shover and Wright, 2001). In a similar vein, recent work has attempted to provide more precise, and from a practical point of view, operational, concepts of state crime. Thus, Green and Ward (2000) propose that the term 'state crime' be restricted to the area of overlap between violations of human rights and state organizational deviance. By using such a definition, they wish to employ a criminological understanding of those acts or omissions that contribute to, or are complicit with, breaches of human rights. Such a concept opens the door to investigation of a wide range of social harms, corruptions, and violations of rights perpetrated by agencies and officials of the state.

Researchers in the area have pointed to the way in which the structure of capitalism itself creates opportunities for crimes of the powerful. Large corporations, most notably the multinational corporations, are in a position to reap considerable gains from their activities at the expense of both the environment and the weakest in society. In addition, certain industries such as the insurance industry may actively support crimes; for instance, an insurance company may gain from the crime of car theft through the sale of wrecked cars complete with high-value identification numbers (Brill, 1993). The market power of these large organizations gives them the opportunity to avoid effective enforcement of laws aimed at curbing their power (Barnett, 1993). Furthermore, it has been argued that law enforcement and criminalization of these activities may in fact have limited value, because the state has an active interest in maintaining good relations with the monopoly capitalists. Other theorists working in this area point to the nature of the dual economy, where the logic of competition pushes smaller, weaker organizations to exploit their workers and spoil the environment. While large organizations have the money to put in place extensive programmes aimed at reducing harm, smaller organizations are forced to cut corners to survive (Haines, 1997). The structure of capitalism is thus directly linked to the harm that organizations perpetrate.

In recent years, interest in international crime or crime between nation states has intensified. This has included an increased focus on the actions of states and/or corporations that participate in actions that contravene international law (Tunnell, 1993; Ross, 2000; Donnelly, 2003; Michalowski and Kramer, 2006). Supernational criminology, therefore, is interested in exploring the impact of **globalization** on the changing nature of crime and violence within, between, and across nation states with a focus on transgressions committed by states and by state-corporate alliances (Barak, 2007: 4). This includes war crimes, genocide, child labour, political imprisonment, slavery, and sexual torture. Jonathon Friedman (2003) describes the relationship between globalization and violence as follows:

> In order to understand the processes involved it is necessary to take seriously the systematic changes occurring in the global political economy that have produced major shifts in forms of control over resources, the relation between capital and states and in the transformation of the conditions of livelihood and labor. The global transformation of capital accumulation is articulated to major reconfiguration of political power in the world, to major dislocations of population, to the disintegration of microsocial forms of life for many, and to the intensification of both everyday domestic, local, and regional violence (xiv).

Yet another area of recent interest is that of green or environmental criminology. Much of this work has been directed at exposing different instances of substantive environmental injustice and ecological injustice. It has also involved critique of the actions of nation-states and transnational capital for fostering particular types of harm, and for failing to adequately address or regulate harmful activity. Drawing upon a wide range of ideas and empirical materials, criminology that deals with environmental harm has ventured across a range of areas of concern. For example, it has documented the existence of law-breaking with respect to pollution, disposal of toxic waste, and misuse of environmental resources (Pearce and Tombs, 1998). Other work has emphasized the dynamic links between distribution of environmental 'risk' (particularly as these affect poor and minority populations) and the claims of non-human nature to ecological justice (Bullard, 1994). It has also considered the specific place of animals in relation to issues of 'rights' and human–non-human relationships on a shared planet (Benton, 1998). Industrial accidents and environmental disasters such as the Love Canal (1978), the Bhopal Disaster (1984), the Westray Mining accident (1992), and the contamination of Lynn Lake (2001) provide examples of the types of issues that environmental criminology may focus on.

In general, and given the pressing nature of many environmental issues, many criminologists are now seeing environmental crime and environmental victimization as areas for concerted analytical and practical attention, that is, as areas of work that require much more conceptual development and empirical attention (see Williams, 1996; Boyd et al., 2002; Lynch and Stretsky, 2003; White, 2003).

There are other examples of critical criminology that illustrate the movement of the perspective beyond a Marxist base. Indeed, some theorists working from a critical standpoint actively reject Marxism as a starting point, most notably those utilizing a

## Box 11.2   The Westray Mining Disaster

On 11 September 1991 Toronto-based Curragn Resources Inc. opened Westray Mine in the small town of Plymouth, Nova Scotia. Touted as a 'state of the art' operation, the mine utilized the latest safety monitoring devices and computerized equipment. The development of Westray Mine was supported by the provincial as well as federal government, despite a history of high fatalities in the Canadian mining industry.

At 5:18 am on 9 May 1992, the Westray mine exploded killing all 26 miners who were underground at the time. The strength of the blast blew the top off the mine and destroyed steel support beams. Plymouth residents felt their homes shake and windows shatter.

The explosion caused the bankruptcy of Curragh Resouces Inc. that had a negative effect on the economy of Nova Scotia, was well as that of the Yukon Territory where Curragh had additional mining ventures. Due to the explosion the company was unable to pay back extensive loans to the province of Nova Scotia as well as the federal government.

In 2002, the names of the 26 miners who died at Westray were read in front of Parliament Hill in an attempt to force the Justice Committee of the House of Commons to make changes to the criminal code. The protestors argued that corporations and their executives should be held more accountable for workplace safety. Although charges of criminal negligence causing death and charges of manslaughter were laid against two mine managers, the trial fell apart due to technicalities.

A memorial commemorating the lost miners sits in a small park in New Glasgow, Pictou County, Nova Scotia. The mine itself was razed in 1998, and its remaining entry points were sealed. In 2000, PanCanadian Petroleum acquired the right to extract methane gas from the Westray mine area.

From 'On this Day: The Westray Mining Disaster', *CBC Archives*, 2006c. http://archives.cbc.ca/on_this_ day/05/09/. Reprinted by permission of the publisher.

postmodern perspective. Postmodernism stresses the plurality of knowledge, and discounts any one 'correct view'. All views, in a sense, have validity. Thus, the focus is on the subjective nature of reality, rather than on objective 'truth'.

Postmodernist writers vary considerably in their opinions regarding the importance of historical context, given their focus on the plurality of existence; this contrasts with the primacy given to history by Marxists. While some postmodern authors accord it considerable importance—for example, Foucault (1977)—others fix only on the (multiple) 'realities' of the present. As such, these approaches tend to negate the possibility of value in anything other than the present (since that is all that is 'knowable'), and it has been argued that past atrocities and social harms can thus melt into insignificance in the postmodernist agenda (Cohen, 1993).

Other writers, however, point to the way postmodernism, like labelling before it, empowers those with little voice (Einstadter and Henry, 1995). In this view, reality is always constituted and reconstituted in the present, but according to very specific discourses. Many postmodern authors, they argue, are concerned with giving a voice to those views that are currently underplayed or ignored by those who have power—for example, the views of indigenous people, women, lesbians and gay men, and so on. Meaning is present in everything we do, but it is the task of postmodernism to unpack the complex nature of everyday 'realities', and the discourses of these realities, including those realities concerned with crime and criminality.

What unifies the many different approaches within the critical criminology perspective is a deep concern with issues of oppression and injustice. These are seen to stem from structural inequalities in resource allocation and decision-making power. Accordingly, institutional reform is not seen as an end in itself, but as part of a more profound transition towards a more equal, fairer society. To take a specific example, a call for the abolition of prisons (or at the least a radical reduction in the prison population) may reflect the position that those who end up in prison are the most vulnerable sections of the population (in terms of income, employment, and educational background) and hence are unfairly criminalized and further penalized for their predicament. But to abolish prisons is not enough. Until the conditions that give rise to the creation of 'surplus populations' and ethnic- and racially-based social divisions are confronted, piecemeal institutional reform will not be sufficient to forestall suffering and pain in the future.

## Critique

Critical criminology, since it has much in common with Marxist criminology, shares some of the same problems. In particular, it shares the problem of the definition of crime. Structuralist criminology, like Marxist criminology, defines crime very broadly, in terms of the oppression of a particular group (e.g., indigenous people or other minority groups) or class (e.g., working people) by those with power. In this, it shares a 'human rights' definition of crime, similar to some Marxist criminologists. The problem with these definitions is how to conceive of differences in the abuse of human rights. For instance, how does one compare discrimination against a person of non-English-speaking background applying for a job to the genocide that occurred in the early 1990s in the former Yugoslavia? As previously discussed, crime/non-crime are dichotomous categories; they do not lend themselves easily to discerning different gradations of harm. Nevertheless, some writers are now systematically addressing these issues. This is particularly the case in respect to definitions of state crime, and definitions of environmental harm (see Green and Ward, 2000; White, 2003). It also is apparent in efforts to create more sophisticated accounts of criminal action (including acts of omission) by the state, such as in the development of a model expressing the multidimensional continuum of state crime complicity (Kauzlarich et al., 2003).

Some critical criminology, like some Marxist criminology, tends to have a simple view of the nature of power. That is, there is a notion that some people have power (the powerful) and others do not (the powerless); there is no serious attempt to analyze the nature of power. This criticism has sometimes been directed at structuralist approaches. While acknowledging the need for further analysis of, and sensitivity to, the dynamics of power at a 'micro' as well as 'macro' level, structuralist criminology nonetheless maintains that social power is best understood as being concentrated in particular directions. It is seen to have substantially different effects according to different groups' resources and capacities, and this, in turn, is related to the institutionalized nature of inequality.

Given the critique of 'capitalism' that lies at the base of structuralist criminology, it needs to be able to spell out in more precise terms the nature of this capitalism in the light of processes of internationalization and globalization, and how its institutions (e.g., transnational corporations, nation-states) impact on the crime debate. Again, many writers are in fact now expanding their analytical horizons with respect to issues of globalization and social and environmental harms (see Findlay, 1999; Haines, 2000) and it can be expected that this will be developed further over time. Yet, it is not always clear whether critical criminology is arguing that the basis of all crime is ultimately economic, or rather that the capitalist system merely exacerbates conflict and tension that exist independently from the economic relations inherent within capitalism. In either case, there is a need to examine the precise way in which capitalism acts to exacerbate tension and both produce and define crime.

Postmodern criminologists do not conceptualize power in the same way as those who adopt a structuralist perspective. Their view tends to draw upon the work of

Foucault (1980), who points to the decentralization of power within modern society; that is, it is not held solely by the state or in one particular class or group of people. Rather, the argument is that power is dispersed throughout society. Furthermore, power is not necessarily seen as always negative but as a generalized feature of social life. Thus, power, when used to oppress, creates resistance, and this in itself is a source of power. According to Foucault, power can be associated with pleasure as well as repression. It can also flow in more than one direction simultaneously.

Foucault's ideas have been highly influential, but at times they have been over-simplified or distorted in some postmodernist work. For example, postmodern criminology emphasizes that language always constitutes, and is constituted by, the relationship between knowledge, power, and resistance. This leads to some logical dilemmas. For instance, it has been pointed out that: 'If all discourses and definitions are power effects involving repression, then power is ubiquitous. It is "everywhere and therefore nowhere"' (Lea, 1998: 173). If power and resistance are always present, then by what criteria are we to discern whether or not any particular social relationship is 'oppressive' or 'liberating'? Here the notion of a power differential becomes central to conceptual analysis. Major problems arise if crucial qualitative distinctions are not made regarding the relative power differences between different individuals and groups.

Additionally, it has been argued that the rejection of 'grand narratives', including those that provide a normative basis for action (such as 'justice', 'rights', and 'equality'), makes it difficult to provide a rationale or justification for specific types of academic analyses or social action on particular criminal justice issues. Although postmodern criminology can expose the power relations exhibited through the languaging of social reality, big questions remain as to what is to be done with this knowledge, given that values themselves may be seen to be subjective and partial, and thus unsuitable as guides to action (Loader, 1998).

Another difficulty with the postmodernist approach is that deconstruction as a method of analysis can lead to infinite regress (Lea, 1998). That is, if there is no 'objective' world, and there really is no reality outside the dynamics of language, then all knowledge is indeterminate and relative. There is no endpoint to the deconstruction process. This can be extremely confusing as words are further defined and interrogated in terms of other words, and the language of analysis becomes ever more complex and obscure. It can also preclude the necessity or capability to actually act on the under-standings we currently have, since these are always changing and are always subject to further deconstruction. Furthermore, if there is no intrinsic foundation to 'facts' about the social world (because these are socially constructed through language), then what criteria can be invoked to determine whose 'voices' should be heard and which groups to support in our work? If the key criterion is that of looking to those voices that have been 'silenced' by the dominant languages of the law, then it raises the prospect of not only enabling oppressed minorities (e.g., ethnic minority groups) to resist better, but also, likewise, supporting extreme right-wing nationalist or white supremacist groups (e.g., neo-Nazis; see Lea, 1998). This can only happen, however, if there is no norma-tive basis to the work of the postmodern criminologist. But implicit in a values frame-work is the idea of some kind of meta-narrative regarding what is deemed to be 'good' and 'right'.

A fundamental challenge to convict criminology results from its main methodology. Because it relies on ethnographic research methodologies, traditional methods of data collection such as surveys are rendered useless. This presents a significant challenge to deeply entrenched analytical paradigms that rely on quantitative data results to provide meta-explanations for predicting behaviours and for causal factors in crime activity.

Critics may also challenge the implied belief that only those who have been directly involved in the criminal justice system and who have been incarcerated are qualified to engage in research projects and the dissemination of research findings in this area. In other words, is it impossible for a trained researcher and academic—without a history of incarceration—to accurately reflect on and give voice to the feelings and experiences of inmates? If so, then one could argue that only women could engage in feminist research, or only Aboriginal people could or should engage in research on issues of importance to Aboriginals. One could also question the ability of an individual incarcerated in a provincial prison to understand and speak for the experiences of someone incarcerated in a federal penitentiary because of the differences that may exist between inmate cultures based on institutional custody levels. This perspective has strong potential to create divisions amongst researchers and critics argue this could significantly weaken criminology's search for knowledge.

Despite these weaknesses, critical criminology (both structuralist and postmodernist) has allowed insight into the diversity of groups that are progressively marginalized by contemporary capitalist societies and, further, how the activities of such groups become criminalized in a way that leads to further marginalization. In doing so, it allows for a number of new voices that have not been previously heard or listened to, such as those of gay men and lesbians, and indigenous people.

Critical criminology forces us to confront issues of the social interests in which the state acts. It highlights the potential long-term conflict that can be produced by a state that prioritizes the interests of one group of society over and above the interests of other groups. In doing so, it gives advance warning of the likely social impact of the dismantling of the welfare state, of the 'racialization' of public order policing, and of the social exclusion of people from basic citizenship rights. The result of such trends may be personalized in the form of high suicide rates (affecting the individual), and collective in the form of riots and general social unrest (affecting whole communities).

## Conclusion

Critical criminology reflects the concerns of many different people in contemporary societies. Generally speaking, it espouses a 'liberation' philosophy that has at its centre emancipatory concerns aimed at allowing all people to participate fully in society, regardless of 'race', ethnicity, sex, class, and sexual orientation. Furthermore, it includes among its concerns issues relating to the environment and animal rights. Ultimately, critical criminology views capitalism as essentially hostile to the promotion of human rights and personal empowerment, and seeks alternative social arrangements and philosophies that can result in a more inclusive society.

In many ways, critical criminology represents the cutting edge of socially progressive criminology in the twenty-first century. It represents an amalgamation of concerns and ideas drawn essentially from socialist and radical viewpoints, and is an attempt to analyze and to develop empowering intervention strategies in a rapidly changing world. As such, it offers a critique of the dynamics of global capitalism, through a mode of investigation that holds the promise of profound social transformation across many domains of social life, including, and especially, that of criminal justice.

## Key Terms and Concepts

- Capitalism
- Convict criminology
- Ethnographic research
- Globalization
- Individualization
- Political economy
- Postmodern critical criminology
- Structural critical criminology

## Further Reading

B. Arrigo and T. Bernard, 'Postmodern Criminology in Relation to Radical and Conflict Criminology', *Critical Criminology* 8.2 (1997): 39–60.

R. Caron, (1978). *GO-BOY: Memoirs of a Life Behind Bars* (Toronto: McGraw-Hill Book Company, 1978).

K. Carrington, and R. Hogg, eds, *Critical Criminology: Issues, Debates, Challenges* (Devon: Willan Publishing, 2002).

E. Comack, ed., *Locating Law: Race/Class/Gender Connections* (Halifax: Fernwood Publishing, 1999).

D. Cook and B. Hudson, eds, *Racism and Criminology* (London: Sage, 1993).

S. Comish, *The Westray Tragedy: A Miner's Story* (Halifax: Fernwood, 1993).

P. Earley, *The Hot House: Life Inside Leavenworth Prison* (New York: Bantam Books, 1993).

M. Foucault, *Discipline and Punish: The Birth of the Prison* (New York: Vintage Books, 1979).

S. Henry and D. Milovanovic, 'The Constitution of Constitutive Criminology: A Postmodern Approach to Criminological Theory', in *The Futures of Criminology*, D. Nelken, ed. (London: Sage, 1994).

J. Lea, 'Criminology and Postmodernity', in *The New Criminology Revisited*, P. Walton and J. Young, eds (London: Macmillan, 1998).

B. Schissel and C. Brooks, eds, *Marginality & Condemnation: An Introduction to Critical Criminology* (Halifax: Fernwood, 2002).

P. Scraton and K. Chadwick, 'The Theoretical and Political Priorities of Critical Criminology', in *The Politics of Crime Control*, K. Stenson & D. Cowell, eds (London: Sage, 1991).

L. Snider, *Bad Business: Corporate Crime in Canada* (Toronto: Nelson, 1993).

L. Taylor, P. Walton, and J. Young, eds, *Critical Criminology* (Boston: Routledge and Kegal Paul, 1975).

S. 'Tookie' Williams, *Life in Prison* (San Francisco, CA: Chronicle Books, 2001).

## Websites

*www.acjnet.org.* A comprehensive Canadian website that contains extensive links to other Canadian and United States criminal justice sites.

*www.amnesty.ca.* The official website for Amnesty International Canada and an excellent source of information regarding human right issues.

*www.bccla.org.* A website for the British Columbia Civil Liberties Association with information about the organization, position papers, press reports, annual report, and membership information.

*www.ccla.org*. A website for the Canadian Civil Liberties Association—a non-profit, non-government law-reform organization dealing with issues of fundamental civil liberties and human rights.

*www.convictcriminology.org*. The official website for convict criminology, providing a comprehensive overview of the principles and practices of convict criminology. It also provides useful links to other sources of information.

*www.crimetheory.com*. This website provides teaching resources offered through the University of Washington.

*www.critcrim.org*. This website is intended to link scholars with interests in critical criminology; it also serves a key function in our efforts to build and support an online community of critical criminologists.

*www.statcan.ca*. Statistics Canada's website provides free and for-fee economic, social, and census data and daily overviews of statistical releases.

*www.TheCorporation.com*. The official website for the film, The Corporation.

## Films/Documentaries

- *Bhopal: The Search for Justice* (National Film Board of Canada, 2004)
- *GO-BOY* (Paradox Pictures, currently in production)
- *Enron: The Smartest Guys in the Room* (National Film Board of Canada, 2005)
- *Quiet Rage: Stanford Prison Experiment* (Phillip G. Zimbardo Inc., 1971)
- *Shawshank Redemption* (Turner Home Entertainment, 1994)
- *The Corporation* (Big Picture Media Corporation MMIII, 2003)
- *The Street: A Film of the Homeless* (National Film Board of Canada, 1997)
- *Unbalanced Scales: Gender Bias in the Justice System* (National Film Board of Canada, 1999)
- *Wards of the Courts* (National Film Board of Canada, 2006)
- *Whose Counting: Marilyn Waring on Sex, Lies, and Global Economics* (National Film Board of Canada, 1995)

## Discussion Questions

1. The authors posit that critical criminology theories can be divided into two separate trends. What are these and how do they work together to create a new way of looking at methods of dealing with crime?
2. Define and discuss the importance of the concept of power to critical criminological theories. Provide examples to support your discussion.
3. What is meant by a risk society?
4. What is the focus of environmental criminology? How has it contributed to the discipline of criminology?
5. Structuralist criminology argues that the response to crime must be built upon a strategy of social empowerment. What does this mean, and how could restorative justice perspectives be incorporated into such a strategy?
6. What factors contributed to the development of convict criminology?
7. What, in your opinion, are the strongest contribution(s) that critical theories offer to the discipline of criminology? What weakness can be found within critical theories? Provide examples to support your answers.

# CHAPTER 12

# Conclusion

The aim of this book has been to provide an introduction to the main concepts and explanations of criminology. In particular, we have reviewed the many and varied ways in which the nature and causes of crime have been defined and analyzed within the field.

As we have seen, the way in which crime is conceived, and thus prevented and controlled, is a matter of considerable dispute. Invariably, the criminological enterprise involves issues of a theoretical, empirical, and political nature. The theories and perspectives we have explored in the book focus on different and often quite specific or distinct aspects of criminal activity and behaviour. Thus, for example, some theories have concentrated attention on the individual characteristics or attributes of the offender, others on the processes whereby an action or person comes to be defined as criminal, and still others on the influence of social structure on personal and group behaviour.

The diverse explanations on offer indicate, at least in part, the interdisciplinary nature of criminology. As a field of study, criminology incorporates ideas, methodologies, and theoretical contributions from disciplines such as psychology, sociology, political science, history, legal studies, and forensic medicine. Different starting points and different conceptual emphases stem from the diversity of academic influences in the field. However, many of the differences within criminology also reflect broader divisions with regard to the level of analysis, and the political perspective.

This is illustrated, for instance, in the debate over whether criminal behaviour is determined or voluntary. At first glance, the debate appears to be fairly straightforward. On the one hand, there are those perspectives, such as the classical, that portray human activity as entirely voluntary—as simply a matter of individual choice. On the other hand, there are those theories that present the view that behaviour is overwhelmingly determined by factors outside the individual's control, whether these are biological, psychological, or social.

Within and across this interpretive divide, however, there is considerable variation. For example, the nature, scope, and extent of determinism and voluntarism often depend upon the level of analysis. A biological approach may stress individual pathology and the fixed features of an individual's genetic make-up as the reason behind certain behaviours. A strain theorist might look at aspects of social situation, and see behaviour as a result of the combination of opportunities available and immediate learning processes. A Left Realist approach could likewise adopt a situational analysis, but with greater emphasis on social conflict and inequality, and the role of institutions of crime control, such as the police, in fostering or dampening working-class criminality. For the critical criminologist, 'choice' is circumscribed by wider structural processes of marginalization and criminalization, or competitive market structures, and criminal activity among both the powerful and the less powerful is seen to reflect the ways in which existing social structures ultimately narrow the scope for the full exercise of human agency.

The complex ways in which the relationship between voluntarism ('free will') and determinism ('fate') is constructed in the criminological field demonstrates the existence of a series of cross-cutting analytical and political differences that transcend strict discipline boundaries.

These differences can be further highlighted by considering the underlying assumptions of criminological theory, as indicated in broad political orientation, and 'popular' conceptions of criminality and the criminal justice system. Table 12.1 outlines how the diverse propensities (or likelihoods), motivations (or drives), and circumstances (or opportunities) underpinning criminality might be conceived according to varying political and analytical focus. The table provides a rough guide to the different outlooks of the conservative, liberal, and radical commentator, and also shows the possible divisions or emphases within each broad political persuasion.

Our presentation of 'needs', 'deeds', and 'greeds' merely indicates general tendencies and, as such, is intended to provide only a schematic conceptual map of the underlying assumptions. Nevertheless, it is useful as an analytical backdrop upon which can be placed most of the theories and perspectives discussed in this book. The relevance of studying criminological theory lies precisely in the way it informs and assists us in understanding the actual source of specific arguments and the ideas of contemporary debates over crime.

We began the book by stating that the relationship between crime and criminology is always reflected in, and reflective of, particular conceptions of society. Each theory or perspective embodies particular values regarding 'what is' the nature of present society, and 'what ought to be' the best way to deal with social issues such as crime.

In the twenty-first century, the debates over crime and criminality look set to intensify as rapid social change continues to transform traditional social, economic, and political relationships. Around the world, great upheavals are taking place, and more often than not these are associated with increasing social polarization. As part of this change, and in this context, 'law-and-order' debates are now constantly at the centre of electoral politics and are standard fare for infotainment and 'serious media' alike.

In the light of current public perceptions about the 'crime threat'—and general unease about the future of jobs, the environment, peace, and respect for human rights—it is more essential than ever to think critically about the nature of crime, how it occurs, who it affects, and what can be done to prevent or control it.

It is our hope that this book will reinforce the fact that there are indeed alternative ways to conceptualize these issues, just as there are various options we can take to deal with them at a practical level. The doing of criminological theory, research, and practical intervention is always at one and the same time a statement about the kind of world each of us would like to see, and a response to the world of which we are an integral part.

**Table 12.1  Underlying Assumptions of Criminological Theory**

| | Different Reform Agendas | |
|---|---|---|
| *Needs* | *Deeds* | *Greeds* |
| *Conservative political perspective* | | |
| Focus on the individual's pathology and need to conform with socially accepted norms and mores. Emphasis on the need to counsel or treat the individual, which may require indeterminate sentencing. | Law and order. Focus on what the individual has done. The extent of harm to the status quo dictates the extent of punishment. Key issues are retribution, punishment, and deterrence. | Motivation to offend, steal, or rob is greed. Focus is on the greed of the 'street criminal' who shirks responsibility to get work and earn money respectably. A focus on 'moral training' and reaffirmation of conservative values. |
| *Liberal political perspective* | | |
| Focus on the needs of both the victim and the offender. Needs tempered by an understanding of social conditions that influence behaviour. Emphasis on restorative justice. | Civil libertarian. Focus on individual rights, determinate sentencing, and due process. Notion of equality and proportionality. All should have access to equal justice, and like offences should be treated in like manner. | Greed is more likely to be associated with those who take 'more than their fair share' from a democratic society. Discussion of white-collar crime relevant here, with a focus on regulation and moral persuasion. |
| *Radical political perspective* | | |
| Focus on the distortions of needs due to the capitalist system. This system places a priority on competition and the market. The result is an emphasis on private profit, rather than social need, which dictates the priorities of the state. | Focus on the deeds of the system, in terms of systematic bias against certain classes or ethnic groups. The degree of harm perpetrated by white-collar crime is juxtaposed against the harm perpetrated by street crime. | Greed is associated with structural competitive pressures, and the widening gap between rich and poor within society. A focus on redistribution of societal resources and radical democracy. |

The key questions that we feel are important for criminologists are:

• What kind of 'work' should we be doing and why? This refers to the means and ends of intellectual production, and raises issues concerning the social implications of our practice.

- What kind of society do we want and why? This implies that, in doing what we do, there is, or ought to be, a vision of an ideal world towards which we can direct our efforts.
- How do we distinguish between 'good' and 'bad' (or 'right' and 'wrong') and why? This is basically a question of the normative or value basis of our work.

It is our belief that attempting to answer these kinds of questions is what makes the criminological endeavour meaningful, both from a personal perspective and from a societal point of view.

The uncertainties of the world we presently inhabit are mirrored in the limitations and uncertainties of contemporary criminological theory. In the end, each theory only fully makes sense when set within an appropriate societal context and values framework. The crucial challenge for the reader, therefore, is to critically question and evaluate the ethical and explanatory basis of each theory or perspective. In so doing, it is our hope that we will be better able to clarify where we stand in relation to the great issues of the day, and to determine what our specific responsibilities and interests are in building a safer, more secure, and healthy future, one in which social harms such as crime are minimized.

# Glossary

**Alienation**: A separation of individuals from control and direction in their social life.

**Androgyny**: A personality that holds a balance of feminine and masculine characteristics.

**Anomie**: An absence, breakdown, confusion, or conflict in terms of the norms of society.

**Atavism**: Concept used by Cesare Lombroso (1835–1909) to describe a type of criminal he called the 'born criminal'. The atavistic criminal was one representing an earlier stage of human evolution. Lombroso identified this type of criminal through several stigmatized physical characteristics, including the length of earlobes and fingers, and the bone structure of the head. This supposed physical degeneracy was associated with moral degeneracy and thus more frequent criminal behaviour.

**Autonomy**: Generally understood as a person's ability to make independent choices.

**Bourgeoisie**: This term was used by Karl Marx to refer to the corporate or capitalist class in modern societies that is thought, particularly in socialist ideas, to be also a ruling class.

**Bureaucracy**: A formal organization with defined objectives, a hierarchy of specialized roles, and systematic processes of direction and administration.

**Captialism**: An economic system where economic activity is primarily directed towards the production of commodities for sale in the marketplace.

**Chicago School**: See Ecological model.

**Civil law**: Civil law has its roots in Roman law and the Enlightenment. The legal system in many civil law countries are based around one or several codes of law, which set out the main principles that guide the law.

**Colonialism**: Political domination of one nation over another that is institutionalized in direct political administration by the colonial power, control of all economic relationships, and a systematic attempt to transform the culture of the subject nation.

**Common law**: In common law legal systems, judges have the authority and duty to decide what the law is when there is no other authoritative statement of the law. The common law forms a major part of the legal systems of those countries of the world with a history as territories or colonies the British Empire.

**Concentric circles**: A term coined by Clifford Shaw and Henry McKay to describe the 'naturally' occurring various and distinct areas that developed in the city of Chicago. Each zone had stable but differing rates of crime.

**Conformity**: A term used by Robert Merton to refer to acceptance of cultural goals and the legitimate or approved means of achieving them.

**Consensus**: Refers to a commonly agreed position, conclusion, or set of values and is normally used in reference to public opinion.

**Conservatism**: A set of ideas that values social stability and the maintenance of traditional community bonds and social hierarchies. There exists the assumption that institutions and values that have lasted a long time represent the collective experience of the community and have persisted because they have fulfilled a valuable and positive role in society.

**Counterculture**: A set of cultural ideas different from and in conflict with the common culture of a society. Similar to a subculture but counterculture stresses the notion of active and open opposition to dominant cultural values.

**Criminal profiling**: The process of using available information about a crime and crime scene to compose a psychological portrait of the unknown perpetrator of the crime.

**Criminalization**: To treat as a criminal, or to make something or some action unlawful.

**Criminology**: A social science that studies crime and crime-related phenomena, such as law-making, criminal behaviour, victimization, and punishment.

**Cultural feminism**: This perspective reverses the assumption that men exhibit the normative forms of behaviour and that women are different and thus 'the other'.

**Dark figure of crime**: The amount of crime that is unreported or unknown.

**Deconstruction**: The process of rigorously analyzing and making apparent the assumptions, judgments, and values that underlie social arrangements and intellectual ideas.

**Defensible space**: A concept which emerged from environmental criminology that suggests public spaces should, and can be, designed to create a sense of ownership in residents and users. This philosophy believes that the type of design can make space easier to defend from potential criminal activity.

**Deterrence**: The attempt to control crime by creating a threat of punishment. This is directed to specific individuals (specific deterrence) or others, and potential offenders (general deterrence).

**Deviance**: A recognized violation of cultural norms.

**Differential association theory**: A theory created by Edwin Sutherland that argues criminality, like any other form of behaviour is learned through a process of association with others who communicate criminal values.

**Discrimination**: Refers to the unfair treatment of a person or group on the basis of prejudice

**Division of labour**: The division of roles, tasks, and duties within a household, workplace, or community.

**Ecological model**: Also referred to as the Chicago School, is an approach that emphasizes the characteristics of population groups and the mapped locations of such groups relative to one another and views the social disorganization that characterizes delinquency areas as a major cause of crime and victimization.

**Environmental criminological theory**: An emerging perspective that focuses on the importance of geographical location and architectural features, as they are associated with the prevalence of criminal victimization.

**Ethnography methods**: A form of qualitative research that uses participant observation as a tool to gather information.

**Ethnomethodology**: A sociological theory developed by Harold Garfinkel that roughly translates into the study of people's practices or methods. This micro-perspective views the social world as something that people must build and rebuild constantly in their thoughts and actions.

**Eugenics**: The eugenics movement, active in many parts of the western world, was driven by the belief that social intervention should occur in order to protect the best gene pool. This was achieved by encouraging people who were considered to represent 'good' genes to breed, and, more importantly, to support interventions by the state to prevent those considered to have 'bad' genes from breeding.

**Feudalism**: Feudalism refers to a general set of reciprocal legal and military obligations among the warrior nobility of Europe during the Middle Ages.

**Forensics**: The study of evidence discovered at a crime scene and used in a court of law.

**Functionalist approach**: This perspective tends to explain features of social life in terms of their function (the part they play) in social life.

**Gatekeepers**: Individuals or groups within the hierarchical structure of organizations who hold crucial positions from which they can control access to goods, services, or information.

**Globalization**: Refers to the development of extensive worldwide patterns of economic relationships between nations.

**Ideal type**: An abstract model of a pure form of social phenomenon. It is a model concept and does not necessarily exist in exact form in reality.

**Ideology**: A linked set of ideas and beliefs that act to uphold and justify an existing or desired arrangement of power, authority, wealth, and status in a society.

**Imperialism**: Domination by one or more countries over others for political and economic objectives. It can be effected by force or arms or through the economic and political power exercised by state and corporate agencies.

**Individualization**: Refers to the process whereby individuals are institutionally made more responsible for their well-being and less reliant upon state or collective support, and to the cultural and ideological prominence given to self-managing one's choices and actions.

**Inequality**: Unequal rewards of opportunities for different individuals within a group or groups within a society.

**Jurisprudence**: Concerned with the law and the principles that lead courts to make the decisions they do.

**Just desert**: A philosophy of punishment usually contrasted with utilitarianism. Rather than justifying punishment in terms of the good it will produce, it justifies punishment solely in terms of what the offender did. The offender is thought to get what he or she deserves.

**Law-and-order**: Strict enforcement of laws, especially for controlling crime.

**Left Realist criminology**: This perspective focuses on the social causes of crime and interaction between agencies of social control, the offender, the victim, and the public. It draws strongly on the concepts of relative deprivation and countercultures.

**Legitimacy**: What is accorded to a stable distribution of power when it is considered valid.

**Legitimation**: Refers to the process by which power is not only institutionalized but more importantly is given moral grounding.

**Liberal feminism**: This perspective posits that the liberal principles of equality, freedom, and equality of opportunity must be fully extended to women. It does not call for specific structural changes to society and it does not identify patriarchy or capitalism as enemies of women.

**Liberal-conflict theory**: This position views society as composed of a variety of groups who compete for, and have, differing amounts of power.

**Liberalism**: Refers to an ideology that upholds private property, individual rights, legal equality, freedom of choice, and democratic government. Supports the role of the state in creating improved equality of opportunity for all in society.

**Marginalization**: A process by which a group or individual is denied access to important positions and symbols of economic, religious, or political power within any society.

**Marxist criminology**: This perspective is concerned with the unequal distribution of resources and how structured social environment gives rise to crime and criminogenic conditions.

**Marxist feminism**: This perspective argues that women's oppression is a symptom of a more fundamental form of oppression. Women are not oppressed by men or by sexism, but by capitalism itself. If all women are to be liberated, capitalism must be replaced by socialism.

**Mechanical solidarity**: Refers to a state of community bonding or interdependency that rests on a similarity of beliefs and values, shared activities, and ties of kinship and cooperation.

**Moral panic**: A term first used by Stanley Cohen in 1972 to suggest a panic or overreaction to forms of deviance or wrongdoing perceived to threaten moral order. Moral panics are usually created or fanned by the media and led by community groups or leaders whose goals are to changes laws or practices.

**New Right criminology**: The fundamentals of this perspective are based on two themes: placing responsibility for crime squarely on the individual, and reasserting the importance of punishment in responding to crime.

**Norms**: A culturally established rule prescribing appropriate social behaviour.

**Ontology**: The study of the categories or an inventory of things that exist or may exist in a specific domain. Each special science is said to have its own ontology. In sociology for example, the ontology includes persons, institutions, relations, norms, practices, structures, and roles, depending on the theory under consideration.

**Oppression**: Unjust or cruel exercise of authority or power.

**Organic solidarity**: Refers to the state of interdependency created by the specialization of roles. Individuals and institutions become dependent on others in a complex division of labour.

**Paradigm**: A framework used in thinking about and organizing an understanding of natural or social phenomenon. Thomas Kuhn (1970) argued that a paradigm was a set of assumptions about the kinds of questions to ask in science and how to go about looking for answers.

**Patriarchy**: Generally refers to a social situation where men are dominant over women in wealth, status, and power. It is associated with a set of ideas, a 'patriarchal ideology' that acts to explain and justify this dominance and attributes it to inherent natural differences between men and women.

**Peacemaking criminology**: A perspective that holds crime-control agencies and the citizens they serve should work to alleviate social problems and human suffering and thus reduce crime.

**Phenomenology**: A sociological approach that seeks to reveal how human awareness is implicated in the production of social actions, social situations, and social worlds.

**Pluralism**: This perspective argues that a multiplicity of values and beliefs exists in any complex society.

**Political economy**: A general approach to social analysis that stresses the interconnectedness of social, political, and economic processes in society.

**Positivism**: One way to think about the relationship between science and society, found in the early writings of Auguste Comte (1798–1857). Positivism places science in a privileged position, assumes the possibility of a scientific understanding of human and social behaviour, assumes the separation of knowledge and power, and assumes the possibility of objectivity and impartiality.

**Postmodern critical criminology**: A critical approach that sees power in terms of language, and the ways that knowledge production shapes human experience.

**Power**: The capacity of individuals or institutions to achieve goals even if opposed by others.

**Precedents**: A rule that will guide judges in making subsequent decisions in similar cases.

**Primary deviance**: Term used by Ervin Goffman to represent actions that contradict the norms of a group or society but are relatively mild and would not impact a person's self-concept. Primary deviance is any general deviance before the deviant is labeled as such.

**Procedural law**: Lays out the rules which representatives of the state must follow when investigating crime and prosecuting offenders.

**Proletariat**: A term associated with Karl Marx that refers to the class of individuals in a capitalist society who have no means of production of their own and must subsist economically by selling wage labour to owners of capital.

**Punitive**: To inflict punishment.

**Radical feminism**: This perspective argues that women's oppression is historically primary, harder to transform, causes more harm, and is more widespread than class oppression. Some radical feminists claim that women's oppression is rooted in biology, and its elimination will require a biological revolution that transforms women's relation to reproduction.

**Rational choice theory**: This perspective argues that criminals are making rational choices to commit crime after examining the likelihood of being caught or convicted.

**Rehabilitation**: An attempt to change or reform a convicted person so that he or she will not commit another criminal act.

**Reintegration**: The process of reintroducing a convicted offender into the community.

**Reintegrative shaming**: Braithwaite's shaming theory posits that reintegrative shaming, a process by which the offender is shamed for his or her actions and then is welcomed back into the community, inhibits future misbehaviour. He also argues that those who participate in the shaming process are less likely to misbehave in the first place.

**Relative deprivation**: Deprivation that is not judges against an absolute level of sustainability but of deprivation in relation to others around you.

**Republican theory**: A theory put forward by John Braithwaite and Phillip Pettit that posits the purpose of the criminal justice system should be promote a republican conception of freedom. Republicanism realizes that law alone cannot achieve structural change, and moreover counsels legal restraint through its adherence to a presumption that intervention by the law should be a measure of last resort. Republican theory emphasizes the importance of non-legal forms of regulation (informal social norms and practices).

**Restitution**: Usually a condition attached to a probation order requiring the offender to pay back the victim or the community in some way.

**Restorative justice**: A process for resolving crime and conflicts that focuses on redressing the harms caused to victims while holding offenders accountable for their actions and engaging the community in a conflict resolution process.

**Retribution**: Punishment deserved because of an offence that fits the severity of the crime.

**Risk society**: The term is not intended to imply an increase of risk in society, but rather a society that is organized in response risks. It is a society increasingly preoccupied with the future (and also with safety), which generates the notion of risk.

**Routine activities theory**: Claims that occurrences of personal victimization are dependent upon the 'routine' of 'daily activities' of people and are the outcome of three elements: motivated offenders, suitable targets, and the absence of suitable guardians.

**Rule of law**: A cornerstone of democratic society. Everyone is subject to law, everyone is equal in law, and no-one is exempt from law.

**Secondary deviance**: Secondary deviance is any action that takes place after primary deviance occurs. This is the stage where the individual begins to internal the label of deviant and it affects their self-concept.

**Self-concept**: This concept may be considered the foundation of symbolic interactionism. It highlights the reflective and reflexive ability of human beings to take themselves as objects of their own thoughts.

**Self-report**: A method for measuring crime involving the distribution of detailed questionnaires to a sample of people, asking them if they have committed a crime during a particular period of time.

**Sexual assault**: A broader classification of sexual offence than 'rape'. It is an assault that violates the sexual integrity of the victim. There are three levels of sexual assault that replace earlier offences of rape and indecent assault.

**Sexualization theory**: This perspective argues that women who deviate from the traditional norms of feminine behaviours or display non-feminine characteristics are seen to be more likely to be offenders.

**Social construct**: This understanding of society rejects the notion that events or social phenomena have an independent and objective existence. Instead, this understanding argues that social reality is created or constructed by its members.

**Social contract**: In essence, this concept means that a group or groups of rational and self-interested individuals came together to form a contract which created society. Social rules were created that meant, while each individual gave up a bit of freedom, their self-interest would be protected.

**Social control theory**: This theory seeks to explain why all individuals do not engage in criminal behaviours. The answer can be found in different dimensions of social control, mainly the ways in which people are controlled by family, school, work, and conscience.

**Social disorganization theory**: The theory that crime and other deviant behaviour is most likely to occur where social institutions are not able to direct and control groups of individuals.

**Social ecology**: An approach to theorizing that attempts to link the structure and organization of any human community interactions to interactions with its localized environment.

**Social order**: Refers to a set of linked social institutions, social structures and social practices that maintain and enforce 'normal' ways of relating and behaving.

**Social structure**: The patterned and relatively stable arrangement of roles and statuses found with societies and social institutions. Social structures are inseparable from cultural norms and values that also shape status and social interaction.

**Socialist feminism**: This perspective examines women's social situation as shaped by both patriarchal gender relations and by the class structure of capitalism. It argues for the equality of women within a society that is not dependant on the exploitation of one group by another.

**Sociology**: A social science that examines the structure, organization, and culture of societies and their processes of social change and social interaction.

**Square of crime**: A fundamental concept in left realism that deals with the relationships between two dyads that exist in crime. The first dyad deals with the criminal act and focuses on the offender and victim. The second dyad focuses on social control, which is made up of social action (reactions of police for example) and social reaction (reaction of the public).

**Standpoint feminism**: This perspective claims that less powerful members of society are able to achieve a more comprehensive view of social reality. Less powerful groups, like women and minorities, may be less incorporated into the reward system of society and more clear-sighted and critical about its inequalities and deficiencies.

**Stigma**: A term used by Erving Goffman to mean a powerfully negative label that radically changes a person's self-concept and social identity.

**Structural critical criminology**: A critical approach that focuses on power as something that is ingrained in social structures and that manifests itself in the actions of institutions and the activities of sectional interest groups.

**Subcultures**: A culture-within-a culture. The concept of subculture implies some degree of group self-sufficiency where individuals can interact, find employment, recreation, and friends within the group.

**Substantive law**: The portion of the Criminal Code that specifies which acts constitute crime and what the punishments should be.

**Symbol**: Objects, characters, or other concrete representations of ideas, concepts, or other abstractions.

**Symbolic interactionist**: A sociological perspective that stresses the way societies are created through the interaction of individuals. George H. Mead (1883–1931), a founder of symbolic interactionism, saw interaction as creating and recreating the patterns and structures that bring society to life.

**Theory**: Theory consists of a set of concepts, and their nominal relationship between these concepts, assumptions, and knowledge claims.

**Transition zones**: Zones that are characterized by frequent changes in population composition, and high levels of social disorganization. Transition zones are typically located in inner cities.

**Typification**: To represent by an image, form, or model an ideal type. Also refers to any basic cognitive process in which some entity comes to stand for or represent something else.

**Values**: Relative, general cultural prescriptions of what is right, moral, and desirable. They provide the broad foundations for specific normative regulation of social interaction.

**Victimization**: An act that exploits or treats someone unfairly.

**Youth culture**: Are explained either by factors in the experience of adolescence or by the manipulation of young people's spending and leisure, through advertising and other mass media. The functional separation of home, school, and work supposedly makes teenagers increasingly distinct from adults and subject to peer-group influence rather than parent and other adult influences.

# References

Abbott, J.H. (1981). *In the Belly of the Beast: Letters from Prison*. New York: Random House.

———. (2002). *Hard Time Blues: How Politics Built a Prison Nation*. New York: St. Martin's Press.

Abel, L. (2007). 'Stop the Violence, Sisters of Slain Plead', *Toronto Star*, 27 July.

Aboriginal Legal Services of Toronto. (2007). *Mandate of Aboriginal Legal Services of Toronto's Community Council Program*. Available at http://www.aboriginallegal.ca/program.

Abu-Jamal, M. (1995). *Live from Death Row*. New York: Avon Books.

Alder, C. (1985). 'Theories of Female Delinquency', in *Juvenile Delinquency in Australia*, A. Borowski and J. Murray, eds. North Ryde: Methuen.

———. (1991). 'Explaining Violence: Socioeconomics and Masculinity', in *Australian Violence: Contemporary Perspectives*, D. Chappell, P. Grabosky and H. Strang, eds. Canberra: Australian Institute of Criminology.

———. (1994). 'Women and the Criminal Justice System', in *The Australian Criminal Justice System: The Mid-1990s*, D. Chappell and P. Wilson, eds. Sydney: Butterworths.

Alder, C., and J. Wundersitz, eds. (1994). *Family Conferencing and Juvenile Justice*. Canberra: Australian Institute of Criminology.

Aldhous, P. (1995). 'Borrowed Genes Caused Cholera Chaos', *New Scientist* 1966 (25 February): 14.

Allen, J. (1990). '"The Wild Ones": The Disavowal of Men in Criminology' in *Dissenting Opinions*, R. Graycar, ed. Sydney: Allen & Unwin.

Amnesty International. 2002. *Without Discrimination: The Fundamental Right of All Canadians to Human Rights Protection*. Brief to the U.N. Committee on the Elimination of Racial Discrimination on the Occasion of the Examination of the Thirteenth and Fourteenth Periodic Reports Submitted by Canada, July.

Anderson, E. (1990). *Streetwise: Race, Class, and Change in an Urban Community*. Chicago: University of Chicago Press.

Arrigo, B., and T. Bernard. (1997). 'Postmodern Criminology in Relation to Radical and Conflict Criminology', *Critical Criminology* 8(2): 39–60.

Audioblox. n.d. "IQ Test: Where Does It Come From", *History of IQ Tests*. Available at http://iq-test.learninginfo.org/iq01.htm.

Austin, J., and J. Irwin. (2001). *It's About Time*. Belmont, CA: Wadsworth, Belmont.

Barak, G. (2007). 'Supranational Criminology: Towards An Integrative Study of International Crimes and State-Corporate Criminality'. Paper from the Expert Meeting at Maastricht University, The Netherlands, 12–15 April.

Barlow, H. (1993). *Introduction to Criminology*. New York: Harper Collins College Publishers.

Barnett, H. (1993). 'Wealth, Crime and Capital Accumulation', in *Crime and Capitalism: Readings in Marxist Criminology*, D. Greenberg, ed. Philadelphia, PA: Temple University Press.

Bartollas, C., and M. Braswell. (1993). 'Correctional Treatment, Peacemaking, and the New Age Movement', *Journal of Crime and Justice* 16(2): 43–58.

Bazemore, G. (1991). 'Beyond Punishment, Surveillance and Traditional Treatment: Themes for a New Mission in U.S. Juvenile Justice', in *Official Responses to Problem Juveniles: Some International Reflections*, J. Hackler, ed. Onati: International Institute for the Sociology of Law.

———. (1997). 'The "Community" in Community Justice: Issues, Themes, and Questions for the New Neighbourhood Sanctioning Models', *The Justice System Journal* 19(2): 193–227.

———. (1998). 'Restorative Justice and Earned Redemption', *American Behavioral Scientist* 41(6): 768–813.

Bazemore, G., and L. Walgrave, eds. (1999). *Restorative Juvenile Justice: Repairing the Harm of Youth Crime*. Monsey, NY: Criminal Justice Press.

Beccaria, C. (1767). *An Essay On Crimes and Punishments*. London: J. Almon.

Beck, U. (1992). *Risk Society: Toward a New Modernity*. London: Sage.

Becker, H. (1963). *Outsiders: Studies in the Sociology of Deviance*. New York: Free Press.

Bell, S.J. (2007). *Young Offenders and Youth Justice: A Century After the Fact*. Toronto: Thomson Nelson.

Benton, T. (1998). 'Rights and Justice on a Shared Planet: More Rights or New Relations?', *Theoretical Criminology* 2(2): 149–75.

Berger, P., and T. Luckmann. (1971). *The Social Construction of Reality*. London: Allen Lane.

Bilchick, S. (1998). *Guide for Implementing the Balanced and Restorative Justice Model*, Washington, DC: Office of Juvenile Justice and Delinquency Prevention.

Birsch, D., and J.H. Fielder, eds. (1994). *The Ford Pinto Case: A Study in Applied Ethics, Business, and Theory*. New York: SUNY Press.

Bohm, R.M. (1999). *A Primer on Crime and Delinquency Theory*. Toronto: Wadsworth.

———. (2001). *A Primer on Crime and Delinquency Theory*, 2nd ed. Toronto: Wadsworth.

Bottomley, S., N. Gunningham, and S. Parker. (1991). *Law in Context*. Sydney: Federation Press.

Bottoms, A., and P. Wiles. (1997). 'Environmental Criminology', in *The Oxford Handbook of Criminology*, 2nd ed., M. Maguire, R. Morgan, and R. Reiner, eds. Oxford: Clarendon Press.

Boyd, S., D. Chunn, and R. Menzies, eds. (2002). *Toxic Criminology: Environment, Law and the State in Canada*. Halifax: Fernwood.

Braithwaite, J. (1989). *Crime, Shame and Reintegration*. Cambridge: Cambridge University Press.

———. (1991). 'Poverty, Power, White-Collar Crime and the Paradoxes of Criminological Theory', *Australian and New Zealand Journal of Criminology* 24(1): 40–58.

———. (1992). 'Reducing the Crime Problem: A Not So Dismal Criminology—the John Barry Memorial Lecture', *Australian and New Zealand Journal of Criminology* 25(1): 1–10.

Braithwaite, J., and P. Pettit. (1990). *Not Just Deserts: A Republican Theory of Criminal Justice*. Oxford: Clarendon Press.

Brake, M. (1985). *Comparative Youth Culture*. London: Routledge and Kegan Paul.

Brill, H. (1993). 'Auto Theft and the Role of Big Business', in *Crime and Capitalism: Readings in Marxist Criminology*, D. Greenberg, ed. Philadelphia, PA: Temple University Press.

Brown, C. (1979). *Understanding Society: An Introduction to Sociological Theory*. London: John Murray.

Brown, D., and R. Hogg. (1992). 'Essentialism, Radical Criminology and Left Realism', *Australian and New Zealand Journal of Criminology* 25(3): 195–230.

Bryne, J., and R. Sampson. (1985). *The Social Ecology of Crime*. New York: Springer Verlag.

Buchanan, C., and P. Hartley. (1992). *Criminal Choice: The Economic Theory of Crime and Its Implications for Crime Control*. Sydney: Centre for Independent Studies.

Bullard, R. (1994). *Unequal Protection: Environmental Justice and Communities of Color*. San Francisco: Sierra Club Books.

Bursik, R.J. Jr. (1988). 'Social Disorganization and Theories of Crime and Delinquency: Problems and Prospects', *Criminology* 26(4): 519–52.

Bursik, R., and H. Grasmick. (1993). 'Economic Deprivation and Neighborhood Crime Rates, 1960–1980', *Law and Society Review* 27: 263–78.

Burton-Rose, D., with D. Pens and P. Wright, eds. (1998). *The Celling of America: An Inside Look at the US Prison Industry*. Monroe, ME: Common Courage Press.

Butcher, K. (2000). 'Review of *On Strike: The Winnipeg General Strike, 1919*. (The People's History of the West Series)', *CM Magazine* 7(4). Available at http://umanitoba.ca/cm/vol7/no4/onstrike.html.

*Canadian Encyclopedia, The.* (2007) 'Eugenics: Keeping Canada Sane'. Available at http://www.thecanadianencyclopedia.com.

Carrington, K. (1993). *Offending Girls*. Sydney: Allen & Unwin.

Carrington, K., and R. Hogg, eds. (2002). *Critical Criminology: Issues, Debates, Challenges*. Devon: Willan Publishing.

Catalano, R., and J. Hawkins. (1996). 'The Social Development Model: A Theory of Antisocial Behavior', *Delinquency and Crime: Current Theories*, in J. Hawkins, ed. Cambridge: Cambridge University Press.

CBC. (2006a). 'On This Day: Remembering the Winnipeg General Strike', *CBC Archives*.

———. (2006b). 'Gap Widens Between Rich and Poor', Available at http://www.cbc.ca/money/story/2006/12/13/wealth.html.

———. (2006c). 'On this Day: The Westray Mining Disaster', *CBC Archives*. http://archives.cbc.ca/on_this_day/05/09/.

Chambliss, W. (1975a). 'A Sociological Analysis of the Law of Vagrancy', in *The Sociology of Crime and Delinquency in Britain*, Vol. 1, W. Carson and P. Wiles, eds. Oxford: Martin Robertson.

———. (1975b). 'The Political Economy of Crime: A Comparative Study of Nigeria and USA', in *Critical Criminology*, I. Taylor, P. Walton, and J. Young, eds. London: Routledge and Kegan Paul.

Chambliss, W., and M. Mankoff. (1976). *Whose Law What Order? A Conflict Approach to Criminology*. Toronto: John Wiley and Sons.

Chamlin, M., and J. Cochran. (1997). 'Social Altruism and Crime', *Criminology* 35: 203–28.

Chesney-Lind, M. (1974). 'Juvenile Delinquency and the Sexualisation of Female Crime', *Psychology Today* (July): 4–7.

Chesney-Lind, M., and R. Shelden. (1992). *Girls, Delinquency and Juvenile Justice*. Belmont, CA: Brooks/Cole Publishing.

Christie, N. (1993). *Crime Control as Industry: Towards Gulags Western Style?* London: Routledge.

Cicourel A. (1976). *The Social Organisation of Juvenile Justice*. London: Heinemann.

Cleaver, E. (1968). *Soul on Ice*. New York: Dell.

Clarke, J., S. Hall, T. Jefferson, and B. Roberts. (1976). 'Subcultures, Cultures and Class: A Theoretical Overview', *Resistance Through Rituals: Youth Subcultures in Post-War Britain*, in S. Hall and T. Jefferson, eds. London: Hutchinson.

Clausen, J.A. (1993). *American Lives*. New York: Free Press.

Cloward, R., and L. Ohlin. (1960). *Delinquency and Opportunity: A Theory of Delinquent Gangs*. Chicago: Free Press.

Cohen, A. (1955). *Delinquent Boys: The Culture of the Gang*. Chicago: Free Press.

Cohen, S. (1973). *Folk Devils and Moral Panics*. London: Paladin.

———. (1979). 'The Punitive City: Notes on the Dispersal of Social Control', *Contemporary Crises* 3: 339–63.

———. (1985). *Visions of Social Control*. Cambridge: Polity Press.

———. (1988). *Against Criminology*. New Brunswick, NJ: Transaction Books.

———. (1993). 'Human Rights and Crimes of the State: The Culture of Denial', *Australian and New Zealand Journal of Criminology* 26(2): 97–115.

Cohen, S., and J. Young. (2004). 'Comments on Simon Cottee's "Folk devils and moral panics: 'Left Idealism' reconsidered"', *Theoretical Criminology* 8(1): 93–7.

Collins, J., G. Noble, S. Poynting, and P. Tabar. (2000). *Kebabs, Kids, Cops and Crime: Youth, Ethnicity and Crime*. Sydney: Pluto Press.

Comack, E. (1999). *Locating Law: Race/Class/Gender Connections*. Halifax: Fernwood.

Comack, E., and G. Balfour, eds. (2004). *The Power to Criminalize: Violence, Inequality and Law*. Halifax: Fernwood.

Connell, R. (1995). *Masculinities*. Cambridge: Polity.

———. (2000). *The Men and the Boys*. Sydney: Allen & Unwin.

———. (2002). 'On Hegemonic Masculinity and Violence: Response to Jefferson and Hall', *Theoretical Criminology* 6(1): 89–99.

Conover, T. (2000). *Newjack: Guarding Sing Sing*. New York: Random House.

Conservative Party of Canada. (2006). Conservative Party of Canada Policy Declaration. National Policy Convention, Montreal, 19 March.

Cook, D., and B. Hudson, eds. (1993). *Racism and Criminology*. London: Sage.

Cordella P., and L. Siegel, eds. *Readings in Contemporary Criminological Theory*. Boston: Northeastern University Press.

Cormier, R., and T. Audette. (2006). 'Chief Puts Thugs on Notice', *Edmonton Journal*, 28 October.

Cornforth, M. (1987). *Historical Materialism*, Vol. 2 of *Dialectical Materialism: An Introduction*. London: Lawrence and Wishart.

Corrado, R., and A. Markwart. (1992). 'The Evaluation and Implementation of a New Era of Juvenile Justice in Canada', in *Juvenile Justice in Canada: A Theoretical and Analytical Assessment*, R. Corrada, N. Bala, R. Linden, and M. LeBlanc, eds. Toronto: Butterworths.

Coser, L. (1977). *Masters of Sociological Thought: Ideas in Historical and Social Context*. New York: Harcourt Brace Jovanovich.

Cottee, S. (2002). 'Folk Devils and Moral Panics: "Left Idealism" reconsidered', *Theoretical Criminology* 6(4): 387–410.

CTV. (2006a). 'Election Day, January 2006', *CTV.ca News*, 20 January.

———. (2006b). 'Report: Prison System Discriminatory to Aboriginals', *CTV.ca News*, 16 October.

Cunneen, C., and R. White. (2002). *Juvenile Justice: Youth and Crime in Australia*. Melbourne: Oxford University Press.

Curry, G.D., and I. Spergel. (1988). 'Gang Homicide, Delinquency, and Community', *Criminology* 26: 381–407.

Daly, K., and M. Chesney-Lind. (1996). 'Feminism and Criminology', in *Readings in Contemporary Criminological Theory*, P. Cordella and L. Siegal, eds. Boston: Northeastern University Press.

Davis, N.J. (1975). *Sociological Constructions of Deviance: Perspectives and Issues in the Field*. Dubuque, IA: Wm. C. Brown.

Dawson, C.A. (1926). *The City as an Organism: With Special Reference to Montreal*. Montreal, QC: McGill University Publications.

DeKeseredy, W.S., M.D. Schwartz, and S. Alvi. (2006). 'Left Realism', in *Current Issues in Critical Criminology*, W.S. DeKeseredy and B. Perry, eds. Lanham, MD: Lexicon Books.

DeKeseredy, W.S., B.D. MacLean, and M.D. Schwartz. (1997). 'Thinking Critically about Left Realism', pp. 19–27 in *Thinking Critically About Crime*, B.D. MacLean and D. Milovanovic, eds. Vancouver: Collective Press.

DeKeseredy, W.S., and M.D. Schwartz. (2005). 'Left Realism Theory', pp. 307–16 in *The Essential Criminology Reader*, 3rd ed., S. Henry and M.M. Lanier, eds. Boulder, CO: Westview Press.

Derksen, W. (2002). *Confronting the Horror: The Aftermath of Violence*. Danbury, CT: Amity Publishing.

De Haan, W., and I. Loader. (2002). 'On the Emotions of Crime, Punishment and Social Control', *Theoretical Criminology* 6(3): 243–54.

Department of Justice Canada. (2001). *Examination of Declining Intimate Partner Homicide Rates: A Literature Review*. Ottawa, ON: Government of Canada.

DiIulio, J. Jr, R.P. George, and T.L. Simmons. (2001). *The Clash of Orthodoxies: Law, Religion, and Morality in Crisis*. New York: ISI Publishers.

Donnelly, J. (2003). *Universal Human Rights in Theory and Practice*, 2nd ed. Ithaca, NY: Cornell University Press.

Doucette, C. (2007). 'Double Murder', *Sun Media*, 6 July.

Dowbiggen, I.R. (1997). *Keeping American Sane: Psychiatry in the United States and Canada, 1880–1940*. New York: Cornell University Press.

Downes, D. (1966). *The Delinquent Solution*. London: Routledge and Kegan Paul.

Durkheim, E. (1979). *Suicide: A Study in Sociology*. London: Routledge and Kegan Paul

Edwards, S. (1990). 'Violence Against Women: Feminism and the Law', in *Feminist Perspectives in Criminology*, L. Gelsthorpe and A. Morris, eds. Milton Keynes: Open University Press.

Eisenstein, H. (1984). *Contemporary Feminist Thought*. London: Unwin Paperbacks.

Einstadter, W., and S. Henry. (1995). *Criminological Theory: An Analysis of Its Underlying Assumptions*. Fort Worth, TX: Harcourt Brace.

Elder, G.H., Jr. (1985). 'Perspectives on the Life-Course', in *Life Course Dynamics*, G.H. Elder Jr, ed. Ithaca, NY: Cornell University Press.

Elliott, D., W.J. Wilson, D. Huizinga, R. Sampson, A. Elliott, and B. Rankin. (1996). 'The Effects of Neighborhood Disadvantage on Adolescent Development', *Journal of Research in Crime and Delinquency* 33: 389–426.

Empey, L. (1982). *American Delinquency: Its Meaning and Construction*. Chicago, IL: The Dorsey Press.

Ericson, R., and P. Baranek, and J. Chan. (1991). *Representing Order: Crime, Law and Justice in the News Media*. Milton Keynes: Open University Press.

Evans, D., N. Fyfe, and D. Herbert, eds. (1992). *Crime, Policing and Place: Essays in Environmental Criminology*. London: Routledge.

Eysenck, H. (1984). 'Crime and Personality', in *Psychology and Law*, D. Muller, D. Blackmann and A. Chapmann, eds. New York: John Wiley and Sons.

Farrington, D. (1996a). 'The Development of Offending and Antisocial Behavior from Childhood to Adulthood', in *Readings in Contemporary Criminological Theory*, P. Cordella and L. Siegel, eds. Boston: Northeastern University Press.

———. (1996b). 'The Explanation and Prevention of Juvenile Offending', in *Delinquency and Crime: Current Theories*, J. Hawkins, ed. Cambridge: Cambridge University Press.

Feeley, M., and J. Simon. (1994). 'Actuarial Justice: the Emerging New Criminal Law', in *The Futures of Criminology*, D. Nelken, ed. London: Sage.

Feldman, P. (1993). *The Psychology of Crime*. Cambridge: Cambridge University Press.

Felson, M. (1994). *Crime and Everyday Life: Insights and Implications for Society*. London: Pine Forge Press.

Feminist Anthology Collective. (1981). *No Turning Back: Writings from the Women's Liberation Movement 1975–80*. London: The Women's Press.

Ferrell, J. (1997). 'Youth, Crime and Cultural Space', *Social Justice* 24(4): 21–38.

Ferrell, J., and C. Sanders. (1995). *Cultural Criminology*. Boston: Northeastern University Press.

Fine, B. (1984). *Democracy and the Rule of Law: Liberal Ideals and Marxist Critiques*. London: Pluto.

Findlay, M. (1999). *The Globalisation of Crime*. Cambridge: Cambridge University Press.

Fishbein, D. (1990). 'Biological Perspectives in Criminology', *Criminology* 28(1): 27–72.

Fitzgerald, G. (1989). *Report of the Commission of Possible Illegal Activities and Associated Police Misconduct*. Brisbane: Queensland Government Printer.

Foucault, M. (1977). *Discipline and Punish: The Birth of the Prison*. London: Penguin.

———. (1980). 'Truth and Power' in *Power/Knowledge: Selected Interviews and Other Writings 1972–1977*, C. Gordon, ed. New York: Pantheon Books.

Fraser, S., ed. (1995). *The Bell Curve Wars: Race, Intelligence and the Future of America*. New York: Basic Books.

Frenette, M., and S. Coulombe. (2007). *Has Higher Education Among Young Women Substantially Reduced the Gender Gap in Employment and Earnings?* Ottawa, ON: Statistics Canada.

Freund, J. (1969). *The Sociology of Max Weber*. New York: Vintage Books.

Friedrichs, D. (1991). 'Introduction: Peacemaking Criminology in a World Filled with Conflict', in *New Directions in Critical Criminology*, B. MacLean and D. Milovanovic, eds. Vancouver: The Collective Press.

———. (1996). *Trusted Criminals: White Collar Crime in Contemporary Society*. Belmont, CA: Wadsworth.

Friedman, J. (2003). *Globalization, the State and Violence*. Walnut Creek, CA: Alta Mira Press.

Fuller, J. (1998). 'Criminal Justice: A Peacemaking Perspective', *Crime, Law, and Social Change* 29(1): 84–5.

Gamble, A. (1988). *The Free Economy and the Strong State: The Politics of Thatcherism*. London: Macmillan Education.

Garland, D. (1988). 'British Criminology Before 1935', *The British Journal of Criminology* 28: 131–47.

———. (1990). *Punishment and Modern Society: A Study in Social Theory*. Oxford: Clarendon Press.

———. (2001). *The Culture of Control: Crime and Social Order in Contemporary Society*. Chicago: University of Chicago Press.

Garton, S. (1991). 'The Convict Origins Debate: Historians and the Problem of the "Criminal Class"', *Australian and New Zealand Journal of Criminology* 24(2): 66–82.

Gaucher, B. (1998). 'Punitive Justice and the Victim's Movement', *Journal of Prisoners on Prisons* 9(2): 2–16.

Geis, G., and C. Goff. (1983). 'Introduction' in *White-Collar Crime: The Uncut Version*, E. Sutherland, ed. New Haven: Yale University Press.

Gelsthorpe, L., and A. Morris, eds. (1990). *Feminist Perspectives in Criminology*. Milton Keynes: Open University Press.

Gibbons, D. (1977). *Society, Crime and Criminal Careers*. Upper Saddle River, NJ: Prentice-Hall.

———. (1979). *The Criminological Enterprise: Theories and Perspectives*. Upper Saddle River, NJ: Prentice Hall.

Gillespie, K., and K. Rushowy. (2007). '$4 Million Safe Haven Plans Open School for Summer', *Toronto Star*, 6 June.

Glueck, S., and E. Glueck. (1960). *Unraveling Juvenile Delinquency*. Cambridge: Harvard University Press.

Goddard, H.H. (1920). *Human Efficiency and Levels of Intelligence*. Princeton: Princeton University Press.

Gordon, R. (1995). 'Street Gangs in Vancouver', in *Canadian Delinquency*, J. Creechan and R. Silverman, eds. Toronto: Prentice Hall.

Gordon, R., and S. Foley. (1998). *Criminal Business Organizations, Street Gangs and Related Groups in Vancouver: The Report of the Greater Vancouver Gang Study*. Vancouver: Ministry of Attorney-General.

Goring, C. (1913). *The English Convict: A Statistical Study*. London: His Majesty's Stationery Office.

Gottfredson, M., and T. Hirschi. (1990). *A General Theory of Crime*. Stanford: Stanford University Press.

Gottfredson, M., R. McNeill, and G. Gottfredson. (1991). 'Social Area Influences on Delinquency: A Multilevel Analysis', *Journal of Research in Crime and Delinquency* 28: 197–206.

Gould, S. (1981). *The Mismeasure of Man*. New York: W.W. Norton and Co.

Government of Canada. (2007a). *An Overview of the Employment and Equity Act*. Ottawa, ON: Human Resources and Social Development Canada.

———. (2007b). *The Evolution of Victim's Rights in Canada*. Available at http://victimsweek.gc.ca.resource_guide.

Grabosky, P., and P. Wilson. (1989). *Journalism and Justice: How Crime Is Reported*. Leichhardt: Pluto Press.

Graycar, R., and J. Morgan. (1990). *The Hidden Gender of Law*. Sydney: Federation Press.

Green, P., and T. Ward. (2000). 'State Crime, Human Rights and the Limits of Criminology', *Social Justice* 27(1): 101–15.

Greenberg, D., ed. (1993). *Crime and Capitalism: Readings in Marxist Criminology*. Philadelphia, PA: Temple University Press.

Grossman, J.R., A.D. Keating, and J.L. Reiff. (2005). *Encyclopedia of Chicago*. Chicago: University of Chicago Press.

Hagan, J. (1987). *Modern Criminology: Crime, Criminal Behavior and Its Control*. Toronto: McGraw-Hill.

Haines, F. (1997). *Corporate Regulation: Beyond 'Punish or Persuade'*. Oxford: Clarendon Press.

———. (2000). 'Towards Understanding Globalisation and Control of Corporate Harm: a Preliminary Criminological Analysis', *Current Issues in Criminal Justice* 12(2): 166–80.

Hall, S. (1980). 'Popular–Democratic vs. Authoritarian Populism: Two Ways of "Taking Democracy Seriously"', in *Marxism and Democracy*, A. Hunt, ed. London: Lawrence and Wishart.

Hall, S., and T. Jefferson, eds. (1976). *Resistance Through Rituals: Youth Subcultures in Post-War Britain*. London: Hutchinson.

Hall, S., and G. McLennan. (1986). 'Custom and Law: Law and Crime as Historical Processes', in *Law and Disorder: Histories of Crime and Justice*. Milton Keynes: Open University Course Material.

Hall, S., and P. Scraton. (1981). 'Law, Class and Control', in *Crime and Society: Readings in History and Theory*, M. Fitzgerald, G. McLennan, and J. Pawson, eds. London: Routledge and Kegan Paul.

Hall, S., T. Jefferson, C. Critcher, and B. Roberts. (1978). *Policing the Crisis: Mugging, the State, and Law and Order*. London: Macmillan.

Hallinan, J.T. (2001). *Going up the River: Travels in a Prison Nation*. New York: Random House.

Hassine, V. (1996). *Life Without Parole: Living in Prison Today*. Los Angeles, CA: Roxbury.

Hayward, K. (2002). 'The Vilification and Pleasures of Youthful Transgression', in *Youth Justice: Critical Readings*, J. Muncie, G. Hughes, and E. McLaughlin, eds. London: Sage.

Heitmeyer, W. (2002). 'Have Cities Ceased to Function as "Integration Machines" for Young People?', in *Youth in Cities: A Cross-National Perspective*, M. Tienda and W.J. Wilson, eds. Cambridge: Cambridge University Press.

Henry, S., and D. Milovanovic. (1994). 'The Constitution of Constitutive Criminology: A Postmodern Approach to Criminological Theory', in *The Futures of Criminology*, D. Nelken, ed. London: Sage.

———. (1996). *Constitutive Criminology: Beyond Postmodernism*. London: Sage.

Herrnstein, R., and C. Murray. (1994). *The Bell Curve*. New York: Basic Books.

Hilbert, R. (1989). 'Durkheim and Merton on Anomie: An Unexplored Contrast in Derivatives', *Social Problems* 36: 242–56.

Hirschi, T. (1969). *Causes of Delinquency*. Berkeley, CA: University of California Press.

Hogg, R. (1988). 'Taking Crime Seriously: Left Realism and Australian Criminology', in *Understanding Crime and Criminal Justice*, M. Findlay and R. Hogg, eds. Sydney: Law Book Company.

Hogg, R., and D. Brown. (1998). *Rethinking Law and Order*. Sydney: Pluto Press.

Howe, A. (1994). *Punish and Critique: Towards a Feminist Analysis of Penality*. London: Routledge.

Huff, R., ed. (1996). *Gangs in America*, 2nd ed. Thousand Oaks, CA: Sage.

Indermaur, D., D. Brown, S. Egger, and R. Hogg. (2002). 'Shadow Boxing with an Imaginary Enemy—A Response to "Law and Order Blues"', *The Australian and New Zealand Journal of Criminology* 35(2): 145–58.

Inverarity, J., P. Lauderdale, and B. Feld. (1983). *Law and Society: Sociological Perspectives on Criminal Law*. Boston: Little, Brown and Company.

Irwin, J. (1970). *The Felon*. Fort Worth, TX: Harcourt Brace.

———. (1980). *Prisons in Turmoil*. Boston: Little, Brown and Company.

Irwin, J., and D. Cressey. (1962). 'Thieves, Convicts, and Inmate Culture', *Social Problems* 10: 142–55.

Jaggs, D. (1986). *Neglected and Criminal: Foundations of Child Welfare Legislation in Victoria*. Melbourne: Phillip Institute of Technology.

James, D. (2001). *Emily Murphy*. Toronto: Fitzhenry & Whiteside.

Jefferson, T. (1997). 'Masculinities and Crimes', in *The Oxford Handbook of Criminology*, 2nd ed., M. Maguire, R. Morgan, and R. Reiner, eds. Oxford: Clarendon Press.

Jessor, R., J. Donova, and F. Costa. (1991). *Beyond Adolescence: Problem Behavior and Young Adult Development*. Cambridge: Cambridge University Press.

Johnson, R. (1996). *Hard Time: Understanding and Reforming the Prison*. Belmont, CA: Wadsworth.

Johnston, E. (1991). *National Report, 5 Vols, Royal Commission into Aboriginal Deaths in Custody*. Canberra: Australian Government Publishing Service.

Jones, T., B. MacLean, and J. Young. (1986). *The Islington Crime Survey*. Aldershot: Gower.

Jupp, V. (1989). *Methods of Criminological Research*. London: Routledge.

Karmen, A. (2001). *Crime Victims: An Introduction to Victimology*. Belmont, CA: Wadsworth.

Katz, J. (1988). *Seductions of Crime: Moral and Sensual Attractions in Doing Evil*. New York: Basic Books.

Kauzlarich, D., C. Mullins, and R. Matthews. (2003). 'A Complicity Continuum of State Crime', *Contemporary Justice Review* 6(3): 241–54.

Kelly, J. (1992). *A Short History of Western Legal Theory*. Oxford: Clarendon Press.

Kinsey, R., J. Lea, and J. Young. (1986). *Losing the Fight Against Crime*. Oxford: Blackwell.

Klein, M., C. Maxson, and J. Miller, eds. (1995). *The Modern Gang Reader*. Los Angeles, CA: Roxbury Publishing.

Klein, M., H-J. Kerner, C. Maxson, and E. Weitekamp, eds. (2001). *The Eurogang Paradox: Street Gangs and Youth Groups in the U.S. and Europe*. Dordrecht: Kluwer Academic Publishers.

Kyle, A. (2007). 'Saskatchewan: Hot Spot for Gang Activity', *Regina Leader Post*, 7 April.

LaGrange, R., K. Ferraro, and M. Supancic. (1992). 'Perceived Risk and Fear of Crime: Role of Social and Physical Incivilities', *Journal of Research in Crime and Delinquency* 29: 311–34.

Law Commission of Canada. (1999). *From Restorative Justice to Transformative Justice*. Ottawa: Law Commission of Canada.

———. (2003). *Transforming Relationships Through Participatory Justice*. Ottawa: Law Commission of Canada.

Lea, J. (1998). 'Criminology and Postmodernity', in *The New Criminology Revisited*, P. Walton and J. Young, eds. London: Macmillan.

Lea, J., and J. Young. (1982). 'The Riots in Britain 1981: Urban Violence and Political Marginalisation', in *Policing the Riots*, D. Cowell, T. Jones, and J. Young, eds. London: Junction Books.

———. (1984). *What is to be Done about Law and Order?* London: Penguin.

Lees, S. (1989). 'Learning to Love', in *Growing Up Good*, M. Cain, ed. London: Sage.

Lemert, E. (1969). 'Primary and Secondary Deviation', in *Delinquency, Crime and Social Process*, D. Cressy and D. Ward, eds. New York: Harper & Row.

Lind, M. (1995). 'Brave New Right', in *The Bell Curve Wars: Race, Intelligence and the Future of America*, S. Fraser, ed. New York: Basic Books.

Litwack, T., and L. Schlesinger. (1999). 'Dangerousness Risk Assessments: Research, Legal, and Clinical Considerations', in *The Handbook of Forensic Psychology*, 2nd ed., A. Hess and I. Weiner, eds. New York: John Wiley and Sons.

Loader, I. (1998). 'Criminology and the Public Sphere: Arguments for Utopian Realism', in *The New Criminology Revisited*, P. Walton and J. Young, eds. London: Macmillan.

Loeber, R., and D. Farrington, eds. (1998). *Serious and Violent Juvenile Offenders: Risk Factors and Successful Interventions*. Thousand Oaks, CA: Sage.

Lombroso, C. (1911). *Crime: Its Causes and Remedies*. Boston: Little, Brown and Company.

Lowman, J., and B. MacLean, eds. (1992). *Realist Criminology: Crime Control and Policing in the 1990s*. Toronto: University of Toronto Press.

Lozoff, B., and M. Braswell. (1989). *Inner Corrections: Finding Peace and Peacemaking*. Cincinnati: Anderson Press.

Lukes, S. (1973). *Emile Durkheim: His Life and Work*. London: Penguin.

Lynch, M., and P. Stretsky. (2003). 'The Meaning of Green: Contrasting Criminological Perspectives', *Theoretical Criminology* 7(2): 217–38.

McEvoy, K. (2003). 'Beyond the Metaphor: Political Violence, Human Rights and "New" Peacemaking Criminology', *Theoretical Criminology* 7(3): 319–46.

MacLean, B. (1993). 'Left Realism, Local Crime Surveys and Policing of Racial Minorities: A Further Analysis of Data from the First Sweep of the Islington Crime Survey', *Crime, Law and Social Change* 19: 51–86.

MacLean, B., and D. Milovanovic, eds. (1991). *New Directions in Critical Criminology*. Vancouver: The Collective Press.

Males, M. (1996). *The Scapegoat Generation: America's War on Adolescents*. Monroe, ME: Common Courage Press.

Mason, G. (2002). *The Spectacle of Violence: Homophobia, Gender and Knowledge*. London: Routledge.

Mathiesen, T. (1990). *Prisons On Trial: A Critical Assessment*. London: Sage.

Matthews, R. (1989). 'Alternatives To and In Prisons: A Realist Approach', in *Paying For Crime*, P. Carlen and D. Cook, eds. Milton Keynes: Open University Press.

Matza, D. (1964). *Delinquency and Drift*. New York: John Wiley and Sons.

Mawby, R., and S. Walklate. (1994). *Critical Victimology: International Perspectives*. London: Sage.

Merton, R. (1957). *Social Theory and Social Structure*. New York: Free Press.

Messerschmidt, J. (1986). *Capitalism, Patriarchy and Crime*. Lanham, MD: Rowman & Littlefield.

———. (1997). *Crime as Structured Action: Gender, Race, Class, and Crime in the Making*. London: Sage.

Mestel, R. (1994). 'What triggers the violence within?', *New Scientist* 1914 (26 February): 31.

Michalowski, R., and R. Kramer. (2006). *State-Corporate Crime: Wrongdoing at the Intersection of Business and Government*. New Brunswick, NJ: Rutgers University Press.

Miliband, R. (1969). *The State in Capitalist Society*. London: Quartet Books.

Miller, J. (1996). *Search and Destroy: African-American Males in the Criminal Justice System*. New York: Cambridge University Press.

Miller, W. (1958). 'Lower Class Culture as a Generating Milieu of Gang Delinquency', *Journal of Social Issues* 14: 51–119.

Milovanovic, D. (1996). 'Post-modern Criminology: Mapping the Terrain', *Justice Quarterly* 13: 567–610.

Moffitt, T. (1996). 'The Neuropsychology of Conduct Disorder', in *Readings in Contemporary Criminological Theory*, P. Cordella and L. Siegel, eds. Boston: Northeastern University Press.

Mooney, J. (1998). 'Moral Panics and the New Right: Single Mothers and Feckless Fathers', in *The New Criminology Revisited*, P. Walton and J. Young, eds. London: Macmillan.

Moore, M., and R.C. Trojanowicz. (1988). *Corporate Strategies for Policing*. Washington, DC: National Institute of Justice.

Morrison, W. (1994). 'Criminology, Modernity and the "Truth" of the Human Condition: Reflections on the Melancholy of Postmodernism', in *The Futures of Criminology*, D. Nelken, ed. London: Sage.

Moyer, I. (2001). *Criminological Theories: Traditional and Nontraditional Voices and Themes*. Thousand Oaks, CA: Sage.

Moyle, P., ed. (1994). *Private Prisons and Police: Recent Australian Trends*. Sydney: Pluto Press.

Muller D., D. Blackmann, and A. Chapmann, eds. *Psychology and Law*. New York: John Wiley and Sons.

Muncie, J., and M. Fitzgerald. (1981). 'Humanising the Deviant: Affinity and Affiliation Theories', in *Crime and Society: Readings in History and Theory*, M. Fitzgerald, G. McLennan, and J. Pawson, eds. London: Routledge and Kegan Paul.

Muncie, J., E. McLaughlin, and M. Langan, eds. (1996). *Criminological Perspectives: A Reader*. London: Sage.

Murray, C. (1990). *The Emerging Underclass*. London: Institute of Economic Affairs.

Naffine, N. (1987). *Female Crime: The Construction of Women in Criminology*. Sydney: Allen & Unwin.

———. (1990). *Law and the Sexes: Explorations in Feminist Jurisprudence*. Sydney: Allen & Unwin.

———. (1997). *Feminism and Criminology*. Sydney: Allen & Unwin.

Nava, M. (1984). 'Youth Service Provision, Social Order and the Question of Girls', in *Gender and Generation*, A. McRobbie and M. Nava, eds. London: Macmillan.

Nettler, G. (1984). *Explaining Crime*. New York: McGraw-Hill.

*New Zealand Herald*. (2005). 'Sensible Sentencing Trust Story: Call to Scrap Free Removal of Criminal's Tattoos', *New Zealand Herald*, 10 October.

Newbold, G. (1982/85). *The Big Huey*. Auckland, NZ: Collins.

Newman, Oscar. (1976). *Defensible Space: Crime Prevention through Urban Design*. New York: Collier.

O'Leary, C., and T. Platt. (2001). 'Pledging Allegiance: The Revival of Prescriptive Patriotism', *Social Justice* 28(3): 41–4.

O'Malley, P. (1983). *Law, Capitalism and Democracy*. Sydney: George Allen & Unwin.

Palmary, I. (2003). Youth Position Paper prepared for Crime Prevention Alliance. Paper presented at the Alliance for Crime Prevention Conference, Cape Town, 2 December. Available at http://www.csvr.org.za.

Parenti, C. (1999). *Lockdown America: Police and Prisons in the Age of Crisis*. New York: Verso.

Payne, S. (2005). Crime Prevention and the Private/Corporate Sector Involvement. A Paper presented to the International Center for the Prevention of Crime 5th Annual Colloquium on Crime Prevention, Santiago, Chile, 27–28 October.

Pearce, F. (1976). *Crime of the Powerful: Marxism, Crime and Deviance*. London: Pluto.

Pearce, F., and S. Tombs. (1990). 'Ideology, Hegemony and Empiricism: Compliance Theories of Regulation', *British Journal of Criminology* 30(4): 423–43.

———. (1998). *Toxic Capitalism: Corporate Crime and the Chemical Industry*. Aldershot: Dartmouth Publishing Company.

Pepinsky, H. (1991). 'Peacemaking in Criminology and Criminal Justice', in *Criminology as Peacemaking*, H. Pepinsky and R. Quinney, eds. Bloomington, IN: Indiana University Press.

Pepinsky, H., and R. Quinney, eds. (1991). *Criminology as Peacemaking*. Bloomington, ID: Indiana University Press.

Pettit, P., and J. Braithwaite. (1993). 'Not Just Deserts, Even in Sentencing', *Current Issues in Criminal Justice* 4(3): 225–39.

Pickering, S., and C. Lambert. (2001). 'Immigration Detention Centres, Human Rights and Criminology in Australia', *Current Issues in Criminal Justice* 13(2): 219–23.

Platt, A. (1977). *The Child Savers*. Chicago: University of Chicago.

Plummer, K. (1979). 'Misunderstanding Labelling Perspectives', in *Deviant Interpretations*, D. Downes and P. Rock, eds. Oxford: Martin Robertson.

Polk, K. (1993). 'Jobs, not Gaols: A New Agenda for Youth', in *National Conference on Juvenile Justice: Conference Proceedings*, L. Atkinson and S-A. Gerull, eds. Canberra: Australian Institute of Criminology.

———. (1994a). 'Family Conferencing: Theoretical and Evaluative Questions', in *Family Conferencing and Juvenile Justice*, C. Alder and J. Wundersitz, eds. Canberra: Australian Institute of Criminology.

———. (1994b). *Why Men Kill: Scenarios of Masculine Violence*. Melbourne: Cambridge University Press.

Potter, H. (1992). 'Crime, Shame and Reintegration: Review, Questions and Comment', *Australian and New Zealand Journal of Sociology* 28(2): 224–32.

Poulantzas, N. (1972). 'The Problem of the Capitalist State', in *Ideology and the Social Sciences*, R. Blackburn, ed. London: Fontana Books.

Presdee, M. (2000). *Cultural Criminology and the Carnival of Crime*. London: Routledge.

Quinney, R. (1970). *The Social Reality of Crime*. Boston: Little, Brown and Company.

———. (1977). *Class, State and Crime: On the Theory and Practice of Criminal Justice*. New York: David McKay Company.

———. (1991). 'The Way of Peace: On Crime, Suffering and Deviance', in *Criminology as Peacemaking*, H. Pepinsky and R. Quinney, eds. Bloomington, IN: Indiana University Press.

Quinney, R., and J. Wildeman. (1991). *The Problem of Crime: A Peace and Justice Perspective*, 3rd ed. Palo Alto, CA: Mountain View Press.

Quinney, R., ed. (1974). *Crime and Justice in America: A Critical Understanding*. Boston: Little, Brown and Company.

Reiman, J. (1998). *The Rich Get Richer and the Poor Get Prison*, Allyn and Bacon, Boston.

Reiman, J. (1999). 'The Rich (Still) Get Richer—Understanding Ideology, Outrage and Economic Bias', *The Critical Criminologist* 9(2): 1, 4–5.

———. (1986). 'Why Are Communities Important in Understanding Crime?', in *Communities and Crime*, A. Reiss and M. Tonry, eds. Chicago: University of Chicago Press.

Reiss, A., and M. Tonry, eds. *Communities and Crime*. Chicago: University of Chicago Press.

Richards, S.C. (1998). 'Critical and Radical Perspectives on Community Punishment: Lessons from the Darkness', in *Cutting the Edge: Current Perspectives in Radical/Critical Criminology and Criminal Justice*, J.I. Ross, ed. Westport, CT: Praeger.

Richard, S.C., and R.S. Jones. (1997). 'Perpetual Incarceration Machine: Structural Impediments to Postprison Success', *Journal of Contemporary Criminal Justice* 13(1): 4–22.

Richardson, G. (2006). 'Report: Prison System Discriminatory to Aboriginals', *CTV.ca News*, 16 October.

Roach, K. (2000). 'Changing Punishment at the Turn of the Century: Restorative Justice on the Rise', *Canadian Journal of Criminology* 42: 249–80.

Rosenthal, R., and L. Jacobson. (1968). *Pygmalion in the Classroom*. New York: Holt, Rinehart and Winston.

Ross, D. (1985). 'A Tattoo Removal Programme in Victoria', *Medical Journal of Australia* 142: 388.

Ross, J.I. (2000). *Varieties of State Crime and its Control*. Monsey, NY: Criminal Justice Press.

Rountree, P.W., and K. Land. (1996). 'Burglary, Victimization, Perceptions of Crime Risk, and Routine Activities: A Multilevel Analysis Across Seattle Neighborhoods and Census Tracts', *Journal of Research in Crime and Delinquency* 33: 147–80.

Rubington, E., and M. Weinberg, eds. (1978). *Deviance: The Interactionist Perspective*. New York: Macmillan.

Russell, S. (1997). 'The Failure of Postmodern Criminology', *Critical Criminologist* 8(2): 61–90.

Rutter, M., H. Giller, and A. Hagell. (1998). *Antisocial Behavior by Young People*. Cambridge: Cambridge University Press.

Sampson, R.J., and J.H. Laub. (1992). 'Crime and Deviance in the Life-Course', *Annual Review of Sociology* 18: 63–84.

———. (2001). 'Crime and Deviance in the Life-Course', in *Life-Course Criminology: Contemporary and Classic Readings*, A. Piquero and P. Mazerolle, eds. Toronto: Wentworth.

———. (2005). 'A Life-Course View of the Development of Crime', *Annals of the American Academy of Political and Social Science* 602(1): 12–45.

Sampson, R., and W. Wilson. (1993). 'Toward a Theory of Race, Crime and Urban Inequality', in *Crime and Inequality*, J. Hagan and R. Peterson, eds. Stanford: Stanford University Press.

Sarre, R. (1994). 'Violence: Patterns of Crime', in *The Australian Criminal Justice System: The Mid-1990s*, D. Chappell and P. Wilson, eds. Sydney: Butterworths.

Schissel, B., and C. Brooks, eds. (2002). *Marginality and Condemnation: An Introduction to Critical Criminology*. Halifax: Fernwood.

Schmalleger, F., and R. Volk. (2005). *Canadian Criminology Today: Theories and Applications*, 2nd ed. Toronto: Pearson Prentice Hall.

Schur, E. (1973). *Radical Non-Intervention: Rethinking the Delinquency Problem*. Upper Saddle River, NJ: Prentice-Hall.

Schwartz, M.D., and W.D. DeKeseredy. (1998). 'Is Left Realism a Useful Theory for Addressing the Problem of Crime?', in *Controversial Issues in Crimminology*, pp. 127–34, J.W. Fuller and E.W. Hickey, eds. Boston: Allyn & Bacon.

Schwendinger, H., and J. Schwendinger. (1975). 'Defenders of Order or Guardians of Human Rights', in *Critical Criminology*, I. Taylor, P. Walton, and J. Young, eds. London: Routledge and Kegan Paul.

Scraton, P., ed. (1987). *Law, Order and the Authoritarian State: Readings in Critical Criminology*. Milton Keynes: Open University Press.

Scraton, P., and K. Chadwick. (1991). 'The Theoretical and Political Priorities of Critical Criminology', in *The Politics of Crime Control*, K. Stenson and D. Cowell, eds. London: Sage.

Scutt, J. (1990). *Women and the Law*. Sydney: Law Book Company.

Segal, L. (1987). *Is The Future Female? Troubled Thoughts on Contemporary Feminism*. London: Virago Press.

Shaw, C., and H. McKay. (1942). *Juvenile Delinquency and Urban Areas*. Chicago: Chicago University Press.

———. (1972). *Juvenile Delinquency and Urban Areas*, rev. ed. Chicago: University of Chicago Press.

Sheldon, W. (1940). *Varieties of Human Physique*. New York: Harper & Row.

Shoemaker, D. (1984). *Theories of Delinquency*. New York: Oxford University Press.

Shonholtz, R. (1984). 'Neighborhood Justice Systems: Work, Structure, and Guiding Principle', *Journal of Mediation Quarterly* 5: 3–30.

Shore, M. (1987). *The Science of Social Redemption: McGill, the Chicago School, and the Origins of Social Research in Canada*. Toronto: University of Toronto Press.

Shover, N., and J. Wright. (2001). *Crimes of Privilege: Readings in White-Collar Crime*. New York: Oxford University Press.

Siegel, L.J., and C. McCormack. (2003). *Criminology in Canada: Theories, Patterns, and Typologies*, 2nd ed. Toronto: Thomson Nelson.

Skogan, W. (1986). 'Fear of Crime and Neighborhood Change', in *Communities and Crime*, pp. 191–232, A. Reiss and M. Tonry, eds. Chicago: University of Chicago Press.

Smart, C. (1976). *Women, Crime and Criminology: A Feminist Critique*. London: Routledge and Kegan Paul.

Smith, D. (2005). 'Our Highway of Tears', *Hiway 16 Magazine*. Available at http://www.bcnorth.ca/magazine/pages/Debi/tears/tears1.htm.

Spelman, W. (1993). 'Abandoned Buildings: Magnets for Crime?', *Journal of Criminal Justice* 21: 481–93.

Spitzer, S. (1975). 'Toward a Marxian Theory of Deviance', *Social Problems* 22: 638–51.

Solicitor General Canada and the Aboriginal Healing Foundation. (2002). *Mapping the Healing Journey in Canadian Aboriginal Communities*. Ottawa, ON: Government of Canada.

Stark, R. (1987). 'Deviant Places: A Theory of the Ecology of Crime', *Criminology* 25: 893–911.

Statistics Canada. (2008). *Study: Firearms and Violent Crime: 2006*. Ottawa: Public Works and Government Services.

Steadman, H. (1973). 'Follow-up on Baxtrom Patients Returned to Hospitals for the Criminally Insane', *American Journal of Psychology* 3: 317–19.

Steinart, H. (1985). 'The Amazing New Left Law and Order Campaign', *Contemporary Crises* 9: 327–33.

Stenson, K., and R. Sullivan, eds. (2001). *Crime, Risk and Justice: The Politics of Crime Control in Liberal Democracies*. Devon: Willan Publishing.

Stuart, C., and J. Eakins. (2003). An Evaluation of the Whitehorse Youth Justice Panel, Yukon, Canada. A Paper Presented at the 6th International Conference on Restorative Justice, June.

Sutherland, E. (1983). *White-Collar Crime: The Uncut Version*. New Haven: Yale University Press.

Sutherland, E., and D. Cressy. (1974). *Criminology*. New York: Lippincott Company.

Sykes, G., and D. Matza. (1957). 'Techniques of Neutralization: A Theory of Delinquency', *American Sociological Review* 22: 664–70.

Tame, C. (1991). 'Freedom, Responsibility and Justice: The Criminology of the "New Right"', in *The Politics of Crime Control*, K. Stenson and D. Cowell, eds. London: Sage.

Tanner, J. (1996). *Teenage Troubles: Youth and Deviance in Canada*. Toronto: Nelson.

Terman, L.M. (1916). *The Measure of Intelligence*. Boston: Houghton Mifflin.

Traub, S.H., and C.B. Little. (1999). *Theories of Deviance*, 5th ed. Toronto: Thomson Wadsworth.

Taylor, I. (1981). *Law and Order: Arguments for Socialism*. London: Macmillan.

Taylor, I., P. Walton, and J. Young. (1973). *The New Criminology*. London: Routledge and Kegan Paul.

———. (1974). *The New Criminology: For A Social Theory of Deviance*. New York: Harper & Row.

Taylor, R., and Covington, J. (1988). 'Neighbourhood changes in ecology and violence', *Criminology* 26: 553–89.

Thompson, A. (1992). 'Foreword: Critical Approaches to Law: Who Needs Legal Theory?', in *The Critical Lawyers' Handbook*, I. Grigg-Spall and P. Ireland, eds. London: Pluto Press.

Tittle, C.R. (1995). *Control Balance: Toward a General Theory of Deviance*. Boulder, CO: Westview Press.

Tomsen, S. (2002). 'Hatred, Murder and Male Honour: Anti-homosexual Homicides in New South Wales, 1980–2000', *Australian Institute of Criminology Research and Public Policy Series* 43.

Tong, R. (1989). *Feminist Thought: A Comprehensive Introduction*. London: Unwin Hyman.

Tory, J. (2006). *Remarks* by John Tory, MPP, Leader of the Progressive Conservative Party of Ontario. Ontario Convenience Store Association Annual Dinner, Monday, 27 February.

Tunnell, K. (1993). *Political Crime in Contemporary America: A Critical Approach*. New York: Garland Publishing.

Vold, G.B., and T.J. Bernard. (1986). *Theoretical Criminology*, 3rd ed. New York: Oxford University Press.

Weatherburn, D. (2002). 'Law and Order Blues', *The Australian and New Zealand Journal of Criminology* 35(2): 127–44.

Weatherburn, D., and B. Lind. (2001). *Delinquent-Prone Communities*. Cambridge: Cambridge University Press.

Weber, L. (2002). 'The Detention of Asylum Seekers: 20 Reasons Why Criminologists Should Care', *Current Issues in Criminal Justice* 14(1): 9–30.

Welch, M. (1994). 'Jail Overcrowding: Social Sanitation and the Warehousing of the Urban Underclass', in *Critical Issues in Crime and Justice*, A. Roberts, ed. Thousand Oaks, CA: Sage.

White, R. (2002). 'Understanding Youth Gangs', *Trends and Issues in Criminal Justice, No.237*. Canberra: Australian Institute of Criminology.

———. (2003). 'Environmental Issues and the Criminological Imagination', *Theoretical Criminology* 7(4): 483–506.

White, R., and S. Perrone. (1997). *Crime and Social Control*. Melbourne: Oxford University Press.

White, R., and J. van der Velden. (1995). 'Class and Criminality', *Social Justice* 22(1): 51–74.

White, R., and J. Wyn. (2004). *Youth and Society: Exploring the Social Dynamics of Youth Experience*. Melbourne: Oxford University Press.

Williams, C. (1996). 'An Environmental Victimology', *Social Justice* 23(4): 16–40.

Williams, III, F.P., and M.D. McShane. (2004). *Criminological Theory*, 4th ed. Upper Saddle River, NJ: Pearson Prentice Hall.

Wilson, J. (1975). *Thinking About Crime*. New York: Vintage Books.

———. (1987). *The Truly Disadvantaged*. Chicago: University of Chicago Press.

Wilson, J., and R. Herrnstein. (1985). *Crime and Human Nature*. New York: Simon and Schuster.

Wilson, W.J. (1996). *When Work Disappears*. New York: Knopf.

Wright, M. (1991). *Justice for Victims and Offenders*. Milton Keynes: Open University Press.

Young, A. (1990). *Femininity in Dissent*. London: Routledge.

Young, J. (1971). 'The Role of the Police as Amplifiers of Deviancy, Negotiators of Reality and Translators of Fantasy: Some Consequences of Our Present System of Drug Control as Seen in Notting Hill', in *Images of Deviance*, S. Cohen, ed. London: Penguin.

———. (1981). 'Thinking Seriously About Crime: Some Models of Criminology', in *Crime and Society: Readings in History and Theory*, M. Fitzgerald, G. McLennon, and J. Pawson, eds. London: Routledge and Kegan Paul.

———. (1986). 'The Failure of Criminology: The Need for a Radical Realism', in *Confronting Crime*, R. Matthews and J. Young, eds. London: Sage.

———. (1991). 'Left Realism and the Priorities of Crime Control', in *The Politics of Crime Control*, K. Stenson and D. Cowell, eds. London: Sage.

———. (1992). 'Realist Research as a Basis for Local Criminal Justice Policy', in *Realist Criminology: Crime Control and Policing in the 1990s*, J. Lowman and B. MacLean, eds. Toronto: University of Toronto Press.

———. (1999). *The Exclusive Society: Social Exclusion, Crime and Difference in Late Modernity*. London: Sage.

———. (2003). 'Merton with Energy, Katz with Structure: The Sociology of Vindictiveness and Criminology of Transgression', *Theoretical Criminology* 7(3): 389–414.

Van Ness, D.W., and K.H. Strong. (2002). *Restoring Justice*, 2nd ed. Cincinnati, OH: Anderson Publishing Company.

Zehr, H. (1990). *Changing Lenses: A New Focus for Crime and Justice*. Scotsdale: Herald Press.

Zehr, H., and B. Toews. (2004). *Critical Issues in Restorative Justice*. Monsey, NY: Criminal Justice Press.

Zehr, H., and H. Mika. (1998). 'Fundamental Concepts of Restorative Justice', *Contemporary Justice Review* 1(1): 47–56.

# Index

NIAGARA COLLEGE LRC